Computational Social Networks

Ajith Abraham
Editor

Computational Social Networks

Security and Privacy

 Springer

Editor
Dr. Ajith Abraham
Machine Intelligence Research Labs
  (MIR Labs)
Scientific Network for Innovation
  and Research Excellence
Auburn, WA
USA

ISBN 978-1-4471-5815-8   ISBN 978-1-4471-4051-1 (eBook)
DOI 10.1007/978-1-4471-4051-1
Springer London Heidelberg New York Dordrecht

Printed on acid-free paper

Springer is part of Springer Science+Business Media (www.springer.com)

Preface

Computational Social Network (CSN) is a new emerging field that has overlapping regions from Mathematics, Psychology, Computer Sciences, Sociology, and Management. E-mails, blogs, instant messages, social network services, wikis, social bookmarking, and other instances of what is often called social software illustrate ideas from social computing.

Social network analysis is the study of relationships among social entities. Very often, all the necessary information is distributed over a number of websites and servers, which brings several research challenges from a data mining perspective. Recently, privacy concerns with social network services have become a much-publicized topic since the creation and increasing popularity of social networking sites such as Myspace and Facebook, etc. Issues relating to stalking, identity theft, sexual predators, and employment consistently arise, as well as the ethics regarding data storage and the management and sharing of such data. This book is a collection of chapters authored by world-class experts focusing on the security and privacy aspects from a computational point of view, with a focus on practical tools, applications, and open avenues for further research.

The main topics cover the design and use of various computational tools and software, simulations of social networks, representation and analysis of social networks, with a focus on security, privacy, and anonymization. Authors present some of the latest advances of in security and privacy issues related to social networks and illustrate how organizations/individuals can be protected from real-world threats. Experience reports, survey articles, and intelligence techniques and theories with specific networks technology problems are depicted. We hope that this book will be useful for researchers, scholars, postgraduate students and developers who are interested in social networks research and related issues. In particular, the book will be a valuable companion and comprehensive reference for both postgraduate and senior undergraduate students who are taking a course in Social Networks. The book contains 13 chapters (including an introductory chapter) and is divided into three parts, and all chapters are self-contained to provide greatest reading flexibility.

Part I deals with six chapters focusing on different research issues related to trust and privacy in social networks. In Chap. 1, Salama et al. provide an overview of a number of social network related concepts from a computational perspective, such as different performance measures, network services and applications. Further the chapter presents an overview of the social networks security and privacy issues and illustrates the various security risks and the tasks applied to minimize those risks. The authors explain some of the common strategies that attackers often use and some possible counter measures against such issues.

Karupannan in Chap. 2 presents detailed research studies in the areas of security, trust, and privacy applicable to social networks. Novel technologies and methodologies for securely building and managing social networks are discussed and the relevant secure applications as well as practical issues are narrated.

In Chap. 3, Kobayashi focuses on the development of blogs and the blogosphere around the globe. The author found that according to various National surveys conducted by numerous international teams of researchers, motivations for blogging and attitudes regarding privacy are strikingly different in countries with large blogging communities. These differences are reflected in the content of blogs and profoundly influence blog-based social networks, which tend to be region-centric.

Beye et al. in Chap. 4 provide deep insight into privacy in social networks. The authors discuss about the associated privacy risks in relation to both users and service providers, and finally relevant research areas for privacy protecting techniques are illustrated. Mappings are made to reflect typical relations that exist between the type of social network, data type, particular privacy risks, and privacy-preserving solutions.

In Chap. 5, Ulbricht analyzes the options users of online social networks like Facebook have to adjust in the privacy settings. The author illustrates how Facebook as a provider of an online social network designs its platform in such a way that their own interests, as many users data to keep visible and searchable, is implemented.

Guo and Kraines in Chap. 6 introduce the role of trust and recommendation in knowledge sharing networks. To infer the trustworthiness of a knowledge sharing "agent," the authors present a reliability-based trust metric for generating locally calculated inferred trust values using recommendations from trusted agents.

Part II deals with four chapters related to security, measurements, and various real-world applications.

In Chap. 7, Gyarmati and Trinh present the various measurements of user behavior in online social networks that also allows measuring diverse facets of human activities. The authors consider both passive and active methods. The measurement frameworks are compared based on several properties including the details of the datasets and the resource consumption of the different methods.

Simoes et al. in Chap. 8 illustrate the usage of clustering techniques to study how user interests group together and identify the most popular users within these groups. The authors used multiple dimensions of user-related data, providing a more detailed process model of how influence spreads within the network according to interest's dependencies.

In Chap. 9, Varga et al. introduce Gedda-Headz, a novel social mobile gaming concept that focuses on multiplayer mobile gaming. The authors discuss how users may cooperate in Gedda-Headz, and how such cooperation might help users to use services that would otherwise be unreachable for them, or greatly decrease the energy cost of certain activities. Finally, the Gedda-Headz spreader, a novel method to spread the word about the network, is also presented.

Silas et al. in Chap. 10 propose an effective framework for service selection of social network. The experimental results on overhead, social service deduction time, average delay, etc., are illustrated.

Part III deals with three chapters related to various anonymity issues in real-world social network environments.

Chertov and Tavrov in Chap. 11 attempt to solve the problem of group anonymity in a social network. Group anonymity refers to a group of people to be indistinguishable within a particular dataset and the authors propose a wavelet transforms approach for solving this difficult issue.

In Chap. 12, Tripathy presents the status of research on anonymization of social networks and introduces a rough set based algorithm for anonymization. The author also describes some recent algorithms, which use isomorphism of graphs for anonymization, and some future research challenges.

Malinka and Hanacek in the last chapter deal with anonymous communication. The authors perform a set of analyses targeting the behavioral patterns of users and their impact on such systems. The analyses are focused on the properties of e-mail communication relevant to the designers of anonymous systems, information about user profiling, and properties of identifiable social networks and their development in time within the context of the security of anonymous systems.

I am very much grateful to the authors of this volume and to the reviewers for their tremendous service by critically reviewing the chapters. Most of the authors of chapters included in this book also served as referees for chapters written by other authors. Thanks go to all those who provided constructive and comprehensive reviews. I would like to thank Wayne Wheeler and Simon Rees of Springer Verlag, London, for the editorial assistance and excellent cooperative collaboration to produce this important scientific work. Finally, I hope that the reader will share our excitement to present this volume on social networks and will find it useful.

Prof. (Dr.) Ajith Abraham

Machine Intelligence Research Labs (MIR Labs)
Scientific Network for Innovation and Research Excellence (SNIRE)
P.O. Box 2259, Auburn, Washington 98071, USA
http://www.mirlabs.org
Email: ajith.abraham@ieee.org
Personal WWW: http://www.softcomputing.net

Contents

Part III   Anonymity

Contributors

Ajith Abraham Machine Intelligence Research Labs (MIR Labs), Scientific Network for Innovation and Research Excellence, Auburn, WA, USA

Michael Beye Information Security and Privacy Lab, Faculty of EEMCS, Delft University of Technology, Delft, The Netherlands

Laszlo Blazovics Faculty of Electrical Engineering and Informatics, Budapest University of Technology and Economics, Budapest, Hungary

Hassan Charaf Faculty of Electrical Engineering and Informatics, Budapest University of Technology and Economics, Budapest, Hungary

Oleg Chertov Kyiv Polytechnic Institute, National Technical University of Ukraine, Kyiv, Ukraine

Ashwini Dalvi Department of Information Technology, K.J. Somaiya College of Engineering, Vidyavihar, Mumbai, India

Yomna Elbarawy Faculty of Computers and Information, BUE, Cairo, Egypt

Zekeriya Erkin Information Security and Privacy Lab, Faculty of EEMCS, Delft University of Technology, Delft, The Netherlands

Kirubakaran Ezra BHEL, Trichy, India

Frank H.P. Fitzek Mobile Device Group, Aalborg University, Aalborg, Denmark

Weisen Guo Science Integration Programme (Human), Department of Frontier Sciences and Science Integration, Division of Project Coordination, The University of Tokyo, Kashiwa, Japan

László Gyarmati Telefonica Research, Plaza de Ernest Lluch i Martín 5, 08019 Barcelona-Spain

Petr Hanáček Faculty of Information Technologies, Brno University of Technology, Brno, Czech Republic

Pieter Hartel Distributed and Embedded Security, Faculty of EEMCS, University of Twente, Enschede, The Netherlands

Aboul Ella Hassanien Faculty of Computers and Information, Cairo University, Cairo, Egypt

Arjan J.P. Jeckmans Distributed and Embedded Security, Faculty of EEMCS, University of Twente, Enschede, The Netherlands

Komathy Karuppanan DCSE, Easwari Engineering College, Chennai, India

Julia Kiseleva St. Petersburg State University, St. Petersburg, Russia

Mei Kobayashi IBM Research-Tokyo, Toyosu, Koto-ku, Tokyo, Japan

Steven B. Kraines Science Integration Programme (Human), Department of Frontier Sciences and Science Integration, Division of Project Coordination, The University of Tokyo, Kashiwa, Japan

Reginald L. Lagendijk Information Security and Privacy Lab, Faculty of EEMCS, Delft University of Technology, Delft, The Netherlands

Kamil Malinka Faculty of Information Technologies, Brno University of Technology, Brno, Czech Republic

Boris Novikov St. Petersburg State University, St. Petersburg, Russia

Mrutyunjaya Panda Department of ECE, Gandhi Institute of Engineering and Technology, Gunupur, India

Elijah Blessing Rajsingh Department of Information Technology, Karunya University, Coimbatore, India

Mostafa Salama British University in Egypt, Cairo, Egypt

Irfan Siddavatam Department of Information Technology, K.J. Somaiya College of Engineering, Vidyavihar, Mumbai, India

Salaja Silas Department of Information Technology, Karunya University, Coimbatore, India

Jose Simoes Fraunhofer FOKUS, Berlin, Germany

Elena Sivogolovko St. Petersburg State University, St. Petersburg, Russia

Qiang Tang Distributed and Embedded Security, Faculty of EEMCS, University of Twente, Enschede, The Netherlands

Dan Tavrov Kyiv Polytechnic Institute, National Technical University of Ukraine, Kyiv, Ukraine

Tuan Anh Trinh Network Economics Group, Department of Telecommunications and Media Informatics, Budapest University of Technology and Economics, Budapest, Hungary

Bala Krishna Tripathy School of Computing Science and Engineering, VIT University, Vellore, Tamil Nadu, India

Max-R. Ulbricht Department of Commercial Information Technology and Quantitative Methods, Computers and Society, Technical University of Berlin, Berlin, Germany

Csaba Varga Faculty of Electrical Engineering and Informatics, Budapest University of Technology and Economics, Budapest, Hungary

Part I
Privacy and Trust

Chapter 1
Computational Social Networks: Security and Privacy

Mostafa Salama, Mrutyunjaya Panda, Yomna Elbarawy,
Aboul Ella Hassanien, and Ajith Abraham

Abstract The continuous self-growing nature of social networks makes it hard to define a line of safety around these networks. Users in social networks are not interacting with the Web only but also with trusted groups that may also contain enemies. There are different kinds of attacks on these networks including causing damage to the computer systems and stealing information about users. These attacks are not only affecting individuals but also the organizations they are belonging to. Protection from these attacks should be performed by the users and security experts of the network. Advices should be provided to users of these social networks. Also security experts should be sure that the contents transmitted through the network do not contain malicious or harmful data. This chapter presents an overview of the social networks security and privacy issues and illustrates the various security risks and the tasks applied to minimize those risks. In addition, this chapter explains some of the common strategies that attackers often use and some possible counter measures against such issues.

M. Salama (✉)
British University in Egypt, Cairo, Egypt
e-mail: mostafa.salama@gmail.com

M. Panda
Department of ECE, Gandhi Institute of Engineering and Technology, Gunupur, 765022, India

Y. Elbarawy
Faculty of Computers and Information, BUE, Cairo, Egypt

A.E. Hassanien
Faculty of Computers and Information, Cairo University, Cairo, Egypt
e-mail: aboitcairo@gmail.com

A. Abraham
Machine Intelligence Research Labs (MIR Labs), Scientific Network for Innovation
and Research Excellence, Auburn, WA, USA
e-mail: ajith.abraham@ieee.org

A. Abraham (ed.), *Computational Social Networks: Security and Privacy*,
DOI 10.1007/978-1-4471-4051-1_1, © Springer-Verlag London 2012

Introduction

The Internet has 1,700 million users [26] and nearly 187 million web pages [8, 15, 42]. In this way, it has become the largest source of information worldwide. Web search engines (WSEs), for example, Google, Bing, etc., are an essential tool for finding specific data among this incalculable amount of information. WSEs are easy to use, and they retrieve search results quickly. Accordingly, it can be argued that these tools have played a crucial role in the success of the World Wide Web [15, 42, 56, 57]. The demand for solid expertise in social network analysis (SNA) has recently exploded [3, 9, 21, 24, 36] due to the popularity of social networking websites such as Facebook, Twitter, Netlog, etc., and automated data collection techniques. The main target in social network security is to enjoy the benefits of social networks while mitigating the security risks. This could be applied through determining the risks and security threats that may affect the organization using these networks. Several threats and security risks are facing the social network media, and the victims of these threats may be the users of these networks, or the community they are related to, or even the city they are living in.

Web 2.0 and social networking are easy targets for attacks as they allow users to upload different types of content. Also the continuing growth of Web 2.0 and social networking adds some new threats every day. The threats could be divided into two forms, an input form through input to the users' information that are not correct like rumors. The second form is an output form, through gathering information from different users and networks to finally get a complete picture. In the first form, social networking sites can be a source of personal and organizational information leaks. Social networks contain a wealth of personal information. People share their date of birth, email address, home address, family ties, and pictures. Some of that information would not be valuable by itself, but having a clear picture of everything about a person can give attackers ideas and information required to perform other attacks such as credit card fraud or identity theft. Any real-life targeted attack can be made much more effective through access to additional information about the intended victim. Or more simple when we post something like looking forward to the family vacation next week at Sharm El Sheikh. Obviously for anyone that our house will be empty for a whole week and as we know most of any social network users are not familiar with all people in their contact list and some of them we even do not know well, and hence, how can we trust that our new 52″ flat-screen TV, which we just purchased, will not be stolen. If an employee in a company posts a message "Our boss just laid off 40 employees, I heard that there may be more next Sunday," this message might indicate that the company is doing poorly and continuing with losses, and shareholders start to sell off their stocks and reduce the company value. So users need to be careful about what information is posted or shared and try to make contact with people only whom we know for sure so that should make us less vulnerable to malicious attacks [3, 24, 36, 40, 55]. Also it is important to provide advices and solutions required to minimize those risks through different procedures like demonstrating the information security policies that may be applied in the organization.

The second form is the vulnerability to malware and harmful attacks through contents transmitted through the network. Users may be tricked into pasting and executing malicious javascript in their browser, which also lead them to unknowingly sharing the content. For example, Facebook Inc. maintained that it is investigating a rash of unsolicited graphic images that hit some users' accounts recently. "We experienced a coordinated spam attack that exploited a browser vulnerability. Facebook engineers have been working to reduce this browser vulnerability," Facebook spokesman Andrew Noyes said in a statement emailed to Reuters [58]. So it is important to manage and track the contents uploaded by different users, and social network security experts should also work on the browser vulnerability.

This chapter has the following organization. Section "Social Networks: Privacy Analysis" briefly describing the social network privacy analysis. Section "Social Network Security Risks" discusses the different risks and attacks that face the social networks. Section "Preventive Measures on Security" introduces some preventive measures on security. Sections "Case Study 1: Social Network Analysis in Terrorist Network Dataset" and "Case Study 2: Social Networks Concepts to Visualize Terrorist Networks" introduce an implemented case study on social network security on terrorist network dataset. Finally, opportunities, challenges, and conclusions are discussed in section "Conclusions."

Social Networks: Privacy Analysis

Privacy concerns with social networking services have become controversial and a much publicized topic since the creation and increasing popularity of social networking sites such as Bebo, Myspace, and Facebook. Issues relating to stalking, identity theft, sexual predators, and employment consistently arise, as well as the ethics regarding data storage and the management and sharing of such data than someone who barely uses the site [23, 39]. A security issue occurs when a hacker gains unauthorized access to a site's protected coding or written language. Privacy issues do not necessarily have to involve security breaches. The potential harm to an individual user really boils down to how much a user engages in a social networking site, as well as the amount of the information they are willing to share. A user with more viewers or a part several groups is a lot more likely to be harmed by a breach than someone who barely uses the site [23].

Online social networks are immensely popular, with some claiming over 200 million users [27]. Users share private content, such as personal information or photographs, using online social networks applications. Users must trust the online social networks service to protect personal information even as the online social networks provide benefits from examining and sharing that information. Several works that address the privacy issue can be found in the literature. For example, authors in [4] presented Persona, an online social network where users dictate who may access their information. Persona hides user data with attribute-based encryption, allowing users to apply fine-grained policies over who may view their data. Persona provides an effective means of creating applications in which users, not the online social networks, defining policy over access to private data. They described group-based access policies and the mechanisms needed to provide decryption and authentication by both groups and individuals. Authors demonstrated the versatility of operations in the proposed Persona, which provides privacy to users and the facility for creating applications like those that exist in current.

Privacy could be used for protection of social networking platforms and protection for social networking APIs [17]. Many researchers tackled this problem. For example, authors in [12] proposed a version of the probabilistic neural network that is privacy-preserving by evaluating a test point by the algorithm without any party knowing the data owned by the other parties. An analysis of the proposed algorithm from the standpoint of security and computational performance is presented. Salonas [54] proposed an NP-hard-based algorithm on data aggregation to solve privacy problem. They suggested the use of a genetic algorithm for solving the microaggregation problem. A comparative analysis of six social network site (SNS) report including Facebook [60], Hi5 [25], LinkedIn [34], LiveJournal [35], MySpace [41], and Skyrock [51] has been reviewed and discussed in [6]. The privacy-specific characteristics of each social network were examined under the following headings: registration information, real identities vs. pseudonyms, privacy controls, photo tagging, accessibility of member information to others, advertising, data retention, account deletion, third-party applications, and collection of nonuser personal information. This report also attempts to identify where sites have made particularly strong or weak choices with regard to privacy and to identify opportunities for improved privacy protection on SNS [6].

Social Network Security Risks

Risks associated with social networks can be classified into two main realms:

1. Risk associated with the organizations uses those social networks for official or personal reasons as if they are vulnerable to anyone of the major attacks, the organization system could fail.
2. Risks to the people (vertices) use those networks associated with identity theft or even more their personal belongings (e.g., home). In 2009, for instance [45], an employee of a Hawaii hospital illegally accessed a patient's electronic medical records, then posted the patient's name and confidential medical details on her MySpace page. This violation of Health Insurance Portability and Accountability Act policy did not deter the employee, who was later sentenced to 1 year in prison.

To minimize risks in social networks, we should (1) only publish information that we are perfectly comfortable with, depending on what we want to accomplish; (2) add only people we trust to our contact list; (3) avoid clicking unexpected links coming from people we do not know; and (4) never fully trust anyone we do not know that well.

Social Networks: Major Malicious Attacks

Social networks contain a wealth of information including birth dates, email addresses, family ties, home addresses, photos, and affiliations, which all the attackers need [47].

- Email addresses are entered into databases that are later used for spam campaigns. Email addresses that are derived from social networks can be further categorized to improve the impact of the campaign–race, age, country, and other factors can be used as filters in such a database so that its market price is higher than just any normal email address database [47].
- Date-of-birth data is used by different companies to confirm people's identities over the telephone. Criminals do not have databases, but they do have tools to automate "date-of-birth" searches in social networking sites [47].

Attackers may use social networking services to spread malicious code, compromise users' computers, or access personal information about a user's identity, location, contact information, and personal or professional relationships. You may also unintentionally reveal information to unauthorized individuals by performing certain actions.

Common Threats to Social Networking Services

The following are some of the common threats to social networking services [38]:

Viruses

The popularity of social networking services makes them ideal targets for attackers who want to have the most impact with the least effort. By creating a virus and embedding it in a website or a third-party application, an attacker can potentially infect millions of computers just by relying on users to share the malicious links with their contacts [38].

Tools

Attackers may use tools that allow them to take control of a user's account. The attacker could then access the user's private data and the data for any contacts that share their information with that user. An attacker with access to an account could also pose as that user and post malicious content [38].

Social Engineering Attacks

Social engineering relies on exploiting the human element of trust [22]. The first step in any social engineering attack is to collect information about the attacker's target. Social networking websites can reveal a large amount of personal information, including resumes, home addresses, phone numbers, employment information, work locations, family members, education, photos, and private information. Social media websites may share more personal information than users expect or need to keep in touch. A study by the University of Virginia cites that out of the top 150 Facebook applications, all of which are externally hosted, 90.7% of applications needed nothing more than publicly available information from members. However, all of these applications were given full access to personal information not necessary for operation but supplied by the user granting the applications' total access to their account [16]. Attackers may send an email or post a comment that appears to originate from a trusted social networking service or user. The message may contain a malicious URL or a request for personal information. By following the instructions, the user may disclose sensitive information or compromise the security of the system. An example of this kind of attack is called phishing, which is a fraudulent attempt to steal personal information such as usernames, passwords, and credit card details. Phishing is usually made through emails and appears to come from a well-known organization and is targeted to steal users' personal information. Often times phishing attempts appear to come from sites, services, and companies with which the users do not even have an account.

The best way to protect from phishing is to learn how to recognize a phish [44]:

- Generic greeting. Phishing emails are usually sent in large batches. To save time, Internet criminals use generic names like "first bank name customer," so they do not have to type all recipients' names out and send emails one-by-one.
- Forged link. Even if a link has a name you recognize somewhere in it, it does not mean it links to the real organization. Roll your mouse over the link and see if it matches what appears in the email. If there is a discrepancy, do not click on the link. Also, websites where it is safe to enter personal information begin with "https" – the "s" stands for secure. If you do not see "https," then do not proceed [16, 22, 44].
- Requests personal information. The point of sending phishing email is to trick you into providing your personal information. If you receive an email requesting your personal information, it is probably a phishing attempt.

- Sense of urgency. Internet criminals want you to provide your personal information now. They do this by making you think something has happened that requires you to act fast. The faster they get your information, the faster they can move on to another victim.

Identity Theft or Fake Identity

Attackers may be able to gather enough personal information from social networking services to assume our identity or the identity of one of our contacts. Even a few personal details may provide attackers with enough information to guess answers to security or password reminder questions for email, credit card, or bank accounts. In addition to this, underground forums sell personal information. The data can be mined and stored somewhere in the dark corners of the Internet waiting for a criminal to pay the right price for it. Criminals can use this information to obtain birth certificates/passports/other documentation and fake real-life identities. Some countries have looser controls than others, but in general, identity theft is something that already happens regularly. An example of this kind of attack is the Sybil attacks. In a Sybil attack, a malicious user takes on multiple identities and pretends to be multiple, distinct nodes (called Sybil nodes or Sybil identities) in the system. With Sybil nodes comprising a large fraction (e.g., more than one third) of the nodes in the system, the malicious user is able to "out vote" the honest users, effectively breaking previous defenses against malicious behaviors. For example, virtually all protocols for tolerating Byzantine failures assume that at least 2/3 of the nodes are honest. This makes these protocols vulnerable to Sybil attacks [14].

To handle these attacks, we may use a central authority that verifies credentials unique to an actual human being can control Sybil attacks easily. For example, if the system requires users to register with government-issued social security numbers or driver's license numbers, then the barrier for launching a Sybil attack becomes much higher. The central authority may also instead require a payment for each identity. Unfortunately, there are many scenarios where such designs are not desirable. For example, it may be difficult to select/establish a single entity that every user worldwide is willing to trust. Furthermore, the central authority can easily be a single point of failure. Finally, requiring sensitive information or payment in order to use a system may scare away many potential users.

A defense against Sybil attacks in social networks is the Sybil guard. Sybil guard leverages the existing human established trust relationships among users to bind both the number and size of Sybil groups. All honest nodes and Sybil nodes in the system form a social network. An undirected edge exists between two nodes if the two corresponding users have strong social connections (e.g., colleagues or relatives) and trust each other not to launch a Sybil attack. If two nodes are connected by an edge, we say the two users are friends. Notice that here, the edge indicates strong trust, and the notion of friends is quite different from friends in other systems such as online chat rooms. An edge may exist between a Sybil node and an honest node if a malicious user (Khaled) successfully fools an honest user (Lyla) into trusting her. Such an edge is called an attack edge, and we use g to denote the total number of attack edges. The authentication mechanism in Sybil guard ensures that regardless of the number of Sybil nodes Khaled creates, Lyla will share an edge with at most one of them (as in the real social network). Thus, the number of attack edges is limited by the number of trust relation pairs that the adversary can establish between honest users and malicious users. While the adversary has only limited influence over the social network, we do assume it may have full knowledge of the social network. The degree of the nodes in the social network tends to be much smaller than n (number of honest nodes), so the system would be of little practical use if nodes only accepted their friends. Instead, Sybil Guard bootstraps from the given social network a protocol that enables honest nodes to accept a large fraction of the other honest nodes. Each pair of friends shares a unique symmetric secret key (e.g., a shared password) called the edge key [63]. The edge key is used to authenticate messages between the two friends (e.g., with a message authentication code) because only the two friends need to know the edge key, and key distribution is easily done out-of-band (e.g., via phone calls). A node can also revoke an edge key unilaterally simply by discontinuing use of the key and discarding it.

Third-Party Applications

Some social networking services may allow you to add third-party applications, including games and quizzes, which provide additional functionality. Social media websites are advanced web applications, as their use requires a high level of inter- action and capabilities. Be careful using these applications, even if an application does not contain malicious code, it might access information in your profile without your knowledge. This information could then be used in a variety of ways, such as tailoring advertisements, performing market research, sending spam email, or accessing your contacts. For example, emerging techniques include using custom Facebook applications to target users. Facebook applications are written by third- party developers and often have minimal security controls [48–50, 53].

Public Comments

Public comments may contain links to false locations designed to make failure of systems of certain organizations which are the target, and as we know, most staffs are using social networks.

Preventive Measures on Security

The attack graph represents collections of possible attack scenarios (sequences of actions) that an intruder might make to lead to a security breach in the network.

Measuring Network Security Using Attack Graphs

A topographical analysis of known critical points in the network can yield measurable data on overall system security. Analysis can produce an attack graph showing most vulnerable paths to/within the network, and hence, the network resistance to attacks can be quantified and measured.

An Ant Colony Optimization Algorithm for Network Vulnerability Analysis

AntNAG (ant network attack graph), an ant colony optimization algorithm for minimization analysis of large-scale network attack graphs. Each ant incrementally constructs a critical set of exploits. Each exploit is associated with a pheromone trail that indicates the desirability of including that exploit into an ant's solution. The first step is to set parameters and initialize pheromone trails. Then repeated iterations of the algorithm are run until some termination condition is met (e.g., a maximum number of iterations is reached). Within each iteration, each ant starts with an empty set and constructs a critical set of exploits by incrementally adding exploits until all attack scenarios are hit. The critical sets of exploits constructed by ants may contain redundant exploits, which are eliminated. After that, the iteration's best solution is improved by a local search heuristic. Finally, the pheromone trails are updated using a global updating rule.

Attack Tree

Attack trees are used to analyze attributes of the security of the network. The root node of the tree is the global target of the attacker, nodes represent the attacks, and the children nodes are refinements of this goal. The example in [37], the tree shows the goal of the attacker is to obtain a free lunch. The tree lists three possible ways to reach this goal. Lower levels in the tree explain how these subgoals are refined as well.

Social Networking Security and Privacy Study (2011)

The study reported in [5] is based on survey results from hundreds of users representing over 20 countries. The research was conducted over a 2-week span between September and October 2011. Users are asked about their experiences and feelings on social networking usage, security, and privacy. The results highlight some deficiencies that must be addressed by social network providers and the security community in order to provide a safe, fertile ground for continued growth and advancement on social platforms [1, 5] (Figs. 1.1–1.3).

Fig. 1.1 Social network users [1]

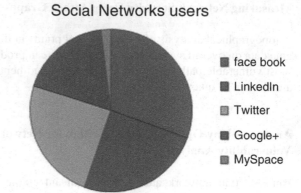

Social Networks users

■ face book
■ LinkedIn
▨ Twitter
■ Google+
▨ MySpace

Fig. 1.2 Problem experienced on social networks [5]

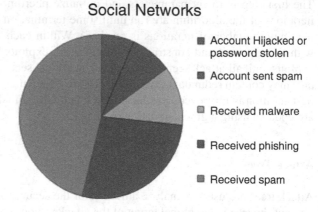

problem experienced on Social Networks

■ Account Hijacked or password stolen

■ Account sent spam

▨ Received malware

■ Received phishing

▨ Received spam

Fig. 1.3 Percentage of people who feel unsafe on the following social networks [5]

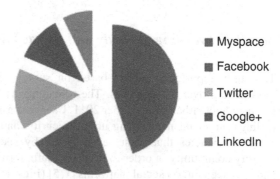

Precentage of people who feel unsafe on the following social networks

■ Myspace
■ Facebook
▨ Twitter
■ Google+
▨ LinkedIn

Case Study 1: Social Network Analysis in Terrorist Network Dataset

Following are the step-by-step procedures that are to be adopted while analyzing a social network.

Algorithm 1 Adopted while analyzing a social network

Step-1: Identification of a suitable target by the investigator.

Step-2: The research on the subject matter should be conducted thoroughly. For example, the investigator should explore who knows whom and how well do they know each other in order to discover the channel of information flow in the network.

Step-3: A database is to be created based on the information gathered from Step-2 in a binary matrix format in a node-by-node manner, as shown in Table 1.1 below.

Step-4: The investigator should investigate the basics of software that are to be used for analyzing the compiled data in order to provide everything from basic knowledge to expert advice.

Step-5: Finally, actual analysis is to be done which further can be used to identify the possible tactics to disrupt or improve the networks under investigation.

The relationship matrix in Table 1.1 is identified based on the number of nodes available in a network, where the data are entered by placing 0's and 1's into a spread sheet. The 0's indicate no connection where 1 represents a link. Sometimes, a signed matrix with +1 (positive relationship), 0 (no relationship), and −1(negative relationship) may also be considered to understand the relationships among the nodes. Further, if there exists a strong relationship, then in place of mentioning +1 in the spreadsheet, we may use 5 or 10, etc., based on their strength in relationships. Once the relationship matrix is obtained, the social network analysis software is then able to interpret them.

Example Scenario

Step-1: Based on the list of Foreign Terrorist Organizations, SNA is used to perform the social network analysis.

Step-2: Open sources are used to collect basic informations about each group, and then their affiliations with other groups are obtained from the list provided.

Step-3: Excel spreadsheet is used for the data compilation by putting 1's and 0's in order to signify the relations and obtain the binary matrix.

Table 1.1 Relationship matrix

	A	B
	1	0
	0	1

Table 1.2 Betweenness
centrality

	Betweenness	nbetweenness
1	213.00	15.123
2	123.00	6.349
3	47.97	2.872
4	42.11	2.981

Table 1.3 Closeness
centrality

	inFarness	inCloseness
1	9	100
2	10	78
3	11	65
4	15	90

Step-4: We then perform the social network analysis using UCINET tool [24] to run the experiments on the data in matrix format and found performance measures like betweenness and closeness centrality [59] in order to interpret the results, as shown below in Tables 1.2 and 1.3, respectively:

From the betweenness property [59], we know that it finds the number of times that a node lies along the shortest path between two others. Hence, the result says that the node-1 poses higher betweenness between all others.

From the result shown, it is quite evident that node-1 with incloseness score of 100 has the lowest total of geodesic distances from other nodes. At the same time, the node-4 with its inFarness score of 15 produces largest geodesic distances from other nodes.

Step-5: Finally, network visualization is made, as shown below for completing our social network analysis.

From Fig. 1.4, it can be seen that Al-Qaeda is the center node, whereas Jaishe-e-ahmed and Hamas are playing the most significant roles in the network. Further, Hezbollah has the highest betweenness because of its link with Al-Qaeda, Hamas, and all others. At the same time, Al-Aqsa Martyre brigade has the highest farness because of its highest geodesic distance from Al-Queda.

Case Study 2: Social Networks' Concepts to Visualize Terrorist Networks

Visualizing social networks are of immense help to the social network researchers in understanding new ways to present and manage data and effectively convert that data into meaningful information [55]. A number of visualization tools have been proposed for effective visualizing social networks including Pajek [18], NetVis, Krackplot, IKnow, InFlow, Visone, JUNG, and Prefuse, to name a few. Another source of online collaboration has also been visualized to better understand interactions that are provided in a discussion form [13]. Visualizing tasks for better

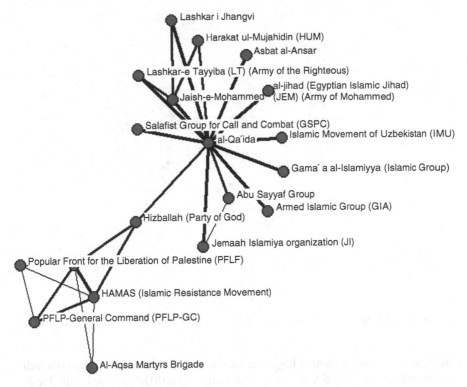

Fig. 1.4 Network visualization of foreign terrorist network data

collaboration during software development has been proposed [13] to address issues of coordination and geographical distribution of developer teams. Visualizing social networks using query interfaces for wikis and blogs [36] is used to provide the end users with more user-friendly alternatives.

Terrorism deals with violent acts aiming to simulate fear, coercion, or intimidation [11, 28, 46]. It is an established fact that terrorism poses both direct and indirect threats to normal life. Even though terrorist strikes destroy only a small fraction of the direct economy of a country, their large effect on economic outcomes is well known [20]. It is sad to note that technical development is not only pulled by the demand for high-tech products but is also highly influenced by some external environments, for example, terrorism. As shown by the aftermath of the 9/11 attacks, Bali, Madrid, and London bombings, some changes have occurred in the day-to-day living of citizens of those countries and around the world [2, 29, 43, 62].

After the 9/11 attacks, lots of efforts have been done to develop effective methods for antiterrorism strategies. Visualization is very important part for analyzing such a network since it can quickly provide good insight into the network structure, major members, and their properties [19]. Analyzing huge networks is not an easy task, and there is a need to reduce the complexity of these networks, which is

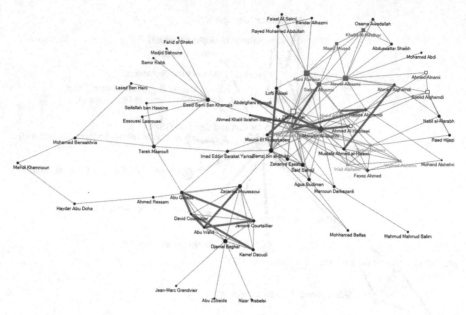

Fig. 1.5 Terrorists network with highlighted link suggestions using SDD reduction (rank 10)

usually depicted in the form of huge matrices. Matrix factorization method is a well-established approach, and Semidiscrete decomposition (SDD) is highly suitable for dealing with huge networks. Empirical results using the 9/11 network data illustrate the efficiency of the proposed approach [52]. The analysis of general complex networks is well described in [7] and [10]. This work is closely related to the link prediction, which is well elaborated by Liben-Nowell and Kleinberg [33]. Koren et al. [30] discussed the usage of matrix factorization methods for recommendation systems.

The obtained experiment is based on the dataset involving 9/11 attacks from [31]. Change from zero to one in the reduced matrix can be in wider sense considered as a link suggestion. In different fields, the suggestion can have different meanings. In the terrorist network, we can consider them as a suggestion to investigate, whether the link truly exists in reality; for more details, a reader can refer to [52]. The results for parameter setting with rank equal to 10 are illustrated in Fig. 1.5. Same coloring is used as in the original paper [31] by Krebs. Green triangles for flight AA #11, which crashed into the WTC North, full red squares for flight AA #77 which crashed into Pentagon, empty blue squares for flight UA #93 which crashed into Pennsylvania, and full purple diamonds for flight UA #175 which crashed into WTC South.

Edges drawn in bold red are suggestions obtained by the mentioned reduction. As evident, the suggested links are in the group of Zacarias Moussaoui, Abu Qatada, David Courtaillier, Jerome Courtaillier, Abu Walid, Kamel Daoudi, and Djamal Beghal. This group is also connected using several subgroups in the original

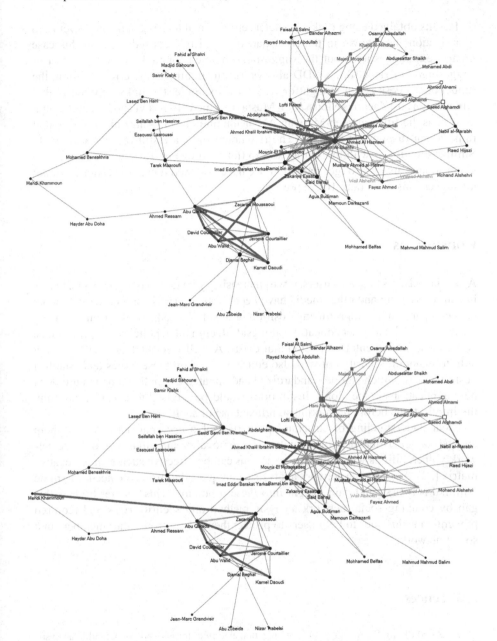

Fig. 1.6 Terrorists network with highlighted link suggestions using SDD reduction (rank 5 and 20)

data; therefore, the proposed method suggests their stronger interconnection. The same holds for the suggested link between Ramzi bin al-Shibh and Lofti Raissi as it connects two different groups of individuals. Remaining suggestions can be explored in a similar way.

Results obtained using rank parameter setting equal to 20 (that means lower ratio of reduction) are shown in the right part of Fig. 1.6. Less reduction in this case means less suggestions, but the suggestion obtained for rank 20 is not subset of suggestions for rank 10. As SDD always tries to minimize the error function, the reduction process is not straightforward – for example, the links between Mehdi Khammoun and Zacarias Moussaoui, Mustafa Ahmed al-Hisawi and Satam Suqami, as well as the link between Marwan Al-Shehhi and Nawaf Alhazmi, are present at rank 20 but disapper at rank 10. The remaining links are still present at rank 10. Similar situation is with the setting $k = 5$ (left part of Fig. 1.6), which gives us 16 suggestions – using stronger reduction, we have obtained more suggestions, but not all suggestions from rank 10 are present.

Conclusions

As social networking gains users, it will increasingly be targeted by attackers, just as instant messaging and other media have been. Security risks can put the individual or a company in a compromising position or at serious risk. Aside from not using these sites at all, end-user education, alongside documented policies and procedures, is the most fundamental protection that exists. A well-informed user will not only help to maintain security but will also educate others on these issues and establish best practices, which can be standardized and updated as applications mature or as new applications come along. Institutions would be advised to consider carefully the implications before promoting significant use of such services.

Clear understanding of structural properties of a criminal network may help analysts target critical network members for removal or surveillance and locate network vulnerabilities where disruptive actions can be effective such as non negative matrix [32]. Appropriate network analysis techniques, therefore, are needed to mine criminal networks and gain insight into these problems. This chapter bridges this gap by combing social network analysis method and security risks and required prevention techniques to help users to protect themselves from other members in a social network.

References

1. Abadi, M., Jalili, S.: An ant colony optimization algorithm for network vulnerability analysis. Iran. J. Electr. Electron. Eng. 2(3), 106–120 (2006)
2. Abadie, A., Gardeazabal, J.: Terrorism and the world economy. Eur. Econ. Rev. 52(1), 1–27 (2008)
3. Antheunis, M.L., Valkenburg, P.M., Peter, J.: Getting acquainted through social network sites: testing a model of online uncertainty reduction and social attraction. Comput. Hum. Behav. 26, 100–109 (2010)

4. Baden, R., Bender, A., Spring, N., Bhattacharjee, B., Starin, D.: Persona: an online social network with user-defined privacy. ACM SIGCOMM Comput. Commun. Rev. **39**(4), 50–55 (2009)
5. Barracuda Networks Inc.: Social Networking Security and Privacy Study. Barracuda Labs, Belgium (2011)
6. Barrigar, J.: Social network site privacy: a comparative analysis of six sites. The Office of the Privacy Commissioner of Canada, Feb 2009. http://www.priv.gc.ca/information/pub/sub_comp_200901_e.pdf. Accessed on Feb 2012
7. Boccaletti, S., Latora, V., Moreno, Y., Chavez, M., Hwang, D.U.: Complex networks: structure and dynamics. Phys. Rep.**424**, 175–308 (2006)
8. Boyd, D., Ellison, N.: Social network sites: definition, history and scholarship. J. Comput. Mediat. Commun. **13**(1), 210–230 (2007)
9. Carley, K.M.: Dynamic network analysis. In: Breiger, R., Carley, K., Pattison, P. (eds.) Dynamic Social Network Modeling and Analysis: Workshop Summary and Papers, pp. 133–145. Committee on Human Factors, National Research Council, Washington, DC (2003)
10. Costa, L.F., Rodrigues, F.A., Travieso, G., Boas, P.R.V.: Characterization of complex networks: a survey of measurements. Adv. Phys. **56**, 167–242 (2007)
11. Czinkota, M.R., Knight, G.A., Liesch, P.W., Steen, J.: Positioning terrorism in management and marketing: research propositions. J. Int. Manage. **11**(4), 581–604 (2005)
12. Das, K., Bhaduri, K., Kargupta, H.: A local asynchronous distributed privacy preserving feature selection algorithm for large peer-to-peer networks. Knowl. Inf. Syst. J. **24**(3), 341–367 (2009)
13. De Nooy, W., AMrvar, A., Batagelig, V.: Exploratory Social Network Analysis with Pajek. Cambridge university press, New York (2004)
14. Douceur. J.: The Sybil attack. In: First International Workshop on Peer-to-Peer Systems, Cambridge, MA, USA, pp. 251–260 (2002)
15. Erola, A., Castell-Roca, J., Viejo, A., Mateo-Sanz, J.M.: Exploiting social networks to provide privacy in personalized web search. J. Syst. Softw. **84**(10), 1734–1745 (2011)
16. Felt, A., Evans, D.: Privacy protection for social networking APIs, In Proceedings of Web 2.0 Security and Privacy (W2SP 2009), Oakland, California (2009)
17. Felt, A., Evans, D.: Privacy Protection for Social Networking APIs. University of Virginia Charlottesville, Virginia (2008)
18. Freeman, L.: Visualizing social network. J. Soc. Struct. **1**(1), 151–161 (2000)
19. Freeman, L.C.: Social network visualization. In: Methods of Encyclopedia of Complexity and Systems Science, pp. 8345–8363 (2009)
20. Frey, B.S.: How can business cope with terrorism? J. Policy Model. **31**(5), 779–787 (2009)
21. Grace, J., Gruhl, D., et al.: Artist remains: through analysis of on-line community comments. In proc. of J. Grace edns, (2007)
22. Granger, S.: Social engineering fundamentals, part I: hacker tactics. (cited 5/12/11). Available on: http://www.symantec.com/connect/articles/social-engineering-fundamentals-part-i-hacker-tactics, (2001)
23. Gross, R., Acquisti, A.: Information revelation and privacy in online social networking sites (the facebook case). Available at: http://www.fastcompany.com/articles/2008/10/social-networking-security.html. Accessed 8 Jan 2012
24. Halgin, D.: An introduction to UCINET and NetDraw. In: Proceedings of the NIPS UCINET and NetDraw Workshop 2008, Harvard University, pp. 1–47 (2008)
25. Hi5: http://hi5.com. Accessed on 2011
26. Internet world stats: http://www.internetworldstats.com/stats.htm (2008)
27. Kadushin, C.: Who benefits from network analysis: ethics of social network research. Soc. Netw. **27**, 139–145 (2005)
28. Koh, W.T.H.: Terrorism and its impact on economic growth and technological innovation. Technol. Forecast. Soc. Change **74**(2), 129–138 (2007)
29. Kollias, C., Messis, P., Mylonidis, N., Paleologou, S.: Terrorism and the effectiveness of security spending in Greece: policy implications of some empirical indings. J. Policy Model. **31**(5), 788–802 (2009)

30. Koren, Y., Bell, R., Volinsky, C.: Matrix factorization techniques for recommender systems. IEEE Comput. **42**, 30–37 (2009)
31. Krebs, V.E.: Uncloaking terrorist networks. First Monday **7**, (2002)
32. Lee, D., Seung, H.: Learning the parts of objects by non-negative matrix factorization. Nature **401**, 788–791 (1999)
33. Liben-Nowell, D., Kleinberg, J.: The link-prediction problem for social networks. J. Am. Soc. Inf. Sci. Technol. **58**, 1019–1031 (2007)
34. LinkedIn: http://www.linkedin.com. Accessed on 2012
35. LiveJournal: http://www.livejournal.com. Accessed on 2012
36. Matsuo, Y., et al.: Polyphonet: an advanced social network extraction system from the web. In: Proceedings of the International Conference on World Wide Web (www 06), New York, pp. 397–406 (2006)
37. Mauw, S., Oostdijk, M.: Foundations of attack trees. In: Proceedings of the 8th International Conference of Information Security and Cryptology (ICISC 2005), Seoul Korea, pp.186–198 (2005)
38. McDowell, M., Morda, D.: Socializing securely: using social networking services. United States Computer Emergency Readiness Team (US-CERT), Washington, DC (2011)
39. Moor, J.H.: Towards a theory of privacy for the information age. SIGCAS Comput. Soc. **40**(2), 31–34 (2010)
40. Moustafa, W., Deshpande, A., Namata, G., Getoor, L.: Declarative analysis of noisy information networks. In: Proceedings of the IEEE 27th International Conference on Department of Computer Science, Data Engineering Workshops (ICDEW), Hannover, pp. 106–111, (2011)
41. MySpace: http://www.myspace.com
42. Netcraft: http://news.netcraft.com (2009)
43. Paraskevas, A., Arendell, B.: A strategic framework for terrorism prevention and mitigation in tourism destinations. Tour. Manage. **28**(6), 1560–1573 (2007)
44. PhishingTank: What is phishing? (cited 6/12/11). Available from: http://www.phishtank.com/what-is-phishing.php
45. PricewaterhouseCoopers: Security for social networking. Available on: http://www.pwc.com/en_US/us/it-risk-security/assets/security-social-networking.pdf, (2010)
46. Reid, E.F., Chen, H.: Mapping the contemporary terrorism research domain. Int. J. Hum. Comput. Stud. **65**(1), 42–56 (2007)
47. Sancho, D.: Security guide to social networks, A Trend Micro White Paper, Aug, (2009).
48. schrock, A.: Examining social media usage: technology clusters and social network relationships. First Monday **14**(1), (2009)
49. Shani, G., Chickering, M., Meek, C.: Mining recommendations from the web. In: Proceedings of the 2008 ACM Conference on Recommender System, Lausanne, pp. 35–42 (2008)
50. Sheldon, P.: The relationship between unwillingness to communicate and students Facebook use. J Media Psychol. Theor. Method Appl. **20**(2), 67–75 (2008)
51. Skyrock: http://www.Skyrock.com. Accessed on 2012
52. Snasel, V., Horak, Z., Abraham, A.: Link suggestions in terrorists networks using semi discrete decomposition. In: Sixth International Conference on Information Assurance and Security (IAS), USA, IEEE, ISBN 978-1-4244-7408-0, pp. 337–339 (2010)
53. Soghoian, C.: Hackers target facebook apps. CNet News, (cited 5/12/11). Available from: http://news.cnet.com/8301-13739-3-9904331-46.html (2008)
54. Solanas, A.: Privacy protection with genetic algorithms. Stud. Computat. Intel. **92**, 215–237 (2008)
55. Tantipathananandh, C., Breger-wolf, T., Kempe, D.: A framework for community identification in dynamic Social network. In: Proceedings of the KDD 2007, San Jose, CA, USA, pp. 717–726 (2007)
56. Thellwal, M.: Social networks, gender and friending, analysis of myspace profiles. J. Am. Soc. Inf. Sci. Technol. **591**(8), 1321–1330 (2008)
57. Tufekci, Z.: Grroming, gossip facebook and myspace: what can we learn about these sites from those who wont assimilate? Inf. Commun. Soc. **11**(4), 544–564 (2008)

58. http://www.facebook.com/note.php?note_id=324110600939875. Accessed on 2012
59. http://en.wikipedia.org/wiki/Betweenness. Accessed on 2012
60. http://www.facebook.com. Accessed on 2012
61. Walther, J., Vander Heide, B., Kim, S., Westerman, D., Tang, S.T.: The role of friends appearance and behaviour on evaluations of individuals on facebook: are we known by the company we keep? Hum. commun. Res. **34**, 28–49 (2008)
62. Wolf, Y., Frankel, O.: Terrorism: toward an overarched account and prevention with a special reference to pendulum interplay between both parties. Aggress. Viol. Behav. **12**(3), 259–279 (2007)
63. Yu, H., Kaminsky, M., Gibbons, P.B., Flaxman, A.: SybilGuard: defending against sybil attacks via social networks. SIGCOMM'06 **16**(3), 576–589 (2006)

Chapter 2
Security, Privacy, and Trust in Social Networks

Komathy Karuppanan

Abstract Millions of people worldwide are connected through networked digital infrastructure that grows increasingly sophisticated and contextually rich. A social network service is an online service, platform, or site that focuses on building and reflecting of social relations among people. A social network service essentially consists of a representation of each user called a *profile*, his/her social links, and a variety of additional services. Recent years have seen exceptional growth in the usage of online social networks and there are about 300 online social networks such as Facebook, Twitter, and MySpace, having more than half a billion registered users worldwide (Wikipedia, Social network service. http://en.wikipedia.org/wiki/Social_network_service. Accessed 25 Jan 2011, 2010). Users can often upload pictures of themselves to their profiles, post blog entries for others to read, search for other users with similar interests and compile and share lists of contacts. The information they share are not only viewed by the trusted users but also by the adversaries. This chapter is to encompass research studies in the areas of security, trust, and privacy applicable to social networks. The contributions relating to novel technologies and methodologies for securely building and managing social networks are discussed here. Also, the relevant secure applications as well as cross-cutting issues are narrated.

Introduction

The social networks, as they disseminate and process massive amounts personal of data on individual behavior, probably lead to the erosion of civil liberties through loss of privacy and personal freedom. Moreover, identity theft invites malicious acts such as phishing, spamming, and sybil attacks. These negative developments

K. Karuppanan (✉)
DCSE, Easwari Engineering College, Chennai, India
e-mail: gomes1960@yahoo.com

A. Abraham (ed.), *Computational Social Networks: Security and Privacy*,
DOI 10.1007/978-1-4471-4051-1_2, © Springer-Verlag London 2012

Fig. 2.1 Names of some of the social network sites

threaten to undermine the potential and beneficial opportunities of Internet. Securing the future Internet becomes a concern of users' community. The real benefits of online social networking should not be lost while working for new security standards. It is like venturing into careful handling of a double-edged sword.

Figure 2.1 has captured a pool of onsite logos, which are currently active social networking websites. According to Boyd and Ellison [1] and Wikipedia [2], an online social network is characterized as follows:

An online social network is a digital representation of its users and a subset of their social connections or relationships in the physical or virtual world, plus networking services for messaging and socializing among its users. It provides a platform to:

- Allow users to construct digital representations of themselves (usually known as user profiles) and articulate their social connections with other users (i.e., lists of contacts)
- Support the maintenance and enhancement of preexisting social connections among users in the physical or virtual world
- Help forge new connections based on common interests, location, activities, and so on

Based on the above definition, an online social network should provide the following functionalities to facilitate users' self-representations and online social interactions [3].

- Personal space management
- Social connection management
- Connectivity to other applications
- Social search
- Social traversal

Friendster is the first popular social networking site (SNS) that allows people to explicitly articulate their social network, present themselves through a profile such as interests and demographics, post public testimonials about one another, and browse a network of people. Friendster's tools support a powerful process of community formation around shared values and tastes. Social groups tend to converse collectively on a coherent presentation style and encourage other participants to follow the collective norms (e.g., regarding photos). Studies on Friendster [4] revealed how people negotiate context when presenting themselves; how the network structure of a SNS spreads and connects people; and the issues involved in articulating one's social network as compared to a behavior-driven network. Boyd [4] listed three forms of constructing fake personas called Fakesters:

1. Cultural characters that represent shared reference points with which people might connect (e.g., God, Buddha, George W Bush)
2. Community characters that represent external collections of people to help collect known groups (e.g., Stanford University, Olympic Games, San Francisco)
3. Passing characters meant to be perceived as real (e.g., duplicates of people on the system, representations of friends who refuse to participate)

Facebook, a social networking site that began with a focus on colleges and universities, has been studied and evaluated by several works [5–7]. These studies have collected profile information from Facebook through the use of a web crawler and through surveys of members. They show that Facebook members reveal a lot of information about them, and they are not aware of privacy options or controls who can actually view their profile [5].

MySpace, the largest social networking site in the world following Friendster, mainly focuses on music and popular culture. Figure 2.2 depicts the popularity of top social networking sites in India. In a comparative study of Facebook and MySpace [8], it is found that Facebook has shown more reputation than MySpace. Schools have attempted to prohibit their students' use of the site, and law enforcement officials allege that MySpace is a space for cyber criminals to lure the school students [8]. MySpace has a stronger evidence of new relationship development beyond the bounds of social networking site, despite weaker trust results. The outcome of the survey [8] also showed that the interaction of trust and privacy concern in social networking sites is not yet understood to a sufficient degree to allow accurate modeling of behavior and activity.

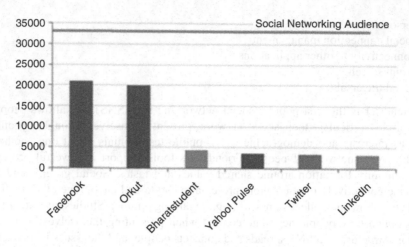

Fig. 2.2 Popularity of top social networking sites in India – July 2010 (Courtesy: comScore, Inc.)

Security, Trust, and Privacy for Social Networking Sites

Trust is a very important aspect of human life. Several people have attempted to define trust and consequently several definitions of trust exist. Oxford English Dictionary defines trust as:

confidence, strong believe in the goodness, strength, reliability of something or somebody

Trust is defined [9] as "the willingness of a party to be vulnerable to the actions of another party based on the expectation that the other will perform a particular action important to the trustor, irrespective of the ability to monitor or control that other party". Trust is a critical determinant of sharing information and developing new relationships [10, 11]. Trust is also an important measure for successful online interactions [12–15]. In social networks, users assign a trust as a single rating describing their connection to others, without explicit context or history. Instead of being a binary value, trust falls within a range. There is some upper threshold above which a person can say another is trusted. Below that threshold, there is a range of values of trust. Gambetta [16] has brought out that the threshold changes not only between people, but for each person depending on their circumstances. Instead of using a single point to decide a person "trusted," allow people to express a value of trust they have for others. The users themselves can determine when that value qualifies as above the threshold for "absolute trust" and when it does not. Gambetta presents a different but unique definition of trust. He defines trust mathematically as follows:

- Trust (or, symmetrically, distrust) is a particular level of the subjective probability with which an agent assesses that another agent or group of agents will perform

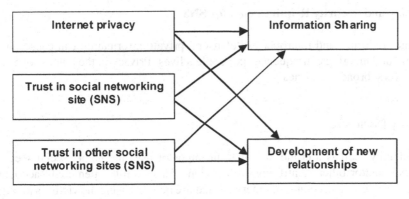

Fig. 2.3 Privacy trust model for SNS

a particular action, both before he can monitor such action (or independently or his capacity ever to be able to monitor it) and in a context in which it affects his own action.

- When someone is trustworthy, it implicitly means that the probability that he will perform an action that is beneficial or at least not detrimental to others is high enough to consider for cooperating with him.
- Correspondingly when someone is untrustworthy, it implies that probability is low enough for us to refrain from doing so.

Confidentiality or Privacy is the security service provided against the illegal disclosure of information of a person, a product or a company and against exploiting their private information. The more *sensitive* the information revealed by a user, the higher his privacy risk. Also, the more *visible* the disclosed information becomes in the network, the higher the privacy risk. If we are able to measure the sensitivity and visibility of a data item exposed in social network site, the control measure to an adequate level can be applied [17].

Figure 2.3 provides a theoretical model used by the study done by Catherine Dwyer et al. [18]. The independent variables are internet privacy concern, trust in the social networking site, and trust in other members of social networking sites. They relate the trust to the outcomes being measured with respect to the use of social networking sites, specifically information sharing and development of new relationships.

Privacy and Security of SNS

To understand the challenges of security and privacy, the standard services of network security such as confidentiality, integrity, and availability with respect to SNS are briefed in this section.

Privacy and Security Requirements for SNS

Illegal disclosure and improper use of users' private information can cause undesirable or damaging consequences in people's lives. Privacy in the context of SNSs has several broad categories:

Identity Disclosure

An Identity theft is a crime in which an impostor uses the name, social security number, and/or other identifying information of a victim to open credit accounts, use existing credit accounts, or otherwise acquire benefits using the victim's identity. Identity theft is classified into five categories:

- Business/commercial identity theft (using another's business name to obtain credit)
- Criminal identity theft (posing as another person when apprehended for a crime)
- Financial identity theft (using another's identity to obtain credit, goods, and services)
- Identity cloning (using another's information to assume his or her identity in daily life)
- Medical identity theft (using another's identity to obtain medical care or drugs)

Identity theft may be used to facilitate or fund other crimes including illegal immigration, terrorism, and espionage. There are cases of identity cloning to attack payment systems, including online credit card processing and medical insurance [19]. Identity management is about the management of data defining a person's identities. The biggest repository of personal images on the internet is Facebook with a staggering several billion images, while few million new images are uploaded every day. Either a Government or Federated Identity Providers have not acquired such a voluminous data warehouse of personal profiles compared to that of the social networking providers.

The protection of a user's identity changes across different types of SNSs. Identity anonymity is not encouraged because most applications in SNSs rely on connecting users' profiles to their public identities. A weak pseudonym method is employed in some of the SNSs such as Facebook and Match.com, where the use of real names and personal contact information is discouraged. A random identifier is used to protect the public identity of a person. SNS provider is also able to have the data of each session the user had such as time and length of connections, location (IP address) of connection, other users' profiles visited, messages sent and received, and so forth. Therefore, in addition to privacy of identity, communication privacy is also lost. Hence, access control measures to protect unauthorized entities against learning the content of the private data and user anonymity are mandatory. Access to information of a user shall only be granted by the user directly, and the access control has to be as fine-grained as each private information item has to be separately manageable. Also, private data files or profile when stored or transmitted should appear random and leak no useful information.

Identity management systems take care not only to store personal data, but also to manage data such as allowing query, transfer, and display of the data. Social network sites provide user-friendly tools which allow users to define how their personal profiles are displayed, both in terms of visual layout and the data fields which are displayed. They also provide sophisticated tools for searching and mining profile data.

Access Control

It assists users to control over who accesses which parts of their personal data. Control measures define the basic credentials of the entities to be authorized. For example, a database of medical records might allow access only to users who can prove somehow that they are doctors. Recently, social networks have added features which allow users to restrict access down to the level of individual friends or business associates for each field of their personal profile. In other words, they are now offering a fine-granular access control. Most identity management systems provide data tracking tools so users can see who has accessed personal data. This functionality is often not fully implemented in SNSs because users browsing other people's profiles generally prefer to remain anonymous. Some SNSs, however, have installed profile trackers to provide statistics on anonymous accesses to user profiles.

Authentication and Data Integrity

Social networking actually represents existing social relationships in real life called *real-life social network* (RSN). The data stored in an SNS can be modeled as an online social graph and there exists a one-to-one mapping from the RSN to the online social graph model [1]. Figure 2.4 shows a sample of online social graph with four user nodes and a single SSN provider node. Any attempt on altering the online social graph model from its corresponding RSN indicates the loss of data consistency or an attack on data integrity. These instances of attack should be detected and corrected with appropriate mechanisms.

From Fig. 2.4, it is evident that attacks on online social graphs are forging nodes or identities and forging social links/connections. Forging a node (e.g., identity theft) is a fundamental problem in SNSs. For example, an attacker can create fake profiles in the name of well-known personalities or brands in order to defame people or to earn profit using their reputation. Also, an attacker can create multiple fake identities to disrupt digital reputation systems for SNSs [20, 21]. Therefore, it is required that the communicating entities in SSN be assured of each other's legitimacy and authenticity.

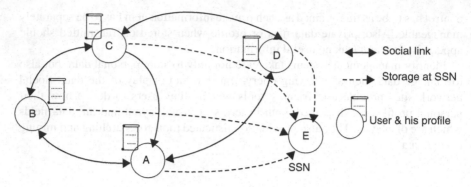

Fig. 2.4 A sample online social graph along with a SSN provider

Security Threats

The relative freedom afforded by social networking services has caused concern regarding the potential of its misuse by individual patrons. In October 2006, a fake MySpace profile has led to the suicide of a person [2]. The event provoked global concern regarding the use of social networking services for harassment purposes. In July 2008, posting a fake page on Facebook falsely claiming the personality of an individual was ordered to pay about USD $44,000 for defamation and breach of privacy [2].

Risk for Child Safety

Citizens and governments have been concerned of misuse by child and teenagers of social network services, particularly in relation to online sexual predators. A certain number of actions have been engaged by governments to better understand the problem and find some solutions. A panel report in 2008 concluded that technological fixes such as age verification and scans are relatively ineffective means of apprehending online predators [22].

Trolling

A common misuse of social networking sites is that it is occasionally used to emotionally abuse individuals. Such actions are often referred to as trolling. Trolling can occur in many different forms, such as defacement of deceased person(s) tribute pages, playing online pranks on volatile individuals and controversial comments with the intention to cause anger and cause arguments. Inherently individuals are given the power to post offensive remarks or pictures that could potentially cause a great amount of emotional pain for another individual.

Digital Profile Aggregation

Profiles on SNSs can be downloaded and stored over time and augmented by third parties, creating a digital dossier of personal data. Information revealed on an SNS can be used for purposes and in contexts different from the ones the profile owner had considered. While profiles can be changed or even deleted, additional storage elsewhere cannot be prevented – thus personal data takes on a life of its own even when the information itself may no longer be accurate or relevant.

Face Recognition

Related to face recognition, content-based image retrieval (CBIR) was originally developed for digital forensics. CBIR is an emerging technology identifying aspects of a room (e.g., a painting) in very large databases of images. Traditional search terms are replaced with a reference image or image template. Search is designed to be resilient to cropping, resizing, rotation, and quality adjustment. According to the report by ENISA [12], this can lead to stalking, unwanted marketing, blackmail, and all the other threats associated with unwanted disclosure of location data. Currently, privacy controls on images uploaded and the advice given on SNSs do not take into account the possibility of CBIR, and few people are aware of the consequences of posting images with location-specific content online.

Network-Based Risks

Unsolicited messages (spam), cross site scripting (CSS), viruses and worms have capitalized on the exponential growth of SNSs and the free traffic they provide. *Phishing* attacks facilitated by the self-created "profiles" are easily approachable in SNSs. SNSs are also vulnerable to social engineering techniques which exploit low threshold to trusted networks and to scripting attacks which allow the automated injection of phishing links. On many SNSs, it is even possible to use scripts to invite friends.

CSS attacks and threats are due to "widgets" produced by weakly verified third parties. A widget [2] is a stand-alone application that can be embedded into third party sites by any user on a page where they have rights of authorship, e.g., a webpage, blog, or profile on a social media site. Widgets allow users to turn personal content into dynamic web apps that can be shared on websites where the code can be installed. For example, a *Weather Report Widget* could report today's weather by accessing data from the weather channel. Should you want to put that widget on your own Facebook profile, you could do this by copying and pasting the embed code into your profile on Facebook. This is a growing phenomenon with several SNS-specific features.

Cyber-stalking is another threatening behavior in which an attacker repeatedly contacts a victim by electronic means such as e-mail, Instant Messenger, and messaging on SNSs. Statistics suggest that stalking using SNSs is increasing.

Sybil attacks, in which a malicious user takes on multiple identities and pretends to be multiple, distinct nodes called *sybil nodes* or *sybil identities* in the system. A trusted central authority that issues and verifies credentials unique to an actual human being can control sybil attacks easily. But in practice, establishing a single identity to each user worldwide is a tedious work. Furthermore, the central authority who issues and maintains the identity can easily be a single point of failure, a single target for denial-of-service attacks, and also a bottleneck for performance, unless its functionality is itself widely distributed. Defending against sybil attacks without a trusted central authority is much harder. Many decentralized systems today try to combat Sybil attacks by binding an identity to an IP address. However, malicious users can readily harvest or steal IP addresses. Spammers, for example, are known to harvest a wide variety of IP addresses to hide the source of their messages, by advertising BGP routes for unused blocks of IP addresses. Beyond just IP harvesting, a malicious user can *co-opt* a large number of end-user machines, creating a *botnet* of thousands of compromised machines spread throughout the Internet. Botnets are particularly hard to defend against because nodes in botnets are indeed distributed to end users' computers. Techniques generally used by spammers include [21]:

- The use of specialized SNS spamming software such as FriendBot [23] to automate friend invitations and note/comment posting. Such tools use the SNSs' search tools to target a certain demographic segment of the users and communicate with them from an account disguised as that of a real person.
- The sending of notes typically including embedded links to pornographic or other product sites designed to sell something.
- Friend invitations, using an attractive profile which is likely to persuade someone to accept the invitation. The profile or the invitation then contains links to external sites advertising products or even phishing for passwords.
- The posting of spam comments on public notes or comments areas of 'friends'. Typically, spammers will create as many 'friends' as possible, focusing on those with public notes or comments areas or message boards and fitting a specific demographic profile (Friendbot has features to automate this) and then post spam messages on their public notes or comments areas.
- Stealing members' passwords to insert and promote their offers on another profile.

Detection and correction techniques to thwart security attacks in SNSs shall include:

- Filtering of malicious or spam comments
- Filtering comments by quality to increase content quality
- Increasing reliability of third party widgets
- Reporting inappropriate or copyrighted content
- Reporting profile-squatting or identity theft

- Recommendation-only sign-up (where new members have to be introduced by an existing member)
- Reporting of inappropriate behavior and posting of high-risk data such as location information

The critical points arising from the above discussion of the privacy and security threats exposed to SNSs are listed below as per the recommendation report given by the European Network and Information Security Agency (ENISA) [12]:

- An effort to have open architectures and data formats for social networks is crucial to improve security and privacy. since business models based on increasing the user base through malicious techniques generally discourage privacy and security whereas open formats create a market for secure and privacy-respecting data storage.
- In opening up these personal data warehouses, it is crucial that the confidentiality and privacy of data continue to be respected; i.e., portable access control and privacy rules must be provided along with portable data. Open standards allow users to "leave the Hotel California" but they also need a secure suitcase to take their data with them.
- Fine-grained authorization schemes which can delegate access are very important in such open architectures.

An Architecture for Trust and Anonymity in Social Networks

Identity theft and authentication are fundamental problems in social networking and they originate due to the lapses in security measures. Though the use of Smart ID cards finds its access including home computers, but the success of the technology is not guaranteed. For example, adults often lend their payment/ID cards complete with PIN to children or friends and there is no way to stop this kind of delegation with ID cards. Another effort could be the use of web-of-trust techniques such as *attribute reputation* for establishing identity. One such model of an attribute reputation for identity assurance is described below [21]:

- Each user is issued a token (e.g., public-private key pair) while joining the social network. It may be managed entirely by the social network provider until the user wants to export his profile. The token is like a social network identity card and it assures the person's name and certain attributes like age, sex, and location (ASL). It is called as key-trust.
- Every time user A is accepted as a friend by another user, the token is given a positive or negative trust rating. No user intervention is required to do this. Trust ratings could also be allocated according to a more sophisticated scheme whereby trust ratings allocated depend on the trust rating of the vouching party.
- If user A suspects that another user B is not as he identifies himself in terms of Name + ASL, then you can explicitly state this by signing a revocation certificate and posting it in a directory. This negates user B's key trust.

- If user A knows user B personally, user A can go through an explicit procedure where user A verifies user B's token and profile together in person and vouches that it is definitely user B's profile. This adds user B's key trust.
- Positive and negative scores are exported through certificates and the user's token are aggregated to give an identity reputation.
- Anyone can examine the score on a user's token to evaluate whether to believe that they are who they say they are.
- If a user wants to leave a specific social network and go to another one, they can take their token with them as a public-private key-pair and a public key certificate from the provider over the key and personal data and the trust score as electronic signatures of other people over that certificate.
- This could be extended from key identity reputation other than name, age, sex, and location. For example, work experience, reliability, or any other attribute one might attach a reputation for. This is an extension of the testimonial system seen in existing social networks.
- Attribute reputation could be exported through public key certificates as above.

The above scheme could also be used as a basis for a smart way of encrypting data in social networks to strengthen privacy so that network members with an adequate trust level in their keys can see the data, but others, including possibly even the service provider, cannot. A typical use-case is:

- Data from social networks are encrypted using the public key from the basic use-case above. This is used to export the data in a secure way and transport it between social networks. The private key corresponding to the public key is used to decrypt the data.
- Data could even be encrypted when inserted into the social network provider's database to provide extra privacy.
- Data in profiles could be encrypted in such a way that only private keys whose public component is signed by the data owner would be able to decrypt the profile data. This provides a portable access control system for social networks.

Privacy Preserving Models and Architectures

Sharing information is one of the most important features of online social networks. Such shared information is often personal and only intended to be shared with certain users or groups of users. Unintended leakage of personal information can result in damage of someone's reputation, identity theft, or can have other bad effects for the user. To share information in a comfortable and secure way, the user needs to know with whom personal data are shared and must be able to restrict who can access it. This section discusses about the design of some of the models and architectures that preserve the privacy of users while they utilize the services of social networks.

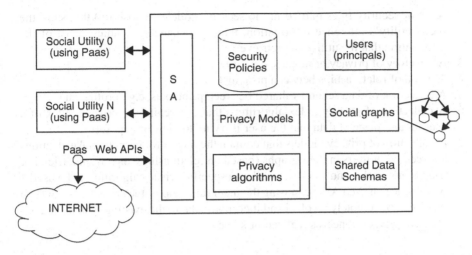

Fig. 2.5 Privacy-as-a-service (PaaS) architecture (Courtesy: IBM Almaden Research Center)

PaaS: Architecture, Model, and Algorithm

A majority of the users are not aware of the implication of using the default privacy configuration that they accept when using these services [24]. Most social network sites provide many utilities for setting the privacy policy [25]. There are some primary concerns over the privacy setting such as:

- Privacy model and engine does not prevent social applications, launched from heterogeneous developers, rather from collecting additional data from users nor does it help these application developers to easily build privacy functionality into their applications [3, 26].
- Growing number of privacy settings multiplied by number of social applications present a significant cognitive burden on end-users who typically accept the defaults and do not revisit their options until damage is done [27].
- Mechanisms for privacy settings are primitive at best, are mostly manual, and do not take full advantage of the social and trust relationships that users build. The platform should leverage the social graphs of its users to help them improve the relative privacy of their data across all social software [28].

IBM research unit [29] has brought out a framework, service, privacy model, and algorithm for social platforms and applications that enables the concept of Privacy-as-a-Service (PaaS). Figure 2.5 shows a typical architecture of PaaS developed by IBM.

The service consists of the following eight components:

1. A Security Assistant (SA) that ensures that access to the information in the PaaS server strictly follows the rules in the Security Policies repository

2. A set of security rules (stored in the security policies repository) that store the social utility's reference information, their associated credentials, a list of the information that the utility can retrieve
3. A directory of privacy principals, e.g., users
4. A graph of relationships between principals
5. A collection of data schemas shared between principals, e.g., profile data
6. A collection of privacy index algorithms that can return the privacy index of a user for any piece of data that the user is trying to view or expose;
7. A collection of privacy models that contain the means for users to make elections between other users in their graphs (based on relationships, e.g., friend, friend of friends, networks, and so on) as well as a specific privacy algorithm to be used
8. A collection of Web APIs exposing the main functions of the privacy system such that it can be remotely invoked and incorporated into the existing systems that do not have privacy concerns realized or solved

Model

A model for an arbitrary social network is defined, which is a set of interconnected entities and containers. Entities are the primary artifacts of a social network, i.e. users, and containers are special structures formed around these entities to foster a community, activity, or for greater purposes, e.g., a social network applications, groups, and networks. It is assumed that entities may opt to be members of containers and each entity interacts with other entities and with other containers.

Social Entity

A social entity is referred to as se. The set of all entities for this particular social network, E, is $\{se_1, \ldots, se_n\}$, where n is the total number of entities in the network.

Descriptor

Let d is a descriptor that is used to describe the attribute utilized to create the profile for an entity. d is a tuple of the form $\{d\_name, d\_type\}$. The set D is the complete set of descriptors used to describe a particular entity and is equal to $\{d_1, \ldots, d_m\}$, where m is the total number of descriptors needed to describe this particular entity. Assume that D^* is the universal set for D. Each entity can be described by a set of descriptors (i.e., attribute-value pairs), e.g. $\{(name, "Kathy"), (birth\_date, 16/06/1960)\}$.

Container

A container c is the set $\{\{a_1,\ldots,a_k\}, \{u_1,\ldots,u_p\}, D_c, \{Du_1,\ldots,Du_k\}\}$, where $\{a_1,\ldots,a_k\}$ are administrators of the container, $\{u_1,\ldots,u_p\}$ are the users of the container, D_c is the set of descriptors for the container and $\{Du_1,\ldots,Du_k\}$ is the data on the users of the container. It should be noted that $\{a_1,\ldots,a_k\} \subseteq \{u_1,\ldots,u_p\}$, and $k \leq p$ and C is defined as the universal set of all containers in the network. A set of applications ($A \subseteq C$), groups ($G \subseteq C$) and networks ($N \subseteq C$) are also defined.

Privacy

Assume that every user has a profile consisting of n profile items (e.g., name, gender, birth date, phone number). For each profile item, users set a *privacy level* that determines their willingness to disclose information associated with this item. The privacy levels picked by all N users for the n profile items are stored in an $n \times N$ response matrix, $\mathfrak{R}$. The rows of $\mathfrak{R}$ correspond to profile items and the columns correspond to users.

Privacy Algorithm

The *privacy index* of a user quantifies the user's privacy risk caused by his privacy settings. The basic privacy risks are the following:

- The more sensitive information a user reveals, the higher his privacy risk
- The more people know some piece of information about a user, the higher his privacy risk

The privacy risk of user j is defined in terms of two parameters: the *sensitivity* of the user's profile items, and the *visibility* these items set. In the following sections, it is described in detail how to compute the sensitivity, the visibility, and the privacy risk score.

Sensitivity of a Profile Item

Let β_i denotes the sensitivity of item i. This sensitivity depends on the nature of the item itself. For example, one's mother's maiden name is usually considered more sensitive than his work phone number.

Visibility of a Profile Item

The visibility of a profile item i due to user j captures how widely known the value of i becomes in the social network; the more it spreads, the higher the item's visibility.

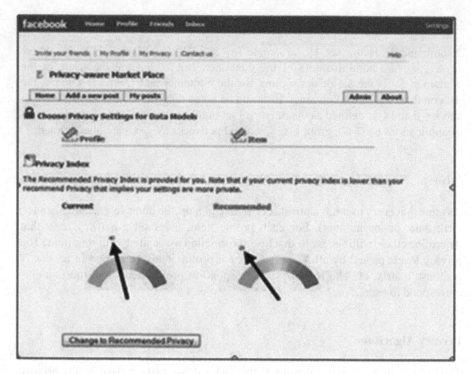

Fig. 2.6 Privacy score index and recommendation applied in Facebook

$V(i,j)$ depends on the user's privacy level setting for item i, $\Re(i,j)$. The simplest possible definition of visibility is $V(i,j) = I_{(\Re(i,j)=1)}$, where $I_{\text{condition}}$ is an indicator variable that becomes 1 when "condition" is true.

Privacy Risk of a User

The privacy risk of individual j due to item i, denoted by $PR(i,j)$, can be a combination of sensitivity and visibility, i.e., $PR(i,j) = \beta_i \otimes V(i,j)$. Operator $\otimes$ is used to represent any arbitrary combination function that respects the fact that is monotonically increasing with both sensitivity and visibility.

$$PR(i) = \sum PR(i,j) = \sum \beta_i \times V(i,j) = \sum \beta_i \times P_{ij} \qquad (2.1)$$

where visibility is equivalent to $P_{ij} = \text{Prob}[R(i,j) = 1]$. Figure 2.6 illustrates a Facebook application using PaaS framework that helps a user to view their settings and to see their current privacy index and also a recommendation of a privacy index based on the other users in his/her network. A user may choose a more secured privacy state if desired.

Relationship Model for Social Networks

Social relationships, in practice, are extremely diverse in terms of strengths and types of relationships. Social networks often represent these connections in simple binary relationships: *friend* or *not* [4]. This results in an inconsistency between the real-life social network and the online social graph model, and violates our security principle of keeping consistency between online and offline social networks. In order to capture multiple aspects of real-life social networks, the relationship model (or link model for an online social graph) should be extended to include, for example:

- *Type of relationships*, which can be roughly categorized into bidirectional relationships such as friend or colleague, and one-directional relationships such as fans or followers
- *Trust strength*, which expresses how much a user trusts other users either with respect to a specific topic (topical trust) or in general (absolute trust)
- *Interaction intensity*, which measures the quality and quantity of interactions between users

An enriched social relationship model developed by Chi Zhang et al. [20] highlighted many ways to improve SNS privacy and security. First, all social relationships should be clearly articulated and treated accordingly in making privacy decisions. Second, trust relationships are the core information on which all security mechanisms are based. By their very nature, trust relationships among users are not equal. Traditional privacy polices based on binary trust relationships ignore the existing strength differences and treat them as equal. Therefore, a fine-grained access control is necessary. Third, interaction intensity can be used as a proxy for relationship quality for the purpose of making privacy decisions. In general, if a pair of users does not interact often, they only want to reveal a limited amount of information to each other. The measurement of interaction intensity also introduces a way to characterize network dynamics. However, the trade-off between accuracy and complexity in describing social relationships must be taken into account. Inaccurate and ambiguous descriptions will introduce security vulnerabilities, but evaluating and processing too complex descriptions may have computational costs that make the SNS infeasible in practice.

Protecting Online Social Graphs

A fundamental feature of social network is the online social graph that connects users. It collects the core information on which all services provided by SNSs are based; therefore, it should be primarily protected. According to the model proposed [3], trust relationships and connection patterns embedded in real-life social networks can be utilized to provide security mechanisms to protect the online social networks and mitigate the attacks on online social graphs mentioned earlier.

Defense Against Social Link Forging Attacks

A social link can be forged if a malicious user (Malory) successfully fools an honest user (Alice) into trusting him. However, the trust strength and interaction intensity introduced in the relationship model can effectively limit the impact of this kind of forged social links. Malory may also try to present as Bob, a good friend of Alice, in order to establish a strong social link with Alice. However, most people can tell quite easily if a friend's profile is faked, and a large proportion of SNS users also meet in person, allowing them to perform a *face-to-face* identity verification.

Defense Against Node Identity Forging Attacks

For many SNSs, it is easy for a malicious user to obtain multiple fake identities and pretend to be multiple distinct users in the SNS. If the social network enforces users to register with government issued identity cards, then launching node forging attacks becomes harder. A node's position in the online social graph can be verified based on trust strengths of paths from the verifier to the claimant. The key point, therefore, is to find a privacy-preserving way to utilize the knowledge of online social graphs. One approach to mitigate the design conflicts is to try to find and utilize *qualitative properties* of real-life social networks. Unlike quantitative properties, qualitative properties are very malleable (i.e., applicable to any secure online social graphs) and reveal no information about individual users. For example, in [30], Yu et al. propose a new defense scheme against Sybil attacks for SNSs based on the fact that it is difficult to forge social links between honest nodes and Sybil nodes, The basic idea is that if malicious users create too many Sybil nodes, the online social graph contains only a small set of social links (the attack edges) whose removal disconnects a large number of nodes (all the Sybil nodes) from the rest of the graph. By utilizing a special kind of verifiable random walk in the online social graph and intersections between such walks, the number of Sybil nodes can be fixed. More and more qualitative properties of social networks combined with privacy preserving cryptographic techniques [31] can be utilized to design novel security mechanisms for SNSs without compromising user privacy.

Safebook

A preliminary analysis of existing online social networks (OSNs) shows that they are subject to a number of vulnerabilities, ranging from cloning legitimate users to sybil attacks through privacy violations. A solution that aims at avoiding any centralized control and leverages on the real-life trust between users has been proposed by Leucio Antonio Cutillo et al. in their model called *Safebook* [32]. It is an anonymization technique based on multi-hop routing among trusted nodes that guarantees privacy in data access and in all OSN operations.

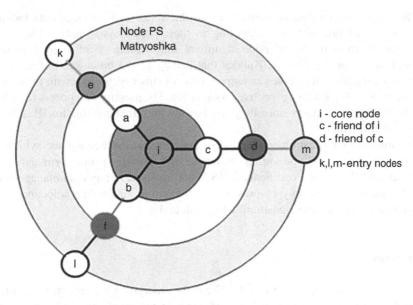

Fig. 2.7 Structure of matryoshka of a user

Architecture of Safebook

The architecture of Safebook consists of two overlays namely the peer-to-peer overlay and the social network overlay. The components of Safebook are:

- Several matryoshkas
- A peer-to-peer substrate
- A trusted identification service (TIS)

Matryoshkas are particular structures providing end-to-end confidentiality and distributed data storage with privacy and the structure is illustrated in Fig. 2.7. The trusted identification service guarantees authentication and provides unique addresses to each member of Safebook.

The Matryoshka of a user is a structure composed by various nodes surrounding the user's node in concentric shells. The user's node is the core of his matryoshka and can also be part of some other users' matryoshkas. The inner shell of a matryoshka consists of nodes belonging to the trusted contacts of the user. The second shell consists of nodes that are trusted contacts of nodes in the inner shell and so on. It is important to note that nodes on the same shell do not necessarily share trust relationships between themselves, except for the inner shell, which all share their relation to the core node. The nodes on the inner shell cache the data for the core and serve requests if the core is off-line. A data request message reaches a node in the inner shell from a node in the outer shell through a path that provides hop-by-hop trust. The reply follows the same path in the reverse direction. Based on this, the matryoshkas assure cooperation enforcement in the OSN.

The peer-to-peer substrate consists of all the nodes and provides data lookup services. Nodes are arranged according to their pseudonyms and lookup keys correspond both to members' node identifiers and to the hash of their attributes, like full names or the likes. All nodes that belong to the outer shell of a user's matryoshka register themselves as entry points for this matryoshka with the nodes that are responsible for the respective lookup keys. The identity of a peer is revealed only to his trusted contacts since they are the only ones that can link his IP address to his node identifier.

The trusted identification service (TIS) guarantees resistance against sybil and impersonation attacks by providing each node with a unique pseudonym and node identifier, and the related certificates. TIS is not involved in any data management activity and it is used only to prevent impersonation and a free selection of a pseudonym and hence their position in the hash table.

Operations

The most important operations of OSN are the matryoshka creation, the profile publication, and the data retrieval. In order to join Safebook, a member V has to be invited by another member U. After this phase, having obtained the necessary credentials from the TIS, V can start building his matryoshka. In the hash table, V is to register his node id and a particular set of lookup keys associated to his identity, e.g., a hash of his full name. At the beginning V has only U in his contact list, so he sends U a signed registration request containing the lookup key(s) he wants to register, his certificate associated to his node id signed by the TIS, and a time-to-live (ttl) counter. This first message presents the node id of the sender instead of his pseudonym. This prevents the node in the hash table responsible for V's lookup key from linking that key with V's pseudonym. Once U receives the registration message it decreases the ttl counter, chooses one (or several) of his trusted contacts, called W, as a next step and sends W the request message signed with his pseudonym. This will prevent the registering node in the hash table from retrieving the social relationships between the OSN members constituting V's matryoshka. It is important to note that no assumption is held about social relationship between V and W. This process runs until the ttl counter expires, when V's lookup key is registered in the table. The node responsible for that key maintains a reference table associating the key with the IP addresses of the nodes belonging to the outer shell of V. The number of contacts each node chooses to forward the registration request is determined by the *spanning factor*. It defines the branching of the tree through the matryoshka whose root is the core and whose leaves are the nodes in the outer shell, starting from the core's direct connections. The higher the spanning factor, the higher is the number of nodes composing the tree, and the higher is thus the probability to have a valid path through the tree, i.e., a path where all the nodes are online. The spanning factor and the number of inner shell nodes each core should have is fundamental to guarantee data availability.

A user's data can be public, protected, or private. Privatedata is only stored by the owner, while public and protected data are stored by the contacts being in the inner shell of the user's matryoshka. All the published data are signed by the owner and encrypted using a simple group-based encryption scheme. Each node can manage the profile information, the trusted contact relations, and the messages. The profile information consists of the data a member wants to publish in the OSN and is organized in atomic attributes. The trusted contact relations represent the friend list of the user and associate each contact with a particular trust level. The messages can be exchanged by each member of the OSN, in this case the communication does not stop at the first matryoshka shell but reaches the core.

The requests are routed according to the P2P protocol until they reach the node responsible for the lookup key. It sends back the list of all the nodes constituting the outer shell of the target node's matryoshka. The requesting node then sends its request to a subset of the outer shell nodes of the target matryoshka. The requests are forwarded through the matryoshka to the inner shell, whose nodes serve it and send a response along the inverse path. To summarize, Safebook offers security and privacy as follows:

- Privacy through layering
- Friendship relations hidden through Matryoshkas
- Untraceability through pseudonyms and anonymous routing
- Cloning and DoS prevention through ID manager
- Access control in terms of data encryption and key management
- Availability as replication at friends' nodes

Privacy Preserving Cryptographic Protocol

This section introduces an efficient cryptographic protocol with which parties can determine shared friends while exposing minimal information about their social contacts. Reliable Email (RE) [33], an email system that reliably accepts mail from senders based on proximity in a social network, is based only on cryptographic hash functions and symmetric encryption. Reliable Email is an automated email acceptance system that white-lists email according to its sender. Existing content-based filters and other spam fighting technologies, while seeking to minimize the amount of spam that reaches a user's inbox, occasionally misclassify legitimate mail as spam. Traditional white-lists suffer from two primary issues. First, a recipient's white-list cannot accept mail from a sender previously unknown to the recipient. Second, populating white-lists requires manual effort distributed.

To overcome these limitations, Michael J. Freedman et al. have examined the privacy of RE among email users and improved the private techniques for verifying social proximity [33]. Specifically, RE allows a user R to *attest* to another user S, which indicates that R is willing to have email from S directly forwarded to his mailbox. In other words, "User R trusts his *friend* S not to send him spam." Such an attestation is a digitally signed statement of the form:

$$\sigma_{R \rightarrow S} = \{H(R), H(S), \text{start, end}\} \, SK_R \qquad (2.2)$$

where H is a collision-resistant cryptographic hash function like SHA-256 operating on the users' email addresses, *start* and *end* define the attestation's validity period, and SK_R denotes user R's signing key. RE leverages these attestations for accepting mail in cases where the sender S and recipient R are *not* already friends, but instead share a *bridging* friend T, resulting in a *friend-of-friend* (FoF) relationship between S and R. By performing an FoF query, a recipient can determine which of his friends, if any, have attested to the sender.

RE provides the following privacy properties:

- The sender S does not learn anything about R's friends. Both learn an upper bound on the number of friends presented by the other.
- The recipient R learns only the intersection of the two sets of friends, *i.e.*, those T for whom R signed $\sigma_{R \rightarrow T}$ and from whom S received $\sigma_{T \rightarrow S}$.
- A third party observing all messages between S and R learns an upper bound on the size of each input, but nothing about their content nor the intersection size.
- Only R can execute the FoF query.

Model

A social network can be modeled as a directed graph $G = (V,E)$, whose vertices represent the users of the system and where the presence of an arc $(R,T) \in E$ (also denoted $R \rightarrow T$) indicates the existence of a social relationship between user R and user T. It is assumed that $R \rightarrow T$ to mean that "T is R's friend". This graph is represented within the system in a distributed fashion: each participant has only a local view of the network, consisting of its incoming and outgoing arcs. Additionally, the system provides a *proximity check* mechanism by which a user S can help R determine whether he is "close enough" to her in the social network. In particular, R can find out all *bridging* friends X such that $R \rightarrow X$ and $X \rightarrow S$. Such mechanism is exposed to a higher-level application, in which users send *requests* to each other, and requests may be treated differently by the recipient according to the social proximity of the sender.

Figure 2.8 illustrates this for a fragment of a social network, where solid arrows represent trust relationships; the dotted arrow highlights a pair of users for which to verify social proximity. R learns that there is exactly one bridging friend between him and S, namely T. Both T and W are directly connected to S, but R should not learn about W since the arc $R \rightarrow W$ does not appear in the graph. To properly address privacy concerns of this kind, the nature of the relationships represented by the social network is elaborated first.

In the context of RE, such relationships were viewed as predominantly unidirectional: $R \rightarrow T$ roughly corresponds to the notion that "user R trusts T not to send

Fig. 2.8 Fragment of a social network

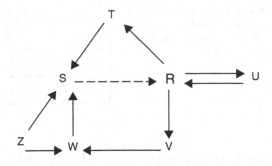

him spam". Under this interpretation, whether the arc $R \rightarrow T$ appears in the social network or not is essentially up to R. Building on the example of Fig. 2.8, an overly curious R could unilaterally augment the social network with arcs $R \rightarrow U$, $R \rightarrow W$, $R \rightarrow Z$. This would "entitle" R to learn about the social link $W \rightarrow S$ when receiving email from S, breaching the privacy of both W and S. To this effect, the presence of social link $R \rightarrow T$ ought to express consent of *both* parties:

- Forward Trust: User R places some form of trust on user T that T can use to demonstrate to some U the presence of a chain $U \rightarrow R$, $R \rightarrow T$.
- Backward Authorization: User T authorizes user R to discover links of the form $T \rightarrow X$ when trying to establish the existence of a social chain such as $R \rightarrow T$, $T \rightarrow S$.

R's trust in T could be expressed via a digitally signed attestation, whereas backward authorization could be implemented as a shared secret key that T gives to R. Under such a setup, one can formalize a system's privacy properties by explicitly pointing out what information is exposed to the users, in terms of guarantees of the form: "During a proximity check with user S, user R learns at most I". Given I and the knowledge held by R (which can be deduced from R's social relationships), it is possible to simulate (or "fake") the content of all messages seen by R during the proximity check. This implies that any other information exposed to R can be derived using only I and R's knowledge.

Hash-Based Construction

Each user R has a signing/verification key pair $SK_R//VK_R$. Additionally, R maintains a secret seed s_R for a cryptographic pseudo-random function F (*e.g.*, 256-bit long for HMAC-SHA-256). Each arc in the social network is associated with a pseudo-random key, termed the arc's a-value. All a-values corresponding to arcs of the form $R \rightarrow X$ are derived from R's secret seed s_R as: $a_{R \rightarrow X} = F_{s_R}(\text{"arc"},R,X)$.

For each social link of the form $R \rightarrow X$, user R creates an attestation $\sigma_{R \rightarrow X}$ for user X, and sends it to X along with $a_{R \rightarrow X}$ (*forward trust*). In return, R receives s_X from X (*backward authorization*). Proximity checks thus are implemented from this

Fig. 2.9 Data structures used for a hash-based proximity check between a sender S and recipient R

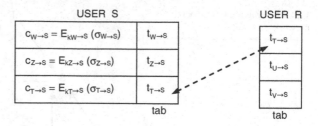

asymmetric exchange of secrets. For Y such that $Y \rightarrow S$, the sender S encrypts the attestation $\sigma_{Y \rightarrow S}$ under a key derived from $a_{Y \rightarrow S}$. In turn, for X such that $R \rightarrow X$, the receiver R tries to read these encrypted attestations using a key derived from the a-value $a_{X \rightarrow S}$ which R can compute given s_X. To help R in his decryption process, S includes a *tab* $t_{Y \rightarrow S}$ along with each encrypted attestation $c_{Y \rightarrow S}$.

Figure 2.9 displays the data structure used for a hash based proximity check between sender S and recipient R. More in detail, for each arc $Y \rightarrow S$, S combines the attestation $\sigma_{Y \rightarrow S}$ and the a-value $a_{Y \rightarrow S}$ into a *tabbed encrypted attestation* ($c_{Y \rightarrow S}$, $t_{Y \rightarrow S}$) as follows. The *tab* $t_{Y \rightarrow S}$ is a pseudo-random hash computed under F keyed with $a_{Y \rightarrow S}$ i.e., $t_{Y \rightarrow S} = Fa_{Y \rightarrow S}$ ("tab",ReqID), where ReqID is a unique identifier supplied by the higher-level application. The ciphertext $c_Y = E_{kY \rightarrow S}$ ($\sigma_{Y \rightarrow S}$) is computed under a secure symmetric cipher E (*e.g.*, AES-CBC), with a key $k_{Y \rightarrow S}$ also derived from $a_{Y \rightarrow S}$: $k_{Y \rightarrow S} = Fa_{Y \rightarrow S}$ ("key",ReqID).

At this point, S creates a list of such tabbed encrypted attestations, one for each of her incoming social relationships, permutes this list in random order, and sends it to R along with her request. User R processes such a list by first looking at the tab component of each entry. In particular, for each relationship of the form $R \rightarrow X$, R holds the seed s_X. So R can form the a-value: $a_{X \rightarrow S} = Fs_X$ ("arc", X, S), and then the F-hash of ReqID under $a_{X \rightarrow S}$. In this way, R computes his own set of tabs, and compares them with those received from S. The cryptographic properties of F prove that it is extremely unlikely that two such tabs will coincide, except when they are created from the same seed. In other words, a match between the tabs guarantees that the same seed was used by both R and S, which in turn reveals the bridging friend(s), say T. At this point, R can compute the proper key $k_{T \rightarrow S} = Fa_{T \rightarrow S}$ ("key",ReqID) and decrypt the corresponding encrypted attestation, thus recovering $\sigma_{T \rightarrow S}$. Finally, R verifies T's signature on $\sigma_{T \rightarrow S}$ before concluding that $R \rightarrow T$ and $T \rightarrow S$.

Peer-to-peer systems may use social networks in order to establish trust between participants, yet they introduce privacy concerns when sharing such information. A privacy model for verifying social proximity has been discussed so far. The features of the hash-based protocol that provide privacy to RE are summarized as follows:

- The hash-based protocol also supports a weak form of detection for longer social paths.
- By uncovering the identity of the linking friend, the protocol provides *auditability*, which enables the decision-maker to review and correct the elements that led to the wrong decision.

- The method employed is a non-interactive, requiring just a single message from S to R. This can significantly reduce system complexity and can facilitate integration with the existing e-mail infrastructure.
- For social networks with symmetric trust relationships (i.e., $X \to Y$ and $Y \to X$) the hash-based construction can be simplified by suppressing the a-values, and having the seed s_Y playing the role of $a_{X \to Y}$, for all of Y's social contacts X.

Identity Anonymization on Social Network Graphs

In a social network graph, nodes correspond to individuals or other social entities, and edges correspond to social relationships between them. The privacy breaches in social network data can be grouped to three categories:

1. *Identity disclosure*: the identity of the individual who is associated with the node is revealed
2. *Link disclosure*: sensitive relationships between two individuals are disclosed
3. *Content disclosure*: the privacy of the data associated with each node is breached

e.g., email message sent or received by the individuals in an email communication graph.

A perfect privacy protection system should in fact consider all of these issues. However, protecting against each of the above breaches may require different techniques. For example, for content disclosure, standard privacy preserving data mining techniques such as data perturbation and k-anonymization can help. For link disclosure, the various techniques studied by the link-mining community can be useful. This section describes a systematic framework for identity anonymization on graph proposed by Kun Liu et al. [17]. It is assumed that the graph is a simple graph, *i.e.*, the graph is undirected, unweighted, containing no self-loops or multiple edges.

Let $G(V,E)$ be a simple graph; V is a set of nodes and E the set of edges in G. Let d_G denotes the *degree sequence* of G. That is, d_G is a vector of size $n = |V|$ such that $d_G(i)$ is the degree of the i-th node of G. We will look into some of the definitions before going into privacy preserving features.

- k-anonymous vector : A vector of integers v is k-anonymous if every distinct value in v appears at least k times. For example, vector $v = [5, 5, 3, 3, 2, 2, 2,]$ is 2-anonymous.
- k-degree anonymous: A graph $G(V;E)$ is k-degree anonymous if the degree sequence of G, d_G, is k-anonymous.

Figure 2.10 shows two examples of degree-anonymous graphs. In the graph in (a), all three nodes have the same degree and thus the graph is 3-degree anonymous. Similarly, the graph on the right is 2-degree anonymous since there is a node with degree 1 and five nodes with degree 2.

Fig. 2.10 (a) Examples of a
3-degree anonymous graph
(b) a 2-degree anonymous
graph

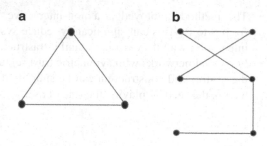

Graph Anonymization

The input to the anonymization problem is a simple graph $G(V,E)$ and an integer k. The requirement is to use a set of graph modification operations on G in order to construct a k-degree anonymous graph $\bar{G}$ $(\tilde{V}, \bar{E})$ that is structurally similar to G. It is required that the output graph is over the same set of nodes as the original graph, that is, $\tilde{V} = V$. Moreover, it is restricted the graph modification operations to edge additions, that is, graph $\bar{G}$ is constructed from G by adding a (minimal) set of edges. Formally, the definition of Graph anonymization is given as follows:

> *Given a graph $G(V,E)$ and an integer k, find a k-degree anonymous graph $\bar{G}(V,\bar{E})$ with $\bar{E} \cap E = E$ such that $GA(\bar{G}, G)$ is minimized.*

A two-step approach for the Graph Anonymization problem is given below for an input graph $G(V,E)$ with degree sequence d and an integer k:

1. First, starting from d, a new degree sequence $\hat{d}$ that is k-anonymous is constructed such that the *degree anonymization* cost $D_A(\hat{d},d) = L_1(\hat{d} - d)$; is minimized. Dynamic programming (DP) is used for solving the Degree Anonymization problem with an optimal timing $O(n^2)$. This can further be improved to $O(n)$ for minimizing the cost.
2. Given the new degree sequence $\hat{d}$, the construction of a graph $\bar{G}(V,\bar{E})$ is done such that $d_G = \hat{d}$ and $\bar{E} \cap E = E$.

Given the original graph $G(V,E)$ and the desired k-anonymous degree sequence $\hat{d}$ output by the DP (or Greedy) algorithm, a k-degree anonymous graph $\bar{G}(V,\bar{E})$ with $\bar{E} \cap E = E$ and degree sequence d with $d = \hat{d}$ is constructed. The three algorithms namely ConstructGraph, Probing and Greedy_Swap are used for solving the graph anonymization.

ConstructGraph Algorithm

It takes as input the desired degree sequence d and outputs a graph with exactly this degree sequence, if such graph exists. Otherwise it outputs a "No" if such graph does not exist. The algorithm is iterative and in each step it maintains the residual degrees of vertices. In each iteration it picks an arbitrary node v and adds edges from v to $d(v)$ nodes of *highest* residual degree, where $d(v)$ is the residual degree of v. The residual degrees of these $d(v)$ nodes are decreased by one. If the algorithm terminates and outputs a graph, then this graph has the desired degree sequence. If at some point the algorithm cannot make the required number of connections for a specific node, then it outputs "No" means that the input degree sequence is not realizable. Algorithm 1 sequences the computational flow required for constructing the graph.

Probing Algorithm

For input graph $G(V,E)$ and integer k, the Probing first constructs the k-anonymous sequence đ by invoking the DP (or Greedy) algorithm. If the subsequent call to the Supergraph algorithm returns a graph $\bar{G}$, then Probing outputs this graph and halts. If Supergraph returns "No" or "Unknown", then probing slightly increases some of the entries in d via the addition of uniform noise. The new noisy version of d is then fed as input to the DP (or Greedy) algorithm again. A new version of the đ is thus constructed and input to the Supergraph algorithm to be checked. The process of noise addition and checking is repeated until a graph is output by Supergraph. Note that this process will always terminate because in the worst case, the noisy version of d will contain all entries equal to $n - 1$, and there exists a complete graph that satisfies this sequence and is k-degree anonymous with $E \subseteq \bar{E}$.

Algorithm 1 The ConstructGraph Algorithm

Input: A degree sequence d of length n.
Output: A graph G(V,E) with nodes having degree sequence d or "No"
if the input sequence is not realizable.

1: $V \leftarrow \{1 \ldots n\}$; $E \leftarrow \Phi$;
2: if Σ d(i) is odd then
3:       Halt and return "No"
4: while i do
5:    if there exists d(i) such that d(i) < 0 then
6:       Halt and return "No"
7:    if the sequence d are all zeros then
8:       Halt and return G(V;E)
9:    Pick a random node v with d(v) > 0
10:   Set d(v) = 0
11:   Vd(v) $\leftarrow$ the d(v)-highest entries in d (other than v)
12:   for each node w $\in V_{d(v)}$ do
13:       E $\leftarrow$ E $\cup$ (v,w)
14:       d(w) $\leftarrow$ d(w) - 1

The Supergraph algorithm presented in the previous section extends the input graph $G(V,E)$ by adding additional edges. It guarantees that the output graph $\bar{G}(V,\bar{E})$ be k-degree anonymous and $E \subseteq \bar{E}$. In many cases, a degree-anonymous graph where $\bar{E} \cap E$ means that most of the edges of the original graph appear in the degree-anonymous graph as well, but not necessarily all of them. Algorithm 2 displays the steps involved in probing.

Algorithm 2 The Probing Scheme

Input: Input graph G(V;E) with degree distribution d and integer k.
Output: Graph $(V; \bar{E})$ with k-anonymous degree sequence đ such that
$E \subseteq \bar{E}$.

1: đ = DP(d)　　　　　　　　/* or Greedy(d) */
2: (realizable, $\bar{G}$ = Supergraph(đ)
3: while realizable = "No" or "Unknown" do
4:　　　d = d + random_noise
5:　　　đ = DP(d)　　　/*or Greedy(d) */
6:　　　(realizable, $\bar{G}$ = Supergraph(đ)
7: Return $\bar{G}$

Greedy_Swap Algorithm

Let đ be a k-anonymous degree sequence output by DP(or Greedy) algorithm. Let us additionally assume for now that đ is realizable so that the ConstructGraph algorithm with input đ outputs a simple graph $\bar{G}_0(V, \bar{E}_0)$ with degree sequence exactly đ. Although $\bar{G}_0$ is k-degree anonymous, its structure may be quite different from the original graph $G(V,E)$. The Greedy_Swap algorithm is a greedy heuristic that given $\bar{G}_0$ and G, it transforms $\bar{G}_0$ into $\bar{G}(V, \bar{E})$ with degree sequence $d = đ = d_0$ and $E \cap \bar{E} \cong E$. Algorithm 3 lists the steps involved in Greedy_Swap.

Algorithm 3 The Greedy_Swap Algorithm

Input: An initial graph $\bar{G}_0(V, \bar{E})$ and the input graph G(V,E).
Output: Graph $\bar{G}(V, \bar{E})$ with the same degree sequence as $\bar{G}_0$, such
that $E \cap \bar{E} \cong E$

1: $\bar{G}(V, \bar{E}) \leftarrow \bar{G}_0(V, \bar{E}_0)$
2: (c, (e_1, e_2, e_1', e_2')) = Find_Max_Swap ($\bar{G}$)
3: while $c > 0$ do
4:　　　$\bar{E} = \bar{E} \setminus \{ e_1, e_2\} \cup \{ e_1', e_2'\}$
5:　　　(c, (e_1, e_2, e_1', e_2')) = Find_Max_Swap ($\bar{G}$)
6: return $\bar{G}$

Algorithm 4 gives the pseudo code representing the whole process of solving the relaxed graph construction problem when the degree sequence đ is realizable.

Algorithm 4 An Overall Algorithm for Solving the Relaxable Graph Construction Problem; The Realizable Case

Input: A realizable degree sequence đ of length n.
Output: A graph $\bar{G}(V, \bar{E}))$ with degree sequence đ and $E \cap \bar{E} \cong E$

1: $\bar{G}_0 =$ ConstructGraph (đ)
2: $\bar{G} =$ Greedy_Swap ($\bar{G}_0$)

In this section, a study done by Kun Liu et al. [17] on a specific graphanonymity notion that prevents the re-identification of individuals by an attacker with certain prior knowledge of the degrees has been brought up. Compared with existing data anonymization and perturbation techniques for tabular data, dealing with graphs is a much more challenging task. In tabular data, each tuple can be viewed as an independent sample from some distribution. However, in a graph, all the nodes and edges are correlated; a single change of an edge and/or a node can spread across the whole network. Moreover, in graphs it is difficult to model the capability of an attacker. Any topological structure of the graph can be potentially used to derive private information. Finally, it is difficult to measure the utility of a graph.

Summary

This chapter has included many research studies in the areas of security, trust and privacy applicable to online social networks such as MySpace and Facebook. Security, privacy, and trust requirements for SNSs are also listed here. Privacy preserving models such as Paas, an enriched relationship model for social graph, Safebook, privacy preserving cryptographic protocol and an identity anonymization model for social network graph are also discussed in this chapter.

References

1. Boyd, D.M., Ellison, N.B.: Social network sites: definition, history and scholarship. J. Comput. Mediat. Commun. **13**(1), 210–230 (2007)
2. Wikipedia: Social Network Service. http://en.wikipedia.org/wiki/Social_network_service (2010). Accessed 25 Jan 2011
3. Zhang, C., Sun, J., Zhu, X., Fang, Y.: Privacy and security for online social networks: challenges and opportunities. IEEE Netw. **24**(4), 13–18 (2010)
4. Boyd, D.M.: Friendster and publicly articulated social networks. In: Proceedings of the SIGCHI Conference on Human Factors and Computing Systems, Vienna, Austria (2004)
5. Acquisti, A., Gross R.: Imagined communities: awareness, information sharing and privacy on the Facebook. In: Proceedings of the 6th Workshop on Privacy Enhancing Technologies, Cambridge, UK, pp. 36–58 (2006)
6. Lampe, C., Ellison, N., Steinfield, C.: A face(book) in the crowd: social searching versus social browsing. In: 20th Anniversary Conference on Computer Supported Cooperative Work, Canada, pp. 167–170 (2007).

7. Stutzman, F.: Student life on the Facebook. http://chimprawk.blogspot.com/2006/01/student-life-on-facebook (2006). Accessed 30 Jan 2011
8. Schrobsdorff, S.: Predators playground?. Newsweek www.newsweek.com/2006/01/26/predator-s-playground.html (2006). Accessed 25 Jan 2011
9. Mayer, R.C., Davis, J.H., Schoorman, F.D.: An integrative model of organizational trust. Acad. Manage. Rev. **20**(3), 709–734 (1995)
10. Fukuyama, F.: Trust: The Social Virtues and the Creation of Prosperity. Free Press, New York (1995)
11. Lewis, J.D., Weigert, A.: Trust as a social reality. Soc. Forces **63**(4), 967–985 (1985)
12. Coppola, N., Hiltz, H.R., Rotter, N.: Building trust in virtual teams. IEEE Trans. Prof. Commun. **47**(2), 95–104 (2004)
13. Jarvenpaa, S., Leidner, D.: Communication and trust in global virtual teams. J. Comput. Mediat. Commun. **3**(4), 0 (1988)
14. Meyerson, D., Weick, K.E., Kramer, R.M.: Swift trust and temporary groups. In: Kramer, R.M., Tyler, T.R. (eds.) Trust in Organizations: Frontiers of Theory and Research. Sage Publications, Thousand Oaks (1996)
15. Piccoli, G., Ives, B.: Trust and the unintended effects of behavior control in virtual teams. MIS Q. **27**(3), 365–395 (2003)
16. Gambetta, D.: Trust: Making and Breaking Cooperative Relations. University of Oxford, pp. 213–237 (2000)
17. Liu, K., Terzi, E.: Towards identity anonymization on graphs. In: SIGMOD'08, pp. 93–106 (2008)
18. Dwyer, C., Hiltz, S.R., Passerini, K.: Trust and privacy concern within social networking sites: a comparison of Facebook and MySpace. In: Thirteenth Americas Conference on Information Systems, Keystone, Colorado (2007)
19. Identity Theft Resource Center (ITRC): http://www.idtheftcenter.org. Accessed 20 Jan 2011
20. Zhang, C.: Security issues and recommendations for online social networks. ENISA. http://www.enisa.europa.eu/doc/pdf/deliverables/enisa_pp_social_networks.pdf (2007). Accessed 10 Jan 2011
21. Hogben, G.: Security issues in the future of social networking. In: W3C Workshop on the Future of Social Networking, Barcelona (2007)
22. Internet Safety Technical Task Force: Enhancing child safety and online technologies. Final Report of the Internet Safety Technical Task Force to the Multi-State Working Group on Social Networking of State Attorneys General of the United States (2008)
23. Friendbot, automated friend adding software. http://www.friendbot.com/. Accessed 20 Jan 2011
24. Bonneau, J., Anderson, J., Danezis, G.: External data collection from online social networks. In: First International Conference on Advances in Social Network Analysis and Mining (2009)
25. Stross, R.: When everyone's a friend, is anything private?. The New York Times. http://www.nytimes.com/2009/03/08/business/08digi (2009). Accessed 25 Jan 2011
26. Blakely, R.: Does Facebook's privacy policy stack up?. UK Times. http://business.timesonline.co.uk/tol/business/industry_sectors/technology/article2430927.ece (2007). Accessed 25 Jan 2011
27. Wurrey, S.: Was the Facebook privacy breach really a surprise?. MediaBullsEye.com. http://mediabullseye.com/mb/2008/03/was-the-facebook-privacy-breac.html (2008). Accessed 25 Jan 2011
28. Grandison, T., Maximilien, E.M.: Toward privacy propagation in the social web. In: Workshop on Web 2.0 Security and Privacy 2008 (W2SP) (2008)
29. Maximilien, M., Grandison, T., Sun, T.: Enabling privacy as a fundamental construct for social networks. In: International Workshop on Security and Privacy in Online Social Networking (SPOSN 2009), pp. 1015–1020 (2009)
30. Yu, H., Kaminsky, M., Gibbons, P.B.: Sybilguard: defending against sybil attacks via social networks. IEEE/ACM Trans. Netw. **16**(3), 576–589 (2008)

31. Mezzour, G.: Privacy-preserving relationship path discovery in social networks. In: CANS'09, Ishikawa, Japan (2009)
32. Cutillo, L.A. Molva, R., Strufe, T.: Leveraging social links for trust and privacy in networks. In: INetSec2009 Open Research Problems in Network Security, pp. 27–36 (2009).
33. Garriss, S., Kaminsky, M., Freedman, M.J., Karp, B., Mazi'eres, D., Yu, H. RE: reliable email. In Proceedings of NSDI (2006)

Chapter 3
Blogging Around the Globe: Motivations, Privacy Concerns, and Social Networking

Mei Kobayashi

Abstract Blogging has become popular since its introduction the late 1990s, and the practice continues to grow. Blogs exemplify internet-age, user-generated content that is changing the way people access information, form social networks, and interact with acquaintances. Moreover, blogs are associated with extensive social communities defined by interconnecting references, and are considered to be one of the early catalysts for propelling the popularity of online social networking. This paper traces the development of blogs and the blogosphere around the globe. National surveys conducted by numerous international teams of researchers indicate motivations for blogging and attitudes regarding privacy are strikingly different in countries with large blogging communities. These differences are reflected in the content of blogs and profoundly influence blog-based social networks, which tend to be region-centric.

Introduction

A *weblog*, or *blog,* isa website that contains periodic, reverse chronologically ordered entries on a common webpage. Each entry or *blog post*, at a *blogsite,* is written and published by a *blogger* (or group of bloggers) who maintain(s) the site. The collection of all blogs is known as the *blogosphere*. Blogs often serve as online diaries [123], evangelical platforms, or as an informal medium for reporting on events. Most are maintained by an individual (individual or single-author blogs). However, blogging by groups of individuals (community or multi-authored blogs) with similar viewpoints or common purpose is increasing [3, 4].

When blogging started in the USA in the late 1990s, participants needed sufficiently strong programming skills to build and maintain their own sites.

M. Kobayashi (✉)
IBM Research-Tokyo, 5-6-52 Toyosu, Koto-ku, Tokyo 135-8511, Japan
e-mail: mei@jp.ibm.com

A. Abraham (ed.), *Computational Social Networks: Security and Privacy*,
DOI 10.1007/978-1-4471-4051-1_3, © Springer-Verlag London 2012

As inexpensive and free software to support the practice became widely available, blogging spread rapidly. The blogosphere has grown and diversified from a white, well-educated, US male-dominated community to ordinary people of both sexes from a wide range of age groups, countries, and socio-economic backgrounds. In March 2005, *Technorati*[1] reported the doubling of blogs every 5 months and approximately 7.8 million blogs with 937 million links in the blogosphere [119]. For example, data from March 2005 are roughly double that from October 2004. By December 2007, *Technorati* was tracking more than 112 million blogs. We tried *blogpulse*[2], another popular blog analysis and search engine on July 13, 2009, and found 112,326,499 blogs in the world. About a year later, on August 3, 2010, blogpulse identified 144,217,571 total blogs. The top five featured people were Lady Gaga (215,732 messages), Lindsay Lohan (62,079), Kim Kardashian (31,572), Angelina Jolie (53,335) and Jessica Simpson (22,267), confirming that blogging is now practiced by the masses, not just computer scientists.

The rise in blogging has been accompanied by a sharp increase in spam-like blogs or *splogs* [64, 67, 68]. A *splog* is "a fake blog created solely to promote affiliated Web sites, with the intent of skewing search results and artificially boosting traffic"[3]. This situation has created new challenges as well as new opportunities for business and internet analysts. In March 2005, *Technorati* estimated that 40,000 new blogs were being created every day (i.e., new blog sites, not to be confused with new postings on existing sites). By the fall of 2005, *Technorati*'s estimates grew to 70,000 new blogs per day, of which 2–8% were splogs. In July 2007, *Technorati*'s estimates grew to 120,000 new blogs per day (i.e., 1.4 new blogs per second), of which 3,000–7,000 were splogs [121]. Splog creation reached a monthly peak in December 2006 when 11,000 new splogs were created every day. Recent actions by some blog hosting services are having a noticeable effect on reducing the overall proportion of splogs.

> Will the negative publicity (from splogs) give blogging a bad name? No more than spam gives e-mail a bad name. ... splogging will rather give sploggers a bad name – meanwhile blogging is here to stay. – B.L.Ochman, President of WhatsNextOnline.com (2005)

Despite the problem posed by splogs, the popularity of blogs and blogging remains strong. A spring 2008 survey by the *Pew Research Center*[4] found that blog readers outnumber writers. Twelve percent of US internet users (9% of adults) have their own blog, while 33% (24% of adults) read blogs. Furthermore, only 5% of bloggers write on a regular, daily basis, while 11% of the readership read blogs on a daily basis [122].

Blogs epitomize the growing mass of user-generated content that is changing the way people access information, make and interact with friends, and form professional communities. Other examples of internet sites that are actively

---

[1] Technorati™, Inc.: http://technorati.com/

[2] blogpulse™ of Nielsen BuzzMetrics: http://www.blogpulse.com

[3] Whatis.com, definition of splog: http://whatis.techtarget.com/definition/0,,sid9_gci1137059,00.html

[4] Pew Research Center: http://pewresearch.org/

promoted or are conducive to social networking include friendship sites (e.g., *Facebook*[5], *hi5*[6], *MySpace*[7], *tagged*[8]); collaborative tagging sites (e.g., *Delicious*,[9] *StumbleUpon*[10]); audio, image, and video-sharing sites (*flickr*[11], *photobucket*[12], *playlist*[13], *YouTube*[14]); and wikis[15]. In 2006, Time magazine named *"You"* as *Person of the Year* for their participation in "a story about community and collaboration on a scale never seen before" [45].

Given the sudden and powerful emergence of blogs as a forum for self-expression, social networking, and dissemination of information, we felt that a survey of this topic would be of interest to a wide audience. At the same time, we realize that a comprehensive review would be impossible due to the widespread influence of blogs and the ever-changing landscape of the blogosphere. Although we whittled the broader topic of blog mining to motivations, privacy concerns, and social networking, it is still too large for comprehensive coverage. We hope that this review will serve as a useful introduction to readers with limited background on blogs, while illustrating the diversity of the international blogging community. We also hope that it will point to some interesting new avenues for research.

This chapter is organized as follows. The remainder of this section summarizes the history of blogs and differences between blogs and general Web pages. The second section examines blogging around the globe, with emphasis on trends in Japan, which has the highest readership and bloggers per capita. It concludes with a summary of statistics and trends about *Twitter*[16], a microblogging service. The third section reviews some basic tools for *social network analysis* (SNA), recent work on SNA of blogs, and analysis of comments on postings. For the most part, these works examine English-based blog sites in the USA. Given wide disparities in motivations and attitudes regarding privacy in different global regions, we speculate on possible extensions and limitations of the methods and their applicability to blogs outside of the USA. We conclude with a discussion on some possible directions for future research.

---

[5]Facebook™: http://www.facebook.om

[6]hi5 Networks™, Inc.: http://www.hi5.com

[7]MySpace.com™: http://www.myspace.com

[8]Tagged™, Inc.: http://www.tagged.com

[9]Delicious™: http://delicious.com

[10]StumbleUpon™: http://www.stumbleupon.com

[11]flickr™: http://www.flickr.com

[12]photobucket™: http://photobucket.com

[13]playlist.com™: http:www.playlist.com

[14]YouTube™: http:www.youtube.com

[15]A *wiki* is a website that allows the creation and editing of any number of interlinked web pages via a browser using a simplified markup language or WYSIWYG (what-you-see-is-what-you-get) text editor. Wikis are typically powered by wiki software and are often used collaboratively by multiple users, from: http://en.wikipedia.org/wiki/Wiki in Wikipedia: http:www.wikipedia.org. Accessed 6 May 2011.

[16]Twitter™, Inc.: http://twitter.com/

Blogging: Motivations and Privacy Concerns

In 1999, *Merriam-Webster On-Line*[17] recognized the neologism:

> **blog** (blog, bläg) *noun*, short for *Weblog*: a Web site that contains an online personal journal
> with reflections, comments, and often hyperlinks provided by the writer; *also*: the contents
> of such a site; **blog·ger** *noun*; **blog·ging** *noun* (entered in 1999)

Blogging as an activity existed in many forms prior to the evolution of the
internet, for example, personal diaries and diaries based on themes (e.g., travel,
cooking, gardening, personal vignettes) were published in book form. One of the
milestones in the history of blogging was the birth of the World Wide Web in
1992, as it enabled anyone with internet access to publish online notes, opinions,
and diaries for view by the general public. Anyone, in principle, could start and
maintain a Web page to publish their unedited thoughts in near real time.

However, there are major differences between blogs and general Web pages. For
example, blogging does not require programming knowledge since many types of
Weblog software (software designed to simplify the creation and maintenance of
blogs) are readily available. Some software tools are free, open source software
(e.g., *Apache Roller*[18], *LiveJournal*[19], *WordPress*[20]). Others that are proprietary may
require purchase of a user license, depending on the intended use (e.g., *Telligent
Community*[21], *Windows Live Writer* and *Windows Live Writer team blog*[22], *Traction
TreamPage*[23]). Blog hosting services that are operated by the developer allow users
to blog without having to install special software (e.g., *Blogger, MySpace, Open
Diary*[24]).

Blogs serve as a friendly facilitator of discussion between the writer and readers
since most blogging software provide simple means to post comments. And there
appears to be a lower psychological barrier in the blogosphere to comment since
there is an expectation of interactivity in the blogging community. This interaction
between bloggers and their readership who comment is regarded as one of the early
forms of online social networking.

There are numerous genres of blogs that cover a wide range of topics (e.g.,
news on scientific conferences and breakthroughs, sports, cooking, diaries, political
commentary, photos and videos). Nowson [99] notes three predominant types in
the blogosphere: news, commentary, and journal (diary-like) blogs; whereas Li [81]

---

[17]Merriam-Webster™ On-Line: http://www.merriam-webster.com/dictionary/blog

[18]Apache Roller™: http://roller.apache.org/

[19]LiveJournal™, Inc.: http://www.livejournalinc.com/index.php

[20]WordPress.org™: http://wordpress.org/

[21]Telligent Systems™, Inc.: http://telligent.com/products/telligent-community/

[22]Windows Live Writer™: http://download.live.com/writer and Windows Live Writer team
blog™: http://windowslivewriter.spaces.live.com/ of Microsoft™ Corporation.

[23]Traction® TeamPage™ of Traction Software, Inc.: http://traction.tractionsoftware.com/traction

[24]Open Diary™: http://www.opendiary.com

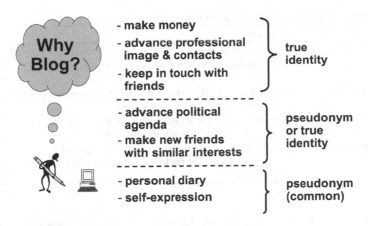

Fig. 3.1 Motivations for blogging and commonly associated privacy levels

notes the three categories: filter blogs, personal journals, and knowledge blogs (or k-logs). Filter blogs "consume, evaluate and select … (content) … they regard as worth commenting (on)," and k-logs consist of "information and content focussed around an external topic, product or project."

Motivations for blogging yield further insight into contents of blogs. Pedersen [107] studied British bloggers and found motivating factors to be similar to those of the international community, but with different rankings of priorities. They include the desire or need to connect with others online; express opinions, vent, share experiences; make money; become a "citizen journalist"; receive validation; and explore professional and commercial opportunities (e.g., publishing one's own blog into a "blook"). A US-centric study by Nardi et al. [92] cited five similar motivations: "documenting one's life; providing commentary and opinions; expressing deeply felt emotions; articulating ideas through writing; and forming and maintaining community forums." Similar findings have been reported in other studies that also examine how personality traits and gender of bloggers influence blog topics and content [43, 81, 99–102] (Fig. 3.1).

The strong will of bloggers to publish their work online may not always match their motivations for blogging, their personality traits, or their views regarding personal privacy. In some countries, a large portion of bloggers remain anonymous or use a pseudonym, overriding any desire (if any) for publicity, fortune, or fame. Some individuals maintain several seemingly unrelated blogs, each on a topic reflective of the blogger's diverse interests. Use of multiple pseudonyms (one for each distinct blog) is not uncommon. To understand motivations of bloggers, Gill et al. [43] examined personalities of bloggers based on a five-factor model of Costa and McCrae [25]. Specifically, Gill et al. [43] examined propensities of bloggers toward *neuroticism, extraversion, openness, conscientiousness*, and *agreeableness* based on the text and language (e.g., words, style of prose) in blogs. They conducted experiments by examining blogs and conclude:

Table 3.1 Features in blogs that facilitate social networking

Feature	Description
Comments	Comments from readers can be input below specific blog posts, facilitating communication between bloggers and their readership
Permalinks	Permalinks are URLs that point to specific blog posts or forum entries that are worthy of discussion
Trackbacks	Trackbacks are linkback methods for authors of blogs to receive notification when their Websites link to their sites
Web feeds	Web feeds are notification mechanisms that provide information to blog readers about recent updates and new postings

high *Neurotic* authors use blogging for cathartic or auto-therapeutic purposes ... high *Extraverts* use blogs to document their life ... Leisure interests related to *Openness*. ... the blogs of high *Openness* scorers appear to represent more of an evaluation or review with greater self-reference and negative emotion words (Sadness). Like *Openness*, *Conscientiousness* influenced blogs in terms of topics of interest to the author ... however (it) appears to be a more mundane commentary regarding life around them. For *Agreeableness*, positive rather than negative emotions are more pleasing to others, but in blogs, self talk is more acceptable, whereas talk about leisure activities is less so.

They conclude that language used in blogs is, for the most part, consistent with the personality of the authors and their behavior in other types of media, "suggesting that bloggers do not generally choose to present themselves differently than they present in other contexts."

Blogs Versus General Web Pages

The content and format of blogs are different from those of general Web pages. Most blogs consist of one, long page, in which the latest article appears on top, i.e., the articles are listed in reverse chronological order of posting. Updates tend to be more frequent for blogs. Three features have enabled blogs to become a successful medium for active participation and discussion between bloggers and their readership: permalinks, comments, and trackback [12, 85].

A *permalink* is a URL that points to a specific blog post or forum entry and provides a *permanent link* to the site. Since permalinks provide readers a means to pinpoint specific topics worthy of comments, they can serve as a vehicle for "turning weblogs from an ease-of-publishing phenomenon into a conversational mess of overlapping communities. For the first time it became relatively easy to gesture directly at a highly specific post on someone else's site and talk about it. Discussion emerged. Chat emerged. ... " [20]. Comments from readers are usually located at the end of blogs, which contributes to readership and "the immediacy of the conversational element of blogs" [12] (Table 3.1).

A *trackback* is a *linkback* method for authors of Web sites to receive notification when other Web sites link to their sites [138]. (Other well-known linkback methods are refback and pingback.) Trackbacks also facilitate communication between blogs by sending *trackback pings* that have summaries of and links to all comments when they links to a blog post. Trackbacks came into common use in blogs around 2002 after *Six Apart* introduced them in their *Movable Type*[25] software. The popularity of the method led competing blogging software services to offer easy-to-implement trackback methods. *Blogger* is one of the few famous services that does not support trackback; instead, it provides *backlinks*, which uses *Google's Blog search*[26] to find blog posts linked to a particular post.

The link structure between blogs (and to general web pages) is different from those associated with general Web pages, so methods developed for analysis of Web communities based on page links may not be applicable to analysis of blogging communities. Many blogs have *Web feeds* to provide readers with information about updates. Examples include *RSS, Atom* and *RDF* files [118].

Despite statistics showing an increase in blogs, some skeptics present a different view. Many sites classified as blogs may not be dynamic and interactive as claimed. Cohen and Krishnamurthy [21] report that most blogs do not change frequently, and a 2003 study by *Perseus*[27] reports that up to two-thirds of blogs may be *inactive*, i.e., not updated within the last 2 months [52]. The study was based on 3,634 blogs on eight leading blog hosting sites (*Blog-City*[28], *BlogSpot*[29], *Diaryland*[30], *LiveJournal*[31], *Pitas*[32], *TypePad*[TM][33], *Weblogger*[34] and *Xanga*[35]). *Perseus* estimates that of the 4.12 million blogs that had been created on these services, 66% or 2.72 million are permanently or temporarily abandoned, and 1.09 million of the abandoned blogs appear are one-time/1-day works. The average active lifespan of the remaining 1.63 million blogs is 126 days. 132,000 blogs were abandoned after more than 1 year of activity. Active blogs were updated, on average, every 14 days, of which only 106,579 were updated daily.

---

[25]Moveable Type[TM] of Six Apart[TM], Ltd.: http://moveabletype.com/

[26]Blog search[M] of Google[TM]: http://blogsearch.google.com/

[27]WebSurveyer[TM] and Perseus[TM] combined to become Vovici[TM] in June 2006: http://www.vovici.com/about/websurveyor-perseus.aspx

[28]Blog-City[TM]: http://www.blog-city.com/community/

[29]BlogSpot[TM]: https://www.blogger.com/start

[30]Diaryland[TM]: http://members.diaryland.com/edit/welcome.phtml

[31]LiveJournal[TM]: http://www.livejournal.com/

[32]pitas.com[TM]: http://www.pitas.com/

[33]TypePad[TM] of Six Apart[TM], Ltd.: http://www.typepad.com/

[34]Weblogger[TM]: http://www.weblogger.com/

[35]Xanga[TM]: http://www.xanga.com/

Blogging Around the Globe

Much that has been written in the USA about blogging pertains to blogs written in English by residents of the USA with a strong bias toward white, male, well-educated bloggers. However, as a wide range of services have become available in many other regions around the globe, blogging has become popular with a more diverse community of individuals. Examples of these services include *Globe of Blogs*[36] and *AboutUs*[37] for multilingual retrieval, *Best Blogs in Asia*[38] directory by *Misohoni*[39] for retrieval, and *kizasi*[40] for analysis of Japanese blogs. A number of recent studies focusing on demographics of bloggers have examined and found gender-based differences in bloggers[41] [7, 54, 109, 114, 143], different characteristics in teenage versus adult bloggers [56, 75–77, 127], and differences with respect to the age groups of bloggers [7, 114]. This section examines blogging around the world, with emphasis on patterns outside of the USA. Statistics on blogs in America compiled by the *Pew Internet Research Center* are available online [122]. Tables 3.2 and 3.3 summarize our findings on motivation for blogging and attitudes on personal identification and anonymity of bloggers in different regions of the globe.

A 2006 internet poll by *goo Research* and *internet.com* found that the practices of bloggers appear to differ according to the language used. For instance, Japanese postings peak around lunch time and midnight, with morning hours (midnight to noon) significantly more active than the late afternoon to mid-evening hours. Postings in English are fairly steady throughout the day with slight dips during commute hours and after dinner. Most Chinese postings take place during the afternoon, with very few posts from 9 p.m to midnight. Postings in Spanish are fairly steadily throughout the day, with a slight increase in activity during the afternoon to an hour or so past midnight. The relatively steady posting rates in English and Spanish indicate that they are taking place throughout the globe, while the sharp increases and decreases of Japanese and Chinese postings indicate that most are posted by native speakers in their country of origin, i.e., in Japan and China. The relatively large number of postings in Farsi (considering the number of native speakers on the language) is interesting. The report "*24 Hours in the Blogosphere*" [57] details posting patterns of bloggers around the world in a typical day.

---

[36]Globe of Blogs™: http://www.globeofblogs.com/

[37]AboutUs™: http://www.aboutus.org/

[38]Best Blogs in Asia: http://www.bestblogs.asia/

[39]Misohoni™: http://www.misohoni.com/

[40]kizasi.jp™: http://www.kizasi.jp/

[41]Determining the gender of author(s) of written text is a centuries-long open problem. A modern-day spin on this problem is to develop computer algorithms for automated gender identification of authors of electronic text (e-books, e-articles, e-mails, blogs, instant messages, etc.).

Table 3.2   Blogs: motivations for writing and readership levels by region

Region	Motivations	Readership
Japan	Personal diary, self-expression	74% internet users average 4.54 times/week, 25% daily, highest in world
Korea	Personal diary or scrapbook, on-line journalism	43% internet users average 2.03times/week, ages 8–24: 4 times/week, ages 25–34: 3 times/week
China	96% personal blogs packed with photos, audio animations, ...	Highest for ages 18–24 (less than 3 times/week) probably friends
US	Make money, promote political or professional agenda	27% internet users avg. 0.9 times/week, lower than Asia, higher than Europe
Germany	For fun, like to write, personal diary	Bloggers are regular readers of other blogs, average 21.15 (standard deviation 39, median 10)
UK	Connect with others, express opinions/vent, make money, citizen journalist, validation, professional advancement	23% internet users average 0.68 times/week
Poland	Self-expression, social interaction, entertainment	Not available

Table 3.3   Blogs: privacy concerns of bloggers and interesting regional facts

Region	Privacy & anonymity	Miscellaneous remarks
Japan	Use of (multiple) pseudonyms common	Access via mobile devices common, low blogger-reader interaction
Korea	Moderate	Political user-generated content banned during elections
China	High, due to government monitoring policies	High. Web-based media rated #2 trustworthy source of info (TV #1)
US	Low	High interaction in blogger-reader community
Germany	Low. 40.9% use real identity, (29.5% anonymous/pseudonym), 35.8% *about me* page	Blogging had late start compared to US, but quickly becoming popular

The *Edelman Omnibus Blog Study*[42] examined the multilingual, worldwide blogosphere. Countries included in the comparison study (with number of participants in parentheses) were Belgium (937), China (1,000), France (940), Germany (1,000), Italy (1,000), Japan (1,000), Poland (1,038), United Kingdom (1,002), United States of America (1,000), and South Korea (1,000). It found that by 2006, blogs had the potential to impact the daily lives of ordinary citizens and affect policy decision making. For example, they could break new stories (e.g., *Sony's* massive laptop battery recall; and *Google's* acquisition of *YouTube*[43]) [78, 83]; influence the worldwide mainstream media; reach influencers; and influence politics [1, 26, 33, 73, 92].

---

[42]http://www.edelman.jp/data/news/JIBS_e.pdf. Accessed 22 Dec 2010.

[43]*YouTube*™: http://www.youtube.com

Japan

Among all nations, blogging is currently most popular in Japan. Although there are only ~127 million native Japanese speakers (compared to ~380 million native speakers of English), more blogs are written in Japanese than any other language [110]. This has not always been the case; blogging first became very popular in the late 1990s in the USA, among white, college-educated males. Around 5–6 years ago (depending on the source), Japan clearly overtook the USA to become the number one blogging nation, measured in total blogs, not just per capita. For instance, quarterly surveys by *Technorati*[44] show Japanese overtook English as the top language for blogging during the latter half of 2006. Languages for blogging for the third quarter of 2006 were English 39%, Japanese 33%, Chinese 10%, Spanish 3%, Italian 2%, Russian 2%, Portuguese 2%, French 2%, German 1%, Farsi 1%, and others 5%, while those for the fourth quarter were Japanese 37%, English 36%, Chinese 8%, Italian 3%, Spanish 3%, Russian 2%, French 2%, Portuguese 2%, German 1%, Farsi 1%, and all others 5%.

In Japan, the primary motivation for writing personal blogs is to reflect on personal topics (music, children, food, daily life) rather than to promote professional or political interests; the latter two motivate many US bloggers [34, 49]. Other studies also found that reasons for personal blogging and how blogging is regarded in Japan differ from other countries. Only 3.8% of the 14,823 respondents in a May 2009 poll of the *MyVoice* internet community viewed blogs as "somewhere to make money through affiliates (and) advertising" Indeed, over two-thirds of active bloggers (67.8%) cited diary as one of the major themes of their blogs, followed by hobbies (29.8%), eating out, sweets, cooking (16.5%), entertainment (14.7%), and introducing products and services (14.6%). Only 4.5% of bloggers attended a corporate-sponsored blogger event.

A 2006 internet poll by *goo Research*[45] and *internet.com*[46] found Japanese bloggers tend to prefer anonymity (93.4% use pseudonyms, while 6.6% do not), and comments from readers and trackbacks were rarer than the USA. Similar findings have been reported by other sources, such as Japanese polls translated and published in *MyVoice*. Orita [104] surveys and presents results from a study of Japanese attitudes on blogging, anonymity/identifiability, linkability (i.e., ability to link a pseudonym of a blogger) and privacy, based on age and gender. Many Japanese bloggers use one or more pseudonyms and anonymity, depending on the blog site. However, use of pseudonyms may not necessarily prevent inquisitive readers willing to use search and pattern matching tools from identifying the writer or linking two

---

[44]Sifry, D. for Technorati, State of the Blogosphere: http://technorati.com/state-of-the-blogosphere/. Accessed 30 June 2010.

[45]goo Research.jp™: http://research.goo.ne.jp/

[46]internet.com™: http://www.internet.com/

pseudonyms to the same writer, because the blogs often describe patterns in daily life (recommended cafes, preferences in food and music), and use of similar phrases, expressions, and slang.

Adversity toward identifiability appears to be a cultural trait of the Japanese internet community and is not restricted to the blogosphere [129]:

> ... in Japan, one of the globe's most wired nations, few people have heard of Mr. Zuckerberg, the Facebook[47] chief executive and co-founder. And relatively few Japanese use Facebook ... fewer than two million or less than 2% of the country's online population. ... in sharp contrast to the United States where 60% of Internet users are on Facebook ... (Each) Japanese social networking site and game portal – like Mixi, Gree and Mobage-town. ... has more than 20 million users, and each offers its own approach to connecting people online. One trait those sites have in common is crucial to Japan's fiercely private Internet users. The Japanese sites let members mask their identities, in distinct contrast to the real-name, oversharing hypothetical user on which Facebook's business model is based. Japanese Web users, even popular bloggers, typically hide behind pseudonyms or nicknames. "Facebook does face a challenge in Japan," said Shigenori Suzuki, a Tokyo-based analyst at Nielsen/NetRatings. "There are powerful rivals, and then there's the question of Japanese Web culture." – The New York Times, January 9, 2011

Blogging as a percentage of Japanese internet users has been examined in a number of recent polls. A July 2008 internet-based poll of 330 members of the *JR Tokai Express* research monitor group (translated and published in *MyVoice*[48]) found the percentage of internet users with an active blog may be as high as 25.8% (an additional 10.9% created but no longer maintain a blog). A May 2009 poll of 14,823 members of the *MyVoice* internet community (translated and published in *MyVoice*) found similar results: 22.3% have an active blog, and 14.2% created but no longer maintain a blog. The top eight blog sites used by bloggers in the two surveys (*JR Tokai Express, MyVoice*) were the same, but the sites had different relative rankings: *FC2*[49] (15.3%, 21.8%), *Livedoor*[50] (14.1%, 6.9%), *Ameba*[51] (14.1%, 18.9%), *Yahoo!* (12.9%, 10.1%), *nifty's cocolog*[52] (11.8%, 6.1%), *Rakuten*[53] (10.6%, 15.2%), *goo* (9.4%, 6.3%), and *Seesaa*[54] (5.9%, 5.9%).

Many Japanese bloggers actively update their sites. A September 2008 poll of 300 blogging members of *Cross Marketing Inc.* and a May 2009 poll of the *MyVoice* community found: (17.3%, 18%) update daily of which 4% do so more than once a day. (25.7%, 30%) update more than twice per week, (9.7%, 14%) once a week,

---

[47]Facebook™: http://research.goo.ne.jp/

[48]Ken Y-N, What Japan Thinks, translations of Japanese opinions polls and surveys, available at: http://whatjapathinks.com, available through MyVoice: http://myvoice.org/. Accessed 1 July 2010.

[49]FC2™: http://blog.fc2.com/

[50]livedoor Blog™: http://blog.livedoor.com/

[51]Ameba™: http://www.ameba.jp/

[52]nifty cocolog™: http://www.cocolog-nifty.com/

[53]Rakuten™: http://plaza.rakuten.cjp/

[54]Seesaa: ™http://blog.seesaa.jp/

and (20.3%, 19%) 2 to 3 times per month. *Cross Marketing* found 8.0% of bloggers update once a month, 8.7% every 2–3 months, and 10.3% once every 6 months or less, while *MyVoice* found 20% of bloggers update once a month or less.

Analysis of results from a survey conducted May 15–22, 2007 through *NTT DoCoMo iMode* mobile phone service with 3,709 respondents indicates that widespread use of mobile phones in Japan along with PCs stimulated the growth of blogging communities [63]. 31.5% of blog readers exclusively use mobile phones for accessing blogs, while 22.7% exclusively use PCs. Among readers who use both devices, 23.3% mostly use mobile phones, while 22.5% mostly use PCs. Although both males and females access blogs most often from mobile phones, the tendency is even more pronounced among females.

As a country, Japan has the highest readership of blogs in the world (74%). A July 2008 internet-based poll of 330 members of the *JR Tokai Express Research* monitor group (translated and published in *MyVoice*[55]) shows an even higher readership rate of 81.8% among internet users. Corporate blogging by *small-to medium businesses* (SMBs) is commonplace in Japan. It is increasingly seen as an essential part of communicating with regular as well as potential customers. Even some larger, famous firms, such as *Sony*[56], *Nissan Motor*[57], and *Uniqlo*[58] are using blogging as a marketing tool [110]. These blogs are written in a friendly and informal style, in striking contrast to the highly formal business culture.

Asia

A study by Edelman [34] uncovered some unexpected data about the Asian blogosphere. Blog readership in the Asian region was exceptionally large in 2006, compared to the USA and Europe. Japan had exceptionally high readership and frequency of reading per week by adults in all age groups (18–24, 25–34, 35–44, 45–54, 55–64, 65+). Although the frequency of reading blogs declined with age, the decline was slight only for Japan, and the age group 65+ has even higher frequency of reading blogs (slightly more than 4 times per week) than the 18–24 age group with the highest frequency in South Korea (about 4 times per week). The next highest were the 25–34 age group in South Korea with (approximately 3 times per week) and the 18–24 age group in China (slightly less than 3 times per week). Males tended to be more frequent readers of blogs than females in all countries except Japan (4.74 per week for females vs. 4.36 per week for males) and Poland (.51 female vs..41 male). In contrast, the male statistics were more than double of those for females in Germany, Italy and Belgium. South Korea's frequency statistics (2.39 male vs. 1.69 female) were markedly lower than Japan's.

---

[55]MyVoice™: http://www.myvoice.co.uk/

[56]Sony™: http://www.sony.co.jp/

[57]Nissan Motor™: http://www.nissan-global.com/JP/

[58]Uniqlo™: http://www.uniqlo.com/jp/

Edelman [34] also reports some interesting local viewpoints on the internet and blogs. For instance, blogs appear to play a larger role in the dissemination of news in China because of tight censorship of traditional news media by the government. Television is rated as the most trustworthy news source (49%) followed by Web-based media (34%), and newspapers (17%). Many famous journalists, established businessmen, executives, tycoons, entrepreneurs, and entertainers maintain active, personal blogs, with comment sections for reader feedback. Although the frequency of reading blogs (39% claim to do so once a week) is lower than Japan and South Korea, it is significantly higher than the USA and Europe. MacKinnon [84] presents results from an in-depth study of Chinese blogging and its citizens, news media and government policies.

In 2005, South Korea was reported to have the highest internet penetration in the world by the OECD, and blogging appears to be strongly influenced by popular on-line scrap booking-like Web pages, known as *hompy* or "personal home pages with photo albums, guest books, avatars, background skins, and background music" [59]. Many of the popular *hompy* service providers also provide blog hosting services. Ito [59] and Yun [144] report approximately ten million *hompy* in 2005. Statistics on South Korean blogs and blogosphere may be significantly undercounting participation rates, because of the policies of these service providers (e.g., absence of support for trackback, RSS, pingback). In 2005, when Technorati was tracking over 35 million blogs, it was not tracking the two dominant South Korean *hompy* and blog sites: *CyWorld*[59] (currently known as *NaverBlog*) and *Daum*[60] [120]. Yun [144] cites three major motivations for blogging in South Korea: making a personal diary, making a personal scrapbook and participating in on-line journalism.

Other studies on blogging and blogs in Asia are: a comparison study of blogging in the USA, China and Korea by Park et al. [106]; a study on the relationship of social networks (hyperlinks) and the political blogosphere in South Korea by Park and Thelwall [105]; a report on censorship of internet content and communications (including blogs) in China by Thompson [132].

Europe

Outside of Asia and the USA, bloggers have the largest and most influential presence in the UK (23% readership) and France (22% readership). Surprisingly, blogging did not have much presence in Germany in 2006. Belgium had the lowest readership of blogs (14%), but those who did were more likely to be spurred into taking action. Italy suffers from a *digital divide*, with only 43.3% of families having PCs and 34.5% access to the internet in 2006, according to the Italian National Institute for

---

[59]CyWorld™ or NaverBlog™: http://www.nate.com/?f=cymain
[60]Daum™: http://www.daum.net/

Statistics. Similar findings were found in a 2006 survey by *The Economist* in which Italy was found to have 31.3 computers for every 100 people compared with 76.2 for the USA.

One of the earlier studies on bloggers in the UK was conducted by Pedersen and Macafee [108]. A follow-up study that compares US and UK bloggers found that the demographic group "males" had notable differences from the rest of the blogosphere [109]. Specifically, US males "dominated" rankings in links, use of images, amount of words, popularity (according to *Technorati* and *The Truth Laid Bear*[61]), and the subject of their blogs tended to be about interests, business, hobbies and external events, and less about personal topics (experiences, personal journals, diaries). They were also less concerned about privacy and tended to use their real name and post "identifiable" photos of themselves. Some differences between UK and US bloggers were: time of blogging (tendency for morning postings in the USA), more use of blog rings in the UK, more international linking in UK blogs, and different views on the role(s) of blogging.

Trammel et al. [135] conducted a study of 500 Polish bloggers by taking a random sample of users from the most popular and well-known Polish blogging service *blog.pl*. Of these sites, only 358 were still active and accessible to the public (some blogs were password protected, while others were "placeholders for blogs set up but never started"). Based on data on the front page, 42.7% blogs were updated several times per week and 41.9% several times per month. The gender of bloggers could be identified using characteristics of the Polish language in 82.4% of the blogs. Of these 74.2% appeared to be female. Some additional statistics on the blogs are: 19.0% contain a "biography statement," only 2.5% had a "topic" or "mission" statement, 21.5% provided contact information, and the average number of posts on the front page was 7 (mean 8.82, std. dev. 6.08, and range 1–30).

Trammel et al. [135] used six categories for motivation to classify blogs, allowing for multiple motivations: self-expression (82.4%), social interaction (59.5%), entertainment (51.7%), passing time (24.3%), information (8.4%), and professional advancement (2.2%). The statistics were fairly equally distributed between male and female bloggers but with slightly higher numbers for self expression, social interaction, and information for female bloggers, and a slightly higher number for professional advancement for male bloggers. The top five categories describing the content of Polish blogs were: feelings and thoughts (80.2%), family and friends (61.7%), record of the day (57.5%), interests and hobbies (39.7%) and communication with others (30.2%). The authors concluded that females tended to be more interested in a record of the day, memories, communicating feelings and thoughts, while males tended to discuss hobbies and interests. Work by Trammel et al. [135] supports previous studies conducted in 2003 of Polish bloggers (in Polish by Cyswinska-Milonas and Olcon) which found that Polish bloggers tend to view blogging more as a vehicle for self-presentation and self-expression, rather than a means for advancing one's career and promoting a professional image.

---

[61]The Truth Laid Bear™: http://truthlaidbear.com/

A study on the practices of the German-speaking blogosphere (Germany, Austria, Switzerland) by Schmidt [115] was based on 5,246 participants. A follow-up study of German user-satisfaction with blogging software was conducted [116] based on data from the first survey with 5,246 participants and follow-up Q&A from 2,701 participants. The median age of the bloggers in the first study was 29.3 years, with a standard deviation of 10.59. They tended to be highly educated and experienced, frequent (weekly or more) internet users (5 years or more), and the gender was fairly balanced (male 54.4% vs. female 45.6%) with the exception of teenagers for whom the female-to-male ratio was 2:1.

The top ten motives for maintaining a blog in the survey by Schmidt [115] were: for fun (70.8%), like to write (62.7%), record ideas and experiences for myself (61.7%), share ideas and experiences (49.0%), get feelings off my chest (44.5%), share my knowledge on certain topics (33.4%), stay in touch with friends and acquaintances (33.2%), make new contacts (27.2%), for professional reasons (12.7%), and others (10.7%). The frequency of updates was impressive: couple of times per day (11.4%), once a day (21.7%), couple of times per week (39.2%), couple of times per month (22.6%), and once a month or less (5.1%). The top ten types of content in blogs were: episodes from private life (74.5%), pictures and photos (63.5%), episodes from professional life, school, university, etc. (58.3%), commented links to other online content (58.2%), current political issues (40.5%), comments on professional, school or academic topics (40.5%), poems, lyrics, short stories (32.1%), other content (19.7%), video clips (4.6%), and podcasts (3.0%).

Germans appear to be less concerned than the Japanese regarding personal information [115]. Only 29.5% used a pseudonym or blogged anonymously, while 40.9% posted or used their actual identity. 35.8% maintained an *"about me"* page, 15.8% of the URLs of the blog contained the author's name, and 11.5% of the bloggers placed a link to their personal homepage. A copy of the survey (and questions) is available in the appendix of the study by Schmidt [115].

He et al. [51] conducted a comparison study of the Chinese and German blogosphere by examining 700 blog pages. They found blog hosting services in both countries are fairly similar since a new, attractive feature will be quickly imitated by other competing hosting sites. The only major difference was the ability to view the last visitor in *Sohu*[62], a Chinese blog service. The authors speculate that the importance of social relationships in China is driving a trend towards "providing further social functions which enable people to interact (via their blogs)."

He et al. [51] found a big difference in gender ratios between Chinese and German bloggers: (40% female, 35% male) for China vs. (22% female, 55% male) for Germany. Ninety six percent of Chinese blogs are personal blogs, while 12% of German blogs are organized by groups and 10% by companies. Chinese blog services provide a wider array of features for enhancing the visual appearance of a blogsite. It is not known whether demand by users drove the increase in features or the features drove greater use of graphic design elements. Specifically, statistics

---

[62]*Sohu:* http://www.sohu.com/

on Chinese vs. German use of graphic design elements in blogs are: animations (39% vs. 4%), photo albums (29% vs. 18%), audio files (39% vs. 2%), clocks (11% vs. 5%), and calendars (46% vs. 33%). German blogs contained more videos (10% compared to 7% for China).

Obradovic and Bauman [103] used the HITS algorithm of Kleinberg [65] to determine the top blogs in the German blogosphere, known as *A-List blogs*, which are "most widely read, cited in the mass media, and receive the most inbound links from other blogs" [53]. They argue that Technorati's rankings need to be modified because "for languages other than English, there exists separate sub-blogospheres that are more cohesively interlinked among each other than the blogosphere as a whole." Other studies of blogging in languages other than English are Esmaili et al. [35] of Persian and Merelo [88] and Tricas-Garcia and Merelo-Garcia [137] of Spanish.

The international blogging community is diverse in many respects. Motivations for and practices regarding reading and writing blogs and interaction with readers may differ in different countries. Interestingly, these general trends and regional differences are mirrored (albeit with a few years delay) by a relatively new player *Twitter*, a microblogging service, the subject of the next section.

Microblogs: Twitter et al

Recently, a fast and nimble new player has emerged in the blogging scene, the *microblog*. In microblogging, authors send or post very short text updates (usually 200 characters or less) to anyone or a small group of intended recipients. Subjects of updates may be about almost anything, such as events in daily life, special activities (e.g., a concert, conference, business meeting), a hobby, or a review of a product or service. Microblogs originally came into being via blogs, and were called, "*tumblelogs.*" However, as many services specially targeted for microblogging were introduced in 2006–2007, the term fell out of favor.

Some of the more popular microblogging services include: *Twitter, Jaiku*[63], *Qaiku*[64] (developed in late 2009 as a replacement to *Jaiku*, which was acquired by *Google*), *Frazr*[65], *Six Apart* (which acquired *Pownce*)[66], *Tumblr*[67], *MySay*[68], *hictu*[69],

---

[63]Jaiku™: http://www.jaiku.com/
[64]Qaiku™: http://www.qaiku.com/
[65]Frazr™: http://frazr.com/
[66]Six Apart™: http://www.sixapart.com/
[67]tumblr™: http://www.tumblr.com/
[68]MySay™: http://www.mysay.com/
[69]hictu™: http://www.hictu.com/

MoodMill[70], *IRateMyDay*[71], *Plurk*[72], *identi.ca*, and *emote.in*.[73] Each offers slightly different features. For example, *Frazr* targets French and German users; *Six Apart* offers beautiful fonts and formatting, supports social networking, and has anti-spam software; *Tumblr* supports adding tags to posts and video posting; *hictu* supports video microblogging; *MoodMill* provides a means for expressing one's current mood or state of being; *IRateMyDay* is for rating one's day; *identi.ca* is like an open source *Twitter*; and *emote.in* is a service on *identi.ca* for attaching emotions to posts.

Currently, the most popular microblogging service in the USA is *Twitter*, which was founded in 2007. *Jaiku* is ranked a distant second. According to a report on digital marketing in the USA in 2009 by *comScore*[74], *Twitter* grew from 2 to 20 million visitors from December 2008 to December 2009, with extraordinary growth from 4 to 17 million visitors between February to April [22]. This period also saw a change in user demographics. In December 2008, the majority of users (65%) were in the 25- to 56-year-old range, and only a small percentage (9%) were young (ages 18–24). By December 2009, the 18- to 24-year-old segment grew by 7.9% and 17-year-old or under by 6.2%. During this period, the percentages of users in older age segments decreased, specifically: 25- to 34-year-olds by 1.3%, 35- to 44-year-olds by 3%, 45- to 54-year-olds by 3%, and 55- to 64-year-olds by 6%. (Note: a follow-up report by *comScore* estimates that in March 2010 *Twitter* had 22.3 million unique visitors up from 524,000 in March 2009.) A June 2009 study of 11.5 million accounts by *Sysmos*[75] also found that most *Twitter* users are very young (31% ages 15–19, 35% ages 20–24, 15% ages 25–29), and a few *Twitter* users account for most of the activity (5% of users account for 75% of all activity, 10% for 86% of all activity, and 30% for 97.4% of all activity) [18].

Twitter was designed to help people keep in contact with one other, by answering the simple question, *"What are you doing?"* using at most 140 characters via instant messaging, texting or the Web. *Twitter* accepts responses from *short messaging services* (SMS), the Web and mobile Web, instant messaging services, and third party API services. Demographics of users and reasons behind its adoption have been studied by sociologists, scientists, governments and businesses [55, 60, 74, 90, 126]. Motivations for *twittering* are similar to those for blogging.

The increasing popularity and use of *Twitter* is following some of the same patterns as that of blogging. *Twittering* by large numbers of people in the general public began in the USA and has spread to other countries (a summary of the "State

---

[70]MoodMill™: http://www.moodmill.com/

[71]IRateMyDay™: http://www.iratemyday.com/

[72]Plurk™: http://www.plurk.com/

[73]identi.ca™: http://identica/, emote.in™: http://identica/emote

[74]comScore™, Inc.: http://www.comscore.com/

[75]Sysmos™: http://www.sysmos.com/

of the Twittersphere" in 2008 is available from *Hubspot*[76]). A May 2010 article in the *New York Times* quotes *Nielson* which found that 12.3% of people in Japan have used *Twitter*, versus 10.2% of people in the USA [128]. A big surge in Japanese users (from 521,000 to 7.52 million) appears to have taken place between April 2009 and March 2010. During the same period, *Nielsen* found a slower rate of growth in the USA (from 13.858 to 20.109 million[77]). A July 9, 2010 post by *Nielson*[78] reports that *Twitter* hit the ten million user mark in Japan, and 16% of internet users in Japan *twitter*, versus 10% for the USA.

Tabuchi [128] reports *keitai* (mobile phones and devices) are important drivers of the growth of *Twitter* in Japan. In addition, the compact nature of the written Japanese language accommodates more information in individual tweets and is less constraining since a few characters can be used to represent many word, concept or name. In short, the 140 character limit is not as constraining as phonetically-based European languages. In March 2010, growth in *Twitter* use in Japan was projected to outpace that in the USA sometime that year, with the help of *Softbank*, which announced an embedded application that displays an icon to jump directly to a customized *Twitter* site on the welcome screen on 14 types of the company's cell phones [128]. In July 2010 *Twitter* released statistics to the Associated Press that showed by June 2010, Asia overtook North America as the region for generating the most tweets (37% vs. 32%). In rankings by country in June 2010, the USA generated the most tweets (25%), Japan generated the most per capita (18%) and ranked second with approximately eight million tweets per day, Indonesia ranked third (10%), and South Korea fourth (2%).

A July 9 post by Nielsen notes the 1900% growth in *Twitter* use in South Korea in the year leading up to May 2009 appears to be supported by the high use of portable devices (particularly advanced cell phones). And *hompy* services have catalyzed this growth. The *Korean Times* reported in July 2009 of the rush to "leap onto the microblogging bandwagon" [133]. In June 2009, Twitter received 600,000 visitors. An "abundance" of other local microblogging services give Koreans more flexibility, such as: no limits on message length; messaging within private member-only communities; easy means to comment of posts; and accommodating uploads of video clips. Some of the popular local services are: me2Day (*me2day.net*), Runpipe (*www.runpipe.com*), Tocpoc(*tocpic.com*), and User Story Net (*userstory.net*). At the time the article went to press, *me2Day* was the only serious competitor to *Twitter* in terms of popularity with the general public.

---

[76]State of the Twittersphere: http://cdnqa.hubteam.com/State_of_the_Twittersphere_by_HubSpot_Q42008.pdf. Accessed 31 May 2010.

[77]Facebook and Twitter post large year over year gains in unique users, May 4, 2010: http://blog.nielsen.com/nielsenwire/global/facebook-and-twitter-post-large-year-over-year-gains-in-unique-users/. Accessed 31 May 2010.

[78]Social media dominates Asia Pacific internet usage, July 9, 2010: http://blog.nielsen.com/nielsenwire/global/social-media-dominates-asia-pacific-internet-usage/. Accessed 30 July 2010.

Despite its success in terms of user volume, there are several concerns regarding *Twitter*. Its initial business model was ambiguous, and its exponential growth has not led to significant revenue. However, in early April of 2010, the company announced a new advertising service based on keyword searches [89]. Companies will be able to purchase keywords. If a user of *Twitter* inputs a "purchased" search term, a promotion or ad will pop up at the top of the screen. It is unclear whether the ads will: impact the business of keyword purchasers, annoy users, or have unforeseen unintended consequences (good or bad). Other concerns with *Twitter* include privacy, security, and integration into corporate culture.

Social Network Analysis: Online Communities and Blogs

Social Network Analysis (SNA) is the study of relationships between various entities (e.g., people, groups, computers, organizations) using network theory [40, 48, 82, 98, 117, 139, 141]. This section examines some basic concepts from SNA and their applications to internet-based social networks: link analysis, models for diffusion of ideas; and blog comment analysis.

Basic Concepts in SNA

Identifying and understanding human networks and their properties is important for tracking the spread of information, ideas and trends. These networks may be based on friendships, professional relationships, or common interests – e.g., politics, volunteer work, sports, hobbies [6, 50, 93, 94, 97]. Network and link analyses are based on fundamental concepts from a number of fields, including: graph, hypertext and web mining [16, 17, 31, 124]. The growth of the internet and social networking sites has attracted greater attention to analysis of personal relationships [8, 14, 32, 38, 39, 41, 61, 140].

Many concepts and tools from conventional network analysis and Web page link analysis can be applied straightforwardly to SNA[79]. However, SNA focuses on the properties of links and networks that represent relationships and communities, such as: the strength and nature of relationships in communities (tightness, openness to outsiders), relationships between communities, and the effect of relationships within and among communities on individuals [15, 30, 66, 131]. In a typical social network, each node represents a person, machine or organization, and each link connecting two nodes represents the relationship between the two nodes. The links may or may not be directional (unidirectional or bi-directional) since relationships may be asymmetrical.

---

[79]orgnet.com, Social Network Analysis, A Brief Introduction: http://www.orgnet.com/sna.html. Accessed 30 July 2010.

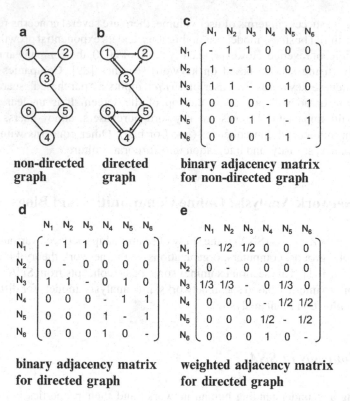

a non-directed graph

b directed graph

c binary adjacency matrix for non-directed graph

d binary adjacency matrix for directed graph

e weighted adjacency matrix for directed graph

Fig. 3.2 Examples of graphs and adjacency matrices for a network of six people. (**a–b**) Non-directed and directed graphs of relationships. (**c–d**) binary adjacency matrices for non-directed and directed graphs. (**e**) adjacency graph for directed graph, in which all edges starting from a node have equal weight and the sum of all weights for edges starting for each node is one

SNA is also concerned with determining connectors, leaders, isolates, core and peripheral members, etc. in a community [96]. Networks with n members (or nodes) are modeled by graphs in which members with relationships are connected by edges. Mathematical analysis of the network begins with construction of an n-by-n *adjacency matrix* $\mathbf{A}$. In the simplest model, all relationships are symmetric and equal, so $\mathbf{A}$ is a symmetric matrix with ij^{th} entry $\mathbf{A}(i,j)$, such that $\mathbf{A}(i,j) = \mathbf{A}(j,i) = 1$ when the ith and j^{th} nodes are connected, and $\mathbf{A}(i,j) = \mathbf{A}(j,i) = 0$ when they are not. In more sophisticated models, the edges are weighted to reflect the strength of relationships between nodes, and the edges may have directionality (i.e., relationships may be asymmetric) so $\mathbf{A}$ is not necessarily a symmetric matrix. An example of a six-person network with its binary and weighted matrices is given in Fig. 3.2.

Centralities are measures to determine the importance of a node in a social network with respect to flow, e.g., of traffic or information [11]. Four commonly used centralities are: degree, eigenvector, betweenness and closeness.

Table 3.4 Four common centralities in social network analysis

Centrality	Measured property/characteristic
Degree	Extent to which node is central player in community based on number of direct links to other nodes
Eigenvalue	Importance of node in community based on number of links to other nodes and importance of the nodes
Betweenness	Ability of node to act as vital bridge between important nodes, (particularly in the absence of a direct link between them)
Closeness	Speed at which node can be accessed (directly or indirectly) measured as the mean of the geodesic distance between the node and all other accessible nodes in the network

1. *Degree centrality* measures if a node is a central player based on the number of direct links a node has to other nodes in the network. In the simple network model (above), the degree of the ith node is the number of edges attached to it, i.e., $\Sigma_j A(i,j)$; where $j = 1, 2, \ldots, n$.

2. *Eigenvector centrality* measures the number of links as well as their quality, i.e., whether a link is to an important node in the network. Let $x(j)$ denote the centrality of node j. Then the eigenvector centrality of node i is the average of the centralities of its neighbors, i.e., $\lambda^{-1}\Sigma_j A(i, j) x(j)$, for $j = 1, 2, \ldots, n$, where λ is a constant. Rewriting the expression as a system of equations in matrix form yields $\lambda x = A\,x$, where x is the eigenvector of the adjacency matrix A with eigenvalue λ. Eigenvector centrality takes the largest eigenvalue λ and the corresponding eigenvector x. Google's *PageRank*^{TM} algorithm is based on a variation of this concept [13, 72].

3. *Betweenness centrality* measures the ability of a node to act as a vital bridge between two important nodes. For instance, a node that lies between two important clusters or nodes with no direct path has high between-ness. It is computed as follows. Find all shortest paths between each pair of vertices. Determine the fraction of the paths that pass through the vertex under consideration. Compute the sum of the fractions for all pairs of vertices. More precisely, let V denote the set of all vertices in a graph of a social network. Let $\sigma_{ts} = \sigma_{st}$ denote the number of shortest paths between two vertices $s,t \in V$. By convention, $\sigma_{ss} = 1$. Let $\sigma_{st}(v)$ denote the number of shortest paths between $s,t \in V$ on which a vertex $v \in V$ lies. Then $C_B(v) = \Sigma_{s,t,v \in V}(\sigma_{st}(v)/\sigma_{st})$ is the betweenness centrality of vertex $v \in V$, where s, t and v are distinct and $s,t,v \in V$.

4. *Closeness centrality* measures the speed at which a node can access another node, directly or indirectly; it is the mean of the geodesic distances between the node and all other accessible nodes in the network.

Identifying peripheral players and their roles in a network is useful for understanding information flow in a network. Other measures of centrality have been proposed for targeted purposes, such as power centrality [10] (Table 3.4).

Examination of networks from a structural perspective may also yield interesting insights. *Structural cohesion* is defined as the minimum members of a group that need to be deleted to disconnect a group. A group is said to be a *clique* if every node is connected to all other nodes in the group. More loosely connected groups are often described as *social circles*. The *structural equivalence* of two distinct nodes measures the extent to which their links to other nodes are similar. A direct link is not required between the two nodes under comparison. A *structural hole* exists between two nodes if links must be introduced between intermediate nodes to establish a connection between the two nodes.

Community Mining and Dissemination of Information

This subsection examines how analysis of networks graphs can help find on-line communities and help understand how information flows in communities. Gibson et al. [42] examined how information on links can help identify on-line communities by invoking the *Hyperlinked Induced Topic Search* (HITS) algorithm of Kleinberg [65]; the original intended application of HITS was identification of Web pages with a high volume of useful information. More specifically, HITS finds important *authority* Web pages (i.e., pages with original, useful information) and important *hub* pages (i.e., pages with links and references to good authority pages), based on the number of in-links and out-links originating from important hub and authority pages. In an SNA context, the nodes correspond to blogs or bloggers. In a separate study, Obradovic and Bauman [103] use HITS to find A-list bloggers and associated communities. In a different approach Newman [95] identifies communities by locating densely connected substructures in static graphs. Chin and Chignell [19] propose a method for finding blog communities based on graphs and nodes and a definition of community by McMillan and Chavis [87] and applies it to find communities in indie music blogs. Note that all of these approaches rely on bloggers to embed links and for readers to comment and embed links to their own blogs in their comments.

Some studies of dynamic networks are [9, 79], and those with applications to SNA are [23, 24, 36, 37, 42, 58, 71, 123, 130, 134]. Studies to understand evolving communities in data streams were conducted by Aggarwal and Yu [5].

Studies aimed at understanding the dynamics of blog-based networks – their evolution and decay – have been conducted by Adamic and Glance [1], Adar and Adamic [2], Gruhl et al. [46], Kumar et al. [70], Leskovec et al. [80], and McGlohon et al. [86]. These works model networks as directed graphs in which nodes are blogs and edges represent links to other blogs. They found that cascades are rare. They proposed a model with popular topics which generate a relatively constant stream of "chatter" along with volatile topics that generate "spikes" of interest. McGlohon et al. [86] conducted an in-depth study of cascade models of blogs in a network and found that communities associated with blogs can be somewhat characterized by the types and numbers of cascades to which they belong, e.g., the associated communities are "humorous" or "conservative."

On-line communities play an important role in the dissemination of information [111, 112]. In a pre-internet model of information flow, Dawkins [27] proposed the concept of a memes (or small idea or concept) to explain and describe the spread and evolution of ideas and cultural phenomenon.

meme (\mēm\) *noun*, an idea, behavior, style, or usage that spreads from person to person within a culture (entered in 1976) [80]

As the term came into general use, it came to symbolize "an idea that, like a gene, can replicate and evolve." Examples of memes and meme systems include political theories, proselytizing religions, and the idea of memes itself[81]. Recently, the phrase "*internet meme*" is used to describe a "catchphrase or concept that spreads quickly from person to person via the internet" (Wikipedia 2011)[82].

A pioneering work by Kempe et al. [62] studied how to efficiently spread memes in social networks. It begins with the standard directed graph model of a social network, in which each individual is represented by a node. In the static, binary model, nodes can be classified as *active* or *inactive*; the former represents an individual who adopted a meme, while the latter represents an individual who has not. In a *progressive* model of a social network, nodes can switch from being inactive to active, but cannot do so in the other direction:

The process (looks) roughly as follows (for) an initially inactive node v: as time unfolds, more and more of v's neighbors become active; at some point, this may cause v to become active, and v ... may in turn trigger further ... nodes to which v is connected.

Granovetter [44] and Schelling [113] introduced node-specific thresholds in subsequent refinements of the model. In the basic linear threshold model, each node v is influenced by each of its neighbors by a weight b. Each node is associated with a threshold θ. If the sum of the weights of all neighbors exceeds the threshold, the node becomes active. The threshold θ for a node represents the latent tendency of the associated individual to adopt a meme. Kempe et al. [62] proposes a solution to the optimization problem: "If we can try to convince a subset of individuals to adopt a (meme), and the goal is to trigger a large cascade of further adoptions, which set of individuals should we target?"

The first large-scale endeavor to gather and analyze contents from blogs for the purpose of understanding the behavior of information propagation in the blogging community was the now defunct *Blogdex project* of *MIT Media Lab*. The project began in 2001 and continued for 4 years, during which time it identified hot topics and tracked their evolution and spread within the blogosphere. Blogdex published rankings of topics according to their recency and popularity.

Another early work on blogs and information diffusion by Gruhl et al. [46] proposed a macroscopic model of information flow in the blogosphere that consists

---

[80]Merriam-Webster On-Line: http://www.merriam-webster.com/dictionary/meme

[81]Drexler K, Engines of creation: http://e-drexler.com/p/06/00/EOC_Cover.html. Accessed 23 Dec 2010.

[82]What is a meme? In The Daily Meme: http://thedailymeme.com/what-is-a-meme/

of long-running *chatter* topics and *spike* topics that are responses to world events or to events in a blog community. They also proposed a microscopic model of information propagation (i.e., from individuals to individuals) based on models of epidemics and propagation of infectious diseases. *Rich site summary* (RSS) blog feeds from publishers and media organizations and hourly data from 14 RSS channels from rss.news.yahoo.com were used to determine whether topic spikes were responses to world wide news events or to events within the blog community. Data from the top 100 blogs (according to blogstreet.com) was used for studies of the microscopic model. This work is closely related to that of Wu et al. [142], who examined information flow in e-mail networks.

Analysis of Comments on Blog Postings

This subsection is a quick review of some of the few works on blog comment analysis for English-based blogs. Although a key characteristic of blogs is the ability of the readership to comment and participate in discussions with the blogger (as well as other readers), study and analysis of blog comments has largely been overlooked. Exceptions include deMoor and Efimova [28, 29], Gumbrecht [47], Krishnamurthy [69], Mishne and Glance [91], Trevino [136] who note that, "comments are regarded by most bloggers as vital to the interactive nature of weblogs." deMoor and Efimova [28, 29] investigated how meaningful weblog conversations about a topic develop and evolve. They cite a model of blog posts and an evolving community proposed by Jenkins in a 2003 *Microdoc News*[83] story, which cites four types of blog posts:

> (1) *opinion posts* that define a topic . . . , (2) *vote posts* where a blogger (dis)agrees with another post, (3) *reaction posts* in which a blogger responds to a single post on another site, and (4) *summation posts* where the blogger summarizes various other blogs.

The dearth of in-depth studies of comments and their role in the blogosphere is due, in part, to the relative difficulty of their extraction and processing (compared to blog postings). Extraction and analysis of blog postings is supported by various types of syndication (e.g., RSS readers) that facilitate direct access of postings (bypassing the need for parsing of HTML and text mining). With a handful of exceptions, syndication of blog comments is not well-supported. However, the situation is expected to be ameliorated as blogging platforms evolve.

Mishne and Glance [91] conducted one of the earlier large-scale analysis of blog comments by constructing a simple wrapper to enable identification of "comment regions" in a blog and to identify individual comments within each comment region (to handle multiple comments corresponding to a post). They found that comments can be a good indicator of the popularity of a post and of the weblogs as a whole. Most comments have at most one link; either none or a link back to the comment

---

[83]Microdoc News: http://microdoc-news.info/

author's blog. However, some weblogs do not permit posting of comments; some bloggers disable the commenting option to circumvent flaming, spamming, and other unwanted annoying or malicious acts. Mishne and Glance [91] cite statistics from a range of studies that indicate that anywhere from 10% up to 57% of blogs do not permit commenting. The authors used tools from text and sentiment analysis (e.g., words and phrases expressing polarity or subjectivity, punctuation, referrals to previous posts, lengthy, and frequency counts of these features) to try to automatically find disputes and debate in posts and comments. Their algorithm found that about 21% of comments were tagged, "disputative," and a list of words in the text as well as manual examination of the text substantiated the automated tagging. However, the number of disputative comments that the algorithm failed find and tag is unknown.

Conclusion

The past decade has seen the emergence of user-generated content on the internet that is changing the way people access information, form social networks, and interact with others. Blogs epitomize these phenomena, and are often cited as having acted as early catalysts for propelling the popularity of on-line social networking. This chapter reviewed statistics that show the growth of blogging and characteristics of bloggers and their readership in different regions. Since the USA served as the early incubator for blogging software, initially, English was the dominant language for bloggers. A good portion of early research on blogs, the blogosphere and social networks used blog data from North America written primarily in English by college-educated, white males who were interested in advancement of their careers and making money. Although current research is shifting its focus towards a more representative cross-section of the blogosphere, it is still mostly about bloggers who write in English or European languages.

Statistics show that Asia – particularly Japan – has overtaken the USA as the top region for blogging, with respect to sheer numbers, not just per capita. Asian bloggers appear to have different motivations for blogging, i.e., less interest in making money and personal and professional advancement. Furthermore, concerns about privacy, personal identification by the general public, appear to be extremely important to a large portion of Japanese bloggers as well as the larger Japanese on-line community. (Chinese bloggers share these concerns, but they appear to be rooted in censorship and fear of government crack-downs and persecution.) Although readership of blogs is very high in Japan, commenting is relatively rare, compared to the USA and Europe.

The striking difference in attitudes of bloggers and their readership is reflected in the use of (possibly multiple) pseudonyms by bloggers and the density (richness or spareness) of the link structures in local blogospheres. Current methods used to study blog-based social betworks are mostly based on link structure analysis. Although these methods have been useful for understanding blogs written by

Americans in English, new methods may be needed to understand properties of the Asian blogosphere and other local blogospheres whose members exhibit different motivations, attitudes towards privacy, and commenting behaviors.

The growth of the blogosphere has created many exciting new opportunities for research. In addition to the topics mentioned above, some important and emerging issues associated with blogs include: corporate-sponsored blogging, blog mining for business intelligence, metrics for blog and newsblog credibility, splog detection, sentiment analysis of blogs, and many more. We hope that this chapter will serve as a useful pointer to interesting and inspiring works for current and future blog researchers.

Acknowledgements The author would like to thank Scott Trent for his encouragement and suggestions, Mikael Onsjoe for helpful comments on early drafts of the manuscript, and Fumio Ando of IBM Research for his thoughtful management and support of this work.

References

1. Adamic, L., Glance, N.: The politicalblogosphere and the 2004 U.S. election: divided they blog. In: Proceedings of the ACM International Workshop on Link Discovery, Chicago, IL, pp 36–43, 21–24 Aug 2005
2. Adar, E., Adamic, L.: Tracking information epidemics in blogspace. In: Proceedings of the IEEE/EIC/ACM International Conference on Web Intelligence, Compeigne University of Technology, France, pp. 207–214, 4–7 Dec 2005
3. Agarwal, N., Liu, H.: Blogosphere: research issues, tools and applications. ACM SIGKDD Explor. **10**(1), 18–31 (2008)
4. Agarwal, N., Liu, H.: Modeling and Data Mining in Blogosphere. Morgan & Claypool, San Rafael (2009)
5. Aggarwal, C., Yu, P.: Online analysis of community evolution in data streams. In: Proceedings of the SIAM Data Mining, New Port Beach, CA, pp. 18–31, 21–23 Apr 2005
6. Albert, R., Barabasi, A.L.: Statistical mechanics of complex networks. Rev. Mod. Phys. **74**, 47–97 (2002)
7. Argamon, S. et al.: Mining the blogosphere: age, gender and the varieties of self-expression. First Monday 12. http://131.193.153.231/www/issues/issue12_9/argamon/ (2007). Accessed 1 Nov 2010
8. Barabasi, A.-L.: Linked: The New Science of Networks. Persus, Cambridge (2002)
9. Barabasi, A.-L., Albert, R.: Emergence of scaling in random networks. Science **286**, 509–512 (1999)
10. Bonacich, P.: Power and centrality: a family of measures. Am. J. Sociol. **92**(5), 1170–82 (1987)
11. Borgatti, S.: Centrality and network flow. Soc. Netw. **27**, 55–71 (2005)
12. Brady, M.: Blogging: personal participation in public knowledge-building on the web. University of Essex, UK. http://www.essex.ac.uk/chimera/publications.html (2005). Accessed 1 Nov 2010
13. Brin, S., Page, L.: The anatomy of a large-scale hypertxual search engine. In: Proceedings of WWW, Brisbane, Australia, pp. 107–117, 14–18 Apr 1998
14. Buchanan, M.: Nexus: Small Worlds and the Groundbreaking Science of Networks. WW Norton & Co, New York (2003)
15. Carrington, P.J., Scott, J., Wasserman, S. (eds.): Models and Methods in Social Network Analysis. Cambridge University Press, Cambridge, UK (2005)

16. Chakrabarti, S.: Mining the Web. Morgan Kaufmann, San Francisco (2002)
17. Chakrabarti, S., Faloutsos, C.: Graph mining: laws, generators and algorithms. ACM Comput. Surv. **38**, 1–69 (2006)
18. Cheng, A., Evans, M., Singh, H.: Inside Twitter: an in-depth look inside the Twitter world, June. http://www.sysmos.com/insidetwitter (2009). Accessed 1 Nov 2010
19. Chin, A., Chignell, M.: Identifying communities in blogs: roles for social network analysis and survey instruments. Int. J. Web Based Commun. **3**(3), 345–363 (2007)
20. Coates, T.: On Permalinks and Paradigms. Blog: Plasticbag.org, June 11. http://www.plasticbag.org/archives/2003/06/on_permalinks_and_paradigms/ (2003). Accessed 1 Nov 2010
21. Cohen, E., Krishnamurthy, B.: A short walk in the Blogistan. Comput. Netw. **50**(5), 615–630 (2006)
22. comScore: The 2009 U.S. digital year in review: a recap of the year in digital marketing, Feb. press@comscore.com (2003). Accessed 1 Nov 2010
23. Cortes, C., Pregibon, D., Volinsky, C.: Communities of interest. In: Proceedings of the International Symposium of Intelligent Data Analysis, Lisbon, Portugal, pp. 105–114, 13–15 Sept 2001
24. Cortes, C., Pregibon, D., Volinsky, C.: Computational methods for dynamic graphs. J. Comput. Graph. Stat. **12**, 950–970 (2003)
25. Costa, P., McCrae, R.: Professional Manual. Psychological Assessment Resources, Odessa (1992)
26. Davis, R.: Typing Politics: The Role of Blogs in American Politics. Oxford University Press, Oxford (2009)
27. Dawkins, R.: The Selfish Gene. Oxford University Press, Oxford (1976)
28. deMoor, A., Efimova, L.: An argumentation analysis of weblog conversations. In: Proceedings of the International Working Conference on the Language-Action Perspective on Communication Modelling, Rutgers University, NJ, USA Univ. 2–3 June 2004. http://communitysense.nl/papers/lap04b.pdf. Accessed 25 June 2012 (2004)
29. deMoor, A., Efimova, L.: Beyond personal webpublishing: an exploratory study of conversational blogging practices. In: Proceedings of the Hawaii International Conference on System Sciences, 3–6 Jan 2005. IEEE Press, Los Alamitos (2005)
30. deNooy, W., Mrvar, A., Batageli, V.: Exploratory Social Network Analysis with Pajek. Cambridge University Press, Cambridge, UK (2005)
31. Desikan, P., Srivastava, J.: Hyperlink analysis: techniques and applications. US Army High Performance Computing and Research Center. Technical Report TR–2003–120 (2003)
32. Dorogovtsev, S., Mendes, J.: Evolution of Networks. Oxford University Press, Oxford (2003)
33. Drezner, D., Farrell, H. (eds.): Blogs, politics and power: a special issue of Public Choice. Public Choice 134: 1–13
34. Edelman.: The Edelman Omnibus blog study, by strategyOne. http://www.edelman.com/image/insights/content/WhitePaper011107sm.pdf (2007). Accessed 1 Nov 2010
35. Esmaili, K. et al.: Experiments on Persian weblogs. In: Proceedings of the Weblogging Ecosystem, Menlo Park, CA. http://www.blogpulse.com/www2006-workshop/papers/persian-weblogs.pdf (2006). Accessed 1 Nov 2010
36. Falkowski, T., Bartelheimer, J., Spiliopoulou, M.: Community dynamics mining. In: Proceedings of the European Conference on Information Systems, Goeteborg, Sweden, CD-ROM, June 2006
37. Falkowski, T., Bartelheimer, J., Spiliopoulou, M.: Mining and visualizing the evolution of subgroups in social networks. In: Proceedings of the IEEE/WIC/ACM Conference on Web Intelligence, Hong Kong, pp. 52–58, 18–22 Dec 2006
38. Feldman, R.: Link Analysis: Current State of the Art (Tutorial). ACM KDD, Edmonton (2002)
39. Feldman, R.: Link analysis: current state of the art and applications for counter terrorism (video). http://videolectures.net/mmdss07_feldman_latm/ (2009). Accessed 1 Oct 2009
40. Freeman, L.: The Development of Social Network Analysis: A Study in the Sociology of Science. Empirical Press, Vancouver (2009)

41. Getoor, L., Diehl, C.: Introduction to the special issue on link mining. SIGKDD Explor. 7(2):1–2; Link mining: a survey. SIGKDD Explor. **7**(2):3–12 (2005)
42. Gibson, D., Kleinberg, J., Raghavan, R.: Inferring Web communities from link topology. In: Proceedings of ACM Conference on Hypertext and Hypermedia, Pittsburg, PA, pp. 225–234, 20–24 June 1998
43. Gill, A., Nowson, S., Oberlander, J.: What are they blogging about? Personality, topic and motivation in blogs. In: Proceedings of the AAAI ICWSM, San Jose, CA, 17–20 May 2009. http://nowson.com/papers/GillNowOber-ICWSM09.pdf. Accessed 10 Jan 2011
44. Granovetter, M.: Threshold models of collective behavior. Am. J. Sociol. **83**(6), 1420–1443 (1978)
45. Grossman, L.: Time's person of the year: you. Time, 13 Dec 2006
46. Gruhl, D., Guha, R., Nowell, D., Tomkins, A.: Information diffusion through blogspace. In: Proceedings of the WWW, New York, NY, pp. 491–501, 17–22 May 2004
47. Gumbrecht, M.: Blogs as "protected space". In: Proceedings of WWW Workshop on Weblogging Ecosystem, New York, 18 May 2004. http://www.blogpulse.com/www2004-workshop.html. Accessed 14 Jan 2011
48. Hannemann, R., Riddle, M.: Introduction to social network methods. In: UC Riverside, Riverside, CA. Online book: http://faculty.ucr.edu/~hanneman/nettext/ (2005). Accessed 4 Jan 2011
49. Harden, B.: Japan's bloggers: humble giants of the Web. Washington Post, 26 Dec 2007
50. Hayes, B.: Graph theory in practice, part I. Am. Sci. **88**(1): 9–13; Graph theory in practice, part II. Am. Sci. **88**(2): 104–109 (2000)
51. He, Y., Caroli, F., Mandl, T.: The Chinese and German blogosphere: an empirical and comparative analysis. In: Proceedings of Mensch und Computer, Weimar, Germany, pp. 149–158, 2–5 Sept 2007
52. Henning, J.: The blogging iceberg: of 4.12M weblogs, most little seen and quickly abandoned. http://findarticles.com/p/articles/mi_m0EIN/is_2003_Oct_6/ai_108559565/ (2010). Accessed 1 Nov 2010
53. Herring, S., Kouper, I., Paolillo, J., Scheidt, L., Tyworth, M., Welsch, P., Wright, E., Yu, N.: Conversations in the blogosphere: an analysis from the bottom up. In: Proceedings of the Hawaii International Conference on System Sciences, Kaui, 3–6 Jan 2005. http://ella.slis.indiana.edu/~herring/blogconv.pdf. Accessed 14 Jan 2011
54. Herring, S., et al.: Bridging the gap: a genre analysis of weblogs. In: Proceedings of the Hawaii International Conference on System Sciences, Kaui, 5–8 Jan 2004. http://csdl.computer.org/comp/proceedings/hicss/2004/2056/04/205640101babs.htm. Accessed 1 Nov 2010
55. Honeycutt, C., Herring, S.: Beyond microblogging: conversation and collaboration via Twitter. In: Proceedings of the Hawaii International Conference on System Sciences, pp. 1–10, 2009
56. Huffaker, D., Calvert, S.: Gender, identity, and language use in teenage blogs. J. Comput-Mediat. Commun. **10**(12). http://jcmc.indiana.edu/vol10/issue2/huffaker.html (2005). Accessed 30 June 2010
57. Hurst, M.: 24 hours in the blogosphere. In: Proceedings of AAAI Spring Symposium. AAAI, Menlo Park, CA, CD-ROM (2006)
58. Imafuji, N., Kitsuregawa, M.: Finding a Web community by maximum flow algorithm with HITS score based capacity. In: Proceedings of the Database Systems for Advanced Applications, Kyoto, Japan, pp. 101–106, 26–28 Mar 2003
59. Ito, J.: Korean bloggers, personal blog. http://joi.ito.com/weblog/2005/06/02/korean-bloggers.html (2005). Accessed 6 Jan 2011
60. Java, A., Song, X., Finin, T., Tseng, B.: Why we Twitter. In: Proceedings of WebKDD, San Jose, CA, 12 Aug 2007. http://ebiquity.umbc.edu/_file_directory_/papers/369.pdf. Accessed 24 Dec 2010
61. Jensen, D., Goldberg, H. (eds.): AAAI Fall Symposium on AI and Link Analysis. AAAI, Menlo Park, CA (1998)

62. Kempe, D., Kleinberg, J., Tardos, E.: Maximizing the spread of influence through a social network. In: Proceedings of ACM KDD, Washington DC, pp. 137–146, 24–26 Aug 2003
63. Ken, Y.-N.: What Japan thinks, translations of Japanese opinions polls and surveys. Available at: http://whatjapathinks.com. Available through MyVoice: http://myvoice.org/ (2007). Accessed 1 July 2010
64. Kesmodel, D.: "Splogs" roil web, and some blame Google. Wall Street J. B1, 19 Oct 2005
65. Kleinberg, J.: Authoritative sources in a hyperlinked environment. In: Proceedings of the ACM-SIAM Symposium on Discrete Algorithms, pp. 668–677, 1998
66. Knoke, D., Yang, S.: Social Network Analysis. Sage, Thousand Oaks (2007)
67. Kolari, P.: Welcome to the splogosphere: 75% of new pings are spings (splogs). http://ebiquity.umbc.edu/blogger/2005/12/15/welcome-to-the-splogosphere-75-of-new-blog-posts-are-spam/ (2005). Accessed 1 Nov 2010
68. Kolari, P.: Pings, spings, splogs and the splogosphere: 2007 updates. http://ebiquity.umbc.edu/blogger/2007/02/01/pings-spings-splogs-and-the-splogosphere-2007-updates/ (2007). Accessed 1 Nov 2010
69. Krishnamurthy, S.: The multidimensionality of weblog conversations: the virtual enactment of September 11. Internet Research 3.0. http://aoir.org/2002/programme.htm (2002). Accessed 14 Dec 2010
70. Kumar, R., Novak, J., Raghavan, P., Tomkins, A.: On the bursty evolution of blogspace. In: Proceedings of ACM WWW, Budapest, Hungary, pp. 568–576, 20–24 May 2003
71. Kumar, R., Raghavan, P., Rajagoplan, S., Tomkins, A.: Trawling the Web for emerging cyber-communities. In: Proceedings of WWW, Toronto, Canada, pp. 1481–1493, Nov 1999
72. Langville, A., Meyer, C.: Google's PageRank and Beyond. Princeton University Press, Princeton (2006)
73. Lawson-Borders, G., Kirk, R.: Blogs in campaign communication. Am. Behav. Sci. **49**(4), 548–559 (2005)
74. Lenhart, A., Fox, S.: Twitter and status updating. Pew Internet Project Data Memo. http://www.pewinternet.org/Reports/2009/Twitter-and-status-updating.aspx (2009). Accessed 1 Nov 2010
75. Lenhart, A., Madden, M.: Teen content creators and consumers. Pew Internet & American Life Project. http://www.pewinternet.org/Reports/2005/Teen-Content-Creators-and-Consumers/3-Teens-as-Content-Creators/10-More-than-half-of-teen-bloggers-update-once-a-week-or-more.aspx?r=1 (2005). Accessed 1 Nov 2010
76. Lenhart, A., Madden, M., Smith, A., Macgill, A.: Teens and social media. Pew Internet & American Life Project. http://www.pewinternet.org/Reports/2007/Teens-and-Social-Media/3-Teens-creating-content/13-Half-of-online-teens-read-blogs.aspx?r=1 (2007). Accessed 1 Nov 2010
77. Lenhart, A., Purcell, K., Smith, A., Zickuhr, K.: Social media & young adults. Pew Internet & American Life Project. http://www.pewinternet.org/Reports/2010/Social-Media-and-Young-Adults.aspx?r=1 (2010). Accessed 1 Nov 2010
78. Leskovec, J., Backstrom, L., Kleinberg, J.: Meme-tracking and dynamics of the news cycle. In: Proceedings of ACM KDD, Paris, France, pp. 497–506, June 2009
79. Leskovec, J., Kleinberg, J., Faloutsos, C.: Graphs over time: densification laws, shrinking diameters and possible explanations. In: Proceedings of ACM KDD, Chicago, IL, pp. 177–187, 21–24 Aug 2005
80. Leskovec, J., McGlohon, M., Faloutsos, C., Glance, N., Hurst, M.: Patterns of cascading behavior in large blog graphs. In: Proceedings of the SIAM Data Mining, Minneapolis, MN, pp. 551–556, Apr 2007
81. Li, D.: Why do you blog: a uses and gratification inquiry into bloggers' motivations. MA thesis, Marquette University (2005)
82. Liben-Nowell, D.: An algorithmic approach to social networks. PhD dissertation, MIT (2005)
83. Lloyd, L., Kaulgud, P., Skiena, S.: Newspapers vs. blogs: who gets the scoop? In: AAAI Spring Symposium. AAAI Press, Menlo Park, CD-ROM (2006)

84. MacKinnon, R.: Blogs and China correspondence: lessons about global information flows. Chin. J. Commun. **1**(2), 242–257. http://journalsonline.tandf.co.uk/ (2008). Accessed 7 Jan 2011

85. Marlow, C.: Audience, structure and authority in the weblog community. In: Annual Conference on International Communication Association, New Orleans, LA, May 2004. http://alumni.media.mit.edu/%7Ecameron/cv/pubs/0401.pdf. Accessed 14 Jan 2011

86. McGlohon, M., Leskovec, J., Faloutsos, C., Hurst, M., Glance, N.: Finding patterns in blog shapes and blog evolution. In: Proceedings of ICWSM, Boulder, CO, Jan 2007. http://www.icwsm.org/papers/2-McGlohon-Leskovec-Faloutsos-Hurst-Glance.pdf. Accessed 12 Jan 2011

87. McMillan, D., Chavis, D.: Sense of community: a definition and theory. J. Community Psychol. **14**(1), 6–23 (1986)

88. Merelo, J.J., Orihuela, J.L., Ruiz, V., Tricas, F.: Revisiting the Spanish blogosphere. In: Burg, T. (ed.) BlogTalks 2. Books on Demand, Norderstedt (2004)

89. Miller, C.: Twitter unveils plan to draw money from ads. New York Times, 12 Apr 2010

90. Miscaud, E.: Twitter: expressions of the whole self. MS thesis, London School of Economics and Political Science (2008)

91. Mishne, G., Glance, N.: Leave a reply: an analysis of weblog comments. In: Proceedings of WWW Workshop on Weblogging Ecosystem, Edinburgh, UK, May 2006. http://www.blogpulse.com/www2006-workshop/program.html. Accessed 14 Jan 2011

92. Nardi, B., Schiano, D., Gumbrecht, M., Swartz, L.: Why we blog. Commun. ACM **47**, 41–46 (2004)

93. Newman, M.: Models of the small world. J. Stat. Phys. **101**, 819–841 (2000)

94. Newman, M.: The structure and function of complex networks. SIAM Rev. **45**, 167–256 (2003)

95. Newman, M.: Detecting community structure in networks. Phys. J. **B38**, 321–330 (2004)

96. Newman, M.: The mathematics of networks. In: Blume, L., Durlauf, S. (eds.) The New Palgrave Encyclopedia of Economics, 2nd edn. Palgrave Macmillan, Basingstoke (2008)

97. Newman, M., Barabasi, A., Watts, D.: The Structure and Dynamics of Networks. Princeton University Press, Princeton (2006)

98. Newman, M., Giravan, M.: Finding and evaluating community structure in networks. Phys. Rev. **E69**, 026114 (2004)

99. Nowson, S.: The language of Weblogs: a study of genre and individual differences. PhD dissertation, University of Edinburgh (2006)

100. Nowson, S., Oberlander, J.: The identity of bloggers: openness and gender in personal weblogs. In: Proceedings of AAAI Spring Symposium on Computational Approaches to Analyzing Weblogs, Stanford University, Stanford, 27–29 Mar 2006. http://www.aaai.org/Papers/Symposia/Spring/2006/SS-0603/SS0603032.pdf. Accessed 24 Dec 2010

101. Nowson, S., Oberlander, J.: Identifying more bloggers: towards large scale personality classification of weblogs. In: Proceedings of ICSWM, Boulder, CO, Mar 2007. http://www.icwsm.org/papers/2-Nowson-Oberlander.pdf. Accessed 24 Dec 2010

102. Oberlander, J., Nowson, S.: Whose thumb is it anyway? In: Proceedings of CoLing/ACL, Sydney, Australia, 17–21 July 2006. http://nowson.com/papers/OberNowACL06.pdf. Accessed 24 Dec 2010

103. Obradovic, D., Bauman, S.: Identifying and analysing Germany's top blogs. In: Dengel, A. et al. (eds.) Proceedings of Knowledge Intelligence, pp. 111–118. Springer LNAI (2008)

104. Orita, A.: Identity (anonymity, pseudonimity) and linkability. Privacy Preserving Data Mining Workshop, University of Tsukuba, based on Orita, A.: Users' attitudes towards anonymity in user generated content based on structure of anonymity. In: Proceedings of IADIS e-Society, Barcelona, Spain, pp. 163–170, 25–28 Feb 2009

105. Park, H.W., Thelwall, M.: Developing network indicators for ideological landscapes from the political blogosphere in South Korea. J. Comput-Mediat. Commun. **13**(4), 856–879 (2008)

106. Park, S., Zhang, Q., Ma, S.: A comparison study on public-hosted blog sites in the U.S., China, and Korea. In: Proceedings of ASIS&T Annual Meeting, Austin, TX (poster), Nov 2006

107. Pedersen, S.: Why Blog?: Motivations for Blogging. Woodhead, Cambridge, UK (2010)
108. Pedersen, S., Macafee, C.: The practices and popularity of British bloggers. In: Proceedings of the ELPUB2006 Conference on Electronic Publishing, Bansko, Bulgaria, pp. 155–164, 14–16 June 2006
109. Pedersen, S., Macafee, C.: Gender differences in British blogging. J. Comput-Mediat. Commun. **12**(4), Article 4. http://jcmc.indiana.edu/vol12/issue4/ (2007). Accessed 1 July 2010
110. Pontin, J.: The Japanese model: blogs as a business tool. The New Commonplace, 19 Oct 2007. http://www.technologyreview.com/blog/pontin/21891/. Accessed 1 Nov 2010
111. Preece, J.: Online Communities: Designing Usability, Supporting Sociability. Wiley, New York (2004)
112. Rheingold, H.: The Virtual Community. Addison-Wesley, Reading (1993)
113. Schelling, T.: Micromotives and Macrobehavior. Norton, New York (1978)
114. Schler, J., Koppel, M., Argamon, S., Pennebaker, J.: Effects of age and gender on blogging. In: Proceedings of AAAI Symposium on Computational Approaches to Analyzing Weblogs, Menlo Park, CA, pp. 199–205, Mar 2006
115. Schmidt, J.: Blogging practices in the German-speaking blogosphere. Research Centre for New Communication Media. http://www.kowi.uni-bamberg.de/fonk/pdf/fonkpaper0702.pdf (2007). Accessed 1 Nov 2010
116. Schmidt, J., et al.: Use and satisfaction with blogging software. Research Centre New Communication Media. http://www.kowi.uni-bamberg.de/fonk/pdf/fonkpaper0604.pdf (2007). Accessed 1 Nov 2010
117. Scott, J.: Social Network Analysis: A Handbook, 2nd edn. Sage, Thousand Oaks (2000)
118. Shea, D.: What is RSS/XML/Atom/Syndication? Mezzoblue Weblog, 19 May 2004. http://www.mezzoblue.com/archives/2004/05/19/what_is_rssx/. Accessed 1 Nov 2010
119. Sifry, D.: State of the blogosphere, part 1: growth of blogs. Sifry's Alerts. http://www.sifry.com/alerts/archives/000298.html (2005). Accessed 1 Nov 2010
120. Sifry, D.: State of the blogosphere, part 2: on language and tagging. Sifry's Alerts. http://www.sifry.com/alerts/archives/000433.html (2006). Accessed 6 Jan 2011
121. Sifry, D.: State of the blogosphere/state of the live web. http://www.sifry.com/stateoftheliveweb/ (2007). Accessed 4 Jan 2011
122. Smith, A.: New numbers for blogging and blog readership. PEW Internet & American Life Project. http://www.pewinternet.org/Commentary/2008/July/New-numbers-for-blogging-and-blog-readership.aspx (2008). Accessed 1 Nov 2010
123. Spiliopoulou, M., Ntoutsi, I., Theodoridis, Y., Schult, R.: MONIC – modeling and monitoring cluster transitions. In: Proceedings of ACM SIKDD, Philadelphia, PA, pp. 706–711, 20–23 Aug 2006
124. Srivastava, J., Desikan, P., Kumar, V.: Web mining – concepts, applications and research directions. In: Lin, T., Chu, W. (eds.) Recent Advances in Data Mining and Granular Computing, Studies in Fuzziness and Soft Computing, vol. 180. Springer, Berlin (2005)
125. Stefanone, M., Jang, C.-Y.: Writing for friends and family: the interpersonal nature of blogs. J. Comput-Mediat. Commun. **13**(1), Article 7. http://jcmc.indiana.edu/vol13/issue1/ (2007). Accessed 30 June 2010
126. Stevens, V.: Trial by Twitter: the rise and slide of the year's most viral microblogging platform. English Sec. Lang. **12**(1). http://www.tesl-ej.org/ej45/int.pdf (2008). Accessed 1 Nov 2010
127. Strandberg, J.: Giving it up for free: teens, blogs, and marketers' lucky break. Social Sciences and Humanities Research Council, Canada. http://idtrail.org/content/view/323/42/ (2006). Accessed 1 Nov 2010
128. Tabuchi, H.: Softbank to help Twitter get even bigger in Japan. New York Times, 18 May 2010. http://www.nytimes.com/2010/05/19/technology/19twitter.html. Accessed 13 May 2011
129. Tabuchi, H.: Facebook wins relatively few friends in Japan. New York Times, 9 Jan 2011. http://www.nytimes.com/2011/01/10/technology/10facebook.html. Accessed 13 May 2011

130. Tantipathananandh, C., Berger-Wolf, T., Kempe, D.: A framework for community identification in dynamic social networks. In: Proceedings of the ACM KDD, San Jose, CA, pp. 717–726, 12–15 Aug 2007
131. Thelwall, M., Thelwall, M.: Link Analysis. Elsevier, Amsterdam (2002)
132. Thompson, C.: Google's China problem (and China's Google problem). New York Times Magazine, 23 Apr 2006. http://www.nytimes.com/2006/04/23/magazine/23google.html. Accessed 13 May 2011
133. Tong-hyung, K.: Micro-blogs taking off. Korea Times, 29 July 2009. http://www.koreatimes.co.kr/www/news/tech/2011/01/129_49296.html. Accessed 6 Jan 2011
134. Toyoda, M., Kitsuregawa, M.: Extracting evolution of Web communities from a series of Web archives. In: Proceedings of the Hypertext, Nottingham, UK, pp. 28–37, 26–30 Aug 2003
135. Trammel, K., Tarkowski, A., Hofmokl, J., Sapp, A.: Examining polish bloggers through content analysis. J. Comput.-Mediat. Commun. 11(13). http://jcmc.indiana.edu/vol11/issue3/trammell.html (2004)
136. Trevino, E.: Blogger motivations: power, pull, and positive feedback. Internet Research 6.0 (2005)
137. Tricas-Garcia, F., Merelo-Garcia, J.: The Spanish-speaking blogosphere: towards the power law? In: Proceedings of the IADIS International Conference on WWW/Web Based Communities, Lisbon, Portugal, pp. 24–26, 24–26 Mar 2004
138. Trott, M., Trott, B.: A beginner's guide to TrackBack. http://www.movabletype.org/documentation/trackback/beginners/ (2008). Accessed 24 Dec 2010
139. Wasserman, S., Faust, K.: Social Network Analysis: Methods and Applications. Cambridge University Press, Cambridge, UK (1994)
140. Watts, D.: Small Worlds. Princeton University Press, Princeton (1999)
141. Wellman, B., Berkowitz, S. (eds.): Social Structures: A Network Approach. Emerald, Bingley (1998)
142. Wu, F., Huberman, B., Adamic, L., Tyler, J.: Information flow in social groups. Phys. A **337**, 327–335 (2004)
143. Yan, X., Yan, L.: Gender classification of weblog authors. In: Proceedings of the AAAI Symposium on Computational Approaches to Analyzing Weblogs, Stanford University, pp. 228–230, 27–29 Mar 2006
144. Yun, C.: Who are Korean bloggers? Personal blog: http://koreacrunch.com/archive/who-are-korean-bloggers (2006). Accessed 6 Jan 2011

Chapter 4
Privacy in Online Social Networks

Michael Beye, Arjan J.P. Jeckmans, Zekeriya Erkin, Pieter Hartel, Reginald L. Lagendijk, and Qiang Tang

Abstract Online social networks (OSNs) have become part of daily life for millions of users. Users building explicit networks that represent their social relationships and often share a wealth of personal information to their own benefit. The potential privacy risks of such behavior are often underestimated or ignored. The problem is exacerbated by lacking experience and awareness in users, as well as poorly designed tools for privacy management on the part of the OSN. Furthermore, the centralized nature of OSNs makes users dependent and puts the service provider in a position of power. Because service providers are not by definition trusted or trustworthy, their practices need to be taken into account when considering privacy risks.

This chapter aims to provide insight into privacy in OSNs. First, a classification of different types of OSNs based on their nature and purpose is made. Next, different types of data contained in OSNs are distinguished. The associated privacy risks in relation to both users and service providers are identified, and finally, relevant research areas for privacy-protecting techniques are discussed. Clear mappings are made to reflect typical relations that exist between OSN type, data type, particular privacy risks, and privacy-preserving solutions.

M. Beye • Z. Erkin (✉) • R.L. Lagendijk
Information Security and Privacy Lab, Faculty of EEMCS, Delft University of Technology,
Delft, The Netherlands
e-mail: m.r.t.beye@tudelft.nl; z.erkin@tudelft.nl; r.l.lagendijk@tudelft.nl

A.J.P. Jeckmans • P. Hartel • Q. Tang
Distributed and Embedded Security, Faculty of EEMCS, University of Twente, Enschede,
The Netherlands
e-mail: a.j.p.jeckmans@utwente.nl; q.tang@utwente.nl; pieter.hartel@utwente.nl

A. Abraham (ed.), *Computational Social Networks: Security and Privacy*,
DOI 10.1007/978-1-4471-4051-1_4, © Springer-Verlag London 2012

Introduction

In recent years, online social networks (OSNs) have attracted many millions of users worldwide. Even though social networks have always been an important part of daily life, now that more and more people are connected to the Internet, their online counterparts are fulfilling an increasingly important role. OSNs have also become a hot topic in areas of research ranging from sociology to computer science and mathematics.

Aside from allowing users to create a network to represent their social ties, many OSNs facilitate uploading of multimedia content, various ways of communication, and sharing many aspects of daily life with friends. People can stay in touch with (physically remote) friends, easily share content and experiences, and stay up to date in the comfort of their own home or when on the move.

However, benefits aside, potential threats to user privacy are often underestimated. For example, due to the public nature of many OSNs and the Internet itself, content can easily be disclosed to a wider audience than the user intended. Users often have trouble revoking or deleting information, and information about a user might even be posted by others without their consent. Privacy in OSNs is a complicated matter and is not always intuitive to users, especially because it is not always similar to how privacy works in real-life interactions.

Ideally, users should be able to trade some privacy for functionality, without their information becoming available beyond the scope they intend. For example, a user of a self-help OSN (e.g., www.patientslikeme.com) would like to meet people with the same medical condition but does not want everyone to know about his ailment. Even in less extreme cases, the importance of privacy is often underestimated.

In this chapter, we will observe the privacy risks OSN users face, what causes them, and which techniques may help to minimize these risks. To this end, we first look at OSNs as they currently exist (section "Classifying Online Social Networks"), leading to a classification of OSNs based on their type and purpose, and a classification of data types in OSNs. We then map these to associated privacy risks in relation to both fellow users and service providers (section "Privacy Concerns in Online Social Networks") and finally give an overview of existing research into privacy-enhancing technologies (section "Existing Research into Privacy-Protecting Technologies"). Through tables, the relationships between these various aspects are mapped, providing a comprehensive overview. In section "Conclusion," conclusions are drawn.

Classifying Online Social Networks

Let us begin by framing the concept of online social networks, and observe how OSNs have become as widely used as they are today. This will help us understand the purpose of OSNs (which forms the basis for our classification) but also help to illustrate the needs of users, the environment they navigate, and potential threats as discussed in further sections.

Definition of an OSN

Boyd and Ellison's widely used definition [10] captures the key elements of any OSN:

Definition 1. An OSN is a Web-based service that allows individuals to:

1. Construct a public or semipublic profile within the service
2. Articulate a list of other users with whom they share a connection
3. View and traverse their list of connections and those made by others within the service

The terms to describe a connected user include, but are not limited to, "friend" (www.facebook.com and www.myspace.com), "professional" (www.linkedin.com), "relative" (www.geni.com), "follower" (www.twitter.com), and "subscriber" (www.youtube.com). Typically a connection is bidirectional (symmetric), but this is not always the case. For example, "following" on Twitter or 'subscribing' on YouTube are one-way relationships.

The Rise of Online Social Networks

The first OSN to see the light of day was SixDegrees in 1997 [3]. SixDegrees allowed users to create profiles, list and message their friends, and traverse friends listings, thus fitting Boyd and Ellision's definition of an OSN. Even though there were millions of users, these did not have that many direct friends, and SixDegrees did not offer much functionality besides messaging. The website finally shut down in 2000 [10].

During this period, other websites started adding OSN features to their existing content, essentially becoming OSNs, with various degrees of success. In the years that followed, new OSNs started from scratch and began to offer functionality beyond simply listing and browsing friends. Ryze.com and later www.linkedin.com tailored to professionals looking to exchange business contacts, while www.friendster.com focused on dating and finding new friends. Friendster became widely used and experienced technical (performance and hardware) and social (fake profiles and friendship hoarding) difficulties due to its rapid growth. The technical issues and actions taken to combat the social difficulties eventually caused many users to seek out other OSNs. Despite this, Friendster is still popular, particularly in the Philippines, Indonesia, and Myanmar [42].

The popularity of Friendster encouraged the creation of other similar "social OSNs," like www.myspace.com and www.orkut.com. While Myspace has become popular among youth worldwide, Google's Orkut has attracted a predominantly Brazilian and Indian crowd [42]. Aside from these clear-cut "social OSNs," a wide variety of niche OSNs have emerged, each catering to a particular interest. Adding the social structure of an OSN to existing services can often enrich them, making them more useful and attractive to users, or binding users to providers. Currently, OSNs form an integral part of the Internet.

As we have seen, not all OSNs are alike: they can serve different uses for disparate target audiences. A clear classification of OSNs can help us to understand what OSNs mean to their users and how they are used, which in turn will help us to structure our thoughts on privacy in OSNs.

Existing Classifications

It is remarkable that hardly any classifications for OSNs exist in scientific literature, even though OSNs are studied in many disciplines. However, some pseudoscientific blogs and marketing resources offer relevant thoughts on the matter, a selection of which are summarized below.

Classifications by Topical Focus

Lovetoknow.com [17] classifies OSNs based on their topical focus:

- *Informational*. Seeking answers to everyday problems
- *Professional*. Helping you to advance within your career or industry
- *Educational*. Collaborate with other students or academic projects
- *Hobbies*. Conduct research on their favorite projects or topics of interest related to personal hobbies
- *Academic*. For important collaboration within the scientific community, over the Internet
- *News*. Those that publish "community content"

Such a topical point of view seems very relevant, although the categories of informational, educational, and academic seem to have some overlap.

Onlinebrandmanager.com [39] first classifies OSNs into four main areas:

- *Dating/friendship*
- *Alumni networks*
- *Career/business related*
- *Hobby/group networks*

They then state that these can be further split up into: *book communities, business networking and professionals, family, friends, hobbies and interests, languages, video sharing, photo sharing, audio sharing, mobile communities, shopping, social bookmarking, students, and travel and locals*. They note that these are broad categories, where a specific OSN may fit several categories. We remark that sub-categories do not always seem logical extensions of the main categories, and their interrelation is not clear-cut. Note, however, that many categories are again topical, while some categories seem to focus on the *purpose* for which users visit the OSN.

Classifications by Topical Specificity

In contrast, www.Hudsonhorizons.com [27] uses topical *specificity* to divide OSNs into two groups:

- *Broad-range.* "Some social networking websites, such as Facebook, fall into the 'general' category; they accommodate folks of *all interests and backgrounds.* On this type of social networking websites, members can often include a list of their interests, and then locate members with similar interests by searching for keywords and key phrases. The main purpose of general social networking sites is to serve as a social platform where people can reunite with old friends, stay connected with current ones, and even make new acquaintances."
- *Niche.* "Other social networking sites have *tight, niche focuses*, and cater to specific groups of people. Social networking sites can revolve around sports, dating, culture, hobbies, ethnicity, education, romance, entrepreneurship and more."

Note that the topic in question, or the goal behind it (dating vs. talking about hobbies vs. learning), does not play a role in their classification.

The following quote is from Enid Burns on www.Clickz.com [13], regarding advertising through OSNs:

> Many of these sites target communities defined by their affinity to a vertical industry, business model, or interactivity type, unlike Myspace and YouTube, which are designed to appeal to the mass population.

Again, the broad distinction made here seems to be on topical specificity.

Liz Gannes on www.Gigaom.com [22] also devotes a blog entry to classifying OSNs. The following three terms form the core of her argument:

- *Blank slates.* Gannes names Myspace and Bebo as typical examples. These seem to be what others might call "broad-range" or "general" OSNs.
- *Target audiences.* Targeted to a specific niche; Gannes compares them to ad verticals.
- *Existing interests/existing communities.* She names www.last.fm as an example, where OSN functionality is well integrated into an existing activity (listening to music). This category seems to center around integrating OSN functionality into an already established, successful community.

Gannes also mentions "social tools": sites that have a certain goal in mind, such as LinkedIn. She describes the difference between a social network and a social tool as "a place to hang out for X kind of people" vs. "a place to get X done." One of her readers states that OSNs seem to have two main purposes: "communication" (networking with preexisting group) and "self-expression" (social network is just a feature). Another reader proposes "community around shared services" (e.g., www.Del.icio.us) as a separate category. We note that this echoes concepts from previously discussed sources: topical specificity (general social OSNs vs. niche OSNs) and the *purpose* of an OSN playing a central role.

Classifications by Other Criteria

Bernard Lunn on www.Readwriteweb.com [33] also divides OSNs into two types, namely, "open networks" and "gated communities." This distinction is centered around trust – in some communities (they name OSNs for relatives, doctors, or models), trust may be more important than in others, and users will wish to interact in a gated community that shields them from the outside world. Lunn notes that this does not directly relate to the size of the OSN or its significance to society, although the concept of gated communities seems related to both Hudsonhorizon's *niche OSNs* and restricted membership OSNs.

Dave Emmett, on his blog [19], looks at the effect an OSN has on users' personal networks:

- *Tightening*. Deepens existing relationships. Examples include Facebook, Dopplr, and Friendfeed.
- *Broadening*. Adds new connections. Examples include Twitter, Brightkite, Flickr, and YouTube.

One of his readers comments that this seems related to the concepts of "bridging and bonding" in social sciences theory. The main difference here lies in the audience that a user intends to reach.

Dominique Cardon on www.internetactu.net [14] discusses the visibility and interactions of users in OSNs. His discussion on the following categories is freely translated from French:

- *The screen*. People only meet through criterion search and are otherwise invisible. Users are matched online and test their compatibility in the real world.
- *The clear-obscure*. People share information on their daily private lives, but mostly to a select audience. These settings are about strengthening preexisting relationships or explore friends-of-friends.
- *The lighthouse*. People portray their identity, preferences or content with the general audience. Uses its high visibility to expand beyond real-life friends and find a larger audience.
- *The post-it*. Users show their presences, and availability through contextual clues, but to a restricted circle. The real and virtual worlds are highly interwoven.
- *The magic lantern*. Users employ personalized avatars as pseudonyms to decouple their online and offline identities. Interactions are mostly virtual and rarely extend into the real world.

Some remarks are made to relate network size, structure, homogeneity, and growth to visibility. Cardon continues to discuss navigation methods, like "criterion referenced search engine," "friend network navigation," and "user-activity-driven search." It is clear that the *goal* of users in an OSN plays an important role throughout Cardon's views.

Finally, Wikipedia [4] offers the following thoughts on OSN classification:

> [...]Although online community services are sometimes considered as a social network service in a broader sense, social network service usually means an individual-centered

service whereas online community services are group-centered. Social networking sites allow users to share ideas, activities, events, and interests within their individual networks.

The main types of social networking services are those which contain category places (such as former school-year or classmates), means to connect with friends (usually within self-description pages) and a recommendation system linked to trust. Popular methods now combine many of these[...]

One can imagine yet other ways to distinguish between OSNs:

- *Source of revenue.* The OSN service provider can earn his revenue through direct or indirect means (subscriptions or micropayments versus advertisements or data sales).
- *Membership type.* This can be open, select, or invitation only.
- *Wideness of user base.* Does the OSN attract a worldwide, national, or regional audience, or does it target a specific demographic or subculture.

New Classification of OSNs Based on Purpose

Recall that our classification is intended to structure our thoughts on privacy in OSNs. We feel that the *purpose that an OSN fulfills to its user base* is the main factor to determine the functionalities it offers, which in turn dictates what sort of data exists in the network and how users can interact – this data and user interaction are what privacy is all about. Therefore, our approach may come to resemble those of [39] and [17] most, although we feel that none of the above classifications provide completeness, nonoverlapping categories, or a true focus on purpose.

For each category, some illustrative examples will be provided. We make our first broad distinction between OSNs that focus on *connections* and those that focus on *content*.

Connection OSNs

Connection OSNs focus on the social connections and interactions between users, by providing users with a social contact list, channels for interaction, or matching services. Their general purpose is usually to connect users to new or existing friends and acquaintances or to provide an easy way to maintain such relationships.

Dating. Dating sites are websites that aim to help users to find the love of their life – many dating sites incorporate OSN aspects these days. Each user has login credentials and usually a profile to attract potential lovers. Connections are typically in the form of love interests, but friendship links are also common; user groups may also exist. Traversing the OSN is often based on browsing, searching, or recommendation generation rather than through navigating existing connections. Messages exchanged between users are often kept private to these users, although in some cases comment sections viewable by others are offered. Behavioral information can be kept by the OSN to provide better recommendations. Example dating sites are www.match.com, www.paiq.nl, and www.plentyoffish.com.

Business. These OSNs aim to provide professionals with useful business contacts. Searching for profiles does not always require signing up. Profiles display users' capabilities and work field as well as a means to contact them. This is usually done through the OSN via personal messaging. Users can also add other users to their network of connections so that other professionals can see who the user is working or has contact with. An example of this class is www.linkedin.com, which requires a subscription for premium services.

Enforcing real-life relationships. These OSNs are not aimed at finding new friends but (re)connecting users with existing friends or acquaintances. Examples include family-oriented OSNs, college or ex-classmate focused networks, such as www.mylife.com, www.odnoklassniki.ru, and www.plaxo.com.

Socializing. Fitting the more traditional view of social networks, what others might call a "blank slate" or "broad-range network." Here users can connect with current friends and find new ones. Most types of information can be found in OSNs of this class; often a lot of this information is (semi-)public. The revenue for the OSN service provider often comes from advertisements and selling information about the OSN but can sometimes be combined with a subscription for additional functionalities (e.g., as with www.hyves.nl). In order to attract new users and bind them, this type of OSN usually has a lot of additional functionalities such as social and competitive games. For a user, the value of a social OSN is often largely determined by the number of friends that use that particular OSN. Some well-known examples of this class are www.facebook.com, www.orkut.com, and www.myspace.com.

Chat/instant messaging. Some (webcam-)chat websites (e.g., www.stickam.com) contain OSN features (friends list and profile). Some sources consider instant messaging (IM) services an OSN, if they allow users to store an explicit "address book" of friends. Popular IM clients include Windows Live Messenger (formerly MSN Messenger), AOL Instant Messenger (AIM), ICQ, Skype, and Yahoo! Messenger.

Content OSNs

Content OSNs focus more on content provided by or linked to by users. This content can be multimedia or information like knowledge, advice, or news. The social interactions with other users usually revolve around and are driven by a search for information or the exchanging of said media.

Content sharing. Sharing of user-generated content can happen within a selected group, such as friends or family, or a far wider audience. Content that is shared is usually multimedia; this is often of potential interest to a wide audience, and even for selected audiences, e-mailing such content is cumbersome and often impossible due to size of the data. Uploading content generally requires users to sign up and log in; sometimes viewing content also requires logging in, or viewing is restricted through the use of hard-to-guess obfuscated URLs. Sometimes messages or tags can be added to the shared content, and especially in more open systems, content tagging and recommendation may be an integral part of the system. User profiles, if any, are usually brief. Examples are Picasa (www.picasaweb.google.com), photobucket.com, and www.youtube.com.

Resource recommendation. In some OSNs, users do not focus on uploading content but on recommending existing (usually professional, external) content or resources. Book-review sites like weread.com and URL-tagging communities like delicious.com are prime examples where external items are discovered, added to the system as links, and finally tagged or rated. No actual content is created or uploaded.

Advice sharing. Offering a place for people to share their experience or expertise in a certain area with others, or to seek help and advice, can be a focus for some OSNs. For example, mothers-to-be (www.babycenter.com), medical patients (www.patientslikeme.com), or students (www.teachstreet.com) can help one another. Other examples include www.advogato.org for software developers, the now discontinued Cake Financial [2] and www.sciencestage.com.

Hobbies/entertainment. Many OSNs focus on audiences that have similar interests and hobbies. Such OSNs may involve multimedia uploads, recommendation, or advice sharing elements, but the main distinguishing feature is their homogeneous audience. This means that the topic of the OSN mainly determines its character and appeal for users. Examples are www.athlinks.com for athletes, www.care2.com for those interested in health and green living, or OSNs tied to gaming communities like Xbox Live (www.xbox.com/en-us/live/) or www.playfire.com. Entertainment OSNs might make money through advertisements or direct sales targeted to their user base's niche or through subscriptions.

"News" sharing. Some OSNs focus on world news or gossip, but a multitude of (micro-)blogging OSNs provide a stage mainly for sharing "personal news," opinions, and experiences. Examples are www.nowpublic.com, www.blogster.com, twitter.com, www.buurtlink.nl, and www.gossipreport.com.

Data in OSNs

Now that we have an idea of the wide variety of OSNs and their purpose, let us take a look at the data that these systems can contain. From Boyd and Ellison's definition, we can already deduce that the following user-related data must exist in an OSN:

Profiles. A profile is tied to a user and is their representation to the outside world. Usually this is a self-description or the description of an alter ego (pseudonym, avatar). This may typically include a short biography, a picture and attributes like age, gender, location, and the like.

Connections. A connection exists between two users and can be of several types, like friend, colleague, fan, etc. A collection of connections can be represented by a graph.

Login credentials. Most OSNs require the user to login to make use of the service. A user account ties a profile to the user behind it, and to sign in, the user needs certain login credentials. Such credentials can also be found in traditional websites, and this chapter will not pay special attention to the security issues surrounding them.

Depending on the goal of an OSN and the additional services it offers, other forms of information related to users can be involved:

Messages. We view messages in the broadest sense of the word. Any piece of data exchanged between a user and another user or a group of users is a message; these may contain text or multimedia. Messages form the basis for additional OSN functionalities. Interaction between users has been recognized as a rich source of information on the underlying social network, even more so than friendship graphs [50]. Note that in some cases a message can be instantaneous and short-lived, as in an instant messaging setting. In other cases, messages may be stored for an indefinite time and be read long after being sent; think of blog posts or messages left on a user's "Wall" on Facebook. Note that in some cases the service provider stores messages, in others fellow users do (as with most instant messaging applications). The sender of these messages often has little control of how long the messages are stored.

Multimedia. Actual content that can be attached to messages but may also be uploaded to private or public data spaces (e.g., Picasa photo album, a blog, Facebook "Wall") or be attached to a profile. Examples are contents of blog entries (text, photos, video) or the photos, video, music, and voice recordings that can be connected to a Myspace or Stickam profile.

Groups. A group is a collection of users, who usually share some common attributes, resources, or privileges, for example, similar preferences or backgrounds, a collaborative document, or access to a common virtual space.

Tags. We define tags in the broad sense, as in collaborative filtering systems: descriptive keywords (metadata) that are attached to content by users (either the uploader or other users). In Facebook terminology, "tagging" refers to the specific case where a user identifies the people depicted in a photo by tags the photo with their names, thus explicitly linking these people to the picture.

Preferences/ratings/interests. Many OSNs provide their users with some type of matching or recommendation functionality for either content or peers. In order to provide relevant recommendations, information on a user's attributes or preferences is required. Often, users are asked to explicitly express their preferences or rate items. The resulting information may be publicly visible (interests on a profile page, ratings for an item shows along with who provided them) or restricted to the service provider only. Sometimes, the service provider will derive (supplementary) information on users' preferences and attributes from their behavioral information.

Behavioral information. By this we mean browsing history, profile settings, and any actions undertaken by the user while performing tasks within the OSN. Benevenuto et al. note that this type of metadata is particularly rich [8]. Information such as preferences, friendships, or even attributes such as physical location or demographic data can be inferred from it. Behavioral data is also found in traditional websites, although behavior there is not related to navigating a social network.

As said, not all OSNs involve information from all of the above categories. Which information is contained in a particular OSN mostly depends on its media richness, the functionality it offers to users, and its business model. Some information is only available to the service provider (i.e., the OSN's software or operators), while other information is also available to (a subset of) the OSN users, or even the public at large.

Furthermore, some information is consciously supplied by users through the OSN's graphical user interface, while other information is implicitly derived by the service provider by observing user behavior.

Summary

People use OSNs for a variety of purposes. In any case, to get the desired functionality (e.g., meeting with friends, attracting an audience, getting advice or recommendations), they will need to provide some personal information to the OSN. The type of user data in question depends on the functionality of the OSN, and its media richness. Table 4.1 gives an impression of which data types may typically be expected in different types of OSNs. In tables, ● represents a likely match ● represents a possible match and · an unlikely match.

Privacy Concerns in Online Social Networks

Because users need to reveal information to make use of the desired functionality of an OSN, there exists a trade-off between functionality and user privacy. Making sure the OSN can provide the desired functionality is one thing, but when sharing a wealth of (personal) data, one should also consider what *undesired* results might occur. We have seen examples where data is potentially sensitive (e.g., medical or dating OSNs), and the open nature of online systems makes privacy a definite issue. In this section, we will look into the concept of privacy, its role in OSNs, and potential threats to users' privacy.

Table 4.1 Data types typically found in different types of OSNs

OSN types ↓	Data types →	Profiles	Connections	Messages	Multimedia	Tags	Preferences/ratings	Groups	Behavioral information	Login credentials
Connection OSNs	Dating	●	•	●	•	·		●	•	●	●
	Business	●	●	●	•	·		•	●	●	●
	Enforcing real-life relationships	●	●	●	•	·		•	●	●	●
	Socializing	●	●	●	•	·		•	●	●	●
	Chat/instant messaging	•	●	●	•	·		•	●	●	●
Content OSNs	Content sharing	•	•	●	●	●		•	•	●	●
	Resource recommendation	●	·	•	●	●		●	•	●	●
	Advice sharing	●	•	●	•	·		•	●	●	●
	Hobbies/entertainment	•	•	●	•	•		•	●	●	●
	"News" sharing	•	•	●	●	•		•	•	●	●

Definitions Regarding Privacy

The word privacy has many subtly different meanings, each with their own definition. This ranges from "personal privacy" (which involves seclusion and bodily privacy) to "information privacy," around which privacy on the Internet in general revolves. Kang [29] uses the wording of the Information Infrastructure Task Force (IITF), as cited below:

> Information Privacy is "an individual's claim to control the terms under which personal information–information identifiable to the individual – is acquired, disclosed or used."

This concept of information privacy is strongly related to the notion of "Confidentiality," from the field of Information Security, but not to be used interchangeably. Confidentiality is concerned with the secrecy or disclosure of individual pieces of information, while information privacy also deals with the individual who is the subject of said information, the effects that disclosure has on this person, and his or her control and consent.

When users collaborate in a Web 2.0 setting, they generally share a lot of (personal) information. When users upload their data to an OSN, they usually have a *scope* in mind (as a quote from Palen and Dourish below illustrates). Privacy involves keeping a piece of information in its intended scope. This scope is defined by the size of the audience (breadth), by extent of usage allowed (depth), and duration (lifetime). When a piece of information is moved beyond its intended scope in any of these dimensions (be it accidentally or maliciously), a privacy breach occurs. So, a breach may occur when information is shared with a party for whom it was not intended (disclosure), when information is abused for a different purpose than was intended, or when information is accessed after its intended lifetime.

We also see this reflected in data protection laws, such as the Data Protection Act 1998 in the United Kingdom [49], where the use of *personal data* is not regulated in an all-or-nothing fashion, but limitations are imposed on the extent and duration of its use.

Palen and Dourish [41] identify three privacy boundaries with which individuals are struggling:

1. The disclosure boundary (managing the tension between private and public)
2. The identity boundary (managing self representation with specific audience, e.g., one will behave differently when at work than when among friends)
3. The temporal boundary (managing past actions with future expectations; user behavior may change over time)

Something to note at this stage is that by no means all information that is uploaded to an OSN is considered personal data and is thus not covered by laws regulating the use of personal data. Personal data is defined in [49] as:

"Personal data" means data which relate to a living individual who can be identified:

(a) From those data
(b) From those data and other information which is in the possession of, or is likely to come into the possession of, the *data controller*

The term Personally Identifiable Information (PII) is related (but not synonymous) and refers to "information that can be used to uniquely identify, contact, or locate a single person or can be used with other sources to uniquely identify a single individual."

Particularly sensitive personal information is often regulated by additional laws, such as the Health Insurance Portability and Accountability Act (HIPAA) for medical data, or *sensitive personal data* under Data Protection Act 1998, the definition of which includes:

The racial or ethnic origin of the data subject, his political opinions, his religious beliefs or other beliefs of a similar nature, [. . .] his physical or mental health or condition, his sexual life, the commission or alleged commission by him of any offense [. . .]

However, the majority of data in an OSN does not clearly fall under these categories, and its storage, processing, and use are not always strictly regulated.

Users and Privacy Management

Weiss [52] states that on the traditional Web, privacy is maintained by limiting data collection, hiding users' identities, and restricting access to authorized parties only, while the reality of OSNs is that data and identity become closely linked and are often visible to large groups of people. It becomes harder for a user to monitor and control his personal information, as more of it becomes available online. Together, this makes managing information and privacy a lot more difficult.

Most OSNs offer their users privacy controls that are simple to use, but coarse, for example, enabling users to set their entire profile as public, visible to friends only, or private (visible only to the user). With growing demand from users and increased attention to privacy in the media, many OSNs (e.g., Facebook) have started offering their users more (apparent) control, like setting the visibility for individual items or allowing users to organize their friends into categories. Another risk lies in the other extreme, when interfaces become overly complicated. If users do not understand the settings or find them too cumbersome, they may either set them incorrectly or ignore them and settle for suboptimal privacy protection.

Gross and Acquisti [24] show in a case study that most users do not change the default privacy settings as provided by the OSN, while sharing a large amount of information on their profile. Tufecki [47] concludes in his case study that privacy-aware users are actually more reluctant to join social networks, but once they do join, they still disclose a lot of information. Another observation is that users' privacy is regulated mostly through visibility, i.e., the privacy settings of the OSN, rather than through selective uploading. In general, users are preoccupied with the current visibility of their information and do not take into account future change and its implications. It seems that users implicitly trust OSN service providers to handle user data in a fair and conscientious way and continue to do so in the future.

Service Providers and Trust

Besides difficulties in managing privacy towards other "users" (registered or not), there exists a completely different type of concern, originating from the user's relationship with the OSN service provider. The main difference between users and the service provider is the type of information they can access. A user or outsider can generally only view public information. The service provider can generally view *all* data in the system, including private uploads, browsing behavior, IP addresses, etc. It is also the service provider who decides which data is stored, how long it is kept, and how it is used or distributed. The user is also dependent on the service provider for tools to protect his privacy. Therefore, trust plays a big role in the relationship between a user and the service provider.

On a related note, the rules with regards to ownership and intellectual property of user-uploaded data can be deceptive. Some OSNs (e.g., Facebook) acquire a license to use such content through their terms-of-use policy. This license gives the OSN free reign to use or sell the data as it sees fit, without worrying about copyrights or other claims by the user. Facebook's statement of rights and responsibilities [20] states:

You own all of the content and information you post on Facebook, and you can control how it is shared through your privacy and application settings. In addition:
For content that is covered by intellectual property rights, like photos and videos ("IP content"), you specifically give us the following permission, subject to your privacy and application settings: you grant us a non-exclusive, transferable, sub-licensable, royalty-free,

worldwide license to use any IP content that you post on or in connection with Facebook ("IP License"). This IP License ends when you delete your IP content or your account unless your content has been shared with others, and they have not deleted it. [...]

This becomes unnerving once we realize that the interests of users and service provider can clash, especially in OSNs where the main source of revenue is not the users, but third-party sales and targeted advertisement.

Finally, we note that many laws, including the Data Protection Act 1998 [49], focus on *"data controllers."* There are no specific regulations for OSNs, and they are currently treated as *"information services"* – online databases of information. The EU article 29 Data Protection Working Party [48] would like to see this changed so that OSN service providers will be treated as "data controllers," which will obligate them to adhere to laws for processing of user data. This should make it easier to guarantee the trustworthiness of OSNs, by forcing them to be more privacy-friendly, ideally without hampering the services they offer to their users.

User-Related Privacy Concerns

In many cases, privacy is breached by fellow OSN users or unregistered visitors. This may be a deliberate act (snooping, hacking), or accidental (mismanagement of privacy settings by the user himself, lingering data), and can have serious consequences. Let us take a look at different privacy threats that involve disclosure to other users:

Stranger views private information. Users can falsely assume some information to be kept restricted to a certain audience, when in reality it is not. This can be due to design flaws on the part of the OSN service provider (e.g., private photos, videos, and blogs being easily "hacked" on Myspace [28]) or a lack of understanding or attention to the privacy controls of the user himself. However, even Internet security experts can make mistakes with disclosing information [53]. When a stranger views such private information, user control over who views the information is lost, and conflict occurs with the *disclosure boundary*. The above can apply to profiles, connections to fellow users, messages, multimedia, tags, group memberships, etc. Rosenblum [44] shows that information in OSNs is far more accessible to a widespread audience than perceived by its owners and can even end up in the mainstream media [26].

Unable to hide information from a specific friend or group. Sometimes one would like to hide some information from a specific friend or a group of friends. Perhaps a user would not like to let a friend know that a surprise party is being planned or hide the pictures of a night out from his parents or employer. In real life, we easily manage the different social contexts that we belong to, but in OSNs the lines that separate them tend to blur [30]. Not many OSNs provide the option to create groups of friends for different social contexts or hide information on a fine-grained level. This problem is related to Palen and Dourish's *identity boundary* as users do not have the control to act differently towards one user or group of users than towards others.

Other users posting information about you. Even if a user is careful in controlling what information she posts to an OSN, she has no control over what other users post in the same OSN. Often, messages contain information about multiple OSN users or even nonusers. This problem is related to the *disclosure boundary* because information is made more public than intended, in this case by others. It can occur when another user posts information about you which you do not want to be uploaded to the OSN, or when information disclosed privately to another user is made available to a larger audience. This can even be a deliberate act [43].

Provider-Related Privacy Concerns

A completely different type of privacy threat involves the relationship between the user and OSN service provider, and in particular the trust that the user puts in the provider. This goes beyond user control of information because the service provider usually designed or configured the systems underlying the OSN. Thus, he has full access to any user-related data, including browsing behavior and message logs. The associated threats are detailed below:

Data retention issues. When posting information to an OSN, it is often impossible or very difficult to remove that information, for several reasons. On one hand, the service provider may intentionally prevent or hinder removal of data. Facebook, for example, does not provide users with the means to delete their profile and has actively blocked third-party software that attempts to remedy this [34]. This is because the capital of an OSN often lies in the number of users, and data sales are sometimes part of the revenue. Facebook would like to store content forever [51]. Secondly, information (especially in a social context) tends to be replicated. People may spread information or multimedia and even store it locally and reupload it at a later time. Finally, information that is apparently erased may still reside elsewhere on the OSN, for example, in backups, to be found by others. Similarly, a resource may be disabled or seemingly deleted, but references to it (thumbnails, messages on friends' pages, etc.) can remain visible to the outside world. An example of this is given by Bonneau [9] who tracked the availability of deleted photos. These are all violations of the *temporal boundary* as information is available longer than intended.

OSN employee browsing private information. The OSN service provider has full access to the data, and its employees might take advantage of this. This is in conflict with the implicit trust that the OSN asks of its users. All information supplied to the OSN is at risk in this issue, up to and including behavioral information. Interviews suggest that some Facebook employees are able to view user information, and it is left to the company to police this [38].

Selling of data. The wealth of information that is stored on the OSN is likely to be of value to third parties and may be sold by the OSN. User preferences, behavior, and friendship connections are all potentially interesting for marketing purposes and research into social dynamics. Data sales can easily be in conflict with the implicit trust the user has in the OSN. Depending on the OSN's business model, it may be in the interest of the OSN to have its users share as much information as possible, to obtain a license or ownership wherever possible, to store it indefinitely and get maximal profits from sales. One example of an OSN that provides user data to third parties is PatientsLikeMe. To quote their website:

PatientsLikeMe offers pharmaceutical companies the opportunity to reach and learn from thousands of patients with chronic diseases. Follow their symptoms, treatments, outcomes and attitudes. Evaluate real-world safety and efficacy data, and conduct targeted clinical trial recruitment. These are just a few examples of how our portfolio of services drives value at each stage of the drug development process.

Even though data is often anonymized before being sold to protect user privacy, reidentification is a remaining threat that is often overlooked or ignored. Backstrom et al. [6] show how users can be reidentified by looking for unusual points within the friendship graph of the actual OSN and locating these in the anonymized dataset.

Targeted marketing. Multiple pieces of information in the OSN can be combined to provide a high-value profile of the user. This high-value profile can then be used or exploited to present targeted marketing to the user. This again is a conflict of the implicit trust in the OSN because information is used for a different purpose than intended by the user. An example of a company which uses OSN data for targeted marketing is TrustFuse [37].

All of this information could come in handy for Rapleaf's third business, TrustFuse, which sells data (but not e-mail addresses) to marketers so they can better target customers, according to TrustFuse's Web site.

Summary

Because OSNs contain massive amounts of useful and interesting data about large numbers of users, they form an interesting target for third parties, both private and commercial. Either through browsing/spidering, hacking attacks, or legitimate data sales, this information could end up in the wrong hands. The fact that the users are not always the source of revenue for an OSN (in the case of advertisement revenue and data sales) can lead to conflicting interests for users and service providers. Given the diverse and often extensive information available on OSNs, and the fact that threats may come from other users or even the service provider itself, the threats are numerous. Table 4.2 attempts to give a comprehensive overview. In this table, concern is high (●), medium (•), or low (·).

Table 4.2 Privacy concerns for user data in OSNs

Privacy concerns ↓	Data types →	Profiles	Connections	Messages	Multimedia	Tags	Preferences/ratings	Groups	Behavioral information	Login credentials
User related	Stranger views private info	●	●	●	●	·	●	●	·	·
	Unable to hide info from specific friend/group	●	●	●	●	·	·	·	·	·
	Other users posting information about you	·	·	●	●	●	·	·	·	·
Provider related	Data retention issues	●	●	●	●	●	●	●	●	·
	OSN employee browsing private info	●	●	●	●	●	●	●	●	●
	Selling of data	●	●	●	●	·	●	·	●	·
	Targeted marketing	●	·	·	·	·	●	·	●	·

Existing Research into Privacy-Protecting Technologies

We have seen that there is a wide variety of privacy issues that play a role in OSNs. Because the type of access differs greatly between users and service providers, the two main categories of threats require their own specific defense mechanisms. Despite the fact that prevention is no simple matter, research is being conducted in many areas to alleviate some of the aforementioned threats. To protect user data from fellow users, awareness and proper tools for managing and enforcing access policies play a leading role [5, 15, 30]. This does not work towards solving issues that involve untrusted service providers. Obscuring and hiding sensitive data from the providers [1, 25, 46] and removing them from the picture entirely [11, 12, 45] are the general approaches here, as we will see. We now proceed to a topical literature overview of research on mitigating privacy issues and tailoring to the privacy needs of users.

Anonymization

As pointed out in sections "Classifying Online Social Networks", sales of information pertaining to the OSN are often a major source of revenue for the service provider. If this were to be done without any further consideration for privacy, users might take offense and leave the network (thus hurting revenue) or take justified legal action. Through *anonymization*, OSN service providers may try to remove the privacy issues associated with data sales by *obscuring the link between users and data sold*.

Basic anonymization involves removing any identifying (or identifiable) information from the data, while preserving other structures of interest in the data. As said, however, different reidentification attacks [6] can be mounted to fill in the missing info from the data sold, for example, by exploiting the topology of the network. Techniques for more thorough anonymization have been proposed, for example, mixing of attributes, or modifying the graph structure in such a way that its properties stay mainly intact, while making reidentification hard or impossible [54]. Zhou et al. [55] give a good overview of this field and its problems. Recently the field of anonymization is shifting towards differential privacy [18], which aims to make users in released data computationally indistinguishable from most of the other users in that data set.

Anonymization techniques are usually simple to implement and need to be performed only once on a given snapshot of the OSN before sales to third parties. The drawback is that it is hard to *formally prove* the security of these methods, as is done in classical cryptography. This mainly stems from the fact that information can only be *partially* removed or obfuscated, while other parts *must be kept intact* for the dataset to remain interesting for after-sale use. Because OSNs are such complex systems, it is nearly impossible to predict which pieces of data can be combined into identifiable information or which external hints may become available for attackers to exploit. This is what makes it hard to definitively prevent (partial) recovery of the private information that was obscured through anonymization.

Decentralization

Research on *decentralization* of OSNs revolves around the concept of untrusted OSN service providers, and tries to prevent privacy issues where the implicit trust in the OSN is abused. Decentralization can be applied to different degrees. Either some of the power is taken away from the service provider, or he is removed from the picture altogether. An example with slight decentralization would be to set up direct links between users when chatting. In this way, the chat data never passes through the server. An extreme form of decentralization would remove the OSN altogether and have all traffic take place through peer-to-peer networks. Generally the more decentralized the solution, the better the protection from aforementioned privacy issues.

Buchegger and Datta [11] list the possible advantages and challenges for shifting to a fully decentralized OSN. One of the major obstacles is that all users will be made responsible for availability (and integrity) of (one another's) information. Because users cannot be expected to remain online constantly, peers or a trusted proxy should keep data available on a user's behalf. Doing this securely (with untrusted peers), reliably, and efficiently poses a big challenge, especially because another of the main challenges in this area of research lies in version control. Given the churn of users and the rate at which data is updated, designing a fully decentralized OSNs is no simple task. Because a decentralized structure works strongly towards taking power away from the OSN service provider, it is contrary to the business model of many existing OSNs. This means that these will not be likely to adopt such a structure, or aid its development.

Some creative proposals have been made with the aim to overcome these challenges. Tootoonchian et al. [46] propose to decouple social relationships from the user data. User data (which they call "social data") will still reside on the OSN's server, but the relationships (the actual graph) will be in the form of attestations. An attestation can prove to a service provider that two users have a social relationship. These attestation can then be used for access control, granting the user access to the proper resources on any such OSN without requiring the user to sign up for every social network.

Freedman and Nicolosi [21] propose a method for verifying social proximity (friend of a friend) and give the list of bridging friends to one of the parties. In this scheme, one of the parties looks forward, while the other looks backwards. With both using a one-way transform, one party compares these relationships. In this directional scheme, the party that is the target of the friend relationship has to consent. This party also has to give up more of his privacy; he sends out a key and receives an attestation. Considering that this party is not the initiator of the relationship, this is a skewed trade-off.

Mezzour et al. [36] propose another method which works for longer paths. This method works by using a token flooding phase in which tokens are spread throughout the social graph. The user whom first sent these tokens can use a look-up to discover the path between him and the other user. However, revoking any of the relationships in the flooded path would require another flooding phase.

Privacy Settings and Management

The research in this field is devoted to finding methods to either give the user more control over their privacy settings or make it easier for the user to manage such settings. In doing so, research in this area hopes to mitigate such problems as unauthorized data access by other users and the inability of users to hide information from a specific friend or group.

Some propose forms of automated assistance to set defaults or adjust privacy settings. Baatarjav et al. [5] propose a system that selects privacy settings according to some basic profile information. This profile information is used to predict a set of expected user preferences, based on statistical data. For example, if most single elderly ladies adopt a certain set of settings, this will be the default for new users in this demographic.

A similar approach is suggested by Maximilien et al. [35], where a privacy score based on the sensitivity and visibility of profile items is computed. This privacy score can then be compared among peers, and the privacy settings of peers can be mimicked if needed.

Goecks et al. [23] have created an overview of the challenges and problems of configuring privacy settings based on this type of collaboration. Most notable is *information cascade*, which is a snowball effect that can lead to the adoption of a certain set of privacy settings by many users. Because this process can also increase the score of an unwanted configuration, this herding behavior can eventually lead all users to share the same unwanted setting. In an extension of their system, Goecks et al. add an "expert set" of advanced users that has higher priority over regular users.

A different suggestion comes from Banks and Wu [7], where an interaction history facilitates privacy settings between users, using trust as a currency. This proposal has not been worked out in detail.

Another interesting research topic is the development of solutions to make information disclosure and privacy settings more gradual, fine-grained, and transparent. The central question here is how to design appropriate tools for such fine-grained control, without overburdening the users or the system.

Privacy awareness among users can be enhanced by showing the user the consequences of his actions. According to Lipford et al. [31] this can be done by showing the user their profile as seen by others. Onwuasoanya et al. [40], study the behavior of users when given the ability to define subgroups among their online friends. An existing system that combines both of these features (and other privacy tools) is Clique (www.clique.primelife.eu), part of the Primelife project. This experimental OSN allows its users to create multiple "faces" to use in different social contexts. Each face has its own collections of contacts (e.g., friends, colleagues, and family), and each piece of information can be made visible to any combination of people [30]. Users can check if the desired result is achieved by viewing their profile from the perspective of other users.

This type of solution is often comparatively cheap to implement and mainly depends on OSN service providers making the right design choices. However, they require user awareness and acceptance in order to reach their full potential. Also, data collection and retention are key to many OSNs' revenue, so acceptance by service providers may be an even bigger issue.

Encryption

Encryption can be used as a tool to provide confidentiality and as the basis for integrity. Depending on how encryption is applied, this can mean protection from unauthorized users or the service provider. It is often used as a building block in other proposals, for example, in decentralized systems or in privacy settings and management tools.

Lucas and Borisov [32] propose to encrypt certain parts of a user's profile using public key cryptography. Keys are derived from user-supplied passwords in order to maintain access flexibility. A potential problem with this approach is the resulting low entropy of the keys.

Guha et al. [25] argue that encrypted messages on a profile are easy to spot by the service provider, which could result in sanctions if the provider disapproves of encryption. Their aim is akin to *steganography* in that the service provider should not even be aware that information hiding is being applied. Their approach uses substitution of "information atoms" (e.g., age or name-and-gender) to hide information. Keys and related material are exchanged out of band. The number of channels that are used for this scheme is high. Also, users that do not employ this system have no way to distinguish users that are hiding their information from users that are not. This makes profiles meaningless to such users and could lead to cases of mistaken identity.

The advantage of cryptographic approaches is that they can solve many issues, if used properly. Through cryptography, one can protect data from other users, as well as the OSN. In addition, the security of such techniques can often be proven or verified comparatively easily. However, key management is a big issue, especially if there is a high amount of churn in friendship relations and group membership. Also, cryptography often involves expensive operations for the user, the service provider, or both. Especially in large OSNs, scalability can easily become an obstacle.

Awareness, Law, and Regulations

Research in this mainly nontechnical field aims to enhance user awareness of the privacy issues that exist within OSNs, as well as compliance of both users and service providers to established laws and social conducts. It can aid users in specifying and respecting privacy boundaries and may alleviate issues like snooping and "other users posting information about you."

Kang and Kagal (2009, Establishing social norms for privacy in social networks, unpublished) propose a social mechanism to prevent data abuse by showing on a profile what is acceptable to do with the data and what is not. This relies on proper social conduct, and no further technical support is provided to enforce it.

Onwuasoanya et al. [40] want to make it a requirement for the user to group his friends and consequently be able to set different privacy settings for each group. The aim is to provide users a simple and intuitive way to manage their privacy settings, thus increasing user awareness and control.

The system that Goecks et al. [23] propose uses social collaboration to make it easier for users to set their privacy settings and make them more aware if their choice is different from the norm.

The Platform for Privacy Preferences (P3P) [16] is an initiative that aims to provide websites with a standardized format in which they can define their privacy policy. Visitors of the website can then, through client-side "user agents" (e.g., plug-ins for their web browser or applets), easily check the details of a privacy policy and see what will happen to data they submit. This system can help to increase user awareness, but only for users that employ agents and if websites properly define their privacy policies and adhere to them.

These nontechnical approaches lack the power to actively enforce the changes they propose. Policies and regulations are not mandatory, and awareness is something that needs time to be raised. Specific laws dealing with personal information

Table 4.3 Privacy concerns and relevant defenses

↓ Privacy concerns	Relevant defenses →	Anonymization	Decentralization	Privacy settings and management	Encryption	Awareness, law, and regulations
User related	Stranger views private info	●	·	●	●	●
	Unable to hide info from specific friend/group	·	·	●	●	·
	Other users posting information about you	·	·	●	·	●
Provider related	Data retention issues	●	●	·	●	●
	OSN employee browsing private info	·	●	·	●	●
	Selling of data	●	●	·	●	●
	Targeted marketing	●	●	·	●	●

as related to the Internet and OSNs form an important and much needed tool but often take long to be developed. Also, laws are generally used to solve matters *after* things go wrong, whereas most technical solutions attempt to *prevent* violations.

Summary

Table 4.3 shows which research discipline can contribute to address which privacy concern: a ● indicates that the technique is helpful to address a particular concern, while a · states that the technique does not seem applicable. None of the disciplines mentioned in this section offer complete privacy for OSN users. Because the issue of privacy is multifaceted, it will require a multifaceted solution. Several techniques will likely need to be combined to develop proper technical solutions to tackle the various privacy issues. In addition, service providers should be encouraged or required to implement such solutions, and users need to be made aware of the benefits of using them.

Conclusion

We have seen that OSNs are used by millions for a wide variety of purposes. In our classification, we chose to make the broadest distinction between *content* OSNs and *connection* OSNs. Users generally either look to share media and information or simply socialize. The purpose of an OSN and its media richness dictate which types of user data reside in the network. For privacy in turn, this implies which data may be at risk and in what ways.

Because OSNs are such complex systems, the privacy issues are myriad. The fact that trust in the OSNs service provider is not always justified further complicates matters. Users are expected to protect their privacy with tools that are designed by a party that does not by definition have the same goals with regards to privacy, and even if they are protected from other users, the service provider could abuse his position of power.

Many areas of research can help to protect user privacy, ranging from technical (e.g., system design and cryptography) to nontechnical (e.g., sociology and law). However, privacy protection should ideally be built into the system, without harming its operation by overburdening users or service provider, or hampering the OSN functionalities. Also, we must realize that "the privacy problem" – if one could even formulate it as a single problem – will not be solved by any single research discipline. Our conclusion is that in order to develop a full solution to protect consumer privacy, the strengths of several research areas will need to be brought together. Only thus can users be educated and empowered, will OSN service providers be forced to comply, and are legal steps possible when prevention fails.

Acknowledgements The research for this work was carried out within the Kindred Spirits project, part of the STW Sentinels research program.

References

1. Anderson, J., Daz, C., Bonneau, J., Stajano, F.: Privacy-enabling social networking over untrusted networks. In: Crowcroft, J., Krishnamurthy, B. (eds.) Proceedings of the WOSN, Barcelona, pp. 1–6. ACM, New York (2009)
2. Anonymous contributor on Wikipedia.org. Cake financial. online, 4 (2010). http://en.wikipedia.org/wiki/Cake_Financial
3. Anonymous contributor on Wikipedia.org. Sixdegrees.com. online, 4 (2010). http://en.wikipedia.org/wiki/SixDegrees.com/
4. Anonymous contributor on Wikipedia.org. Social network service. online, 4 (2010). http://en.wikipedia.org/wiki/Social_network_service
5. Baatarjav, E.-A., Dantu, R., Phithakkitnukoon, S.: Privacy management for facebook. In: Sekar, R., Pujari, A.K. (eds.) International Conference on Information Systems Security, Hyderabad. Lecture Notes in Computer Science, vol. 5352, pp. 273–286. Springer, Berlin (2008)
6. Backstrom, L., Dwork, C., Kleinberg, J.: Wherefore art thou r3579x?: anonymized social networks, hidden patterns, and structural steganography. In: WWW '07: Proceedings of the 16th International Conference on World Wide Web, Banff, pp. 181–190. ACM, New York (2007)
7. Banks, L., Wu, S.F.: All friends are not created equal: an interaction intensity based approach to privacy in online social networks. In: IEEE International Conference on Computational Science and Engineering, Vancouver, pp. 970–974 (2009)
8. Benevenuto, F., Rodrigues, T., Cha, M., Almeida, V.A.F.: Characterizing user behavior in online social networks. In: Feldmann, A., Mathy, L. (eds.) Internet Measurement Conference, Chicago, pp. 49–62. ACM, New York (2009)

9. Bonneau, J.: Attack of the zombie photos. online (2009). http://www.lightbluetouchpaper.org/2009/05/20/attack-of-the-zombie-photos/
10. Boyd, D., Ellison, N.B.: Social network sites: definition, history, and scholarship. J. Comput. Mediat. Commun. **13**(1), 210–230 (2007)
11. Buchegger, S., Datta, A.: A case for p2p infrastructure for social networks – opportunities and challenges. In: WONS 2009, 6th International Conference on Wireless On-demand Network Systems and Services, Snowbird, pp. 161–168 (2009)
12. Buchegger, S., Schiöberg, D., Vu, Le H., Datta, A.: Peerson: P2p social networking: early experiences and insights. In: SNS '09: Proceedings of the Second ACM EuroSys Workshop on Social Network Systems, pp. 46–52. ACM, New York (2009)
13. Burns, E.: Marketing to social networking sites, targeted. online, 4 (2007). http://www.clickz.com/3625536
14. Cardon, D.: Le design de la visibilit : un essai de typologie du web 2.0. online, 2 (2008). http://www.internetactu.net/2008/02/01/le-design-de-la-visibilite-un-essai-de-typologie-du-web-20/
15. Carminati, B., Ferrari, E., Perego, A.: Private relationships in social networks. In: ICDE Workshops, Istanbul, pp. 163–171 (2007)
16. Cranor, L., Langheinrich, M., Marchiori, M., Presler-Marshall, M., Reagle, J.: The platform for privacy preferences 1.0 (p3p1.0) specification. online (2002). http://www.w3.org/TR/P3P/
17. Dube, R., Adomaitis, M.B.P.: What types of social networks exist. online, 3 (2009). http://socialnetworking.lovetoknow.com/What_Types_of_Social_Networks_Exist
18. Dwork, C.: Differential privacy. In: Automata, Languages and Programming, 33rd International Colloquium, ICALP 2006, Venice, 10–14 July 2006, Proceedings, Part II, pp. 1–12 (2006)
19. Emmett, D.: Taxonomy of social networks. online, 6 (2009). http://davemmett.wordpress.com/2009/06/15/taxonomy-of-social-networks/
20. Facebook.com. Statement of rights and responsibilities. online (2011). http://www.facebook.com/terms.php
21. Freedman, M.J., Nicolosi, A.: Efficient private techniques for verifying social proximity. In: Proceedings of the 6th International Workshop on Peer-to-Peer Systems (IPTPS07), Bellevue, pp. 1–7 (2007)
22. Gannes, L.: A taxonomy of social networks? online, 2 (2007). http://gigaom.com/2007/02/09/social-network-taxonomy/
23. Goecks, J., Edwards, W.K., Mynatt, E.D.: Challenges in supporting end-user privacy and security management with social navigation. In: Cranor, L.F. (ed.) Symposium on Usable Privacy and Security, Mountain View. ACM International Conference Proceeding Series, pages 1–12. ACM, New York (2009)
24. Gross, R., Acquisti, A.: Information revelation and privacy in online social networks. In: WPES '05: Proceedings of the 2005 ACM workshop on Privacy in the electronic society, Alexandria, pp. 71–80. ACM, New York (2005)
25. Guha, S., Tang, K., Francis, P.: Noyb: privacy in online social networks. In: Proceedings of the First Workshop on Online Social Networks (WOSN), Seattle, pp. 49–54. ACM, New York (2008)
26. Hernandez, N.: President apologizes for questionable photos, 10 (2007). http://www.washingtonpost.com/wp-dyn/content/article/2007/10/17/AR2007101702244.html
27. Hudsonhorizons.com. Types of social networking websites. online, (2010). http://www.hudsonhorizons.com/Custom-Website-Solutions/Social-Networking/Types-of-Social-Networks.htm
28. Jacob, A.: How to hack myspace private profile picture and video. online, 4 (2007). http://www.clazh.com/how-to-hack-myspace-private-profile-picture-and-video/
29. Kang, J.: Information privacy in cyberspace transactions. Stanf. Law Rev. **50**(4), 1193–1294 (1998)
30. Leenes, R.: Context Is Everything – Sociality and Privacy in Online Social Network Sites, vol. 320/2010, chapter 4, pp. 48–65. Springer, Boston (2010)

31. Lipford, H.R., Besmer, A., Watson, J.: Understanding privacy settings in facebook with an audience view. In: UPSEC'08: Proceedings of the 1st Conference on Usability, Psychology, and Security, San Francisco, pp. 1–8. USENIX Association, Berkeley (2008)

32. Lucas, M.M., Borisov, N.: Flybynight: mitigating the privacy risks of social networking. In: Proceedings of the 7th ACM Workshop on Privacy in the Electronic Society (WPES), Alexandria, pp. 1–8. ACM, New York (2008)

33. Lunn, B.: Social network types, motivations, and the future. online, 9 (2007). http://www.readwriteweb.com/archives/social_network_types_motivations.php

34. MacNamara, P.: Facebook blocks 'web 2.0 suicide machine'. online, 1 (2010). http://www.networkworld.com/news/2010/010410-buzzblog-facebook-blocks-suicide-machine.html

35. Maximilien, E.M., Grandison, T., Liu, K., Sun, T., Richardson, D., Guo, S.: Enabling privacy as a fundamental construct for social networks. In: Proceedings of the International Conference on Computational Science and Engineering CSE '09, Vancouver, vol. 4, pp. 1015–1020, 29–31 Aug 2009

36. Mezzour, G., Perrig, A., Gligor, V.D., Papadimitratos, P.: Privacy-preserving relationship path discovery in social networks. In: Garay, J.A., Miyaji, A., Otsuka, A. (eds.) Cryptology and Network Security. Lecture Notes in Computer Science, vol. 5888, pp. 189–208. Springer, Berlin/New York (2009)

37. Olsen, S.: At rapleaf, your personals are public. online, 8 (2007). http://news.cnet.com/At-Rapleaf,-your-personals-are-public/2100-1038_3-6205716.html

38. O'Neill, N.: "anonymous" facebook employee interview: fact vs fiction, 1 (2010). http://www.allfacebook.com/2010/01/anonymous-facebook-employee-interview-fact-vs-fiction/

39. Onlinebrandmanager.com. Types of online social networks. online (2011). http://onlinebrandmanager.org/social-media/social-network-types/

40. Onwuasoanya, A., Skornyakov, M., Post, J.: Enhancing privacy on social networks by segregating different social spheres. Rutgers Gov. Sch. Eng. Technol. Res. J. **3**, 1–10 (2008)

41. Palen, L., Dourish, P.: Unpacking "privacy" for a networked world. In: CHI '03: Proceedings of the SIGCHI Conference on Human Factors in Computing Systems, pp. 129–136. ACM, New York (2003)

42. Pingdom.com. Social network popularity around the world. online (2008). http://royal.pingdom.com/2008/08/12/social-network-popularity-around-the-world/

43. Riddle, W.: Cyberbullied teen sues ex-classmates, their parents, and facebook, 3 (2009). http://www.switched.com/2009/03/04/cyberbullied-teen-sues-ex-classmates-their-parents-and-faceboo/

44. Rosenblum, D.: What anyone can know: the privacy risks of social networking sites. IEEE Secur. Priv. **5**(3), 40–49 (2007)

45. Shakimov, A., Varshavsky, A., Cox, L.P., Cceres, R.: Privacy, cost, and availability tradeoffs in decentralized osns. In: Crowcroft, J., Krishnamurthy, B. (eds.) Proceedings of the WOSN, Barcelona, pp. 13–18. ACM, New York (2009)

46. Tootoonchian, A., Saroiu, S., Ganjali, Y., Wolman, A.: Lockr: better privacy for social networks. In: CoNEXT '09: Proceedings of the 5th International Conference on Emerging Networking Experiments and Technologies, Rome, pp. 169–180. ACM, New York (2009)

47. Tufekci, Z.: Can you see me now? audience and disclosure regulation in online social network sites. Bull. Sci. Technol. Soc. **28**(1), 20–36 (2008)

48. Turk, A.: Opinion 5/2009 on online social networking. Technical report 01189/09/EN WP 163, article 29 data protection working party, 6 (2009). http://ec.europa.eu/justice_home/fsj/privacy/docs/wpdocs/2009/wp163_en.pdf

49. UK Parliament. Data protection act 1998, (1998). http://www.legislation.gov.uk/ukpga/1998/29/contents

50. Viswanath, B., Mislove, A., Cha, M., Gummadi, P.K.: On the evolution of user interaction in facebook. In: Crowcroft, J., Krishnamurthy, B. (eds.) Workshop on Online Social Networks, Barcelona, pp. 37–42. ACM, New York (2009)

51. Walters, C.: Facebook's new terms of service: "we can do anything we want with your content. forever." 2 (2009). http://consumerist.com/2009/02/facebooks-new-terms-of-service-we-can-do-anything-we-want-with-your-content-forever.html
52. Weiss, S.: The need for a paradigm shift in addressing privacy risks in social networking applications. In: The Future of Identity in the Information Society. IFIP International Federation for Information Processing, vol. 262, pp. 161–171. Springer, New York (2008)
53. Williams, D.M.: Online identity expert loses control of nsfw r-rated online pics, 3 (2009). http://www.itwire.com/your-it-news/home-it/23975-online-identity-expert-loses-control-of-nsfw-r-rated-online-pics.html
54. Ying, X., Wu, X.: Randomizing social networks: a spectrum preserving approach. In: Proceedings of the SIAM International Conference on Data Mining, Atlanta, pp. 739–750. Society for Industrial and Applied Mathematics, Philadelphia (2008)
55. Zhou, B., Pei, J., Luk, W.: A brief survey on anonymization techniques for privacy preserving publishing of social network data. Spec. Interest Group Knowl. Discov. Data Min. Explor. **10**(2), 12–22 (2008)

Chapter 5
Privacy Settings in Online Social Networks as a Conflict of Interests: Regulating User Behavior on *Facebook*

Max-R. Ulbricht

> *We are all regulated by software now.*
>
> James Grimmelmann [15]

Abstract This chapter shall analyze the options users of online social networks like Facebook have to adjust privacy settings. As the theoretical background of this evaluation, an institutional economics point of view shall be applied.

Against this background, the following analysis of how Facebook as a provider of an online social network designs its platform in such a way that their own interests, as many users' data to keep visible and searchable, are implemented.

Both the GUI of the platform (website) and the various possibilities for mobile use, such as special "mobile" versions of the website and smartphone applications (apps) for various platforms, will be evaluated.

Introduction

This chapter deals with conflicts of interest concerning privacy in social networks. The parties with potentially different interests are operators of social networking sites and their users. Depending on their reasons for using social networking sites, users want as much control as possible over who they grant access to their various personal data, operators want to allow as much information as possible to remain publicly accessible and searchable.

Max-R. Ulbricht (✉)
Department of Commercial Information Technology and Quantitative Methods,
Computers & Society, Technical University of Berlin, Berlin, Germany
e-mail: phaser@cs.tu-berlin.de

A. Abraham (ed.), *Computational Social Networks: Security and Privacy*,
DOI 10.1007/978-1-4471-4051-1_5, © Springer-Verlag London 2012

I will examine these issues from a perspective that regards software as an institution. This has the advantage that it allows institutional attributes to be ascribed to software and thus makes it easier to demonstrate that software can actually perform regulatory functions.

As a matter of fact, software can wield a much more direct influence on behavior than conventional institutions such as social norms, national law, or contracts. This is due to the fact that software always restricts (i.e., regulates) users' options ex ante, i.e., prior to or during use, simply because rules for use are defined while the software is being developed.

In the following, I will analyze what forms such regulation of behavior can take. I have chosen to do so using the example of *Facebook* because it is currently the social networking site with the largest number of members.

Regulating Human Behavior

An appropriate theoretical framework is required to analyze the influence of software systems on human behavior. Because research into institutions is concerned with analyzing the modes of operation of regulatory systems and their effects on society [24], it makes sense to approach the subject from this perspective.

Research into institutions is conducted in a variety of academic disciplines, such as political science, law, and economics, as well as sociology, (political) philosophy, and new institutional economics [24]. Each of these subdisciplines researches different aspects of how institutions influence individuals within a society.

Institutions can be understood as generally accepted systems of rules that either facilitate, structure, or limit human interactions [17]. However, this study will focus not only on the rules but also on the mechanisms that enforce the rules ([31] quoted from [24]).

To regulate human behavior, institutions can establish rules, enforce them, and penalize those who violate them. Thus, anything that regulates the individuals' possibilities for action in a community can be regarded as an institution.

That said, institutions can take on a variety of different forms. On the one hand, institutions can comprise formal rules, as is the case with national laws and written contracts. On the other hand, unwritten behavioral norms and social conventions also count as institutions [24]. The common denominator among all these forms is that they encompass rules that are applied, monitored, and enforced whenever individuals make a decision regarding their future actions ([25] quoted from [27]).

Thus, by establishing and enforcing rules, institutions determine the options for action open to individuals in a society. In the following, I will set out why software can also be viewed as an institution.

Regulating Options for Action

Human behavior is influenced by numerous factors. These factors are of various origins and regulate the social behavior of individuals within a community in different ways. When attempting to classify these factors, it is helpful to analyze what can influence the behavior of individuals in specific situations. In his book, *Code* [19], L. Lessig sketches out such an analysis, which I will describe below.

The rules that a society establishes have a major influence over the behavior of its members. Some of these rules are laid down as laws and apply equally to all members of the society – and in the case of laws, the rules are always limited to the national territory of the society in question. Other regulatory factors are also confined to a clearly defined scope of application, although identifying the boundaries of the spheres of action in which these regulations apply is not always as clear-cut as it is with national legislation. Thus, within its specific scope of application, legislation regulates behavior through laws.

Social norms can influence a person's behavior just as strongly as laws can, but it is far more difficult to precisely define the sphere of action in which their regulatory power applies. The range of possible behaviors in a specific social situation can differ widely depending on the location (e.g., in many situations, the norms that apply in Europe do not apply in the USA, and vice versa). However, at the point in time an individual chooses to take a specific action, it is not just the relevant society as a whole that influences his or her behavior but also the social group, subculture, and community. Thus, in certain situations, people are likely to behave differently when they are with their family than when they are among colleagues at work.

Another factor that influences human behavior is the market, which determines the options for action for transactions between different actors, in this case market participants. Mechanisms, such as prices (or costs) or even just the presence or absence of supply or demand, provide the actors with specific options for action. For example, if the price of a particular product is too high or if the market simply does not offer it, a person might have to forgo or at least delay satisfying the need to buy that product.

But it is not only the market, norms, and legislation (in the form of laws) that regulate behavior. Another, highly influential, factor is the architecture[1] surrounding the actor. In the physical space, architecture regulates access to places and spaces and therefore also to spheres of action. The rules of the market, norms, and legislation might make it perfectly acceptable to enter a particular building, but a locked door is highly effective in preventing anyone from doing so. Therefore, by determining the scope for movement in a given environment, architecture regulates the options for action open to the individuals in that environment.

---

[1]Regulation by physical architecture can be found in, for example, urban and transport planning, and in the design of public spaces such as shopping malls and supermarkets (cf., e.g., [3]).

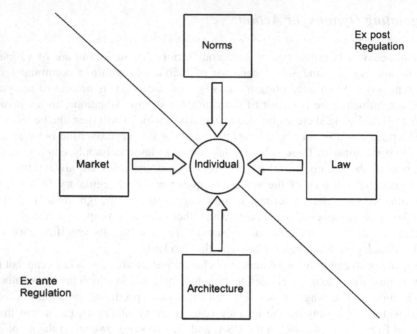

Fig. 5.1 Modalities of regulation according to lessig

According to Lessig [19], this means that individuals' options for action are determined and/or regulated by the modalities of laws, norms, the market, and (physical) architecture (see Fig. 5.1 on page 118).

Regulation Through Software

The dawn of globally networked systems like the Internet brought with it the need to reflect on the possibilities for regulating such systems. Territorial state law is clearly not particularly suited to the task, since the sphere of action that these networks offer goes far beyond national boundaries.[2] There was therefore a need to find a way of establishing and enforcing rules with a scope of application that reaches much further than that of national laws.

Joel R. Reidenberg provided the first reflections on this issue in 1998, when he published *Lex Informatica* [26]. In it he points out that the limited scope of

---

[2]One example of the difficulties in regulating globally networked systems became apparent during the political upheavals in Egypt in early 2011. Because the government in power at the time was unable to limit access to the websites being used for communication and coordination among the opposition movement, it decided that its only course of action was to shut off access to the entire Internet.

the application of laws, and their regulatory character penalizing violations after the fact (ex post), can prove obstructive to handling global systems. Therefore, Reidenberg developed a framework that encourages incorporating rules directly into the informational and technical structures of systems. This would make it possible to establish rules that would apply throughout the system, irrespective of the user's location. This approach also means that the system could be designed in such a way as to prevent undesirable activities from the outset. This kind of *ex ante regulation* circumvents the need for retroactively punishing misconduct because the system architecture prevents it from happening in the first place.

Given these properties of regulations integrated into technical systems, software can influence user behavior in a variety of ways.

Software can be used to enforce established law, as is the case with digital rights management (DRM) systems. DRM systems use informatic structures (systems that comprise hardware and software) to enforce the rules of law, in this case the provisions of copyright law.

The region codes on Digital Versatile Disks (DVDs) provide a good example of this technology. These rules are a combination of hardware and software that ensures that DVD content can only be played back within the framework conditions set out by the owner of the exploitation rights. The rights owner establishes which DVD can be played under which conditions. This involves saving a region code in the metadata of every DVD and requiring all manufacturers of DVD players to implement routines in their devices that can read the DVD code. A device will then use the code to decide whether it is permitted to play a given DVD in the region for which this specific device was produced. If the DVD region code is not compatible with the player, it will be impossible to play back the content. Owners of the exploitation rights use this system to prevent violations of copyright law and as a price-discrimination[3] tool [8].

In this situation, hardware and software are used to implement a technical system for enforcing rights.

Much more common than systems for enforcing rights, however, is software that can (through its developers) define and enforce new rules that are designed independently of rights and laws or other norms [24].

Users of software systems can only interact with the system according to the rules previously established by the manufacturer, i.e., the software itself regulates its users' behavior with predefined rules that determine their options for interaction. Thus, it is virtually impossible to write texts using pocket calculator software because text processing is not a function provided for in the rules established and enforced by the programmer [15].

I would like to stress here that any analysis of the architecture of a software system can only be a "snapshot" of a particular moment in time because of course,

---

[3]Although I will not go into DRM systems in any further detail, this example shows that technologically supported regulation does not only shape the specific regulatory area but can also have far-reaching effects on other legally protected rights (cf., e.g., [18]).

unlike physical architecture, software architecture is malleable and can be adapted at any time [15]. Nevertheless, we can establish the fact that software manifestly determines its users' possibilities for action.

Software as an Institution

When considering software as an institution, it is helpful to bear in mind the process by which it is developed.

Software developers' goal is to harness computers to solve specific problems or perform certain tasks. So that computers can do what they are supposed to, they must be supplied with specific instructions that are written in a language they can "understand." In other words, developers need to translate the solution to the problem they have devised into information that can be processed by a machine.

Computers work deterministically, i.e., the same input will produce the same output every time. That means developers need to structure their instructions in a way that will ensure that the computer processes them in a certain order for the achievement of the desired result. In other words, developers not only need to write instructions in a form computers can understand, they also determine the order in which these instructions are carried out.

During this process, they must also determine what forms of interaction the software needs to make available to users in order to enable them to use the functionalities offered by the program.

In other words, software developers not only establish rules as to how and in what order the program performs which operations in the work process, they also determine how users can later interact with the software.

Software programs offer users certain functionalities on the one hand, while limiting them in their ability to act on the other. In making a number of functions available to them, they automatically eliminate the possibility of using other functions not included in that number [15].

Accordingly, software can be seen as a system of rules that not only controls the program sequence but also regulates users' possibilities for interaction.

If software is a system of rules that can facilitate, structure, or limit the interaction of individuals, we can regard it as an institution in the sense of the definition set out by Hodgson and Calatrava [17] and referred to in the introduction to this section.

Discussion: Software as Architecture or as a Separate Modality

Lessig's approach of describing the various possibilities for regulation offered by software in terms of physical architecture is a legitimate subject for debate, as mentioned at the end of section "Regulation Through Software".

It appears logical that software, much like architecture, can influence the behavior of its users by determining spheres of action according to rules defined by its designer [19].

On the other hand, properties can be assigned to software systems that differ significantly from those of physical architecture, raising the question of whether the regulatory possibilities of software can legitimately be compared with those of physical architecture.

Thus, software, unlike physical architecture, can regulate users' behavior in ways that are not necessarily transparent to them [15]. While the rules of physical architecture are apparent to those it regulates ("That door is locked, so I can't go that way."), it is not always evident to the users of software systems why they are supposed to utilize certain functionalities of the system, while others are withheld from them.

Moreover, rules imposed by software cannot be ignored, while this is certainly possible in the case of physical architecture [15]. Thus, a barrier or gate in the physical world can generally be bypassed fairly easily, while the average software user usually cannot ignore a request for a password, for example.

In addition, unlike physical architecture, most software programs are flexible and can be adapted even after they have been written [15]. For example, a software developer can change the interface of his system should it become clear that users do not interact with the system in the way intended. A highway, on the other hand, cannot simply be moved somewhere else if it turns out that it is not used to the extent the builder assumed it would be.

Lessig does refer to this last point as representing a major limitation of the comparison between the possibilities of regulating software architecture and physical architecture. He argues [19] that not only can individual behavior be regulated *by* software, but the regulation *of* software itself can also be effected by major social institutions, such as the market or by government regulations (see Fig. 5.2 on page 122). The analogy to "building regulations" could therefore certainly be applied. In the case of physical architecture, however, regulations can only be used to influence the shape of the future architecture, whereas in the case of software, regulations can also require software to be changed after it has been designed so that software systems that are already in place then have to be adapted to the requirements of the regulations.

For the following analysis in this study, however, the points addressed above are not relevant for the time being. The aim of the study is to investigate in what way the architecture of a system influences the users' scope of action through its interface design. This can only be a snapshot which evaluates the current state of a platform so it is not necessary, in this context, to take account of the discrepancies identified above between regarding software as architecture and as a regulation mode in its own right.

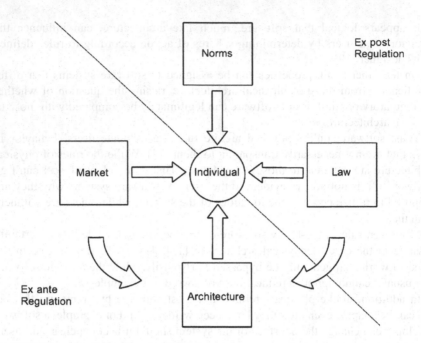

Fig. 5.2 Indirect regulation according to lessig

Regulating Behavior on Facebook

In recent years, the popularity of social networking websites has exploded. One of the most popular and best known of these sites is Facebook.

On July 21, 2010, Facebook founder Mark Zuckerberg posted an entry on the Facebook blog announcing that his company had reached a major milestone in its history: Facebook now had over 500 million active users [32].

This announcement led a number of media to compare Facebook to real countries. Indeed, according to the size of its (virtual) "population" of over 500 million users, Facebook could be considered the third biggest nation on earth, behind India (with 1.18 billion inhabitants) and ahead of the USA (with a population of 308 million) [22, 29].

If we follow this line of reasoning through to its logical conclusion, the question arises if the regulation of the behavior of Facebook's "inhabitants" by the website software can be mapped onto the modalities discussed in section "Regulating Options for Action". In the same way that the regulation of human behavior in the real world can (see Fig. 5.3 on page 123).

In the case of the Facebook system, the Facebook Principles [10] could be interpreted as social norms, while the Terms of Use [12] and Facebook Privacy Policy [11] apply on the site in more or less the same manner as laws, i.e., anybody who violates them can be penalized.

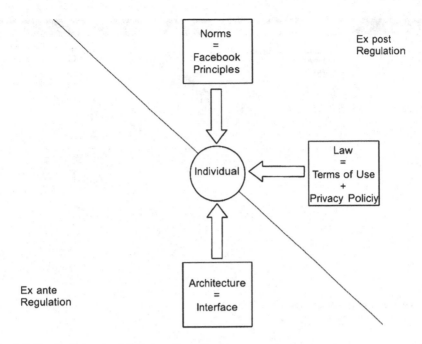

Fig. 5.3 Regulation on facebook according to lessig

The modality I wish to analyze in the following, however, is the architecture of the website; as I use it here, the term architecture refers to all the various ways users can interact with the system, whereby the system consists primarily of the website www.facebook.com, in addition to various special versions of the site designed for mobile devices and client applications (apps) for smartphones, whose use has skyrocketed over the past few years.

The specific object of investigation I will focus on in this section is the options given users to adjust their privacy settings to their individual requirements and preferences.

Website

The most common way to use the Facebook platform is to access it via its website www.facebook.com, which provides the interface for users to interact with the platform.

In principle, Facebook users have the option of adjusting all privacy settings to their own preferences. However, only a small percentage of users take advantage of that option [9, 16]. More than 30% of Facebook users are not even aware of the fact that the platform offers them the option of determining who is allowed to search for and find their profile information. And at least 22% of the site's users claim that they know nothing about privacy settings or cannot recall ever having changed them [2].

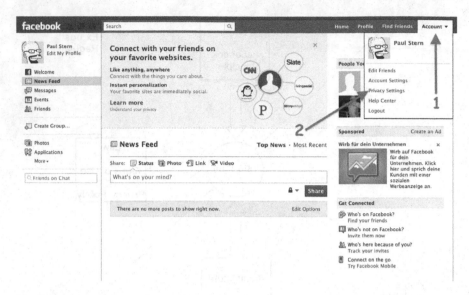

Fig. 5.4 Access privacy settings

But why is that the case? The primary reason is to be found in the architecture or rather the design of the website, in which the options for fine-tuning privacy settings are not immediately apparent. These can be only accessed via a link within a menu in the upper right-hand corner of the user's profile page. As with traditional software menus, the individual items on the menu are only visible once the menu is explicitly activated.

As you can see in Fig. 5.4, users must first (1) open the *Account* menu to be able to access the privacy settings (2). Thus, the interface of the platform poses a hurdle ensuring that users only find the option of changing privacy settings that is potentially available to them if they specifically look for them.

Once users have located and called up the menu, they are shown a page with a fairly clear overview (see Fig. 5.5 on page 125) of the privacy settings. However, this page only allows very basic adjustments to be made. It offers only three options (*Everyone, Friends Only, Friends of Friends*) to limit access to all personal information (with some exceptions; see the next section) and provides no possibility for customizing settings. The option users select applies to all their information on the site.

Many users, however, feel that these options for limiting access are inadequate because they are forced to choose between revealing all their information to everyone and to completely block it from being publicly accessible. Since the selective sharing of information is not possible, users view changing the privacy settings as an *all-or*-nothing-process [28] and therefore often make no changes at all [9, 16].

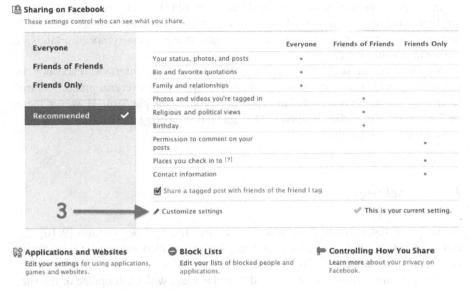

Fig. 5.5 Overview privacy settings

Alternatively, privacy settings can be left at the default setting, which is labeled here as *Recommended*. This option will be described in more detail in the section after the next.

Settings Options

Of course, Facebook does offer its users the possibility to customize their privacy settings and determine precisely which data they wish to make available to whom. For that purpose, users have to click on an inconspicuous link on the overview page of the privacy settings mentioned in the last section (see (3) in Fig. 5.5).

The page that opens when they click on the link then offers truly comprehensive options to define precisely who can access the various kinds of personal information on the user's Facebook page. The only exceptions are the user's name, gender, friends list, and profile picture; access to this information cannot be restricted, and it thus remains visible to everyone [14].

However, the number of options offered on this page frequently leaves users feeling overwhelmed, and surveys have revealed that many describe the interface for customizing privacy settings as confusing and time-consuming [28].

Persistent criticism from users and negative coverage in the media have led Facebook to revise the interface several times, but at least in the view of users, the new versions were no real improvement. According to more recent surveys, the new interface was also felt to be confusing [7] so that many users refrained from changing the standard settings [9].

In addition, respondents complained that the page offers only very limited visual feedback and uses confusing language and that, even after settings have been changed, it is not apparent how these changes affect access to specific kinds of personal information [20].

So far, we can state the following: Via the website interface, Facebook in principle provides its users with all necessary options to exercise precise control over access to all their personal information stored on the platform. However, these options are not immediately apparent [2], and it is confusing and time consuming to exercise them [9, 20, 28].

Default Settings

Considering that only few Facebook users change their privacy settings [9, 16], the default privacy settings, i.e., those settings that are applied automatically to newly registered users, are especially important.

These default settings have changed over the years with each update of the site. That each change has also been accompanied by the release of a new version of the privacy policy [11] indicates that Facebook's stance on this issue has continued to shift as the company weighs its own economic interests against users' right to privacy. An analysis of this development suggests that Facebook has evolved from a platform for people to communicate with groups of their own choosing into a company driven by profit that shares the personal data of its users with business partners and allows it to be used for targeted advertising [23].

This transformation can easily be traced by analyzing how Facebook's terms of use, privacy policies, and default privacy settings have evolved [21]. Such an analysis clearly demonstrates that the default privacy settings have been modified with each updated version of the platform to make more and more of users' personal information visible to the public if the settings are not changed.

The analysis also shows that until 2009, Facebook's default settings merely made users' personal information visible to as many other Facebook members as possible rather than to the larger public. This changed in November 2009, when the platform opened up such information and made it generally accessible on the Internet. From that time on, it was no longer necessary to be registered and logged in as a Facebook member to access information about Facebook users; anyone could simply use a search engine to locate personal data such as users' names, gender, and profile pictures.

If users do not change the default privacy settings, anyone can use a search engine to gain access not only to those data for which visibility cannot be restricted in any case (name, gender, friends list, and profile picture) but also to all status updates, photos, posts, and family and relationship information, as well as the user's biography and favorite quotations (see Fig. 5.5).

Mobile Use

According to Facebook, around 200 million of its members currently access the platform from mobile devices [13]. Facebook provides number of possibilities to allow mobile access, such as special versions of the website designed for small displays and applications (apps) for various smartphone operating systems.

In other words, Facebook provides mobile users with a different architecture for interacting with the platform. Just as the architecture of the website regulates users' behavior, this architecture regulates mobile users' behavior in relation to the information on the platform.

Since the interface of special mobile versions of the website and Facebook smartphone applications have not yet been the subject of academic research, I will merely provide a descriptive analysis in the following.

Mobile Versions of the Website

When the website www.facebook.com is accessed from a mobile device, the platform recognizes that it is a device with a small display from the user agent string. The user is then automatically redirected to a version of the website designed especially for mobile devices, either to m.facebook.com (for devices with traditional small displays) or to touch.facebook.com (for mobile devices with a touch screen).

While users are provided with no options to change the privacy settings on touch. facebook.com, in principle such options are available on *m.facebook.com*, although the same restrictions described in section "Website" apply here, as well.

Users can access the options for customizing privacy settings once they have logged in, but they will only find the menu item *Settings* (see (1) in Fig. 5.6 on page 128) after scrolling down all the way to the bottom of the page.

When you click on the link, a new page opens up where the menu item for changing the privacy settings is located in the middle (see (2) in Fig. 5.6 on page 128). This link leads to another new page containing an overview like that described in section "Website". However, the difference here is that, besides the familiar options (*Everyone, Friends of Friends, Friends Only*), the option for user-defined settings (*Costum*) is featured relatively prominently (see (3) in Fig. 5.7 on page 128). The fact that it is less "hidden away" than on the regular website apparently has to do with the lower resolution of mobile device displays.

In other words, users of the mobile version of Facebook at *m.facebook.com* are in principle provided with all options for adapting privacy settings to their preferences that are offered through the interface of the regular version of the site. However, usability and user acceptance studies will be needed to determine if and to what extent users avail themselves of these options.

In addition, we need to take technological progress into account when it comes to mobile devices; in particular, we must address the progress of smart phones.

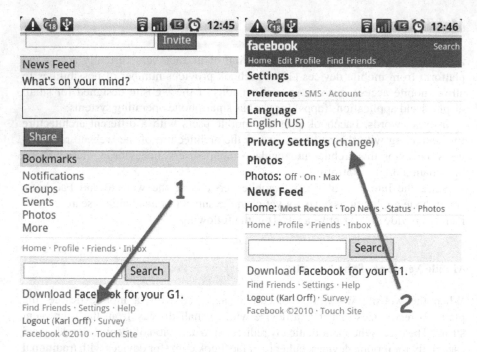

Fig. 5.6 Access privacy settings on *m.facebook.com*

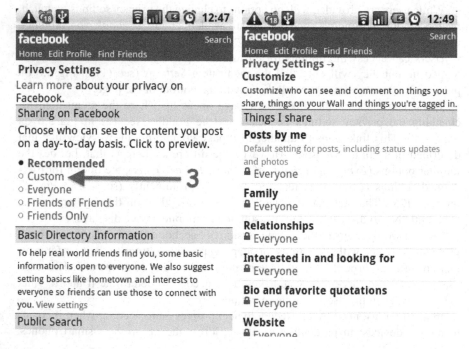

Fig. 5.7 Overview privacy settings on *m.facebook.com*

Since the use of touch screens in mobile devices is bound to increase rapidly in the future (+44% within the past year [1]), the fact that users calling up Facebook from devices with such displays are automatically redirected to *touch.facebook.com*, which offers no options whatsoever for customizing privacy settings, means that a growing number of users will be kept away from these options.

Applications for Smartphones

So-called client applications for smartphones represent another possibility of interacting with the Facebook platform. Statistics confirm that these so-called apps for accessing Facebook are immensely popular, regardless of which smartphone operating system is used [30].

Apps promise users convenient access to the platform with a user interface perfectly adapted to the respective device/display. According to some statistics, over 100 million people already use smartphone applications to access Facebook today [4–6].

Two applications were available to me for the purposes of this study, one for Apple's iPhone and the other the Android operating system developed by Google. The Android app lacks any options for modifying privacy settings. The menu of the iPhone app explicitly offers a *Privacy Settings* option, but you have to leave the app to make use of it. Clicking on the option opens a browser window showing the privacy settings page of the regular Facebook site. This not only has the disadvantages discussed in section "Website", but these are compounded by the fact that the interface – which is confusing enough already – has to be navigated using a tiny screen with relatively low resolution.

Thus the design of the smartphone applications also puts obstacles in the way of Facebook users wishing to modify the privacy settings according to their own needs and preferences.

Summary

The analysis of the architecture of various interfaces for interacting with Facebook revealed that while they offer options for customizing privacy settings in principle, the design of these interfaces serves to make it difficult for users to avail themselves of these options.

Many users find the interface of the website confusing and time consuming so that they frequently refrain from making any changes to the standard settings. Facebook pursues the same strategy in its versions for mobile devices. A version designed primarily for older models does provide access to the full range of options for customizing privacy settings, even if it is difficult to spot at first glance.

Users with newer models, on the other hand, are automatically directed to a version that does not even offer the possibility of modifying privacy settings at all. The situation is no different when it comes to smartphone applications.

It would seem that Facebook, by structuring its architecture and designing its interfaces in the way it does, intends to deter users from making discriminating, informed choices about whom they will allow to have access to the various kinds of personal data stored on the platform.

Conclusion

Users of social networking sites need comprehensive options for restricting the visibility of the personal information they provide on the platform. Facebook does provide its members with all the information they need to determine precisely who can access various personal data and who cannot. My analysis of the options for interaction Facebook provides its users showed that all necessary options for customizing privacy settings are available in principle.

However, Facebook's interfaces seem to be designed with the aim of ensuring that users do not modify these settings or do so only to a limited extent, i.e., that most users simply accept the default settings predetermined by the platform's operators. Thus, if users do not change these standard settings, the result is that not only their names but also their profile photos and other sensitive personal data are accessible to the public at large through the Internet.

In selecting the default settings, Facebook's operators determine which of its users' personal data they would prefer to be generally accessible – and the design of the interfaces they provide ensures that precisely these personal data are indeed generally accessible for the majority of the site's users.

Seen in this light, the first sentence in the preface to the Facebook Principles – "We are building Facebook to make the world more open and transparent. . ." – would seem to be the guiding principle according to which decisions on the design of the user interface are made, with the aim of enforcing that goal even, if necessary, if that runs counter to the interests of its users.

On the face of things, Facebook does nothing that would open it up to criticism. In the documents they make available to users, the site's operators profess that safeguarding the privacy of their users is important to them, point out different possibilities for users to protect their data on the site from unwanted access, and place all functions they need to do so at their disposal on the site.

On the other hand, through the architecture of the site, they regulate their users' behavior in a certain way, i.e., they make it difficult for them to take advantage of the options available to them. Thus, Facebook's operators impose their views of how much and what kinds of their users' information should be publicly accessible on the website by the rules they themselves previously established and enforce through the design of the user interfaces.

In other words, Facebook establishes rules for dealing with users' personal information and is at the same time in a position to impose these rules on users through the design of the website architecture. In this sense, according to the theories outlined in section "Regulating Human Behavior", Facebook meets the definition of an institution that influences the behavior of individuals in its own interest by determining their options for action and is thus analogous to physical architecture.

References

1. Accenture: Mobile Web Watch 2010.   website: http://www.accenture.com/Countries/Germany/Services/By_Industry/Electronics_and_High_Tech/R_and_I/Mobile-Web-Watch-2010.htm (2010) [Online; last visit: 03.03.2011]
2. Acquisti, A., Gross, R.: Imagined communities: awareness, information sharing, and privacy on the Facebook. In: Privacy Enhancing Technologies, Cambridge, pp. 36–58. Springer, Berlin (2006)
3. Allen, J.: Ambient power: Berlin's pOtsdamer platz and the seductive logic of public spaces. Urban Stud. **43**(2), 441 (2006)
4. allfacebook.com.   Facebook for android statistic.   website: http://statistics.allfacebook.com/applications/single/facebook-for-android/350685531728/ (2010)   [Online; last visit: 03.03.2011]
5. allfacebook.com. Facebook for blackberry statistic. website: http://statistics.allfacebook.com/applications/single/facebook-for-blackberry-smartphones/2254487659/ (2010) [Online; last visit: 03.03.2011]
6. allfacebook.com.   Facebook for iphone statistic.   website: http://statistics.allfacebook.com/applications/single/facebook-for-iphone/6628568379/ (2010) [Online; last visit: 03.03.2011]
7. Brandtzæg, P.B., Lüders, M., Skjetne, J.H.: Too many facebook "Friends"? content sharing and sociability versus the need for privacy in social network sites. Int. J. Hum. Comput. Interact. **26**(11), 1006 (2010)
8. Camp, L.J.J.: DRM: doesn't really mean digital copyright management. SSRN Electron. J. 78–87 (2002)
9. Debatin, B., Lovejoy, J.P., Horn, A.-K., Hughes, B.N.: Facebook and online privacy: attitudes, behaviors, and unintended consequences. J. Comput. Mediat. Commun. **15**(1), 83–108 (2009)
10. Facebook.   Facebook principles.   website: http://www.facebook.com/principles.php (2010) [Online; last visit: 03.03.2011]
11. Facebook.   Facebook privacy policy.   website: http://www.facebook.com/policy.php/ (2010) [Online; last visit: 03.03.2011]
12. Facebook.   Facebook terms of use.   website: http://www.facebook.com/terms.php?ref=pf/ (2010) [Online; last visit: 03.03.2011]
13. Facebook.   Platform statistics.   Website: http://www.facebook.com/press/info.php?statistics (2010) [Online; last visit: 03.03.2011]
14. Facebook.   Privacy explanation.   website: http://www.facebook.com/privacy/explanation.php (2010) [Online; last visit: 03.03.2011]
15. Grimmelmann, J.: Regulation by software. Yale Law J. **114**(7), 1719–1758 (2005)
16. Gross, R., Acquisti, A.:   Information revelation and privacy in online social networks.   In: Proceedings of the 2005 ACM Workshop on Privacy in the Electronic Society, Alexandria, pp. 71–80. ACM, New York (2005)
17. Hodgson, G.M., Calatrava, J.: What are institutions. J. Econ. Issues **40**(1), 1 (2006)

18. Kerr, I., Bailey, J.: The implications of digital rights management for privacy and freedom of expression. J. Inf. Commun. Ethic Soc. **2**(2), 85–95 (2004)
19. Lessig, L.: Code version 2. 0. Basic Books, New York (2006)
20. Lipford, H.R., Besmer, A., Watson, J.: Understanding privacy settings in facebook with an audience view. In: Proceedings of the 1st Conference on Usability, Psychology, and Security, San Francisco, pp. 1–8. USENIX Association, Berkeley (2008)
21. McKeon, M.: The evolution of privacy on facebook. website: http://mattmckeon.com/facebook-privacy/ (2010) [Online; last visit: 03.03.2011]
22. Mostyn, S.: Facebook population equivalent to third-biggest country on earth. website: http://www.thetechherald.com/article.php/201029/5922/Facebook-population-equivalent-to-third-biggest-country-on-Earth/ (2010) [Online; last visit: 03.03.2011]
23. Opsahl, K.: Facebook's eroding privacy policy: a timeline. website: http://www.eff.org/deeplinks/2010/04/facebook-timeline (2010) [Online; last visit: 03.03.2011]
24. Orwat, C., Raabe, O., Buchmann, E., Anandasivam, A., Freytag, J.-C., Helberger, N., Ishii, K., Lutterbeck, B., Neumann, D., Otter, T., Pallas, F., Reussner, R., Sester, P., Weber, K., Werle, R.: Software als institution und ihre gestaltbarkeit. Inform. Spektrum **33**(6), 626–633 (2009)
25. Ostrom, E.: Die Verfassung der Allmende: jenseits von Staat und Markt. Mohr Siebeck, Tübingen (1999)
26. Reidenberg, J.R.: Lex informatica: the formulation of information policy rules through technology. Tex. Law Rev. **76**(3), 553 (1998)
27. Richter, R., Furubotn, E.G.: Neue Institutionenökonomik: Eine Einführung und kritische Würdigung. Mohr Siebeck, Tübingen (2003)
28. Strater, K., Lipford, H.R.: Strategies and struggles with privacy in an online social networking community. In: Proceedings of the 22nd British HCI Group Annual Conference on HCI 2008: People and Computers XXII: Culture, Creativity, Interaction-Volume 1, Liverpool, pp. 111–119. British Computer Society, Swindon (2008)
29. techxav: If facebook were a country. website: http://www.techxav.com/2010/03/19/if-facebook-were-a-country/ (2010) [Online; last visit: 03.03.2011]
30. The Nielsen Company: The state of mobile apps. website: http://blog.nielsen.com/nielsenwire/online_mobile/the-state-of-mobile-apps/ (2010) [Online; last visit: 03.03.2011]
31. Zippelius, R.: Juristische Methodenlehre: Eine Einführung. Beck, München (1985)
32. Zuckerberg, M.: 500 million stories. blog: http://blog.facebook.com/blog.php?post=409753352130 (2010) [Online; last visit: 03.03.2011]

Chapter 6
A Reliability-Based Metric for Inferring Trust from Recommendations in Knowledge Sharing Networks

Weisen Guo and Steven B. Kraines

Abstract As knowledge sharing on the Web becomes widespread, it becomes more difficult to know the trustworthiness of the knowledge source. Trust and recommendation have been used for inferring the trustworthiness of unknown entities in many different domains. We introduce trust and recommendation in the EKOSS knowledge sharing network to infer the trustworthiness of a knowledge-sharing agent. We present a reliability-based trust metric for generating locally-calculated inferred trust values using recommendations from trusted agents. The effectiveness of our method is demonstrated through simulation experiments on artificially generated social networks. The advantages and disadvantages of using this method on different kinds of Web-based knowledge sharing networks are discussed.

Introduction

Knowledge sharing is a fundamental process in knowledge-based societies. For example, because research publication is one of the main criteria for performance evaluation, researchers have at least as much incentive to share the knowledge that they have created as users have to seek that knowledge [21]. Previously, we proposed a four level architecture for a Web-based framework to support the sharing, discovery, and integration of scientific knowledge [20]. The framework is intended to form the basis for a network of independently distributed knowledge repositories on the Web. The four levels of the framework consist of a base of knowledge resources in the form of scientific papers, computational models, databases, and so on at the first level [20], a set of tools for allowing experts to create semantic descriptors of their knowledge resources at the second level [21], a Web-based

W. Guo (✉) • S.B. Kraines
Science Integration Programme (Human), Department of Frontier Sciences and Science
Integration, Division of Project Coordination, The University of Tokyo, Kashiwa 277-8568, Japan
e-mail: gws@scint.dpc.u-tokyo.ac.jp; sk@scint.dpc.u-tokyo.ac.jp

A. Abraham (ed.), *Computational Social Networks: Security and Privacy*,
DOI 10.1007/978-1-4471-4051-1_6, © Springer-Verlag London 2012

platform for discovering matches between the knowledge resources based on the semantic descriptors at the third level [19], and a Web-based environment for integrating knowledge such as computational models at the fourth level.

We have developed EKOSS (available at website www.ekoss.org), which stands for Expert Knowledge Ontology-based Semantic Search, as an implementation of the second level of the framework [21]. The network of distributed knowledge repositories described above would then be populated by multiple distributed and independent EKOSS servers. We have created a prototype implementation of the third level of the framework that uses software agent technologies together with ontology-based inference technologies for supporting the searching and sharing of knowledge between distributed and independent agents each representing an EKOSS server [19]. However, the prototype system that we described required that each participating agent register with a service repository agent, and so the system did not treat the issue of how agents can discover information about each other in a decentralized way.

A network for realizing knowledge sharing between geographically distributed and independently operated EKOSS servers must be open and decentralized. Because new EKOSS servers will be constantly appearing in the network, it is likely that an agent representing an EKOSS server on the network will want to interact with an unknown agent with whom it has had no previous interactions.

In order to support an open and decentralized knowledge sharing network we apply the concepts of trust and recommendation. Trust and recommendation are social concepts, and our knowledge sharing network is essentially a Web-based social network populated by people creating and seeking knowledge. In this network, each node is an agent representing one of the knowledge creators/seekers. Each directed link shows that a particular agent knows about another agent, and the links are labeled with the level of trust the first agent has for the second. When an agent A wants to use knowledge shared by an unknown agent B, agent A can first ask the agents that it knows and trusts for recommendations about the trustworthiness and reliability of agent B. This process is repeated until one or more chains are established between agent A and agent B. Each chain can be used to obtain an inferred trust value. We used Multi-Agent System technologies to develop a trust-recommendation model in the EKOSS knowledge sharing system that assesses the accuracy of an inferred trust value for particular unknown agent [14]. If the accuracy is high enough, then the source agent can consider the inferred trust value to be the actual trust value. Otherwise, the inferred trust rating should be discarded.

This chapter presents a new trust metric, reliability-based trust metric (RTM), to calculate the most reliable inferred trust value for an agent unknown to the agent requesting trust information. Our formulation of the metric is based on the following three premises. First, in actual human interactions the recommendation from the most reliable recommender is often more likely to be correct than the average of all recommendations. Consequently, the widely adopted technique of using the average of all recommendations may not give the best results. Second, if there is more than one chain leading to the same inferred trust value for an unknown entity then the aggregate reliability of the inferred trust value should be higher than the reliabilities of each individual chain. Third, if one intermediate recommender occurs in more than one chain, then it should be assigned the same inferred trust value in each chain rather than different inferred trust values based on the different intervening agents. Based on these three premises, we have designed the RTM with the goal of obtaining accurate inferred trust values for target agent.

The rest of the chapter is organized as follows. Section "Background and Related Work" discusses the background and related work. Section "Reliability-Based Trust Metrics" introduces the Reliability-based Trust Metric. In section "Experiments," we generate some small-world scale-free networks, and we conduct simulations on those networks to analyze the proposed Reliability-based Trust Inference (RTI) algorithm together with a conventional averaging algorithm. In section "Discussion," we discuss the advantages and disadvantages of the RTM and suggest potential applications. Finally, in section "Conclusion and Future Works" we conclude the chapter with a summary and description of directions for future work.

Background and Related Work

The work presented here is multidisciplinary, being related to research on knowledge sharing systems, small-world scale-free networks, reputation-based trust, and trust metrics in a trust network. We briefly review the related work in each of these disciplines in the following subsections.

Knowledge Sharing Systems

There are two main directions in the development of knowledge sharing systems. One is decentralization; the other is increasing search system intelligence.

The first knowledge sharing systems were single-machine systems. However, along with the development of Information Technologies and Network Technologies, knowledge sharing systems have evolved from single-machine systems to multi-machine systems, from centralized systems to decentralized systems, and from closed systems to open systems. Peer-to-Peer (P2P) Technologies and Multi-Agent System (MAS) Technologies facilitated this evolution. Several knowledge sharing systems based on these technologies are currently available on the Web [7, 8, 25, 29].

Most of the early knowledge sharing systems represented knowledge in a format that was human-understandable but not computer-understandable. With the emergence of Semantic Web technologies, many researchers are exploring methods and technologies to realize greater system intelligence. Generally, the approach is to use meta data or logic-based knowledge representation languages to enable computers to understand the meanings of the information shared on the Web and other computer-based media [3, 17].

EKOSS is a knowledge sharing system that uses Semantic Web technologies. Expert knowledge is represented by formal descriptors called semantic statements, which are created using domain ontologies based on description logics. Consequentially, expert knowledge is shared on EKOSS using not only human-understandable, but also computer-understandable descriptors. EKOSS is designed as an open and decentralized system. The concept is that multiple EKOSS servers will appear on the Web to serve different communities (possibly with different ontologies). These EKOSS servers will form a network where the links are connections between EKOSS servers that know and trust each other. Each EKOSS server shares its knowledge with and requests knowledge searches from the EKOSS servers it knows and trusts. However, through the links formed by this knowledge sharing network, it is possible that one EKOSS server will want to obtain knowledge from or be asked to give knowledge to an unknown EKOSS server. In that case, the EKOSS server will want to get information on the trustworthiness and reliability of the unknown EKOSS server. The aim of the work presented here is to propose a solution to this problem.

Small-World Scale-Free Networks

A small-world network is a type of mathematical graph where, although most nodes are not neighbors of one another, most nodes can be reached from every other node by a small number of links. A small-world network captures many of the small-world phenomena that occur in social networks, the connectivity of the Internet, and gene networks [1, 18]. For example, social networks, where nodes represent people and links connect people who know each other, often show the small world network characteristic of strangers being linked by one or two mutual acquaintances.

A scale-free network is a type of random network where most nodes have only a few connections but a few nodes are highly connected. The structure and dynamics of scale-free networks are independent of the system's size. In other words, a network that is scale-free will have the same properties no matter how many nodes it has. Scale-free networks have been shown to have a power law degree distribution similar to that observed in many real networks, such as social networks, the Internet, and gene networks [5, 31].

The EKOSS knowledge sharing network is a Web-based social network, so we expect that it will also exhibit characteristics of both small-world networks and scale-free networks. Therefore, in order to evaluate the predicted performance of the EKOSS knowledge sharing network, such as the fraction of EKOSS servers that will be within a certain number of links of each other, we must consider these network characteristics.

Reputation-Based Trust

Trust is an integral part of many kinds of human interaction, allowing people to act under uncertainty and with the risk of negative consequences [4]. Trust has been introduced into computer science from many fields. For example, trust is an essential component of the vision for the Semantic Web [6]. Reputation-based trust uses personal experience, the experiences of others, or both to make a trust decision about an entity.

Issues of trust and reputation on the Web have been around since its conception. Formal methods for rating the reputation of a site or of a user are in common use. The eBay rating system uses positive and negative feedback ratings of sellers made by customers as a measure of a seller's reputation [27]. A consumer reviews website, Epinions, which also allows customers to rate the transaction with sellers, has been used in the study of trust on the Web [23, 24]. The PageRank algorithm [29], used by the Google search engine, treats the number of links pointing to a particular page as votes for that site's reputation.

In a knowledge sharing network, an agent A may want to decide how to interact with another agent B based on its own estimate of the trustworthiness of B. This estimate is normally based on the historical interactions of A with B. However, even if A has not interacted with B before, it can get some recommendations from other agents that have interacted with B and use those recommendations to make its decision. Not all recommendations need to be considered equally valid. For example, A may choose to use only recommendations from agents that have good reputations as the basis for evaluating the reliability or trustworthiness of B.

Trust Metrics in a Trust Network

A trust metric is defined as the quantification of trust together with the algorithms that use that quantification for evaluating trust [4]. Trust is a human, subjective and qualitative concept. That is, when someone says that one person is more trustworthy than another, the evaluation is both subjective and qualitative. It is difficult for a computer to handle qualitative trust values directly. However, if we can quantify the trust value for different entities, then the computer can easily compare the trustworthiness of those entities [11]. A trust decision can be considered a transitive process, where trusting a piece of information or an information source might require trusting another intermediate source [12]. For example, a person might trust a piece of knowledge on a particular EKOSS server because that person trusts the EKOSS server, and one EKOSS server may trust another because of a recommendation from a third highly trusted EKOSS server.

The majority of research on transitive trust computation has focused on the use of reputation. In TrustMail, each entity maintains reputation information on other entities, where reputation is defined as a measure of trust. This creates a trust network [10]. Golbeck and Hendler formulated algorithms to make a trust decision about any two entities based on the reputation information. In our work, we prefer to use the term "reliability" rather than "reputation" to describe a quantitative measure of trust. "Reputation" implies an estimation of an agent by the entire community, whereas our reliability-based trust system uses individual or local estimations of an agent.

Another area of research considers trust decisions made on a given trust network. A link between two entities means a trust decision has been made and the value of that trust is known. How trust decisions are made does not matter, as long as the resulting trust values can be quantified. If there is no link between a pair of entities, it means no trust decision has yet been made. Because the trust decision can be considered a transitive process, trust transitivity can be used to infer the trust decision between a pair of entities without a direct link. Many researchers are exploring ways to transfer trust information within a trust network. We consider some of the research closest to our work in the following.

Singh and Sinha [30] presented a new trust model using a Hidden Markov Model based mixture of experts. They used a coarse-grain Hidden Markov Model to calculate a dynamic trust value for the target agent, where the trust value can vary over time. They calculated the trust value based on the direct trust and recommended trust from the neighbors of the source agent. However, their model does not put the trust and recommendation into a social network environment. For the case where the source agent and its neighbors do not know the target agent, their model cannot calculate an inferred trust value from "friends of friends."

Massa and Avesani [23] studied the problem of controversial users. Controversial users are users who are sometimes trusted and sometimes distrusted. Their work showed that in some cases a locally computed trust value is more accurate than the globally computed trust value.

Golbeck and Hendler [10] addressed the accuracy of metrics for inferred trust and reputation in social networks on the Semantic Web. They described an algorithm for generating locally calculated reputation ratings from a trust network and showed both mathematically and experimentally that the algorithm can accurately infer the trust value of an entity on the trust network.

Richardson et al. [28] provided a means of aggregating trust information that is robust to noise. This approach is described as a generalization of PageRank to the Semantic Web. It avoids computing global values by altering the algorithm to produce personalized results for each entity.

The accuracy of a metric for inferred trust is an important aspect in the trust metrics field. In the reputation inference algorithm used by Golbeck and Hendler's trust metric, when a node is requested to provide a reputation rating for a particular node that it does not know directly, the node will average the ratings provided by all of the nodes immediately downstream. If a node is encountered in two chains from a source node to a sink node, it is considered in each chain. However, they do not provide a way to establish which of the ratings from the intermediate nodes are most reliable. We propose that a metric based on selecting the rating from the most reliable intermediate nodes as the inferred rating for a particular node in question will be more accurate than simply averaging the ratings.

We have developed a metric for trust inference, called the Reliability based Trust Inference (RTI) algorithm, that implements this idea. The RTI algorithm was briefly introduced and evaluated using a random network in previous work [13]. Here, we explicitly define the RTI algorithm and reevaluate it using a small-world scale-free network, which is considered to be a more realistic representation of an actual social network than a random network.

Reliability-Based Trust Metrics

Trust Model

Our trust metric is based on the following three basic premises:

- First, in actual human interactions the recommendation from the most reliable recommender is often more likely to be correct than the average of all recommendations. For example, consider that we want to buy a car, and we find that David is a car dealer. David is a bad car dealer, but we do not know that. We ask three persons that we know for recommendations about David: one trusted and reliable friend Amy, one casual acquaintance Ben, and one trusted but overly trusting friend Carl. Amy tells us "David is a bad car dealer." Ben and Carl tell us "David is a good car dealer." In fact, Ben is a cohort of David, and moreover Ben has fooled Carl into believing that David is a good car dealer. If we use the average of the three recommendations, which rounds off to good, as the final inferred trust value for David, then we will get the wrong answer. However, if we believe that one recommendation from a trustworthy friend is more reliable than the average from all of the recommenders, we would believe the recommendation from Amy. In general, we assume that the more reliable the recommender is, the more weight should be placed on that recommender's recommendations.
- Second, if we receive the same recommendation from two or more recommenders or chains of recommenders, the actual reliability of that recommendation will be higher than that of each of the individual recommenders. In other words, if there is more than one chain leading to the same inferred trust value for an unknown entity then that inferred trust value should have a higher reliability than the reliability of each chain.
- Third, if we receive recommendations from two or more chains of recommenders that pass through the same intermediate recommender, we should assign the same inferred trust value to that recommender for each chain even though there may be different recommenders connecting us to that intermediate recommender. For example, even if we can find a trust chain through a particular recommender that assigns a positive inferred trust value to that recommender, if another chain through that recommender gives us a more reliable recommendation not to trust the recommender, we should use the second recommendation.

Because we want to calculate a local or personal inferred trust value for an unknown entity on the Internet, we place highest priority on the reliability of the recommender. Therefore, we select the most reliable recommendations as the inferred trust value. Furthermore, we increase the reliability of an inferred trust value that has more than one recommendation, according to the second premise. Finally, we increase the accuracy of the inferred trust value for the final unknown entity by calculating the most reliable inferred trust values for the intermediate recommenders occurring in more than one chain, according to the third premise. Based on these three premises, we have formulated our trust model as follows.

There are two basic types of trust in our trust model for knowledge sharing networks: trust in an agent's ability to recommend and trust in an agent's domain knowledge. Trust in the ability to recommend means that an agent can trust or not trust the ability of a known agent to recommend trust values for other unknown agents. For example, when agent A receives a recommendation from agent B that "agent C provides accurate knowledge," A will decide whether or not to trust B's recommendation according to its degree of trust in B's ability to recommend. If A believes that B has a low ability to recommend, B's recommendation may not be enough for A to trust that C provides accurate knowledge.

In the knowledge sharing network application we are targeting, each agent wants to find other agents that provide trustworthy domain knowledge. Trust in an agent's domain knowledge means that an agent can trust or not trust the ability of an agent, known or unknown, to provide accurate knowledge. If the agent does not know the agent in question directly, it may get recommendations from other agents that it does know. For example, if agent A, who knows another agent C, receives some domain knowledge from agent B and confirms that the domain knowledge is good, A can decide to recommend B's domain knowledge to C. Agent C will decide whether or not to trust B's ability to provide good domain knowledge based on its trust in A's ability to recommend together with any other information it has about B.

In order to support the concept of levels of trust or reliability, we use four trust values in our trust model: one distrust value (D) and three trust values of low, medium and high (L, M, H). We only use one distrust value because we consider that dishonest agents that should be distrusted will generally be competent entities that use the best of their abilities to sabotage the system. Furthermore, while a knowledge user wants to know how trustworthy an honest agent is, for a dishonest agent, the user should avoid it no matter what level of dishonesty it has. Finally, we use one more value (U) in this trust model to indicate the status of an agent when it is unknown whether the agent should be trusted or distrusted.

A trust network may contain many agents. Each agent knows some other agents, and it maintains the trust information for these known agents, including the level of trust in ability to recommend and the level of trust in domain knowledge. When one agent (source) wants to decide whether or not to trust an unknown agent (sink), the source agent asks its trusted agents for recommendations. When an agent receives a request for a recommendation about a sink agent, if it knows the sink agent and

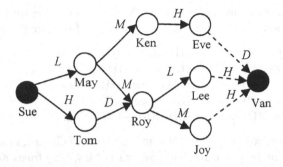

Fig. 6.1 A fictional trust network. The *nodes* denote the agents labeled in normal font. An *arrow with a solid line* denotes the origin agent's trust in the destination agent's ability to recommend. An *arrow with a dashed line* denotes the origin agent's trust in the destination agent's domain knowledge. The *italic letters close to each arrow* denote the origin agent's trust value for the destination agent as described in the text

has a trust value for it, then it can return that trust value to the agent requesting the recommendation. Otherwise, it may ask the agents it trusts for recommendations. This process continues until a recommendation is found or the length of the trust chain reaches the given limit. The recommendations are transmitted back to the source agent through the intermediate agents in the trust chains. When the source agent receives all of the recommendations, it uses that collected trust information together with its own information about the reliability of the agents giving the recommendations to calculate the inferred trust value for the sink agent.

There are many ways to calculate the inferred trust value. In order to obtain an accurate inferred trust value, we have developed the RTI algorithm. We explain the algorithm in the following section.

Reliability-Based Trust Inference Algorithm

We describe the RTI algorithm as being made up of three levels. In the first level, the reliability of each trust chain from the source agent to the sink agent is considered independently. In the second level, if there is more than one trust chain leading to the same inferred trust value for the sink agent then these trust chains are combined and given a higher reliability. In the third level, if an agent appears in more than one chain then the source agent chooses the most reliable inferred trust value for that agent and uses that value in each chain.

In order to explain the RTI algorithm, we use the fictional trust network shown in Fig. 6.1, which is comprised of nodes representing agents and links representing trust relationships between the agents. This trust network includes nine agents: named Ken, Eve, Lee, Joy, Roy, May, Tom, Sue, and Van.

In this trust network, the agent labeled "Sue" wants to determine the trust value of the agent labeled "Van." There are five trust chains from Sue to Van:

Sue – (L) ->May – (M) ->Ken – (H) ->Eve – (D) ->Van
Sue – (L) ->May – (M) ->Roy – (L) ->Lee – (H) ->Van
Sue – (L) ->May – (M) ->Roy – (M) ->Joy – (H) ->Van
Sue – (H) ->Tom – (D) ->Roy – (L) ->Lee – (H) ->Van
Sue – (H) ->Tom – (D) ->Roy – (M) ->Joy – (H) ->Van

If we just consider one level of trust and one level of distrust, then based on the trust transitivity, in the first trust chain, Sue trusts May, May trusts Ken, Ken trusts Eve, and Eve rates Van's domain knowledge "distrust." The second and third trust chains lead to "trust" for Van's domain knowledge. The fourth and fifth trust chains contain a distrust value for recommendation ability: although Sue trusts Tom, Tom does not trust Roy. In general, we consider the presence of a distrust link to break a trust chain, so these two trust chains are discarded.

In our trust model, which has three levels of trust (high, medium, and low) and one level of distrust, the trust transitivity is more complex. When we consider multiple levels of trust, we need to determine which trust chain in the trust network is most reliable. To do this, we introduce a new factor, reliability, as a quantification of the levels of trust in the RTI algorithm.

We define the reliability to be a value between 0 and 1, where a reliability of 1 means that the recommendation is always correct, and a reliability of 0 means that the recommendation is always incorrect. The assignment of quantitative reliability values to qualitative trust values is arbitrary - the only constraints are that trust reliabilities are between 0.5 and 1.0, and distrust reliabilities are between 0.0 and 0.5.We consider that even the most cautious agents will be mistaken occasionally, so we assign a reliability of 0.9 to the high trust value, which means that if A trusts B with high trust value, then A believes that B's recommendations are correct 90% of the time. We assign a reliability of 0.8 to the medium trust value and 0.7 to the low trust value. Finally, similar to the cautious agent, we consider that even a dishonest agent will occasionally end up recommending the correct trust value by mistake. Therefore, we assign a reliability of 0.1 to the distrust value, meaning that if A distrusts B, then A believes that B's recommendations are incorrect 90% of the time. Analysis of the sensitivity of our algorithm to these reliability values will be addressed in future work.

As trust is transferred down a trust chain, the reliability will decrease. For example, in the first trust chain in Fig. 6.1, Sue believes May's recommendations have a reliability of 0.7, May believes Ken's recommendations have a reliability of 0.8, and Ken believes Eve's recommendations have a reliability of 0.9. From the three reliabilities, the aggregated reliability of Eve's recommendation from the point of view of the Sue can be calculated using the Chain Rule for Bayesian Networks (we use the term "aggregated reliability" because the meaning of the probability value derived from the chain rule is not the same as the original meaning of "reliability" given in the previous paragraph):

Table 6.1 The process of combining two trust chains giving the same recommendation

RECs	R1	R2	R3	Validity	Reliability	Unreliability
H	F	T	F	0.392	$0.7 \times 0.8 \times 0.7$	$1-(0.7 \times 0.8 \times 0.7)$
H	F	F	T	0.448	$0.8 \times 0.8 \times 0.7$	$1-(0.8 \times 0.8 \times 0.7)$
H	F	T	T	0.664	$1-(1-(0.7 \times 0.8 \times 0.7))$ $\times (1-(0.8 \times 0.8 \times 0.7))$	$(1-(0.7 \times 0.8 \times 0.7))$ $\times (1-(0.8 \times 0.8 \times 0.7))$

$$P(\text{May}, \text{Ken}, \text{Eve}) = P(\text{Eve}|\text{May}, \text{Ken}) \times P(\text{Ken}|\text{May}) \times P(\text{May})$$

$$= 0.9 \times 0.8 \times 0.7 = 0.504$$

The basic idea of the RTI algorithm is to use the aggregated reliabilities to determine the best choice for the inferred trust value.

It is possible that one agent will appear in more than one trust chain, such as the situation with May and Roy in Fig. 6.1 where May trusts Ken and Roy, Roy is trusted by May and Tom, and Roy trusts Lee and Joy. In the first level of the RTI algorithm, we consider that each trust chain is independent. So the reliabilities of May and Roy are considered independently in each trust chain from Sue to Van. Using the Chain Rule for Bayesian Networks, we can calculate the aggregate reliabilities of first three trust chains (the last two trust chains are discarded because they include a distrust trust value for a recommend ability link):

R1 $= 0.9 \times 0.8 \times 0.7 = 0.504$, the trust value for Van is D
R2 $= 0.7 \times 0.8 \times 0.7 = 0.392$, the trust value for Van is H
R3 $= 0.8 \times 0.8 \times 0.7 = 0.448$, the trust value for Van is H

Comparing the aggregated reliabilities of the three trust chains, we find that the first trust chain is most reliable. Therefore, in the first level of the RTI algorithm we would assign the inferred trust value for Van to be D from the first trust chain.

Sometimes more than one trust chain will give the same recommended trust value for the sink agent. In the first level of the RTI algorithm, we calculate each trust chain independently. But if there are two trust chains giving the same recommendation, the reliability of that recommendation being correct can be considered to be higher than the reliabilities of each individual trust chain. So, in the second level of the RTI algorithm, if there is more than one trust chain leading to the same inferred trust value, then we combine those trust chains to get a higher aggregated reliability. In Fig. 6.1, the second and third trust chains give the same recommendation "the trust value for Van is H." We combine these two trust chains to increase the reliability of that recommendation using the noisy-OR model for Bayesian Networks. Table 6.1 shows the process of computing the combined reliability.

By combining the second and third trust chains, we find that the new aggregated reliability of the recommendation "the trust value for Van is H" given by the second level of the RTI algorithm, is 0.664. This is higher than the aggregated reliability of the recommendation "the trust value for Van is D," so using the second level of the RTI algorithm, we choose H for the final inferred trust value for Van.

In the third level of the RTI algorithm, we consider the situation where the same agent appears in more than one trust chain. The source agent should have the same degree of trust in that agent's ability to recommend for each of the different trust chains. So, in the third level, we calculate the inferred trust value of each inner agent (for ability to recommend, not for domain knowledge) appearing in more than one trust chain between the source agent and the sink agent. We then use these inferred trust values to calculate the aggregated reliability of each trust chain as in levels one and two of the RTI algorithm.

For example, in Fig. 6.1, there are two different trust chains leading to Roy, each of which give a different trust value for Roy's ability to recommend: Sue – (L) ->May – (M) ->Roy, and Sue - (H) ->Tom - (D) ->Roy

We get the inferred trust value of Roy's ability to recommend in the same way as we get inferred trust values for domain knowledge, by calculating the reliabilities of the trust recommendations:

From Sue -(L)->May -(M)->Roy, the reliability that the trust value for Roy is M is 0.7

From Sue -(H)->Tom -(D)->Roy, the reliability that the trust value for Roy is D is 0.9

We choose D for the inferred trust value for Roy because the second trust chain is more reliable.

Next, we replace the original trust value for Roy with D in each trust chain:

Sue – (L) ->May – (M) ->Ken – (H) ->Eve – (D) ->Van
Sue – (L) ->May – (D) ->Roy – (L) ->Lee – (H) ->Van
Sue – (L) ->May – (D) ->Roy – (M) ->Joy – (H) ->Van
Sue – (H) ->Tom – (D) ->Roy – (L) ->Lee – (H) ->Van
Sue – (H) ->Tom – (D) ->Roy – (M) ->Joy – (H) ->Van

The last four trust chains are discarded because they include a distrust value for the ability to recommend. So the final inferred trust value for Van is D from the first trust chain. Because the third level uses all available information to infer a single trust value for inner agents that appear in more than one trust chain, we hypothesize that it can improve the accuracy of inferred trust value for the sink agent.

In the case that there is the same number of equally reliable recommending chains telling the source agent to trust and not trust the sink agent, we will consider the inferred trust value to be unknown (U).

We compare our RTI algorithm with a variation of the averaging method used by Golbeck and Hendler in [10]. The averaging method by Golbeck and Hendler used only 0 and 1 as reputation values, where reputation values are equivalent to the trust values in an agent's domain knowledge in our trust model. They average all of the reputation values and round the average to 0 or 1. In other words, the resulting value is either 0 (distrust) or 1 (trust). Our trust model has three trust values (L, M, H), and one distrust value (D). Therefore, we modify the averaging method by Golbeck and Hendler as follows. We assign the unknown value a numeric value of 0, the high trust value a value of 3, the medium trust value a value of 2, the low trust value a value of 1, and the distrust value a value of -2 (corresponding to the average of the three positive trust values). We use the trust values from each final recommender in each trust chain that does not have a distrusted agent in it. Even if multiple trust chains lead to the same final recommender, we just count it once. We round the average of trust values to an integer between -2 and 3. The average values -2 and -1 are considered distrust values, 0 is unknown, 1 is low trust, 2 is medium trust, and 3 is high trust. For the example of the fictional trust network in Fig. 6.1., there are three trust values $(-2, 3, 3)$ from three final recommenders (Eve, Lee and Joy). The rounded average is 1. Therefore, using the averaging method, we would assign the inferred trust value for Van to be L.

Experiments

Both human social networks and networks on the Internet have been shown to exhibit both small-world behavior [1, 18] and scale-free behavior [5, 31]. Because the EKOSS knowledge sharing network is a Web-based social network, it should also exhibit characteristics of both small-world networks and scale-free networks. We have created a small-world scale-free network generation model [16]. The model can be tuned with the following parameters: in degree power law exponent, out degree power law exponent, and average clustering coefficient. The model uses a modification of the algorithm proposed by Newman [26], which can generate disconnected networks. We believe that this results in a more realistic network than growth models, which always result in connected networks. At the initial stages of the growth of the network, the number of links will be small, so it is likely that there will be many disconnected groups of nodes in a Web-based knowledge sharing system. In fact, one of our main interests in studying network models is to determine the conditions whereby the fraction of nodes that are connected exceeds a certain given threshold.

We created several test networks for evaluating the RTI algorithm using values for the tuning parameters taken from studies of actual networks. We set the size of the test networks to be 1,000 agents, which is large enough to show small-world and scale-free characteristics but still small enough for analysis. We set the number of links to be 3,000 or 4,000 to generate sparsely connected and densely connected networks, respectively. We set the clustering coefficient power law exponent to be 1 based on recent findings reported by Dorogovtsev et al. [9]. Most actual scale-free networks have a power law exponent for degree distribution in the range $(2, 3)$ [9]. In order to compare the performance of the RTI algorithm on different kinds of networks, we used two sets of power law exponents for in- and out-degree distributions. One kind of network is intended to represent a Web graph, so we set the in-degree power law exponent to be 2.1 and the out-degree power law exponent to be 2.72 based on the findings of Kumar et al. [22]. The other network is intended to represent social interactions between individuals, so we set both the in-degree power law exponent and the out-degree power law exponent to be 2.1 based on the study of a massive graph of telephone calls by Aiello et al. [2].

Table 6.2 The tuning parameters for four different types of networks

	A	L	CCPE	IDPE	ODPE
Type A	1,000	4,000	1	2.1	2.72
Type B	1,000	4,000	1	2.1	2.1
Type C	1,000	3,000	1	2.1	2.72
Type D	1,000	3,000	1	2.1	2.1

A denotes the number of agents, *L* denotes the number of links, *CCPE* denotes clustering coefficient power law exponent, *IDPE* denotes in degree power law exponent, *ODPE* denotes out degree power law exponent

Fig. 6.2 An example of a small-world scale-free network using the tuning parameters for type C in Table 6.2. Each *node* represents one agent. Each *directed link* indicates that the origin agent knows the destination agent. There are eight small components and one giant component in this network. The *circle blow up* shows one small component of the network. The *square blow up* shows the typical connectivity features of small-world scale free networks, including the presence of a few highly connected hubs and a large number of agents having only one or two links

Using our small-world scale-free network generation model, we created four types of networks. The tuning parameters used to generate each type of network are listed in Table 6.2. Figure 6.2 shows one example of a type C network. Figure 6.3 shows the distributions of in-degrees, out-degrees, and clustering coefficients for the network in Fig. 6.2.

After generating a small-world scale-free network, we add trust information. In order to calculate the accuracy of the inferred trust value, we need know the actual trust value of each agent. So, we first randomly assign an actual trust value to each agent according to a prescribed distribution. We evaluated the performance of the RTI algorithm for six different distributions of trust values as shown in Table 6.3.

Next, we assign the trust information to each link in the network. Because the network structure is determined by the small-world scale-free network generation model, we know which agents are known directly by each agent in the network. Our generation model creates directed links, so even if agent *A* knows agent *B*, it is possible that agent *B* does not know agent *A*. We believe that this is more realistic than requiring that all links be bidirectional. Each link must be assigned a trust value that is the value believed to be correct for the destination agent by the origin

Fig. 6.3 The distributions of in-degrees, out-degrees, and clustering coefficients for the small-world scale-free network shown in Fig. 6.2. The *x*-axis is the number of nodes having a particular coefficient. The "*r*" is the measured power law exponent for each distribution. This plot confirms that the generated network shown in Fig. 6.2 has an in-degree power law exponent of 2.1, an out-degree power law exponent of 2.72, and a clustering coefficient power law exponent of 1

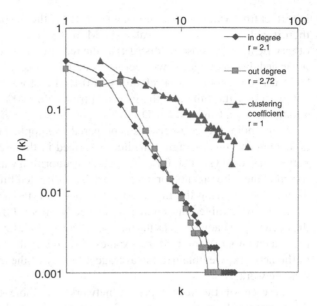

Table 6.3 The numbers of agents having each level of trust in the six cases studied

		Numbers of each level of trust		
		Trust		
Cases	Distrust	High	Medium	Low
1	0	330	340	330
2	100	300	300	300
3	200	260	280	260
4	300	230	240	230
5	400	200	200	200
6	500	160	180	160

agent. If the origin agent has a high actual reliability, it should have a high chance of believing the correct trust value for the destination agent.

We have assumed that an origin agent with a reliability of 0.9 will choose the correct trust value to believe for the destination agent 90% of the time. If the origin agent chooses the wrong trust value, it will assign one of the other trust values with equal probability to the link with the destination agent. Therefore, for network links with origin agents having a high trust level, we assign the correct value 90% of the time and a random value chosen from the remaining trust values 10% of the time. Similarly, if the origin agent has a medium trust level, we assign the correct trust value for links beginning at that agent 80% of the time and a randomly chosen incorrect trust value 20% of the time, and if the origin agent has a low trust level, we assign the correct value 70% of the time and the incorrect value 30% of the time. Finally, if the origin agent has a trust level of "distrust," then it is a dishonest agent and will try to disrupt the trust network by choosing an incorrect trust value for the destination agent to communicate to the agents asking it for a recommendation. The incorrect trust value is chosen using the rule "If the destination agent is "distrust," then it will choose one trust value (H, M, or L) randomly as the recommendation, otherwise it will choose D (distrust) as the recommendation." However, even a well informed dishonest agent will get it wrong on occasion, so we have assumed that "distrust" corresponds to a reliability of 0.1. Therefore, we assign the correct trust value 10% of the time and the incorrect trust value 90% of the time to links from agents having a trust level of D.

At this point the trust network is prepared. We applied the three levels of the RTI algorithm and the averaging method described in the previous section to the trust network as follows. First, for each agent, the algorithm was used to infer trust values for all of the other agents for which there is no directed link from the selected agent. Then, by comparing the inferred trust values with the actual reliabilities for each agent, we determined the number of correctly inferred trust values. We calculated the accuracy of each agent as the number of correctly inferred trust values divided by the total number of inferred trust values. Averaging all the accuracies of the agents in the network, we obtained the average accuracy of the algorithm on the particular trust network.

For each of the four types of networks in Table 6.2 and each of the six distributions of agents in Table 6.3, we first examined the percentage of agents for whom inferred trust values can be calculated using the RTI algorithm and the conventional averaging method with a maximum chain length of six. The conditions for being able to successfully infer a trust value for a sink agent are (1) there must be at least one trust chain to the sink agent that does not include an agent believed by the source agent to have a value of distrust, and (2) the method must give a trust value not equal to "unknown."

One important characteristic of the trust network and trust algorithm is the percentage of agents for whom a given source agent can infer a trust value that is not unknown. We calculate this percentage by dividing the total number of agents for whom a trust value not equal to "unknown" could be inferred by a given source agent using each method by the total number of agents in the network minus the source agent. Figure 6.4 shows the average of the percentages calculated from the multiple simulation runs of 300 agents chosen randomly from the 1,000 agents in each network for each combination of network type and fraction of distrust agents. The results show that for the same fraction of distrust agents, more agent trust values can be inferred on the networks with higher power law exponents for out degree distributions. This is as expected because a network with a higher degree distribution power law exponent has a smaller average path length, which means that more of the agents are within the given path length. Similarly, for the same fraction of distrust agents, more agents can be inferred in the networks with more links because more links means each agent knows more other agents on average, so for a given path length, more agents can be found and their trust values inferred. Finally, the results show that more agents are inferred when there are fewer distrust agents. This is also as expected because all of the methods discard all chains containing an agent believed by the source agent to have a value of distrust, which results in a decrease in connectivity of the network.

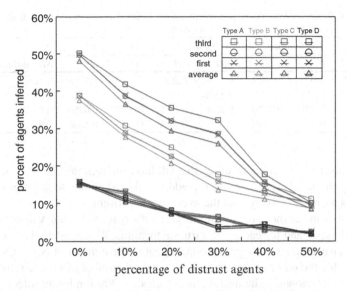

Fig. 6.4 Percentage of agents having inferable trust values using the three levels of the RTI algorithm and the averaging algorithm in the four kinds of networks in Table 6.2 and the six distributions of agents in Table 6.3

Considering each network separately, we find that the third level of the RTI algorithm results in successful inference of trust values for the most agents, followed by the second level and the first level, with the averaging algorithm giving inferred trust values for the fewest agents. The number of agents that can be found is determined by the network connectivity, which is the same for the three levels of the RTI algorithm and the averaging algorithm. Therefore, we can conclude that it is the ability of each method to infer trust values of other agents that are different, the third level being highest and the averaging method being lowest. The averaging method for inferring trust values often results in a value of 0 or "unknown" which is treated as an unsuccessful inference. All levels of the RTI algorithm use the most reliable recommendation as the inferred trust value, so fewer "unknown" values are generated. The first level and the second level are similar, but the second level is slightly higher because it combines recommendations for the same trust value to get higher reliabilities for that recommendation, which results in slightly fewer "unknown" trust values than the first level. The third level has the highest ability to infer trust values because it infers trust values for each inner agent in the trust chains and uses those values instead of the individually recommended trust values for each chain to calculate the inferred trust value for the sink agent, which results in fewer "unknown" trust values than the second level.

Figure 6.4 also shows that the networks with more links and higher out-degree power law exponents result in a greater difference in the performance of the third level of the RTI algorithm and the conventional averaging method (Table 6.4). This is because the more links and higher degree power law exponent the network has,

Table 6.4 The difference in percent of agents inferred between the third level RTI algorithm and the averaging method for each type of network

	The number of distrust agents						
	0	100	200	300	400	500	Max difference
Type A	2.03%	5.37%	6.10%	6.20%	3.80%	1.67%	6.10%
Type B	1.23%	2.97%	4.13%	3.93%	3.87%	2.40%	4.13%
Type C	0.27%	0.87%	0.83%	0.77%	0.30%	0.07%	0.87%
Type D	0.27%	0.93%	0.80%	0.53%	0.60%	0.13%	0.93%

the more trust chains each pair of agents will have on average. The RTI algorithm, particularly the third level, can use the additional trust chains to get more inferred trust values more effectively than the averaging algorithm.

Next, we examine the accuracy of the successfully inferred trust values in each of the network types and for each of the trust algorithms. We calculate the accuracy of the inferred trust values for a given source agent as the number of correctly inferred trust values for the other agents divided by the total number of inferred trust values that are not "unknown." The average accuracies for 300 randomly selected agents of the inferred trust values for agents found in the three levels of the RTI algorithm and the averaging method for each kind of network are shown in Fig. 6.5. In general, the accuracy of the third level is highest, followed in order by the second level, the first level, and the averaging method. The third level of the RTI algorithm gets more accurate inferred trust values because the original trust values for each inner agent in the trust chains between the source agent and the sink agent are replaced with trust values calculated using all of the available information. These calculated trust values are the "best guesses" for the real trust values of the inner agents, so the final inferred trust value for the sink agent can be calculated more accurately. Also, the accuracy of the inferred trust values appears to be robust for networks having up to 40% distrust agents for all algorithms, including the averaging method.

Discussion

All simulation experiments were performed on a PowerEdge 2,900 server with two 1.6 GHZ dual-core Intel® Xeon® CPUs, 2.0 GB main memory, running Fedora 7 (x86_64). We calculated the runtime of each level of the RTI algorithm and the averaging method for each type of network based on multiple simulation runs. For each combination of network type and fraction of distrust agents, we calculated the average runtime for 300 of the 1,000 agents. The results show that the first and second levels of RTI algorithm and the average method have similar runtimes, but the third level of RTI algorithm takes five to ten times longer on average (Table 6.5).

The third level RTI algorithm is a highly accurate but computationally expensive algorithm due to the requirement for massive iterations of communication and

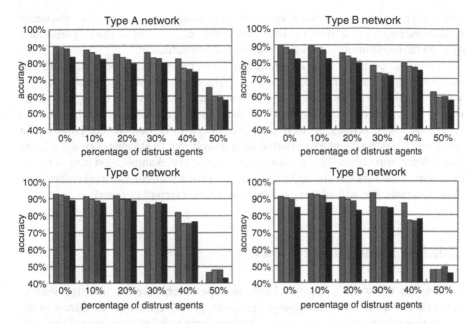

Fig. 6.5 Accuracy of the inferred trust values for agents whose trust values could be inferred in the four kinds of networks and the six percentages of distrust agents. The *red bars* denote the results of the third level of the RTI algorithm. The *green bars* denote the results of the second level of the RTI algorithm. The *blue bars* denote the results of the first level of the RTI algorithm. The *black bars* denote the results of the averaging method

Table 6.5 Runtime for the calculation of a single agent in each level of the RTI algorithm and the averaging method for each type of network. The unit is millisecond

	Third	Second	First	Average	Third/Average
Type A	26,952	5,821	5,820	5,813	5
Type B	43,992	7,065	7,063	7,056	6
Type C	7,250	727	727	725	10
Type D	8,887	1,180	1,180	1,177	8
Average	21,770	3,698	3,697	3,693	6

calculation. Therefore, the third level of the RTI algorithm is likely to be most useful for applications that need to be as accurate as possible and that can afford the additional computational cost. Examples include relatively small networks of highly heterogeneous entities where accurate trust assessment is crucial, such as decentralized systems for identifying knowledge consultants who charge high prices for their services and deal with potentially sensitive information. In those systems, it is essential that the system provide highly accurate recommendations for consultants. Furthermore, the buyer of expensive consultant services is generally willing to wait longer for a more accurate recommendation. If the application does not require high accuracy but needs to be fast, such as a book, film, or restaurant recommending service, then the first level or the second level of the RTI algorithm or even the conventional averaging method may be sufficient.

Another issue about trust recommending systems is privacy protection [15]. In order to achieve higher accuracy, the RTI algorithm transfers the believed trust values together with the trust chain information between all of the agents in the network. Therefore, the RTI algorithm described in this chapter applies only to situations where privacy protection does not need to be considered. However, in some situations, an agent may want to keep its believed trust values private, sharing that information only with the agents that it trusts. For example, you may not want everyone in the office knowing how much you trust a particular coworker, just your closest friends. We will address this issue in the next step of our work.

Conclusion and Future Works

In order to construct a decentralized and open web-based knowledge sharing network where each node is a knowledge source provider, the trustworthiness of the knowledge source must be addressed. We have introduced the concepts of trust and recommendation in our knowledge sharing system, EKOSS. One important issue is the accuracy of the inferred trust value. Previous work on trust in knowledge sharing systems has focused on small-world scale-free networks, reputation-based trust, and trust metrics in a trust network. We described a new approach to handle the issue of accuracy through a reliability-based trust metric. We presented the RTI algorithm as an implementation of this approach. We evaluated the performance of the RTI algorithm compared to a conventional averaging method using simulation analysis on test networks generated with characteristics of both small-world networks and scale-free networks. The results showed that the third level of the RTI algorithm outperformed the second and first levels as well as the conventional averaging method. However, due to the added computational cost of the third level RTI algorithm, care must be taken in deciding what applications would benefit from the full RTI algorithm.

There are two main directions that we intend to pursue in our future work. One direction is to develop mechanisms for protecting the privacy of trust information in the RTI algorithm. The other direction is to improve the performance of the third level RTI algorithm and analyze the sensitivity of the algorithm to various parameters of both the algorithm and the network.

Acknowledgements Support for this work was provided by the Knowledge Failure Database project at the Japan Science and Technology Agency, the Alliance for Global Sustainability Promotion Office at University of Tokyo, and the Office of the President of the University of Tokyo.

References

1. Adamic, L.: The small world web. In: Proceedings of the European Conference on Digital Libraries, (ECDL), Number 1696. Springer, Berlin (1999)
2. Aiello, W., Chung, F., Lu, L.: A random graph model for massive graphs. In: STOC'00, Proceedings of the Thirty-second Annual ACM Symposium on Theory of Computing, Portland, 21–23 May 2000
3. Aroyo, L., Stash, N., Wang, Y., Gorgels, P., Rutledge, L.: CHIP demonstrator: semantics-driven recommendations and museum tour generation. In: Lecture Notes in Computer Science, vol. 4825, pp. 879–886. Springer, Berlin (2007)
4. Artz, D., Gil, Y.: A survey of trust in computer science and the semantic web. J. Web Semant. **5**(2), 58–71 (2007)
5. Barabasi, A., Albert, R., Jeong, H.: Mean-field theory for scale-free random networks. Physica A **272**, 173–187 (1999)
6. Berners-Lee, T., Hendler, J., Lassila, O.: The semantic web. Sci. Am. **2001**, 34–43 (2001)
7. Bonifacio, M., Cuel, R., Mameli, G., Nori, M.: A peer-to-peer architecture for distributed knowledge management. In: Proceedings of the 3rd International Symposium on Multi-Agent Systems, Large Complex Systems, and E-Businesses MALCEB, Erfurt, Germany, 2002
8. Chen, J., Wolfe, S., Wragg, S.: A distributed multi-agent system for collaborative information management and sharing. In: Proceedings of the Ninth International Conference on Information and Knowledge Management (CIKM), McLean, VA, 6–11 Nov 2000
9. Dorogovtsev, S., Goltsev, A., Mendes, J.: Pseudofractal scale-free web. Phys. Rev. E **65**, 066122 (2002) (4 pages)
10. Golbeck, J., Hendler, J.: Accuracy of metrics for inferring trust and reputation in semantic web-based social networks. In: Lecture Notes in Computer Science, vol. 3257, pp. 116–131. Springer, Berlin (2004)
11. Golbeck, J., Parsia, B., Hendler, J.: Trust networks on the semantic web. In: Klusch, M. et al. (eds.) CIA 2003, LNAI 2782, pp. 238–249. Springer, Berlin (2003)
12. Grodzinsky, F.S., Miller, K.W., Wolf, M.J.: Developing artificial agents worthy of trust: "Would you buy a used car from this artificial agent?". Ethic. Inf. Technol. (2010). doi:10.1007/s10676-010-9255-1. Published online 05 Dec 2010
13. Guo, W., Kraines, S.: Inferring trust from recommendations in web-based knowledge sharing systems. In: Advances in Soft Computing – Advances in Intelligent Web Mastering, vol. 43, pp. 148–153. Springer, Hiedelberg (2007)
14. Guo, W., Kraines, S.: Knowledge sharing in multi-agent systems through a trust-recommendation network. Int. J. Knowl. Syst. Sci. **4**(4), 1–11 (2007)
15. Guo, W., Kraines, S.: Recommendation privacy protection in trust-based knowledge sharing network. In: Proceedings of Privacy Enforcement and Accountability with Semantics workshop held at the 6th International Semantic Web Conference, Busan, Nov 2007
16. Guo, W., Kraines, S.B.: A random network generator with finely tunable clustering coefficient. In: Proceedings of 1st International Conference on Computational Aspects of Social Networks, CASoN 2009, Fontainebleau, France, pp. 10–17, 24–17 June 2009. IEEE Computer Society
17. Heath, T., Motta, E.: Revyu.com: a reviewing and rating site for the web of data. In: Lecture Notes in Computer Science, vol. 4825, pp. 895–902. Springer, Berlin (2007)
18. Kleinberg, J.: The small-world phenomenon: an algorithmic perspective. Cornell Computer Science, Technical Report, pp. 99–1776
19. Kraines, S., Batres, B., Kemper, B., Koyama, M., Wolowski, V.: Internet-based integrated environmental assessment, part II: semantic searching based on ontologies and agent systems for knowledge discovery. J. Ind. Ecol. **10**(4), 1–24 (2006)
20. Kraines, S., Batres, B., Koyama, M., Wallace, D., Komiyama, H.: Internet-based collaboration for integrated environmental assessment in industrial ecology – part 1. J. Ind. Ecol. **9**(3), 31–50 (2005)

21. Kraines, S., Guo, W., Kemper, B., Nakamura, Y.: EKOSS: a knowledge-user centered approach to knowledge sharing, discovery, and integration on the semantic web. In: Lecture Notes in Computer Science 4273, vol. 4273, pp. 833–846. Springer, Berlin (2006)
22. Kumar, R., Raghavan, P., Rajagopalan, S., Sivakumar, D., Tomikins, A., Upfal, E.: The web as a graph. In: Proceedings of the Nineteenth ACM SIGMOD-SIGACT- SIGART Symposium on Principles of Database Systems, New York, 15–18 May 2000
23. Massa, P., Avesani, P.: Controversial users demand local trust metrics: an experimental study on epinions.com community. In: Proceedings of the 25th American Association for Artificial Intelligence Conference, Palo Alto, CA (2005)
24. Massa, P., Bhattacharjee, B.: Using trust in recommender systems: an experimental analysis. In: Lecture Notes in Computer Science, vol. 2995, pp. 221–235. Springer, Berlin (2004)
25. Miliard, M.: Wikipediots: who are these devoted, even obsessive contributors to Wikipedia? Salt Lake City Weekly, 1 Mar 2008
26. Newman, M., Watts, D., Strogatz, S.: Random graph models of social networks. Proc. Natl. Acad. Sci. USA (PNAS) **99**, 2566–2572 (2002)
27. Resnick, P., Zeckhauser, R.: Trust among strangers in internet transactions: empirical analysis of eBay's reputation system. In: The Economics of the Internet and E-commerce, Advances in Applied Microeconomics, vol. 11. Elsevier, Amsterdam (2002)
28. Richardson, M., Agrawal, R., Domingos, P.: Trust management for the semantic web. In: Lecture Notes in Computer Science, vol. 2870, pp. 351–368. Springer, Berlin (2003)
29. Sergey, B., Lawrence, P.: The anatomy of a large-scale hypertextual web search engine. Comput. Netw. ISDN Syst. **30**, 107–117 (1998)
30. Singh, S.I., Sinha, S.K.: A new trust model using Hidden Markov Model based mixture of experts. In: Proceedings of the 6th International Conference on Next Generation Web Services Practices, NWeSP 2010, Gwalior, India, pp. 58–63, 23–25 Nov 2010
31. Vazquez, A., Pastor-Satoras, R., Vespignani, A.: Large-scale topological and dynamical properties of the internet. Phys. Rev. E **65**(066130) (2002)

Part II
Security and Applications

Chapter 7
Measurement Methods of User Behavior in Online Social Networks

László Gyarmati* and Tuan Anh Trinh

Abstract The measurements of user behavior in online social networks have recently received special attention from the social, psychological, and networking research communities. Applying different measurement techniques allows to measure diverse facets of human activities. To overview the existing measurement methods and to motivate the development of novel measurement schemes, we review the most prevalent measurement techniques that are used in case of online social networks. Both passive and active methods are considered; the measurement frameworks are compared based on several properties including the details of the datasets and the resource consumption of the methods. In addition, state-of-the-art applications of the measurement ideas are given for illustration purposes.

Introduction

The novel Internet services of the last decade, the so-called Web 2.0 services, caused a paradigmatic change in the Internet ecosystem. Earlier, the prevalent relationship was centralized in case of Web services, i.e., the end users accessed the Web servers. Accordingly, relations among the end users were hard to be expressed explicitly; e-mail messages offered limited capabilities to measure and investigate human interactions, more specifically the social relation of the users.

*This work was done while László Gyarmati was a graduate student at Telecommunications and Media Informatics, Budapest University of Technology and Economics

L. Gyarmati (✉)
Telefonica Research, Plaza de Ernest Lluch i Martín 5, 08019 Barcelona - Spain
e-mail: laszlo@tid.es

T.A. Trinh
Network Economics Group, Department of Telecommunications and Media Informatics,
Budapest University of Technology and Economics, Magyar tudósok körútja 2, Budapest,
H-1117, Hungary
e-mail: trinh@tmit.bme.hu

A. Abraham (ed.), *Computational Social Networks: Security and Privacy*,
DOI 10.1007/978-1-4471-4051-1_7, © Springer-Verlag London 2012

The Web 2.0 services, online social networks in particular, allowed their users to get in touch with other end users; thus, online communities were formed with implicit and explicit relationships. The widespread adoption of online social networks has given an effective way to investigate the social structure of both local and global communities.

In order to investigate and analyze the structure of the societies and the mechanisms within, thoroughly designed measurements have to be carried out to produce the input for these analyses. Several measurement frameworks have been proposed recently; every method has its pros and cons. Moreover, the prerequisites of the measurement are quite diverse; thus, some methods can be applied in case of a specific type of online social networks while the others are useful in other cases.

This chapter presents a structured overview of the measurement frameworks of online social networks. The goal of the chapter is to describe the methods of the measurements, emphasize their preferred properties, and shed light on the drawbacks of the specific methods. The chapter is structured as follows. First, passive measurement techniques are presented in section "Passive Measurement Techniques", where the measurement data is derived by passively collecting information, e.g., by monitoring the data packets of the end users. Section "Active Measurement Techniques" reviews methods where information about user behavior is collected by actively querying the social networks for specific data. In case of both types of measurement techniques, publications are cited where the ideas of the specific measurement frameworks were used. Section "Discussion" discusses and compares the properties of the methods while section "Conclusions" concludes the chapter.

Passive Measurement Techniques

The behavior of the users of online social networks can be measured with passive measurements. In case of passive measurements, the information is derived by observing the communication of the system; there is no need to actively query or extract data either from the server or from the user of the online social networks. In the following, we present two passive measurement frameworks, where the packet flows between the endpoints are monitored by a network equipment (e.g., by a router) or by a proxy server. In addition, we shortly mention a bit odd passive measurement technique when the datasets are obtained from the operators of the online social networks.

Network Monitoring

The most common way to measure the behavior of an online system is to monitor its performance based on network traces. The plain-old network monitoring

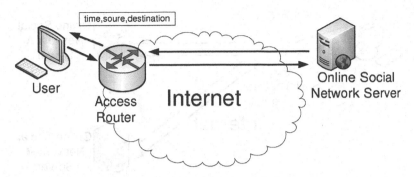

time,soure,destination

User

Access
Router

Internet

Online Social
Network Server

Fig. 7.1 Measuring user behavior based on network monitoring; in this case, the monitoring device is an edge router

measurement framework can be applied in case of online social networks too. The prerequisite of this measurement framework is to have access to network equipments, i.e., to network routers. If the communication between the user and the application server goes through the monitoring router, the users' behavior can be measured in details.

We illustrate the framework of the network monitoring-based measurements in Fig. 7.1. The user requests a page from the application server; the request is sent via the access router of the network. The access router can be used not only to forward the packets to the application server but also to monitor the details of the communication. Analogously, the properties of the response sent by the application server can be measured at the access router. Due to the large traffic volume between the application server and the users, the monitoring access routers store only the descriptors of the flows like time stamps and addresses, the whole packets are not collected.

Golder et al. [17] presented an analysis of interactions among Facebook [9] users based on a large-scale measurement. The measurement was carried out using network equipment; the headers of the communication packets were monitored and stored. The measurement focused on the messages sent by Facebook users to each other. The dataset contains the headers of 326 million messages exchanged by 4.2 million users; information of 26 months is stored in the datasets. The vast majority of the monitored users were university students as Facebook originally started as a service for these students. The analysis of the datasets revealed strong daily and weekly patterns and showed that the communication of the users is clustered mostly based on the universities. Interactions happened almost exclusively among friends; however, only a small fraction of friends sent messages to each others. In addition, the authors showed that the number of messages sent by a user followed a power-law distribution.

Schneider et al. [37] conducted an in-depth analysis of user behavior based on network traces across several online social networks. The clickstream data of the usage were measured across multiple points of the networks of two international Internet service providers. The datasets contained the usage patterns of

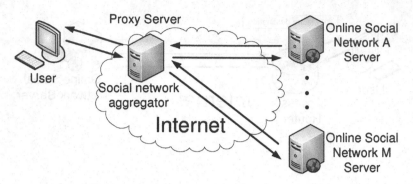

Fig. 7.2 Measuring user behavior using proxy servers

tens of thousands of users of four different online social networks, specifically Facebook [9], Hi5 [20], LinkedIn [24], and StudiVZ [39]. Although the durations of the measurements were limited, e.g., mostly less than 2 days, it is interesting that only a subset of the monitored DSL users actually used any of the social networks, i.e., less than 30% of the subscribers. The authors proposed a procedure to identify the sessions of the users in the clickstream-based datasets. The measurement data showed that users tend to be online for significant amount of time, e.g., more than 30 min. The traffic volumes of online social network sites were mostly driven by photo sharing. In addition, it had been shown that the number of accessed profiles within a session had highly skewed distribution. However, most users only accessed a few profile pages; thus, the friendship graphs may not indicate properly the number of profiles accessed during a session.

Proxy Servers

Measuring user behavior via proxy servers is analogous to the previous method, where the network equipment monitored the flows of the users. In case of proxy servers, the communication between the user and the application server goes through the proxy server; accordingly, even packet level measurements can be carried out. The proxy server often offers additional services to the users, e.g., aggregating the services of several online social networks. Figure 7.2 depicts the proxy server-based measurement framework. The user communicates with the proxy server; its requests are processed by this aggregation point. The proxy server queries data from multiple online social networks via separate connections and combines the received data into a response. Finally, the proxy server sends the response back to the user. As the flows are forwarded throughout the proxy server, the whole behavior of the users can be monitored by placing the measurement tools on the proxy server. The limitation of the method is that only those users can be monitored in this way who connect to the proxy server, i.e., utilize the additional services of the proxy server.

Benevenuto et al. [3] measured the behavior of online social networks' users applying the proxy server-based measurement framework. They monitored the users' traffic at a server of a social network aggregator site, which allows its users to utilize the services of multiple social networks from a single point, specifically Hi5 [20], LinkedIn [24], MySpace [29], and Orkut [33]. The derived datasets contained summarized information of HTTP sessions of more than 37,000 users; the measurement lasted for 12 days. The datasets stored data like user identifiers, IP addresses, URLs, session cookies, and traffic sizes. As we mentioned above, the drawback of this measurement method is that the number of monitored users cannot be controlled, e.g., the derived datasets contained mostly usage patterns of Orkut users (98%). Moreover, the datasets were biased towards the users of social aggregator sites; thus, it might happen that the behaviors of other users differ from the measured ones.

As the datasets stored the details of the HTTP request, e.g., the name of the requested pages, not only the time stamp of the event, an in-depth analysis of users' behavior had been carried out. The authors revealed that more than 90% of user activities are browsing inside the social networks; this behavior can hardly be measured with active measurements as it is not common to display such information on public pages. The measurements provided a ground to develop an accurate model of user behavior in online social networks. Additional user characteristics are revealed such as diurnal usage pattern, heavy-tailed session durations, and intersession times.

Data from Operators

Measurement data may be received from the operator of the online social networks; however, this is rather an exceptional case than a usual one. Although the operators possess detailed datasets regarding the usage patterns of the users, e.g., the logs of the application servers, they usually do not have an intention to share these data with the research community owed to the following reasons. First, the usage characteristics are sensible information, sharing it publicly would cause competitive disadvantages for the operators. Second, the users of the services may not be pleased if their operators make their usage patterns publicly available due to privacy concerns.

One of the exceptions is the work of Chun et al. [6] which presented a comparison of the static social graph and the activity graph of Cyworld [7], a Korean online social network. The operator of Cyworld gave the analyzed datasets to the researchers. The users of Cyworld have their own guestbooks whereto anybody can post messages. Based on the messages written to each others guestbooks, an activity graph can be created. The datasets consisted of the identifier of the user to whose guestbook a message was written, the identifier of the user who posted the entry, and the time stamp when the message was posted. Resulting from the way how the data were obtained, the size of the datasets is remarkable since it contains information about the guestbook entries of 16 million users for more than 2 years. The main findings of the work were that the social interactions are highly reciprocal and that the social and the activity networks have similar characteristics.

Leskovec et al. [23] received and analyzed the activity of the complete user population of the Microsoft Messenger [26] instant-messaging system. The datasets contained the properties of conversations among 240 million users. Based on the datasets, the authors revealed among others that the average distance between two users is 6.6 hops and that communication happened more frequently among users with similar ages, locations, and languages.

Active Measurement Techniques

After presenting the most widely used passive measurement techniques, in this section, we review those methods where the active involvement is necessary to obtain measurement data from online social networks. In case of active measurements, special tools have to be developed to measure the behavior of the users. In the following, we introduce three different active measurement procedures, which (1) utilize the programming interfaces of the online social networks, (2) are integrated into the system throughout the application development platforms of the social networks, and (3) crawl and process the publicly accessible information of the social network sites.

Utilizing Application Programming Interfaces

The operators of online social networks often allow third-party developers to develop custom applications utilizing the data of the social networks. Usually, a subset of the online social network information base is made available by publishing application programming interfaces (APIs). The APIs consist of several methods and functions that can be used to create third-party applications.

The application programming interfaces can be utilized not only for creating profitable applications but also to measure the behavior of the online social networks' users. Throughout the API, data can be gathered about the users; however, only those information is accessible that is made public by the operators. Figure 7.3 illustrates a measurement framework where the capabilities of the API are exploited. The list of callable functions of the APIs is made public; therefore, the measurement application is able to request data from the application server explicitly. The application server may check whether the requesting party has proper permissions to access the required information; afterward, the data are sent back to the monitoring machine. For example, we may query the age of a specific user or the number of its friends. We note that most of the operators constrain the number of API requests for a specific time duration; therefore, this should be considered during the design of the measurement.

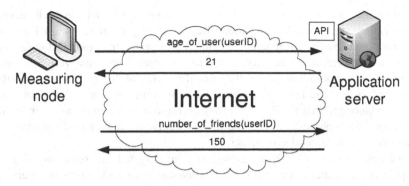

Fig. 7.3 Measuring user behavior via application programming interfaces (APIs)

Utilization of the application programming interfaces of the online social networks is widely used by the research community to measure the behavior on online social networks. Cha et al. [5] investigated the information spreading in social networks, particularly in case of Flickr [10], a photo-sharing site. The users of Flickr can highlight their favorite photos; based on the favorite photos, the dynamics of the information spreading was analyzed. The API of Flickr was utilized to download the list of favorite photos of selected users. Along with the identifier of the favorite photo, a time stamp is also stored by Flickr and made accessible throughout the API; thus, the dynamics of information dissemination can be measured. For example, let us assume that a user marked a photo as favorite. The friends of this user are notified about this when they log into Flickr; thus, they may mark the specific photo as favorite too. If this happens with a larger time stamp, it can be assumed that the information had spread along the social link between the two users. Using this measurement setup, more than 34 million favorite markings were measured. Based on the dataset, it was revealed in a quantitative way that the social graph has a significant impact on the information propagation in online social network.

Mislove et al. [28] exploited the application programming interface of Flickr [10] too. The users of Flickr can form a directed social network, e.g., a user may like the photos of another user. Mislove et al. measured and investigated the social graph of the users; due to the length of the measurement (3 months), the growth of the social network was also measured on a daily basis. To scale the measurement, a cluster of 58 computers was allocated to measure the social graph of Flickr. During the measurement, more than 900,000 users joined Flickr and formed over 9.7 million new links. The measurement showed that users tend to create friendships reciprocally. The growth of the social network had similar characteristics that of preferential attachment; however, the growth model of Barabási and Albert did not fit the dataset entirely. The authors made the datasets publicly available for the research community.

Valafar et al. [43] focused on the users' interactions in case of online social networks, particularly Flickr [10]. The favorite photos of randomly selected Flickr users where queried using the API of Flickr. The scale of the measurement was limited by the fact that only ten queries are responded by Flickr in each second. However, the favorite photos and therefore the activity of more than 4.1 million users were measured in aggregate. Utilizing the information regarding the favorite photos of the users, a fan activity network was created and analyzed. The main findings of the work include that only a small fraction of the users are responsible for the majority of the fan interactions, that only a tiny portion of the photos are marked as favorites, that there is not strong correlation between the number of fans and the age of the photos, and that the photos receive the most fans during the first week after they are uploaded to Flickr.

Krishnamurthy et al. [22] measured and investigated the behavior of Twitter's [42] users. Twitter is a microcontent online social network, where the users can post short, at most 140-character-long messages. In addition, a user can subscribe to follow the posts of other users; thus, a directed social network is formed. The data collection method utilized the API of Twitter; the size of the measurement was limited only by the policy of Twitter, i.e., the number of queries per hours is constrained. One of the datasets was created by querying, and processing the so-called public timeline of Twitter, which shows the last 20 posts. The user identifiers were extracted from these posts; afterward, the partial list of the users being followed by this user was retrieved. Thus, a portion of Twitter's social network can be extracted. Not only the social graph of the users was crawled, but also the activity of the users was measured. The authors downloaded the public timeline of Twitter, extracted the identifiers of the users, and recorded the activity of the users; this process was iteratively conducted for 3 weeks. At the end of the measurement, the usage characteristics of more than 35,000 users were monitored. The datasets revealed three different groups of users based on their activities, namely, broadcasters with numerous followers, acquaintances with almost the same number of followers and followed users, and miscreants who follow significantly more users than the number of followers they have. Users having more followers tend to post updates more often than users with fewer followers. Moreover, national usage patterns are explored based on the datasets, e.g., more friendships were formed by Japanese users.

Galuba et al. [13] also utilized the API of Twitter [42] in order to analyze the information propagation in microblogging services. More than 2.7 million users' posts were measured for 300 h; afterward, the authors investigated the propagation of URLs through posts. The posting frequencies followed a power-low distribution across users and URLs. Based on the datasets, the authors proposed a model that predicts the propagation of information.

Similarly, Ghosh et al. [15] exploited the capabilities of Twitter to gather data about the social graph of the users and examine the effects of the restriction on the maximal number of friends applied by Twitter.

Garg et al. [14] analyzed the evolution of a social network aggregation service called FriendFeed [12]. The analyses are carried out based on datasets, derived by querying the FriendFeed's API. FriendFeed aggregates the services of more than 50 social networks including Twitter [42], Flickr [10], and YouTube [46]. The users of FriendFeed form a directed social graph, which had been explored via the API.

The social graph was measured once in every 5 days based on a breadth-first search method. In total, more than 200,000 users and their connections were measured. In terms of limitations of the measurement, the time granularity of the measurement was 5 days as FriendFeed's API does not return time stamps; thus, the exact time of the link or user creation cannot be queried. The datasets showed that the linear preferential attachment cannot describe the behavior of recently joined members and that common interests increases the probability of creating a new friendship between two users.

Song et al. [38] evaluated their proposed proximity measures based on real-world measurement data of online social networks including Digg [8], LiveJournal [25], and MySpace [29]. In case of the formers, the APIs of the services were used to extract the social graphs in three different times; in aggregate, more than two million connected users were stored in the datasets. In addition, the authors crawled the publicly accessible profile pages of MySpace to extract the social graph; section "Crawling Publicly Accessible Information" will show the idea behind such measurements.

Scellato et al. [36] presented an analysis where the relation of social and geographic distances is addressed based on real-world measurement datasets. Four online social network sites were measured based on their public APIs, namely, BrightKite [4], FourSquare [11], LiveJournal [25], and Twitter [42]. The aggregate number of users whose geographic location had been measured was more than one million.

Service-Specific Applications

Similar to the previous measurement methodology, online social network-specific applications utilize the programming platform of the services. However, these applications are able to measure additional user-specific properties not only those that are accessible throughout the APIs. One may consider measurements based on service specific applications as passive measurements because during the monitoring, there is no need for an active involvement; however, the development of the application requires definitely an active participation of the researchers.

The separate application-based measurement framework is illustrated in Fig. 7.4. The user of the online social network starts to use a third-party application. The user sends its request to the server of the social network (step 1). The server receives this request, processes it, and determines the location of the application server (step 2). Due to privacy and security issues, e.g., to protect users from malicious contents, the online social networks allow only indirect communication between the users and the third-party application servers. Thus, a request is sent to the application server by the server of the social network (step 3). The application-specific tasks are carried out on the application server (step 4). In terms of measurement, the behavior of the users can be measured at this point since the identifiers of the users are forwarded to the server in order to use the application. In practice, the list of the friends can

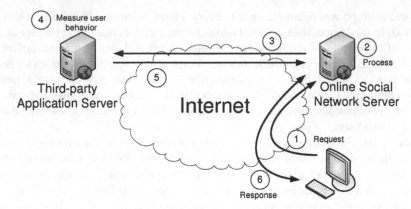

Fig. 7.4 Measuring user behavior via service-specific applications, often developed by a third party

also be utilized and therefore measured by the third-party application. Afterward, a response is sent back to the server of the online social network (step 5). Finally, the required data are transferred to the user (step 6). The advantage of this measurement method is that it focuses on the behavior of the users not exclusively on the structure of the social graphs.

Nazir et al. [30] developed three applications for Facebook [9] to measure the behavior of the users. The three applications had measured the behavior of more the eight million users in total for 3 weeks. The idea of the measurement was similar to the presented; however, the authors were able to capture even the IP addresses of the application users by forcing the users to create a direct HTTP connection to the application server using special HTML tags, namely, iFrames.

The authors identified communities based on the datasets; the members of the communities frequently interact with each other; however, the communication outside the community is limited. Due to the diverse genre of the applications, different kinds of human activities were monitored, e.g., in case of a gaming application, the structures of the communities were weaker. Based on the measurements, it had been shown that the popularity of the applications follows a power-law distribution with an exponential decay. In addition, the datasets of the measurement are made publicly available.

A follow-up work of Nazir et al. [31] presented a more detailed measurement of online social networks focusing on the performance and the workload of Facebook, specifically on the characteristics of delays. Contrary to the former work, the authors carried out not only application but also network-level measurements at the third-party application servers. The network traces were captured with *tcpdump*; the datasets had been made publicly available. The application-level measurement provided a more accurate representation of the load of the application servers.

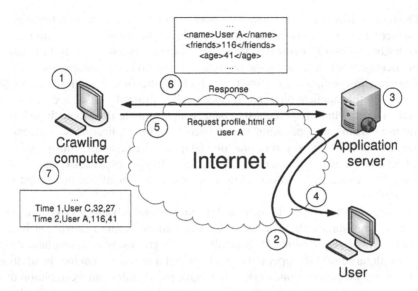

Fig. 7.5 Measuring user behavior by crawling publicly accessible information

Crawling Publicly Accessible Information

Online social networks offer diverse services to their users; the prevalent platform of these services is the World Wide Web. Every social network applies privacy mechanisms, i.e., the visibility of the online social networks' information is controlled. Some data are only accessible for the specific user, who is the owner of this content, others can be shown to the friends of the user or to the members of the online social network. However, online social networks present some information like profile pages publicly, i.e., without any access control. Accordingly, properly designed measurement frameworks are capable to crawl, i.e., iteratively access and download these pages, process the text of the pages, and extract several information about the users of the online social networks. In this way, the behavior of the users can be monitored.

In the following, we review this measurement technique in more details. Figure 7.5 illustrates the idea behind the crawling based online social network measurements. In this measurement framework, three entities are present, namely, the users of the online social network, the application servers, and the machines that crawl the publicly accessible pages on the service. To measure the behavior of the users, a service-specific crawling script has to be deployed in the local machine (step 1). This script knows the exact syntax of the pages that it will monitor. For example, the crawling script processes the profile page of several users; thus, it is acquainted with the structure of the profile page, which is given mostly in HTML. Moreover, the identifiers of the users to be monitored have to be known by the crawling script.

The users utilize the online social networks; they require data from the application server (step 2). The application server produces the required information based on its databases (step 3). In the meantime, the application server records the behavior of the users (step 4). Afterward, the required information is returned to the user.

The crawling scripts can extract a subset of the information stored in the databases of the application servers, specifically, those data that are accessible publicly. The crawling script requests a page, which contains data about the behavior of the user, from the application server (step 5). The application server sends a response back to the monitoring machine (step 6); the response consists of text-based data with the known syntax. Finally, the crawling script processes the received response and extracts the information about the behavior of the monitored user (step 7).

The proposed measurement methodology has several advantages over the usual trace-based measurements. The user behavior can be monitored without having access to network equipments, thus, small research groups, who cannot have cooperation with large network operators, can carry out a measurement too. In addition, based on the proposed framework, whole groups of users can be monitored; if some of the users do not access the OSN through the server where a packet-based measurement is carried out, the behavior of the group cannot be analyzed.

Based on the presented measurement framework, several research groups were able to measure and analyze the behavior of the users of online social networks. Next, we shortly present how the crawling-based framework was used and the key findings of these works.

On the one hand, the crawling framework can be used to measure the static properties of online social networks. In this case, the focus of the measurement is to extract the details of the social graph. Mislove et al. [27] presented the first measurement results of online social networks at a large scale. The structure of multiple online social networks was studied, namely, Flickr [10], YouTube [46], LiveJournal [25], and Orkut [33]. In total, more than 11 million users and their connections were identified. Based on the datasets, properties like power-law, small-world, and scale-freeness were confirmed. Moreover, the authors showed that the in-degrees and the out-degrees of the users have similar characteristics and that the social graphs have strongly connected cores consisting of high-degree nodes. During the measurement, the crawling scripts extracted the identifiers of the friends of the actual user; thus, they iteratively updated their list of user identifiers and extracted the social graphs via a breadth-first search-like mechanism. Due to the size of the measurement, 58 monitoring machines were utilized. The measurement datasets are made publicly available.

Gjoka et al. [16] measured the popularity of online social network applications based on publicly available information. The characteristics of Facebook [9] applications were analyzed based on datasets derived from two sources. Facebook users can install and use several third-party applications; daily statistics of applications' popularity in terms of the number of active users are published by Facebook. Adonomics [1] aggregates the daily statistics and can be queried for earlier usage data; therefore, crawling and processing the data presented at the Adonomics site offers a detailed view about the popularity of Facebook applications. On the other hand, Gjoka et al. developed a crawling tool to measure the popularity of the applications based on the public information presented on the profile pages of the users. In this way, 300,000 users and their applications were measured. It was a challenging task to crawl Facebook profiles as Facebook established several methods to protect its users from automated data mining attempts. Thus, a user can access only its own profile pages, the profile pages of its friends, and the profiles of users located in the same community, e.g., students of the same university. By selecting popular communities and utilizing 20 accounts, which were eventually banned by Facebook, the profiles of significant number of users were processed. The applicability of this measurement framework is limited by the privacy settings of the users; the application usage of a user cannot be measured if the accessibility of its profile page is restricted. The key findings of the work include that the popularity of the applications had a highly skewed distribution (follows power-law), the genres of most popular applications were messaging and friends related services.

On the other hand, the dynamic behavior of the users can also be measured with the crawling-based measurement framework by repeatedly accessing the same information of the users. Torkjazi et al. [41] measured the activity of the users of MySpace [29] in terms of the last logins. More than 360,000 profile pages were downloaded; then the dates of the last logins were extracted from the HTML files. In addition, the status of the profile page, whether it is public or private, and the list of the friends were also obtained. Based on the dataset, it had been derived that a significant portion of the users were either deleted from the system or had not logged in for more than 3 months. Moreover, one third of the user accounts were abandoned shortly after the creation; thus, the users had not found the site's services fascinating enough.

Viswanath et al. [44] compared the social graph and the activity network of Facebook [9] users. Several accounts were created and added to the New Orleans community of Facebook; thus, the profile pages and the information walls of this specific community were crawled and processed. In total, more than 60,000 users were monitored along with their activities and social networks; the anonymized datasets—containing the ids of the owners of the walls, the ids of the users written to the walls, as well as the time stamp of the activity—had been made publicly available. The most interesting findings of the work are that the structure of the activity graph is highly dynamic, i.e., links come and go rapidly; that the volume of activity between two users decreases over time; and that the macroscopic properties of the activity network do not alter regardless of the highly dynamic behavior of the individual activity links. Moreover, the datasets revealed that more than half of the user interactions were owed to the birthday notification service of Facebook.

Similar measurement had been carried out by Wilson et al. [45] who crawled the profile pages of more than ten million Facebook users. Both the social graph and the activity network of the users were investigated based on the measurement datasets.

Gyarmati et al. [18, 19] crawled the public part of users' profile pages, which contained online status information of the users. The online status of users is handled differently by OSNs: some OSNs do not display status information, some

OSNs display it for authorized members (e.g., friends, group members, or logged-in users), while the others handle it publicly if this is allowed by the user. Four OSNs were selected, namely, Bebo [2], MySpace [29], Netlog [32], and Tagged [40], where the status information was publicly available. The sampling time of the measurement had to be selected carefully because of feasibility problems as the time of downloading and processing a single user was not negligible. As the applied measurement method is an active measurement, the resources necessary to conduct the measurement are proportional to the number of monitored users and the sampling time. In total, the online activity of more than 80,000 users were monitored for more than 6 weeks on 1-min basis; more than 500 PlanetLab [34] nodes, a cluster of computers, were involved in the measurements due to scalability reasons. A minor limitation of this measurement framework was that if a user spent less than a minute online, it might not have been identified as an online user. The monitored users of the OSNs were selected randomly; the user search feature of the OSNs was used to get the user identifiers to be monitored. Not only the uptimes of the users, the time duration when the user was online, were extracted from the profiles but also the number of friends, the number of embedded objects (like videos, music, and photos), and the membership history of the users. It was revealed among others that the time spent online by users can be modeled with Weibull distributions that a fraction of users tend to lose interest surprisingly fast soon after subscribing to the service, and that the length of users online sessions power-law characteristics. The measurement datasets were made publicly available.

Jaing et al. [21] presented a large-scale measurement of latent user interaction in case of the Renren [35] social network; the datasets are created by crawling the accessible pages of Renren. A special feature of Renren is that profile pages not only present information about the specific user but also about which users have accessed the profile page recently. Accordingly, the measurement datasets contain the latent interactions of users as well, e.g., browsing the profile pages of other users. In total, the activities of more than 61,000 users were monitored for 90 days. The findings of the research were that latent interactions were more frequent than visible ones, that latent interactions were nonreciprocal, and that the popularity of profile pages was uncorrelated with the frequency of content updates.

Discussion

As we have seen in the former sections, numerous and diverse measurement techniques have been developed in the recent years in order to measure the user behavior in online social networks. In this section, the measurement frameworks are compared; moreover, the applicability of the methods is discussed.

First, the relationships of the research group determine what type of measurement techniques may be used to conduct an online social network measurement. To apply passive measurement frameworks, the research group has to make an agreement with a party whose resources would be utilized during the measurement. In case of network monitoring, the agreement has to be signed by an Internet service provider or the operator of a local network. In both cases, the measurement will be done on the network equipment of another party. Similarly, to measure the user behavior on a proxy server, e.g., on a server of a social network aggregation service, a deal with the operator of the proxy server has to be made. Moreover, datasets can only be received from the operator of online social networks when an agreement is signed. On the contrary, active measurement techniques do not require a permission of another entity; the operators of the online social networks or of the networks would not know about the conducted measurements.

Second, the methods offer different possibilities to control which users to be monitored. If the behavior of the users is measured using network equipment, the user base of the measurement cannot be controlled. All the users who access the online social network via the monitoring network equipment can be monitored; however, the activity of users outside this scope will be missed. Analogously, the monitored users cannot be selected in case of the proxy server-based measurement; the behavior of users who utilize the proxy server can only be measured. The largest user base can be analyzed if the measurement datasets are received by the operators of the online social networks. The application programming interfaces of the social networks allow to query some data about all the users who allow this. A subset of the users and their activities can be observed when a service-specific application is developed and used for measurement purposes. In particular, the behavior of those users can be measured who use the application. The information gathering by crawling public information of the social networks may allow to retrieve data about all the users if the identifiers of the users are known.

Third, a crucial aspect is the scalability of the applied measurement framework, i.e., how does the volume of the used resources alter while increasing the number of monitored users. The resource consumption of network equipment-based measurement depends only slightly on the size of the monitored user base. Until reaching the maximal capacity of the monitoring devices, it is indifferent how many users' activity is monitored. The resource consumption of proxy server-based measurements follows the same characteristic. Naturally, the datasets received from the operators of the online social networks have the best scalability properties. The active measurement frameworks have similar resource consumption characteristics, namely, the required volume of the resources is proportional to the number of the monitored users.

Probably, the details of the measurement dataset describe best the goodness of a framework. From this viewpoint, the best source of data is the operator of the online social network; the datasets store ready-to-use information. The other passive measurements offer also quite detailed activity descriptions as the packets of the users are monitored. In case of these frameworks, the measurement data have to be processed before analyses. The details of the measurements are limited in case of the API-based techniques; only those activities can be monitored that can be queried through the API. The applications developed for the social networks are capable to measure a facet of the user behavior, which is related to the usage of the applications. The details of the crawling-based datasets depend on the status of the

Table 7.1 The properties of the measurement techniques

Property	Network based	Proxy servers	Data from operators	API	Specific applications	Crawling public information
Type	Passive	Passive	Passive	Active	Active	Active
Monitorable users	In the scope of the network equipment	Who utilize the proxy server	All	All	Who use the application	With public informations
Resource consumption	Nearly constant, moderate	Nearly constant, moderate	Low	Proportional to the number of users	Proportional to the number of users	Proportional to the number of users
Details of the datasets	Packet level	Packet level	Most detailed	Limited shared by the API	A facet of behavior	Publicly available information
Publicity of the datasets	Based on agreement	Based on agreement	Usually not	Yes	Yes	Yes
Used in case of	Facebook, Hi5, LinkedIn, StudiVZ	Hi5, LinkedIn, MySpace, Orkut	Cyworld	BrightKite, Digg, Flickr, FourSquare, FriendFeed, LiveJournal, Twitter	Facebook	Bebo, Facebook, Flickr, LiveJournal, MySpace, Netlog, Orkut, Renren, Tagged, YouTube

pages on the online social networks. In case of public pages, any kind of data can be extracted after the page is downloaded. In the contrary, the depth of the dataset is limited if the access of the pages is restricted.

Finally, the measurement techniques have different implications concerning the publicity of the datasets. In general, the datasets of the passive measurement frameworks can only be made available to the research community if the other party of the measurement approves this, e.g., the operator of the network or the service. Moreover, if the data are received directly, the usual procedure is not to make the datasets public.

We summarize the discussed properties, on which the measurement techniques can be compared, in Table 7.1. In addition, the names of the online social networks are given where the specific measurement frameworks were utilized successfully.

Conclusions

In this chapter, we presented a structured overview of measurement techniques applied recently to measure the user behavior in online social networks. In terms of passive measurements, the datasets are either generated using network equipment, e.g., a router or a proxy server, or provided by the operator of the social network. These measurement techniques offer the most detailed datasets; however, in general, an agreement is required to carry out the measurement. Contrarily, active measurement can be made separately, i.e., without involvement of other organizations. The produce of the datasets is harder as additional steps have to be made to extract the required information from the online social networks. Albeit diverse methods are proposed and used across multiple online social networks to measure user behavior, new techniques should be developed in the forthcoming years in order to focus the measurement on the dynamic parts of user behavior and relations not only on the static properties of the social networks.

References

1. Adonomics: http://www.adonomics.com (2007)
2. Bebo: http://www.bebo.com (2005)
3. Benevenuto, F., Rodrigues, T., Cha, M., Almeida, V.: Characterizing user behavior in online social networks. In: ACM SIGCOMM Internet Measurement Conference, pp. 49–62. ACM, New York (2009)
4. BrightKite: http://www.brightkite.com (2007)
5. Cha, M., Mislove, A., Adams, B., Gummadi, K.P.: Characterizing social cascades in Flickr. In: Proceedings of the First Workshop on Online Social Networks – WOSP '08, pp. 13–18. ACM, New York (2008)
6. Chun, H., Kwak, H., Eom, Y.-H., Ahn, Y.-Y., Moon, S., Jeong, H.: Comparison of online social relations in terms of volume vs. interaction : a case study of Cyworld. In: 8th ACM SIGCOMM Conference on Internet Measurement, pp. 57–69. ACM, New York (2008)

7. Cyworld: http://www.cyworld.com (1999)
8. Digg: http://www.digg.com (2004)
9. Facebook: http://www.facebook.com (2004)
10. Flickr: http://www.flickr.com (2004)
11. FourSquare: http://www.foursquare.com (2009)
12. FriendFeed: http://www.friendfeed.com (2007)
13. Galuba, W., Aberer, K., Chakraborty, D., Despotovic, Z., Kellerer, W.: Outtweeting the twitterers-predicting information cascades in microblogs. In: Proceedings of the 3rd Workshop on Online Social Networks, Paris, pp. 1–9. USENIX Association, Boston, MA (USA) (2010)
14. Garg, S., Gupta, T., Carlsson, N., Mahanti, A.: Evolution of an online social aggregation network : an empirical study. In: Proceedings of the 9th ACM SIGCOMM Conference on Internet Measurement – IMC '09, pp. 315–321. ACM, New York, (2009)
15. Ghosh, S., Korlam, G., Ganguly, N.: The effects of restrictions on number of connections in OSNs: a case-study on twitter. In: Proceedings of the 3rd Workshop on Online Social Networks, Paris, pp. 1–9. USENIX Association, Boston, MA (USA) (2010)
16. Gjoka, M., Sirivianos, M., Markopoulou, A., Yang, X.: Poking facebook: characterization of OSN applications. In: Proceedings of the First Workshop on Online Social Networks, pp. 31–36. ACM, New York (2008)
17. Golder, S.A., Wilkinson, D.M., Huberman, B.A.: Rhythms of social interaction: messaging within a massive online network. In: Steinfield, C., Pentland, B.T., Ackerman, M., Contractor, N. (eds.) Communities and Technologies, pp. 41–66. Springer, London (2007)
18. Gyarmati, L., Trinh, T.A.: Characterizing User Groups in Online Social Networks. Volume 5733 of Lecture Notes in Computer Science, pp. 59–68. Springer, Berlin/Heidelberg (2009)
19. Gyarmati, L., Trinh, T.A.: Measuring user behavior in online social networks. IEEE Netw. 24(5), 26–31 (2010)
20. Hi5: http://www.hi5.com (2003)
21. Jiang, J., Wilson, C., Wang, X., Huang, P., Sha, W., Dai, Y., Zhao, B.Y.: Understanding latent interactions in online social networks. In: ACM SIGCOMM Internet Measurement Conference, pp. 369–382. ACM, New York (2010)
22. Krishnamurthy, B., Gill, P., Arlitt, M.: A few chirps about twitter. In: Proceedings of the First Workshop on Online Social Networks, pp. 19–24. ACM, New York (2008)
23. Leskovec, J., Horvitz, E.: Planetary-scale views on a large instant-messaging network. In: Proceeding of the 17th International Conference on World Wide Web – WWW '08, pp. 915–924. ACM, New York (2008)
24. LinkedIn: http://www.linkedin.com (2003)
25. LiveJournal: http://www.livejournal.com (1999)
26. Microsoft Messenger: http://messenger.msn.com (2001)
27. Mislove, A., Marcon, M., Gummadi, K.P., Druschel, P., Bhattacharjee, B.: Measurement and analysis of online social networks. In: Proceedings of the 7th ACM SIGCOMM Conference on Internet Measurement – IMC '07, p. 29. ACM, New York (2007)
28. Mislove, A., Koppula, H.S., Gummadi, K.P., Druschel, P., Bhattacharjee, B.: Growth of the Flickr social network. In: Proceedings of the First Workshop on Online Social Networks, pp. 25–30. ACM, New York (2008)
29. MySpace: http://www.myspace.com (2003)
30. Nazir, A., Raza, S., Chuah, C.-N.: Unveiling facebook: a measurement study of social network based applications. In: ACM SIGCOMM Internet Measurement Conference, pp. 43–56. ACM, New York (2008)
31. Nazir, A., Raza, S., Gupta, D., Chuah, C.-N., Krishnamurthy, B.: Network level footprints of facebook applications. In: Proceedings of the 9th ACM SIGCOMM Conference on Internet Measurement – IMC '09, pp. 63–75. ACM, New York (2009)
32. Netlog: http://www.netlog.com (2003)
33. Orkut: http://www.orkut.com (2004)
34. PlanetLab: http://www.planet-lab.org (2002)
35. Renren: http://www.renren.com (2005)

36. Scellato, S., Mascolo, C., Musolesi, M., Latora, V.: Distance matters: geo-social metrics for online social networks. In: Proceedings of the 3rd Workshop Online Social Networks, Paris, pp. 1–9. USENIX Association, Boston, MA (USA) (2010)
37. Schneider, F., Feldmann, A., Krishnamurthy, B., Willinger, W.: Understanding online social network usage from a network perspective. In: Proceedings of the 9th ACM SIGCOMM conference on Internet Measurement – IMC '09, pp. 35–48. ACM, New York (2009)
38. Song, H.H., Cho, T.W., Dave, V., Zhang, Y., Qiu, L.: Scalable proximity estimation and link prediction in online social networks. In: Proceedings of the 9th ACM SIGCOMM Conference on Internet Measurement – IMC '09, pp. 322–335. ACM, New York (2009)
39. StudiVZ: http://www.studivz.net (2005)
40. Tagged: http://www.tagged.com (2004)
41. Torkjazi, M., Rejaie, R., Willinger, W.: Hot today , gone tomorrow : on the migration of MySpace users. In: Proceedings of the 2nd ACM Workshop on Online Social Networks, pp. 43–48. ACM, New York (2009)
42. Twitter: http://www.twitter.com (2006)
43. Valafar, M., Rejaie, R., Willinger, W.: Beyond friendship graphs: a study of user interactions in Flickr. In: Proceedings of the 2nd ACM Workshop on Online Social Networks, pp. 25–30. ACM, New York (2009)
44. Viswanath, B., Mislove, A., Cha, M., Gummadi, K.P.: On the evolution of user interaction in facebook. In: Proceedings of the 2nd ACM Workshop on Online Social Networks, pp. 37–42. ACM, New York (2009)
45. Wilson, C., Boe, B., Sala, A., Puttaswamy, K.P.N., Zhao, B.Y.: User interactions in social networks and their implications. In: Proceedings of the Fourth ACM European Conference on Computer Systems – EuroSys '09, pp. 205–218. ACM, New York (2009)
46. YouTube: http://www.youtube.com (2005)

Chapter 8
Exploring Influence and Interests Among Users Within Social Networks

Jose Simoes, Julia Kiseleva, Elena Sivogolovko, and Boris Novikov

Abstract The spread of influence among individuals in a social network is one of the fundamental questions in the social sciences. In this chapter we consider the main definitions of influence, which are based on a small set of "snapshot" observations of a social network. The former is particularly useful because large-scale social network data sets are often only available in snapshots or crawls. In our work, considering a rich dataset of user preferences and interactions, we use clustering techniques to study how user interests group together and identify the most popular users within these groups. For this purpose, we focus on multiple dimensions of users-related data, providing a more detailed process model of how influence spreads. In parallel, we study the measurement of influence within the network according to interest dependencies. We validate our analysis using the history of user social interactions on Facebook. Furthermore, this chapter shows how these ideas can be applied in real-world scenarios, namely for recommendation and advertising systems.

Introduction

For more than 20 years we have been living in a society of online social relationships, where people tend to connect and share with others. Despite the fact that we have not yet seen its true utility, we are facing an era of social functionality where social context can be used to personalize multimedia content and services [23].

J. Simoes (✉)
Fraunhofer FOKUS, Kaiserin-Augusta-Allee 31, 10589 Berlin, Germany
e-mail: jose.simoes@fokus.fraunhofer.de

J. Kiseleva • E. Sivogolovko • B. Novikov
St. Petersburg State University, Peterhof Campus, St. Petersburg, Russia
e-mail: julianakiseleva@gmail.com; efecca@gmail.com; borisnov@acm.org

A. Abraham (ed.), *Computational Social Networks: Security and Privacy*,
DOI 10.1007/978-1-4471-4051-1_8, © Springer-Verlag London 2012

These assumptions are explained by the fact that social networks are validated by shared perceptions of worth and maintained by agreement on objectives, social values or even by choice of entertainment. These reciprocal responsibilities and roles that may be altruistic or self-interest based, make network members trust and rely on each other, and provide information that other members might find useful and reliable.

Although the behavior of individuals in online networks can be slightly different from the same individuals interacting in a more traditional social network (reality), it gives us invaluable insights into the people we are communicating with, how often this happens, which groups we are engaged with and what our preferences are. To overcome this discrepancy between online and "offline" networks, data mining techniques can be empowered to approximate both worlds, providing awareness about people's actual behavior. Such techniques typically analyze different types of data to extract subtle patterns that may contain relevant information. The applicability of such studies can be seen in different industries. However, the most relevant are probably marketing and advertising, where identifying customer preferences, desires and needs is a key challenge in the conception and design of products and services. Furthermore, because of the variety of existing marketing strategies, it is important to identify the key peers in a network which will improve the efficiency of such approaches. Nevertheless, these two tasks cannot be seen as separate, as the most influential users for a concrete offering (let us say consumer electronics), are not necessarily the same ones for another (e.g., clothing). In this sense, identifying influence and similarity within different communities of interest is still an unsolved challenge.

To understand how different user contexts can bundle together, we use collective intelligence. Basically, we gather data from a large group of people, which lets us draw statistical conclusions about the group that no individual member would have known by him/herself [22]. Here, by context we mean any user-associated data. In our experiments we worked with a dataset generated from the social network Facebook, which allowed us to collect information about users' groups, pages, events, albums, photos, comments and tags, as well as, personal information. Altogether, this set of contexts provides a great insight into users' preferences and interactions. Then by using different clustering techniques, we show how different user interests correlate, and identify the most popular users within each cluster.

The remainder of this chapter is organized as follows. A concise survey of other initiatives to address calculation of social influence and preferences is covered on section "Related Work". A special focus on the concept and methodology behind this system is presented in section "Methodology". Section "Proof of Concept" introduces some use cases and gives a practical overview of the implemented proof of concept. Then, section "Results and Validation" shows the evaluation methods and results obtained from the tests performed. Finally, section "Conclusions and Future Work" concludes the chapter by outlining future work.

Related Work

Before getting deep into what has been done in these areas, it is important to introduce some basic concepts, terminologies, and definitions that will be used throughout the remaining article. Furthermore, whenever relevant, these will be re-defined within the light of a specific work, application, or context.

Concepts and Definitions

One of the reasons why it is important to explore influence and user preferences within social networks relates to their ability to help understand and predict human behavior. Although this term can have a myriad of definitions, herein, we consider it as an extrapolation of an individual's potential futures. On the basis of an interactive analysis process, a carefully crafted system using artificial intelligence, data mining processes and behavior adaptive features can generate contextualized interactive personal future simulations in the form of interconnected microfuture scenarios, containing, alternative future paths and recommendations based on an individual's personal circumstances and environment [13].

In this sense, being able to collect different types of user-related context became a priority for major mobile and web service/content providers. By user context we mean any kind of information that enhances an individual's awareness of the consequences of his/her existence, by connecting his/her personal and social actions to a wider social, cultural, political, economical, and ecological (environmental) context. Throughout this chapter, we will be dealing mainly with social data (but also personal) and for a better technical comprehension we will call each dimension of this data (context) a feature.

Regarding the term social network, our article will make a distinction from three different perspectives. The first, personal, reflects a specific users own network, composed by him/herself and his first level peers (nodes). A first level peer, denotes that there is a direct connection (edge) between the first user, and a second one. The second type of network will be called global, and refers to all the existing nodes and respective edges in the system. The last, in particular, will refer to a subset of nodes and respective edges. This selection can be the outcome of a clustering operation, or more simply, a specific customization for a special application.

Throughout the chapter, there will be some references to the term "popularity of the user." Although its connotation is easy to follow, the term is ambiguous and therefore needs to be contextualized and redefined according to the situation. Most times, the term relates to popularity, similarity, or influence, which are key topics underlying the understanding and prediction of human behavior. In this sense, it is also important to present a definition for these social forces. Obviously, there are other forces due to confounding factors (e.g., external influence from elements in the environment), which can drive such metrics; nevertheless, they are outside the scope of this work.

A fundamental property of social networks is that people tend to have similar contexts (e.g., interests) to their friends. There are two underlying reasons for this. First, the process of social influence leads people to adopt behaviors exhibited by those they interact with; this effect works in many settings, where new ideas diffuse by word-of-mouth or imitation through a network of people [26]. A second, distinct reason is that people tend to form relationships with others who are already similar to them. This phenomenon, which is often termed selection, has a long history of study in sociology [18], but is outside the scope of our research. The two forces of social influence and selection are both seen in a wide range of social settings: people decide to adopt activities based on the activities of the people they are currently interacting with; and people simultaneously form new interactions as a result of their existing activities [5].

Therefore, influence, in its broad sense relates to the ability of one person performing an action causing his/her contacts to do the same. This can happen, either because more information is provided, or, simply because it increases the value of the action to them. More precisely, given a particular action "A" (e.g., buying a product, joining a community, etc.), an agent who performs "A" is called "active." Consequently, Bob has influence over Alice if Bob performing "A" causes or increases the likelihood that Alice performs "A." In this sense, influence is a directed metric between two nodes. Although there are different types of similarity, the key concept is simple. In social psychology, similarity refers to how closely attitudes, values, interests, and personality match between people. In real systems, it can be seen in the form of opinions, interpersonal styles, amount of inter-communication, demographics, and values [14]. However, generalizing it to a more mathematical concept, it can be seen as a correlation between two or more entities, where its value increases with the number of attributes these have in common. Unlike influence, similarity is an undirected metric, meaning that the value of similarity between two entities is always the same, although it can vary through time. Regarding popularity, it refers to the quality of being well liked or common, or having a high social status. This metric is a property of a single peer and is not associated with any link (edge).

To improve the readability and understanding of the article, all the aforementioned definitions will be further redefined to accommodate the specific requirements of our goals, methodologies, and data. Nevertheless, the following subsection presents previous research work performed on these areas, where the concepts introduced can be easily related to.

Influence, Preferences, and Clustering

Especially over the last 10 years, there has been significant interest in online networks and communities. Indeed, with the rise of social networks, activities within the research and industrial communities expanded significantly. Herein, we will give a brief overview of what has been done before in terms of exploring preferences, interactions, or relationships, how they can be measured over time, and also where they can be applied to real-world applications. Furthermore, we will introduce some of the methodologies, algorithms, and techniques used by other works.

Initially, the work done within sociology and statistics suffered from a lack of data and focused almost exclusively on very small networks, typically in the low tens of individuals. However, there is a long history of empirical work on this topic in sociology [26], through studies of effects such as opinion formation and the diffusion of innovations. In economics [28], theoretical models have been developed to cast social influence as a process by which individuals in a social network tend to coordinate (or anti-coordinate) their decisions. Later, when data started to become available, computer scientists began to develop models for influence in social networks, motivated by applications such as viral marketing. They work on the premise that targeting a few key individuals may lead to strong "word-of-mouth" effects, wherein friends recommend a product to their friends, who in turn recommend it to others, and so forth, creating a cascade of recommendations. In this way, decisions can spread through the network from a small set of initial adopters to a potentially much larger group. Given a probabilistic model for the way in which individuals influence one another, the influence maximization problem consists of determining a set A of k individuals yielding the largest expected cascade. The influence maximization problem was proposed and studied by Domingos and Richardson [6] and Richardson and Domingos [20], who gave heuristics for the problem in a very general descriptive model of influence propagation. Later [11], obtained provable performance guarantees for approximation algorithms in several simple, concrete, but extensively studied models from mathematical sociology. A continuation of the same work [12], showed that the influence maximization problem can be approximated in a very general model (using a greedy algorithm) termed: the decreasing cascade model.

On the basis of the previously mentioned ideas, the work done in [16] developed a scalable algorithm and set of techniques to illustrate the existence of cascades, and to measure their frequencies. In their experiments, they found (1) that most cascades are small, but large bursts can occur, (2) that cascade sizes approximately follow a heavy-tailed distribution, (3) that the frequency of different cascade subgraphs depends on the product type, and (4) that these frequencies do not simply decrease monotonically for denser subgraphs, but rather reflect more subtle features of the domain in which the recommendations are operating. This last finding is particularly relevant to the work we are focusing on.

A slightly controversial study [2], states that "ordinary influencers" are under many circumstances the more cost-effective alternative for cascading behaviors. However, they pointed out a curious fact: that cascading structures and behaviors change according to content or topic, reinstating the importance of understanding the domain being focused upon. Also interesting, is that all the research initiatives focused their work on collective behavior analysis. More recently, the work from [4] considers two of the most fundamental definitions of influence – one based on a small set of "snapshot" observations of a social network and the other based on detailed temporal dynamics – and studies the relationship between these two ways of measuring influence, in particular establishing how to infer the more detailed temporal measure from the more readily observable snapshot measure. In their results, the correspondence between fine-grained ordinal data and the approximation of it made from snapshots is not perfect, but it appears close enough to make useful comparisons. This is particularly important for our research, as we are unable to retrieve all types of data in an ordinal manner. Despite all the advances made in previous work, very little is known on how influence relates to multi-context or multi-feature environments, because most studies were either performed at a theoretical level or within specific applications. Nevertheless, in [5] some techniques are developed for identifying and modeling the interactions between social influence and similarity, using data from online communities where both social interaction and changes in behavior over time can be measured. Their results find clear feedback effects between the two factors, with rising similarity between two individuals serving, in aggregate, as an indicator of future interaction. They also consider the relative value of similarity and social influence in modeling future behavior.

Regarding preferences, research has been mostly focused on user interests and the relationships between each other – similarity. Trying to infer usability of user preferences for recommendation systems, the work developed in [15] examines how similar are interests of users connected by self-defined relationships in the collaborative tagging system Citeulike. Interest similarity was measured by the number of items, metadata and tags users shared between themselves. Their study shows that users connected by social networks exhibit significantly higher similarity on all explored levels (items, metadata, and tags) than nonconnected users. This similarity is the highest for directly connected users and decreases with the increase of distance between users. Although it may seem logical, it is not necessarily true for all types of social networks. Another aspect is that preferences are very restrictive in such systems and rely on user self-defined tags, which are very likely to contain errors. Furthermore, it is very difficult to relate interests between people not using the same language. Focusing on a similar approach, but on a real user social network (Facebook), the research performed by Bhattacharyya et al. [3] developed a model to relate user profile keywords based on their semantic relationship, and define similarity functions to quantify the similarity between a pair of users. Their concept introduced a 'forest model' to categorize keywords across multiple categorization trees and define the notion of distance between keywords. After, it used the keyword distance to define a couple of similarity functions between a pair of users. Then, they analyzed a set of Facebook data according to the model to determine the effect of homophily in online social networks. Although their results were similar to previous initiatives (direct friends share more interests/preferences), they made a striking observation: except for direct friends, similarity between users is approximately equal, irrespective of the topological distance between them. Again, this approach relies on user self-assigned data, which is very prone to errors. Furthermore, only a few percent of the users usually fill their entire profile. Heading towards our work vision is the work developed by Spertus et al. [25], which evaluates user communities (indirect interests) to understand similarity between users. They assert that, just as we can estimate communities similarity through common users, we can estimate users similarity through common community memberships (e.g., user A might be similar to user B because they belong to n of the same communities). Besides being a not so computationally expensive approach, it can even introduce better results as explained in [21].

Another important metric within this area is popularity. Despite its broader concept, within our online society, it is usually associated with people or content (e.g., multimedia, products, services, etc.). The broad distributions of popularity and user activity on many social media sites was demonstrated to arise from simple macroscopic dynamical rules [27]. However, another approach [10] focuses instead on the microscopic dynamics, modeling how individual behavior contributes to content popularity. Although examples from both concepts can be found in the literature, it is rare to find studies that examine the opposite direction, that is, which people are popular among a specific topic, content or in a broader sense, interest. In fact, the existing works usually focus on a single dimension of data or feature. Therefore, it is necessary to introduce new methodologies that allow the exploration of multi-feature settings/environments.

To allow a better understanding of how different types of data (features or dimensions) can be linked together, we can recur to clustering analysis. In short, this process represents the assignment of a set of observations (objects) into subsets (called clusters) so that observations in the same cluster are similar in some sense. An example of such an idea was presented by Levine and Kurzban [17]. Although the study focused on a single dimension (user relationships), it came out with interesting observations. It explained that clusters feature network externalities, which are not possible in sparse networks, thus conferring cascading benefits on the actors (peers or features) contained in those clusters. In this sense, a complex implementation of such an algorithm allows not only clustering of the objects but also the features of the objects. That is, if the data (features) are represented in a data matrix, the rows and columns are clustered simultaneously. One example of such a methodology is introduced by consensus clustering [19]. In conjunction with resampling techniques, it provides a method to represent the consensus across multiple runs of a clustering algorithm (or different algorithms) and assess the stability of the discovered clusters. The method can also be used to represent the consensus over multiple runs of a clustering algorithm with random restart, so as to account for its sensitivity to the initial conditions. Furthermore, it can be seen as a great approach to reconcile clustering information concerning the same data set that comes from different sources [9].

In this section we presented some of the work being done on influence, preferences, popularity, and similarity across social networks. In addition, we focused on some of its strengths and limitations to address the future understanding and prediction of human behavior (by exploring social networks). Grounded on what has been presented, the next section introduces some alternative paths of research by combining some of the aforementioned techniques.

Methodology

After introducing the motivation and some of the studies that have been carried out, this section defines our research goals and the adopted methodology. In addition, it extends previously introduced concepts with analytical definitions.

Requirements and Objectives

With the purpose of understanding and predicting human behavior for improving next generation services, our work defines some goals, requirements, and challenges:

- Discover the most popular users given a particular set of interests. This analysis should be available from both a particular and user personal network perspective.
- Infer relationships between different user contexts. This will help us to understand what kind of user interests might be correlated.
- Understand how user preferences vary and how influence spreads according to time. This relates to the variation of user importance within a previously identified set of interests.
- Highlight the applicability of the previous points, towards an intelligent recommendation system. Show how the mix of influence and similarity (correlated interests) can increase its effectiveness.

On the basis of the aforementioned ideas, the following subsections describe the data model used to verify such conditions. Furthermore, it describes the methodology, the design decisions, and the limitations of our work.

The Data Model

One of the biggest challenges when working with data mining technologies is to find an appropriate dataset that allows scientists to make, or take, significant and meaningful inferences, or conclusions, respectively. The difficulty of such a task is even higher when dealing with datasets obtained from real data, where the latter is usually not captured without errors. In addition, when the information contained within the dataset is related to humans, the sensitivity of the data raises complex privacy protection issues. Therefore, finding a dataset that allows us to study the previously presented (section "Requirements and Objectives") ideas, is practically impossible.

In this sense, we had to collect our own dataset. To accomplish such a task, we used a Facebook application that crawled users personal information, relationships, interactions, and related data. As seen before, with the rise of popularity among

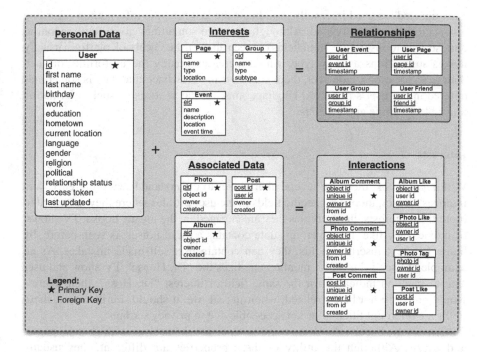

Fig. 8.1 Representation of the data structure used for our dataset

social networks, these tend to contain several pieces of relevant information regarding users. In fact, most of it reflects a very accurate representation of the users' interests, behaviors, and demographics. An informal representation of the retrieved data, as well as, its taxonomical categorization, can be found in Fig. 8.1 (it also gives an informal illustration of the database structure). A more formal representation of the data can be found in the following subsections. All data was collected with strict user consent. Although outside the scope of this work, an architecture and methodology to assure security and protect user privacy concerning this type of data has been proposed here [24].

Personal Data

This type of data is a mere representation of users' demographics, simple preferences, and orientations. This can be particularly useful to extract correlations with interests. For example, it may allow inferring that mostly male users between 18 and 25 are interested in Football. However, its applicability can be further extended to other use-cases. Despite the fact that some of the attributes are directly provided by the user in a free text form (first and last name, work, education, hometown, current location, religion and political orientations), others are standardized by Facebook (id, birthday, language, gender, relationship status, and access token). The field "last updated" is used internally to indicate the last time the information regarding a specific user was refreshed. Although users are sometimes given the freedom to choose what to insert in certain fields (as seen above), the Facebook platform usually makes suggestions as they type, which increases greatly the uniformity of such data (e.g., location). However, there is always the drawback that data is sometimes entered in the user's preferred language, making the analysis of such information unusable for some applications.

Interests

Within Facebook, there are several alternatives to understand users preferences and interests. In fact, there are specific fields in the user profiles where they are asked to input their interests, the activities they are engaged in, the music, books, TV shows, or movies they like. However, this data contains a lot of noise. As seen before, by being free text insertion fields, they can contain user self-made mistakes. As an example, if user John Smith mentions he likes the "Dr. House" TV show and user Maria Angelina indicated for the same field of interest "Dr. Hose," their interest would probably not be correlated, when in real life, it should. Furthermore, these fields are often not filled in or not accessible due to privacy settings.

Conversely, Facebook allows users to associate themselves with groups, pages, and events. Although the utility of these properties are different, they usually establish a relationship between users and their interests. While groups are self-explanatory, where they represent a set of people with a particular interest, concern, or affection, pages are usually used to connect people with their favorite brands, personalities, products, services or inclusively, groups. Events are adopted to organize gatherings, parties, or meetings with users friends, as well as let people in a community know about upcoming events. The main advantage of all these data, is that it is standardized, and therefore, interests are easy to correlate between users. Moreover, each of them contains more precise information about users interests such as location, time, or category (type and subtype). This level of detail can leverage the inference of new relationships not yet established between the different types of user preferences and interests.

Relationships

One data type deriving from the combination of users and their interests, is "relationships." This gives invaluable insight into who likes or engages with what. Furthermore, it gives the relationship between the different users. Because we are analyzing an undirected network (Facebook), the "User Friend" relationship does not differentiate between the fields "user_id" and "friend_id." Moreover, the "timestamp" attribute does not relate to the time this relationship started or took place, but indicates the time it was crawled by our system. Although not optimal for a continuous analysis of data, this value can be interesting for snapshot analysis as explained later in section "Influence Calculation".

Related Data

This kind of data is usually related to user-specific actions. In Facebook, this reflects the pictures and albums that a user owns/creates. At the same time, the content created by the user is stored under posts. This type of action can be an update to their status, a shared link, video or photo, or a comment in a friend's wall (profile). Throughout this chapter, we will define the aforementioned data type as objects (albums, photos, and posts). Although we could get extended semantic information from such data (the content of the photos or posts), currently, the crawling only includes basic information that will help us to find interactions between different users inside these objects.

Interactions

Interactions map "Related Data" with the users themselves. It allows us to track, which users communicate with each other and how they interact. Herein, an analogy can be made with the "relationships" introduced earlier. While the first shows which users are interested in which things, the latter illustrates which users are interested in each other. However, there is a big difference here. As apposed to "relationships," "interactions" give us a directed indication. In fact, although classified above as "Related Data," "Posts" are already a sort of interaction. As before, semantic data could be collected to increase the quality of information (e.g., by knowing the content of the interaction, we could see if it was positive, negative, or neutral). Nevertheless, this is out of the scope of this work.

Architecture and Methodology

With the purpose of enabling the aforementioned objectives and based on the restrictions imposed by the previously presented data model, this subsection introduces the methodology used within our research. Furthermore, it provides a detailed explanation of each of the steps involved in this data mining process. In this sense, as depicted in Fig. 8.2, the system is composed of four main parts:

- *One-Dimensional clustering* (individual features)
- *Multi-dimensional clustering* (several features)
- *Popularity calculation* (based on interactions)
- *Influence calculation* (study how clusters evolve)

For a better understanding of the clustering processes and based on the data model described in section "The Data Model", we sort data types into three main categories. Each of them is then composed of different types of features, which will initially be clustered separately, but after in synergy. *Stable features* relate to users'

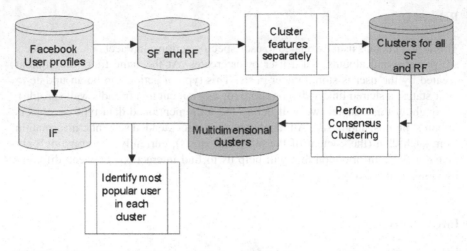

Fig. 8.2 Methodology used in the system that was developed

Table 8.1 Categories of features used for clustering

Stable features	Dynamic features	Interaction features
Home location	Current location	User connections
Gender	Group membership	Common tags
Date of birth (age)	Events attended	Posts
Education history	Pages association	Comments
	Work history	

personal information, which is rarely modified. *Dynamic features* are associated with users' interests. *Interaction features* include the relationships between the different user actions. Table 8.1 details the aforementioned.

One-Dimensional Clustering

As previously mentioned, this research is aimed at analyzing users' behavior in order to predict their interests over time, as well as, identify how these relate between themselves. To accomplish such a task, in a first step, all features are analyzed separately. There are two main reasons why this should be done:

- *Better data understanding.* It is important to have a notion about the structure of the selected features. This is particularly important because data needs to be standardized for later stages of multi-dimensional clustering. For this purpose, we consider text and numbers as valid entries. In addition, it is important to assess whether or not it makes sense to cluster a specific feature. For data types such as "gender," where only two values are expected, categorization may be more appropriate (as it is less expensive), where data is assigned to previously known categories (e.g., gender can be *male* or *female*). Conversely, for features like "age," "group," or "page membership," clustering is necessary.

- *Prepare features for multi-clustering.* On the basis of the outcome of each "one-dimensional" clustering process, data (cluster structures) can be uniformly used as input for the multi-clustering process. In other words, for each user feature vector, instead of using the actual feature value, we use the identifier of the cluster they belong to.

As an example, consider V_a and V_b, to be feature vectors before and after "one-dimensional" clustering, respectively.

V_a = (home location = "Lisbon, Portugal", gender = "female", age = "25", education = "Cornell University", current location = "New York, USA", groups = "Cosmopolitan magazine and MTV")

V_b = (home location = "0, 0, 0, 0, 1", gender = "1", age = "0, 0, 1, 0, 0, 0", education = "1, 0, 0, 0, 0, 0, 0", current location = "0, 1, 0, 0, 0, 0, 0", groups = "0, 1, 1, 0, 0, 0, 0")

From the previous example, it is easy to understand the utility of the standardization process and consequent decision of using independent clustering for each feature. This stage is applied to both "Stable" and "Dynamic" feature categories. Only "gender" is excluded from this operation, as it is categorized using the values "1" and "0," to identify "male" and "female," respectively.

Regarding which clustering technique to apply, we opted for a density-based algorithm, DBScan [8]. One of the reasons for this decision relates to the fact that this technique allows us to discover clusters with arbitrary shape, and still achieve good efficiency. Furthermore, it does not require the specification of the desired number of clusters as an input parameter. As this method depends on a distance function to perform clustering, we opted for Euclidian distance when the features were numbers and Manhattan distance otherwise (for text). Therefore, by varying some of the parameters (e.g., epsilon, minPts) used as input for the algorithm, we can "control" (influence) the way clusters are created (e.g., number of clusters, accuracy, etc.). At the end of this process, the system will obtain cluster structures for each feature and apply their feature vector as illustrated by V_b.

Multi-dimensional Clustering

When all one-dimensional feature vectors are available, we need to apply a specific technique to transform different cluster structures (each coming from its own feature) into a unified one. In this step, we use the Consensus clustering [19] methodology, previously described in section "Influence, Preferences, and Clustering". When this process finishes, the system produces clusters of mixed features, resulting in combinations of demographics and interests. This happens because some features relate to user demographics (e.g., age, location, and gender), while others to their interests (e.g., groups, events, and pages). To illustrate this step, Fig. 8.3 exemplifies how single feature cluster structures are transformed into a single cluster structure.

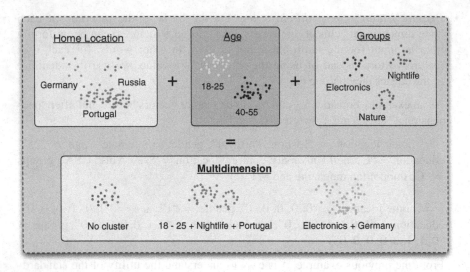

Fig. 8.3 Exemplification of how the multi-clustering process works

As a result, the final cluster structure, allows an understanding of what kind of features and how their specific attributes can cluster together. In the example given by Fig. 8.3, it is possible to see a correlation in users between 18 and 25, living in Portugal with an interest in nightlife. Similarly, users born in Germany are more likely to be interested in technology. It is, however, important to notice that not all users born in Germany will like technology. However, the ones included in the cluster are likely to. Lastly, it is necessary to mention that the clustering structures in the upper part of the figure relate to features, while the multi-dimensional structure refers to users.

Popularity Calculation

Once we have a comprehension of which interests and demographics group together, it is important to identify the key users within these clusters. Although the term popularity can have different meanings, its connotation is usually associated with influence. In this sense, we define popularity as a measurement of user importance within a cluster or a network (depending on the perspective), where importance is related to the number of interactions between the peers inside the cluster. Herein we use the term interaction to classify all activities that involve some sort of reciprocity between two users. In our case we consider: common photos (users tagged together), common friends (connections), comments or posts directed to the user being analyzed. Consequently, the popularity of a user u inside a cluster j, is defined by Eq. 8.1,

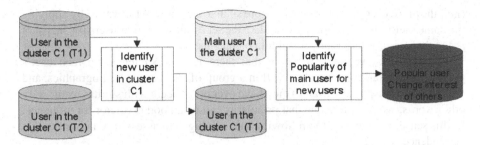

Fig. 8.4 Case 1: how popularity affects influence within a cluster, through time

$$P(u_j) = \sum_{i=0}^{T} \lambda_i \times \frac{n_{i,u}}{L_i} \quad \text{with} \quad L_i = \sum_{a=0}^{S} n_{i,a} \quad \text{and} \quad \sum_{0}^{T} \lambda_i = 1 \quad (8.1)$$

where i indicates an interaction type, $n_{i,u}$ the total number of interactions for user u, $n_{i,a}$ the total number of interactions for user a, T the total number of interactions, S the total number of users in a cluster, a, a user belonging to the cluster, L_i the total number of interactions from type i, and λ_i the weight given to interaction of type i.

Alternatively, the term importance can be associated with user position inside a specific cluster (e.g., a metric based on cluster density and the relative distance between the peers). Another approach could be based on network theory analysis, where one could use different centralities to infer the nodes best located in the network/cluster. This is particularly interesting because different metrics could be used for different types of targeting. Betweenness is one example of a centrality measure that tries to find the central points in a network. However, in some cases, these values may be misleading measures of a node's importance.

Influence Calculation

In order to understand how influence changes through time and how it relates to a user's popularity, we analyze how data changes within a determined time interval. Figure 8.4 depicts this process (for Case 1). It is done in the form of snapshots, where these represent an image of the dataset at a specific point in time, t. In this sense, for each snapshot, the following steps are executed: one-dimensional and multi-dimensional clustering (sections "One-dimensional Clustering" and "Multi-dimensional Clustering", respectively), and consequent popularity calculation for each of the clusters identified. The set of most popular users in cluster j, at a time t will be denominated as $P_{t,j}$. To proceed with influence calculations, we need to identify how the user's popularity changed in time. Therefore, the first thing to be done is to make sure we can map the clusters from snapshot t_1 and t_2. As the resulting clusters contain users, we use this as a criteria to verify the similarity (i.e., the more users in common, the more similar they are). Afterwards, by applying the same methods as before, we calculate the set of most popular users for snapshot t_2. At this point we are ready to calculate influence.

In our work, we want to show that there is a dependence between user's popularity (explanatory variable) within a group of interests or demographics, and the influence (response variable) they have over other peers with similar features. In other words, we want to show that popularity can be a good predictor for influence. In this sense, we propose the following methodology[1] to assess whether or not this dependence exists:

1. *New users in the cluster:* for each cluster, identify who are the new users (not existing in t_1 but present in t_2). Then, for each new user, we need to compare the number of recent interactions (i.e., that occurred between t_1 and t_2) with all the other peers in the cluster. If the number of observed interactions is significantly bigger between the new users and the most popular users in t_2, than with the remaining users in the cluster, and this tendency is verified across the overall cluster structure (result of the multi-dimensional clustering operation), we can prove this dependency. Therefore, dependency is given by Eq. 8.2, where, $n_{r,u}$ is the number of interactions between the new user r and another user u and $L_{r,a}$ the total number of interactions between the new user and all the other users in the cluster.

$$D_{r,u} = \frac{n_{r,u}}{L_{r,a}} \quad \text{with} \quad L_{r,a} = \sum_{a=0}^{S} n_{r,a} \tag{8.2}$$

2. *Users no longer in the cluster:* if a user used to belong to a cluster in t_1, but it no longer does in t_2, then it is important to understand what happened. Did the user join a new cluster? If yes, repeat the methodology presented in (1). If not (meaning that it does not belong to any cluster), check if some of the users belonging to P_{t1} are no longer in P_{t2}. Again, if yes, repeat step (1) and check if the dependency between these is higher than the remaining users.

3. *Others:* the list of tests could continue, but instead of focusing on a test definition, which would evidence the observation (of how popularity can be used as a predictor for influence), we give some more examples of the situations that could be explored.

   (a) Evaluate if users follow popular users from one cluster to another over time (for this we need more snapshots of the data).
   (b) Investigate if a cluster disappeared. In this case, it would be interesting to note if the most popular users in t_1 are still popular in t_2 but in another cluster. In addition, see how many of the remaining users followed this behavior. This would show that popular users are capable of shifting user interests.

---

[1]Because of time constraints, in our validation we only considered Case 1.

(c) Check if new clusters where formed. In parallel, understand if the most popular users where previously popular (in t_0 or t_1) in any other cluster. This will show that besides the known influence types, popular users are also capable of setting trends or groups of interest.

As we can see, independently from the observation in question, we always use the same metric (dependence) to assert influence. The only thing that changes is the way data is analyzed. Although it is widely known that metrics like correlation or dependence do not necessarily imply causation, it increases the degree of certainty in such belief. Furthermore, if it is possible to prove a dependency in all of the aforementioned methods (from 1 to 3), the likelihood that popularity can be used to infer influence, is higher.

Proof of Concept

While the previous sections enabled the understanding of the concepts being proposed, it is not yet clear how these ideas could be applied into the real world. In this sense, in here, we introduce a concrete use-case, the settings under which the analysis was performed, the data collected for this exercise, as well as, the limitations of our experiments.

Use-Case: Intelligent Recommendation

Advertising is definitely one of the most successful revenue models today. In fact, due to its preponderance, it is one of the services that evolved most in the last few years. Today, most products or services are very well described and from a digital standpoint, this information is usually presented in a standardized way in any metadata format. Consequently, if there is a way to technically match advertising with users' profile information, interests and affiliations, it is possible to improve targeting accuracy and user satisfaction. Nevertheless, this information alone is not very useful. A user may like sports but that does not mean he/she is interested in receiving advertising about it. Therefore, the main change must occur in the way advertising is perceived by the end user. What if we could shape it into a recommendation enhanced with the word-of-mouth effect?

Indeed, online social networks provide most of the required data to make this vision a reality. As explained earlier, within social networks there are a couple of algorithms that might be preponderant in reasoning new knowledge. Within this context, similarity between users (by matching profiles, affiliations, friends in common, shared media, etc.) can be used as a predictive factor of interest. It is likely that people with similar profiles like the same things. Likewise, analyzing how user interests group together enables marketeers and advertisers to explore new ways of engaging with their customers. Therefore, applying data mining technologies might help to identify what is or are the common denominators between people, communities, or interests and explore this link in future reasoning processes. Lastly, if advertisers can measure the influence users have on each other, they can differentiate and prioritize offers accordingly. Inside social networks this is usually possible to infer based on the amount of interactivity between peers (e.g., number of comments on a wall, photos or groups and participation in similar events) and the number of shared multimedia objects (e.g., photos, videos, and links). This is particularly relevant if these influencers can be further segmented into different categories of preferences. Furthermore, when combining this data with external sources of context information, the advertising experience can be revolutionized. Advertisements (ads) are no longer limited to static demographic information. Instead, it would be possible to dynamically target users according to external context information such as weather, location, traffic, devices, influence among his peers, or other reasoned data. In addition, this information could be delivered in a personalized and adapted way (if the multimedia content is available in such a format), as it is possible to know at each moment what type of devices the user has currently enabled.

Therefore, advertising and marketing should shift their approaches towards intelligent recommendations, where these should only occur when user-predicted needs, intents, or desires match a specific advertising offer (I am hungry vs. I offer food).

Other Applications

By using attributes such as influence, popularity, and similarity derived from Social Network Analysis (SNA), we may address one of the biggest concerns of major companies worldwide, reduce churn and increase sales. This is particularly important as even a small reduction in churn can mean big savings, as the cost of retaining a customer is estimated to be only one-fifth that of acquiring one. And these customers could ultimately help decrease the churn within their own social circles. Additional marketing opportunities can even be derived from SNA for broadening the scope of existing customers by identifying cross-sell and up-sell opportunities. The social status and position of key individuals in a network can have a profound effect on how their cohorts make decisions. Therefore, the ability to quickly and easily target those influential people can trickle scores of additional profit opportunities across and beyond the entire contact circle. In other words, these concepts could be integrated into Customer Relationship Management (CRM) products, to improve the way companies interact with their customers. Alternative applications based on these data are starting to be seen in the following industries: military, banking, insurance, warehousing, and wholesale, among others.

The Prototype

From the aforementioned use-case, by using collaborative filtering techniques, our work contributes with a few features, bringing innovation to both the user and advertiser perspectives.

Users

- Introduces alternative interests, which are correlated with existing ones.
- Allows users to find which of their peers are more similar to them, as well as other peers not yet befriended.
- Shows them how influent they are among their circle of friends and interests.

Advertisers

- Segment users/groups by different sorts of interests.
- Understand how different user interests group together among different types of demographics.
- Identify key influencers within each area of combined interests.
- Visualize how user preferences vary according to influence.

With the purpose of allowing the aforementioned features, we extended the existing functionalities of our old social enabler prototype [23]. In short, it is composed of a PHP Facebook application (http://apps.facebook.com/socialenabler), which collects user data and stores it into a MySQL database. To analyze the data we used WeKa[2] open source machine learning software. To perform the algorithmic operations presented in section "Architecture and Methodology", we used the following library [9]. The logic responsible for the data cleaning and mining process was developed using JAVA. Section "Results and Validation", shows some examples of the outputs produced by our prototype.

The Dataset

As explained earlier, the dataset was collected from the Facebook application and stored according to the data model presented in section "The Data Model". To allow a better understanding of how information changes through time, we consider two different snapshots. The snapshots are incremental; therefore, Snapshot 2 contains all the information contained in Snapshot 1 plus the extra information collected within the interval t between both. In this work, we considered t as a 3 week period.

In both snapshots, we consider the same number of users. In this sense, the only values that will change are the relationships, interests, interactions, and user associated data. Therefore, Table 8.2 shows the total number of the overall user

---

[2]http://www.cs.waikato.ac.nz/ml/weka/

Table 8.2 Total number of overall user interests (snapshot 2)

Users	Groups	Pages	Events
12,346	1,288	2,500	1,053

Table 8.3 User profile completeness of data (relevant data)

Attribute	Valid(#)	Percentage (%)
Birthday	8,432	67.8
Work	3,346	26.9
Education	5,821	46.8
Hometown	4,777	38.4
Current location	3,304	26.6
Language	12,346	100
Gender	10,090	81.1
Religion	54	0.4
Political	49	0.4
Relationship status	5,055	40.6

Table 8.4 Data resume for snapshot 1

Data type	Total(#)	Data type	Total (#)
Album	426	Photo comment	9,756
Photo	10,780	Photo like	4,379
Post	6,025	Photo tag	3,763
Album comment	497		

interests (spread over groups, event, and pages). Conversely, Table 8.3 gives an overview of the completeness of the data associated with the user personal profile.

By analyzing the previous table, it is clear that some of the data may not be statistically relevant if some correlations are to be made. Nevertheless, that is also not the goal of this work, although some conclusions might be drawn. In this sense, for data analysis (clustering) purposes, the following attributes were excluded from the evaluation: "religion" and "political." As for the remaining data types (relationships, interests, interactions, etc.), all data was complete as all fields considered, are mandatory on the Facebook platform. The following subsections show a detailed resume of the data used in our experiments.

Snapshot 1

In order to better understand what data was collected, Table 8.4 provides a resume of the entries associated with each data type for Snapshot 1.

Snapshot 2

Similarly to what was presented for Snapshot 1, Table 8.5 details the total amount of data considered for Snapshot 2. Furthermore, it also shows the total number of different entries – New – in both cardinal and percentage values.

Table 8.5 Data resume for snapshot 2

Data type	Total(#)	New (#)	New (%)
Album	445	19	4.3
Photo	11,179	399	3.6
Post	6,577	522	7.9
Album comment	509	12	2.4
Photo comment	10,017	261	2.6
Photo like	4,599	220	4.8
Photo tag	4,588	825	18.0

Limitations

Throughout the design of the overall experiments, we found a series of difficulties, which in some cases were not possible to solve. To help in understanding the obtained results, in the following subsections, we describe some of the limitations we faced.

Of the Prototype

On the basis of the use-case presented, it was our intent to provide an example of a recommendation system based on our methodology. However, to allow such deployment, it would be necessary to have a list of advertisements that could be classified into the categories/clusters of interest identified by our system. If existing, the recommendation could be made using the methodology proposed in [5], where the modeling of activities (what to advertise) and interactions (who and when to advertise) is highly dependent on correlated interests/preferences, influence and past activities/interactions of both the user and their friends (or influencing peers). Another limitation is that a feedback channel is not available to measure the accuracy of our interests correlation predictions, as well as, the reach of our cascades. Either way, this is an open door for future work.

Of the Dataset

Despite the fact that one of the main strengths of this work is its detailed dataset, this is also where most of the limitations arise. Because of the sensitivity of the data being collected, Facebook is forced to protect the privacy of their users. In this sense, when crawling data there is no way for the system to know, which of the users granted permission to each of the attributes being requested. In addition, most of the data collected is based on a small set of active users (the ones that actually used our application), representing approximately 0.4% of the total number of users. Therefore, the amount of data being collected depends also on the privacy settings between the users themselves. This limitation raises a concern with the data reliability, as the relationships and interactions may not be as accurate as they should be (e.g., user A might not be able to access the entire collection of photo comments from user B). As a consequence, the level of granularity in the information may vary from user to user. As an example, assuming we make the crawl from user A's account, the system can check which friends A has in common with user B, but it is not allowed to get the entire list of user B friend relationships. The same principle applies to other types of data (e.g., other relationships and interactions). This may lead the results to be biased towards the users that installed our application.

As seen in section "Architecture and Methodology", some of the data related to the user personal profile is missing. This might be because of privacy issues, or simply because users do not want to share this information. Even worse, as the users themselves type most of these fields, they may contain misspellings, might be written in different languages, or filled out improperly on purpose. As a consequence, if no correlation (or proper clusters) can be found, these attributes are excluded from the multi-feature (dimension) clustering process. However, the biggest limitation comes from the Facebook platform itself. Because of the number of friends, relationships and interactions that some users possess, together with the complexity of the queries performed by our application, in some cases, the application can only obtain a subset of the results. Moreover, by analyzing the data in snapshots, we are letting our results be dependent on the time window between snapshots. A short window might not be enough to capture a cascade event, while a long one might obfuscate some evolutions (cascades) due to other factors. Another issue relates to the fact that we might not capture the ordinarily of data entries, and therefore miscalculate our predictions. Nevertheless, these problems can be minimized due to successive crawls, which are promptly time stamped by our system. This is only possible because the users allowed the application to make offline queries about their data.

Of the Processing Power and Memory

While performing consensus clustering, we faced a limitation in terms of processing power and memory. While the first would only delay the clustering operation, the memory outage could not be fixed. Therefore, as reducing the number of users would change the expected results, we decided to perform two separate consensus clustering operations. In this sense, features related with interests (e.g., groups, pages, events) and others related to demographics (e.g., age, gender, location) were clustered independently. Still, the results were limited to five clusters per type of features.

Results and Validation

Evaluation Techniques

With no public benchmark available, it is not possible to compare our results with other works in this area. Therefore we created 'gold standards' by ourselves. The following subsections show the methodologies used for both one- and multi-dimensional clustering.

Pooling

In order to estimate the accuracy of the obtained clusters, we used a well-known pooling technique [1]. Consequently, our benchmark consisted of the following operations:

1. Randomly select 10% of clusters from a result.
2. From these 10%, if a cluster has less than ten elements, evaluate all of them. Otherwise, randomly select ten elements plus 10% of the cluster and evaluate it.

The evaluation consists of human monitoring of the obtained results (cluster structures). More concretely, it consists of assigning two types of labels: "true" (1) or "false" (0), which correspond to "it's a right answer" or "it's not a right answer," respectively. Then, we use accuracy as a metric to decide whether the cluster structure is valid or should be discarded from further analysis. Its value is given by Eq. 8.3.

$$\text{Accuracy} = \frac{\text{Num}_{\text{True}}}{\text{Num}_{\text{True}} + \text{Num}_{\text{False}}} \tag{8.3}$$

Therefore, when the accuracy value is above a determined threshold "gold standard," the cluster is considered as valuable or valid.

Davies and Bouldin's Validity Index

Consensus clustering validity can be measured in several ways:

- Use classical validity indexes on data representation in original space
- Use validity indices rely on the agreement between the consensus partition
- Use modified validity indexes on similarity space
- Use statistical indexes based on pair-wise similarity

In our case we can not use the first methodology because we have different original spaces for each single feature cluster structure. Therefore, there is no common original space. Regarding the statistical methodology, it is too expensive due to the enormous size of the dataset. In this sense, we suggest the use of Davies

Table 8.6 Resume of one-dimensional clustering process (snapshot 2)

Dimension	Algorithm	Epsilon	minPoints	Clusters	Accuracy (%)
Age	Euclidian	0.1	5	20	100
Gender	Euclidian	0.1	3	2	100
Language	Euclidian	0.1	7	13	100
City	Manhattan	0.5	15	29	100
Country	Manhattan	0.4	10	26	100
Work	Manhattan	0.1	5	29	100
Education	Manhattan	0.3	44	19	90.3
Relationship	Euclidian	0.1	9	9	100
Group	Manhattan	0.5	3	42	76.5
Page	Manhattan	0.5	3	65	68.7
Event	Manhattan	0.5	3	41	59.4

and Bouldin's validity index in similarity space in order to measure multi-clustering validity. This index is easy to calculate and it produces good results in consensus clustering evaluation [7].

One-Dimensional Clustering

One of the most important procedures for clustering is tuning the input parameters. Because each feature contains different types of data, this task must be performed for every single feature. As a consequence, these parameters will vary the accuracy of each cluster structure. To better understand the obtained results, Table 8.6 shows the distance function and respective parameters used, the total number of clusters, as well as, their accuracy for every single feature (dimension of data). The accuracy of the results was calculated using the methodology described in section "Pooling".

From the following results it is possible to see that some features are more stable than others. Another important aspect is that the number of clusters depends on the initial parameters, and these were sized to prevent too big or small cluster structures, as the first would not allow further consensus clustering (see section "Limitations"), while the last would limit the final multi-dimension clustering results.

Multi-dimensional Clustering

As mentioned in section "Limitations", because of computational and memory limitations, multi-dimensional clustering is performed in two separate classes. The first refers to user demographics, while the second to their interests. Herein, we used Snapshot 2 as the data source for the presented results.

Table 8.7 Resume of the multi-dimensional clustering process

Demographics	Features	Users	Interests	Features	Users
Cluster 1	4	3,137	Cluster 1	2	3,563
Cluster 2	18	941	Cluster 2	2	2,115
Cluster 3	4	1,797	Cluster 3	73	101
Cluster 4	15	3,401	Cluster 4	70	182
Cluster 5	23	623	Cluster 5	149	3,045

Concerning demographics, we decided to use age and relationship status. As demonstrated in Table 8.6, the total number of clusters were 20 and 9, respectively, covering a total of 9,899 users. Regarding interests, we used the features from groups, pages and events, containing 42, 65 and 41 clusters, respectively, resulting in a total of 9,006 users. The parameters used for consensus clustering were: no sampling and Self-Organizing Map (SOM) algorithm with 200 iterations. Table 8.7 resumes the obtained results.

Because of the limitation of five clusters per type of data, it makes no sense to validate these results, as we know beforehand that these would not be satisfactory. However, based on the method described in section "Davies and Bouldin's Validity Index", it would be possible to assert it. Despite the limitations, it is possible to verify some interesting facts. Clusters containing a large amount of users, usually have less features associated with it. These are the less interesting ones, because they do not provide much information about the users. Moreover, the few pieces of information they provide are very generic and therefore less interesting for our use-case (advertising). Conversely, clusters with a smaller amount of users are generally associated with more features, meaning that it is possible to know more about these users, in a more personalized way. In addition, it is possible to see what kind of features (coming from different dimensions) are normally seen together. This can be very interesting for advertisers, as they can not only better contextualize their ads but also understand their customer's behaviors.

As future work, it will be necessary to include all the available features in the clustering process (specially for demographics), to improve the accuracy of the results. Moreover, to overcome the computational limitations, the proposed methodology should be explored within a cloud computing environment.

Popularity

As explained in section "Popularity Calculation", popularity is calculated within a specific cluster to understand which are the most "important" users. Although the method can be applied to one-dimensional clusters, in our work we decided to evaluate the user's impact on a multi-dimensional level. To simplify the interpretation of the results, we separate the analysis of popularity for user demographics and interests. Figures 8.5 and 8.6 represent the aforementioned, respectively. For a better representation, all users with a popularity value of 0 were excluded from

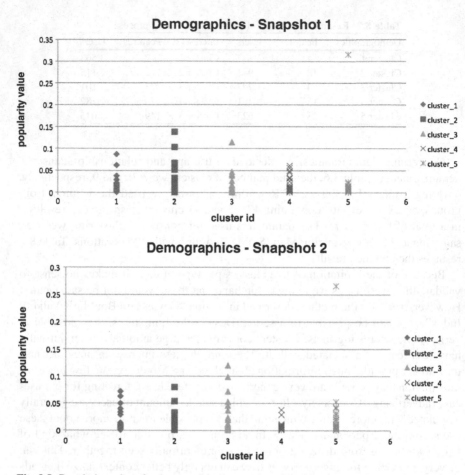

Fig. 8.5 Popularity values for demographics in snapshots 1 and 2

these graphs. Moreover, for both cases, we present snapshot 1 and 2 to facilitate the study. From both figures it is possible to verify that independently of their source, it is possible to identify some users with a significantly higher value of popularity. These, we call leaders.

In order to identify relationships between the data in different snapshots, it is necessary to find a match between clusters over time. These were identified by the maximum number of users in common between both samples. This means that cluster 1 in snapshot 1 does not necessarily correspond to cluster 1 in snapshot 2. Despite the sample not being optimal, the average correlation found between both snapshots was 0.79 for demographics and 0.80 for interests. Furthermore, although not visible here, the leaders are likely to maintain their presence over time, that is, leaders of a cluster in snapshot 1 are more or less the same as the ones in snapshot 2. Despite not having enough data to make assertions, this trend was verified in our results. Depending on the application, the number of users considered as leaders

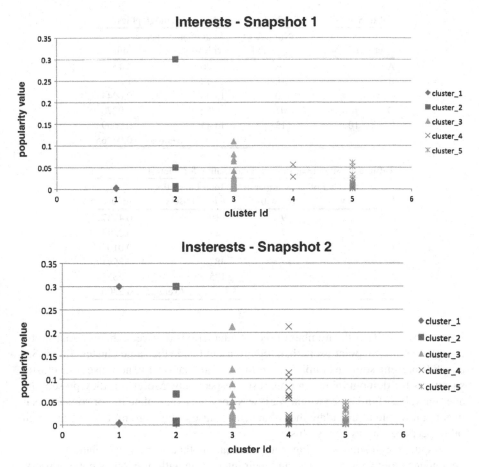

Fig. 8.6 Popularity values for interests in snapshots 1 and 2

may vary. For our experiments, we considered a popularity value of 0.002 as a threshold, meaning that all users with values above this number are considered as leaders. On the basis of these data, it is possible to understand, which peers are more "important" within a specific group of interests or demographics.

In the future, these results should be compared with other strategies to calculate popularity, namely those based on known network analysis metrics, such as, centralities (e.g., degree, betweenness, closeness, etc.), which evaluate relationships between all the peers belonging to one cluster.

Influence

As mentioned in section "Architecture and Methodology", the evaluation of influence will only focus on the analysis of new users joining a previously known cluster.

Table 8.8 Sample of influence calculation for demographics

User	Number of I_{t1} with P_u	Number of I_{t2} with P_u	Total interactions with all users	Influence
A	2	3	20	0.15
B	16	18	18	1
C	39	40	1,645	0.0243
D	706	707	762	0.9278
E	100	115	1,645	0.0699
			Average	0.06465

Table 8.9 Sample of influence calculation for interests

User	Number of I_{t1} with P_u	Number of I_{t2} with P_u	Total interactions with all users	Influence
F	7	9	19	0.4737
G	5	7	27	0.2593
H	0	1	60	0.0167
I	12	13	482	0.2691
J	78	79	135	0.5851
			Average	0.2306

In short, we verify if the number of recent interactions (between the two snapshots) is higher among popular users than regular users inside the same cluster. Tables 8.8 and 8.9 present some examples of influence calculation for new users in cluster structures for demographics and interests, respectively. Moreover, they present the average value of influence whenever it was possible to calculate it. For some users it was not possible to calculate the influence because there were no interactions with other peers belonging to the cluster.

Despite the results showing some indication that there is a relationship (of dependence) between new users and their interaction with previously popular users, this correlation is not that high. However, this value is particularly interesting for demographics. Nevertheless, we cannot forget that these values only account for users, where some sort of interaction occurred, and if we were not to account for this factor the average would be even lower. There are two main reasons for this behavior. The first relates to our initial limitation of five clusters, which obviously does not gather the necessary granularity level. As a consequence, clusters are very big and the number of interactions among their peers is also reduced. The other relates to the amount of features we were able to cluster. It is obvious that age and relationship status alone, aren't good indicators of influence. Nevertheless, when adding location, education, work or language, these results might be completely different (more targeted). Therefore, in the future, by taking advantage of cloud computing or any environment without computational limitations, we intend to explore further combinations of features and play with a higher number of clusters.

Conclusions and Future Work

This chapter proposed a methodology that allows a better understanding on how user related contexts (demographics or interests) group together. Likewise, it introduces a way to measure, which are the most popular users among these groups. Furthermore, it provides some evidences that popularity can be a good predictor for influence within a set of users with similar contexts. More concretely, we have seen that being able to gather user related context from online social networks can be very informative but also very challenging, namely due to privacy issues and technical limitations from the network side (allowing the crawl of big amounts of data). Despite these limitations, we were able to find correlations among user contexts (e.g., which groups are similar) and group them with an average accuracy of 90.4%. Unfortunately, the same was not possible to verify for different groups (consensus clustering), due to a five cluster limitation as expected results. Nevertheless, using these same results, we showed how popularity within a group of users (cluster) can be used to identify leaders. We also noticed that leaders, can be used to identify clusters of user contexts (interests or demographics) across different snapshots (time intervals). However, this may not be truth if the time interval is larger than 1 month. Altogether, by using this methodology, we also introduce a way to compress data and make it available in a very interpretable way, that is, identify relationships between different contexts and at the same time, which users belong to each category. In the future, we need to repeat our calculations with a larger number of snapshots to confirm the trends identified in this chapter. Moreover, it is necessary to overcome some of the limitations covered throughout this chapter, in order to obtain more satisfactory results. In addition, it will be very interesting to see how interests and demographics cluster together. Lastly, this methodology should be benchmarked against other data mining approaches to assess its efficiency.

References

1. Aslam, J.A., Pavlu, V., Savell, R.: A unified model for metasearch, pooling, and system evaluation. In: Proceedings of the Twelfth International Conference on Information and Knowledge Management, CIKM '03, pp. 484–491. ACM, New York (2003)
2. Bakshy, E., Hofman, J., Mason, W., Watts, D.: Everyone's an influencer: quantifying influence on twitter. In: Proceedings of the fourth ACM international conference on Web search and data mining, WSDM '11, pp. 65–74. ACM, New York (2011). 10.1145/1935826.1935845
3. Bhattacharyya, P., Garg, A., Wu, S.: Analysis of user keyword similarity in online social networks, Soc. Netw. Anal. Min. 1(3), 143–158 (2011). 10.1007/s13278-010-0006-4
4. Cosley, D., Huttenlocher, D.P., Kleinberg, J.M., Lan, X., Suri, S.: Sequential influence models in social networks. In: ICWSM, Washington (2010)
5. Crandall, D., Cosley, D., Huttenlocher, D., Kleinberg, J., Suri, S.: Feedback effects between similarity and social influence in online communities. In: Proceedings of the 14th ACM SIGKDD, KDD '08, pp. 160–168. ACM, New York (2008)
6. Domingos, P., Richardson, M.: Mining the network value of customers. In: KDD '01: Proceedings of the Seventh ACM SIGKDD, pp. 57–66. ACM, New York (2001)

7. Duarte, J.M.M., Fred, A.L.N., Lourenço, A., Duarte, F.J.F.: On consensus clustering validation. In: Proceedings of the 2010 Joint IAPR International Conference on Structural, Syntactic, and Statistical Pattern Recognition, SSPR&SPR'10, pp. 385–394. Springer, Berlin/Heidelberg (2010)
8. Ester, M., Kriegel, H.-P., Jörg, S., Xu, X.: A density-based algorithm for discovering clusters in large spatial databases with noise. In: KDD, pp. 226–231. Available at: http://dblp.uni-trier.de (1996)
9. Goder, A., Filkov, V.: Consensus clustering algorithms: comparison and refinement. In: ALENEX, San Francisco, pp. 109–117 (2008)
10. Hogg, T., Lerman, K.: Social dynamics of digg. In: ICWSM, Washington (2010)
11. Kempe, D., Kleinberg, J., Tardos, E.: Maximizing the spread of influence through a social network. In: Proceedings of the 9th ACM SIGKDD, KDD '03, pp. 137–146. ACM, New York (2003)
12. Kempe, D., Kleinberg, J., Tardos, E.: Influential nodes in a diffusion model for social networks. In: ICALP, Lisbon (2005)
13. Koponen, J.: Futureself: emerging digitized life patterns and a personal future simulation system. Futures J. Policy Plann. Futures Stud. **42**(9), 981–994 (2010)
14. Larkey, L.B., Markman, A.B.: Processes of similarity judgment. Cogn. Sci. **29**(6), 1061–1076 (2005)
15. Lee, D.H., Brusilovsky, P.: Social networks and interest similarity: the case of CiteULike. In: Proceedings of the 21st ACM conference on Hypertext and hypermedia, HT '10, pp. 151–156. ACM, New York (2010). 10.1145/1810617.1810643
16. Leskovec, J., Singh, A., Kleinberg, J.: Patterns of influence in a recommendation network. In: Advances in Knowledge Discovery and Data Mining, pp. 380–389. Springer Berlin/Heidelberg (2006). 10.1007/11731139_44
17. Levine, S., Kurzban, R.: Explaining clustering in social networks: towards an evolutionary theory of cascading benefits. Manag. Decis. Econ. **27**, 173–187 (2006)
18. McPherson, M., Smith-Lovin, L., Cook, J.M.: Birds of a feather: homophily in social networks. Ann. Rev. Sociol. **27**(1), 415–444 (2001)
19. Monti, S., Tamayo, P., Mesirov, J., Golub, T.: Consensus clustering: a resampling-based method for class discovery and visualization of gene expression microarray data. Mach. Learn. **52**, 91–118 (2003). 10.1023/A:1023949509487
20. Richardson, M., Domingos, P.: Mining knowledge-sharing sites for viral marketing. In: KDD '02: Proceedings of the Eighth ACM SIGKDD International Conference on Knowledge Discovery and Data Mining, pp. 61–70. ACM, New York (2002)
21. Sarwar, B., Karypis, G., Konstan, J., Reidl, J.: Item-based collaborative filtering recommendation algorithms. In: WWW '01: Proceedings of the 10th International Conference on World Wide Web, pp. 285–295. ACM, New York (2001)
22. Segaran, T.: Programming Collective Intelligence: Building Smart Web 2.0 Applications. O'Reilly, Beijing (2007)
23. Simoes, J., Lampe, S., Magedanz, T.: Enabling next generation multimedia social services. In: IEEE Global Telecommunications Conference, IEEE, Miami (2010)
24. Tselentis, G., Galis, A., Gavras, A., Krco, S., Lotz, V., Simperl, E., Stiller, B., Zahariadis, T.: Towards the future internet, IOS Press, Amsterdam, The Netherlands (2010)
25. Spertus, E., Sahami, M., Buyukkokten, O.: Evaluating similarity measures: a large-scale study in the orkut social network. In: Proceedings of the Eleventh ACM SIGKDD International Conference on Knowledge Discovery in Data Mining, KDD '05, pp. 678–684. ACM, New York (2005)
26. Strang, D., Soule, S.A.: Diffusion in organizations and social movements: from hybrid corn to poison pills. Ann. Rev. Sociol. **24**(1), 265–290 (1998)
27. Wilkinson, D.M.: Strong regularities in online peer production. In: EC '08: Proceedings of the 9th ACM Conference on Electronic Commerce, pp. 302–309. ACM, New York (2008)
28. Young, P.H.: Individual Strategy and Social Structure: An Evolutionary Theory of Institutions. Princeton University Press, Princeton (1998)

Chapter 9
User Cooperation, Virality and Gaming in a Social Mobile Network: The Gedda-Headz Concept

Csaba Varga, Laszlo Blazovics, Hassan Charaf, and Frank H.P. Fitzek

Abstract Social networks and mobile systems are both rapidly developing areas nowadays. In this chapter, we will introduce Gedda-Headz, a novel social mobile gaming concept that brings these two areas together. Gedda-Headz is a social mobile network that mainly focuses on multiplayer mobile gaming. First we will thoroughly discuss how users may cooperate with each other in Gedda-Headz, as cooperation is very important in a mobile environment. Among other benefits, it may help users to use services that would otherwise be unreachable for them, or greatly decrease the energy cost of certain activities. Finally, as virality is very important in social networks, we will describe the viral elements of Gedda-Headz. We will also introduce the Gedda-Headz spreader, a novel method to spread the word about the network, increasing the virality further.

Introduction

In the last few decades, the mobile world has been developing rapidly. At first, establishing and maintaining any kind of wireless connection at all was the main challenge and the focus of research. However, nowadays both the cellular networks (2G and 3G) and short-range communication technologies (e.g. Bluetooth and WLAN) have reached a point, where conveying bits over the air is no longer a problem. Now the main question is what to do with those bits. Current discussions in the mobile world are dominated by terms such as apps, in-app purchase,

C. Varga (✉) • L. Blazovics • H. Charaf
Faculty of Electrical Engineering and Informatics, Budapest University of Technology and Economics, Magyar Tudosok korutja 2, 1117 Budapest, QB-207, Hungary
e-mail: csaba.varga@aut.bme.hu; laszlo.blazovics@aut.bme.hu; hassan@aut.bme.hu

F.H.P. Fitzek
Mobile Device Group, Aalborg University, Niels Jernes Vej 12, 9220, Aalborg, Denmark
e-mail: ff@es.aau.dkl

A. Abraham (ed.), *Computational Social Networks: Security and Privacy*,   207
DOI 10.1007/978-1-4471-4051-1_9, © Springer-Verlag London 2012

in-app advertisements and many more, although many standard communication and embedded problems are still not solved. One of the biggest problems is the energy consumption of the mobile devices for handset producers. The long operational times that users expect are in contrast with the huge number of services running on a phone, draining the batteries. Energy consumption is driven by Moore's law and therefore doubling every 2 years, as discussed many times in [1] and [2], while the energy capacities of batteries is doubling less than once every decade.

Therefore, Fitzek and Katz [1, 2] introduce a novel communication architecture, known as user cooperation. This architecture enables new services and offers a solution to the problems of spectral efficiency [3], low data rates [4] and energy consumption [5] at the same time. The main idea of user cooperation is that the phones communicate with each other using short-range communication technologies (e.g. Bluetooth, or WLAN), while they maintain a connection to the 2G or 3G network. In future systems the 2G and 3G networks may be replaced by WiMAX or LTE. The cooperation among users is not based on pure altruism, each user is expected to behave egoistically. So far cooperative services have focused on scenarios where the pay-off tolerance can be zero. However, in case we assume a larger pay-off tolerance among cooperative users, they can expect a much larger profit in the end. Pay-off tolerance basically means when users would expect something in return for their cooperative help in the past. For example, cooperative video services or download services have a pay-off tolerance of zero as their cooperative gain is achieved in the very same moment. But in other cases, for example in multiplayer games, cooperative help may not pay off right away. Fitzek [6] and Fitzek et al. [7] introduce user cooperation in such games, while [8] shows that combining user cooperation with a social mobile network, the benefits of cooperation can be increased further.

Brosnan et al. [9] discusses an interesting behaviour of monkeys: their pay-off tolerance towards family members is larger towards strangers. This is in line with our daily human experiences. The main challenge now is creating and maintaining trust among mobile devices. One method is to start the cooperation and use the cooperation itself to build up trust while it takes place. It has the advantage of not using any memory, although it may cause inefficient use at the beginning of the cooperative phase. The opposite approach is storing and maintaining a full-blown database of all mobile devices on each phone, which would consume a tremendous amount of memory, need a lot of additional compute time and capacity, resulting in increased energy consumption. Therefore we are looking into the combination of cooperative networks with social mobile networks.

Web-based social networks are spreading rapidly all over the world, and they are becoming a more and more important part of our everyday lives, as it is deeply discussed in [10]. For example, networks like Facebook or MySpace offer their users the possibility to present themselves and get to know other people, thus increasing the importance of virtual friendship. For these networks, it is only a logical step to move into the mobile world, offering their services to mobile users too. There are also social mobile networks that take the mobile aspect into account already, having dramatically growing communities, with the users forming part of a family.

So the assumption is that whenever I meet people of my community, it is more likely that those people will help me. For example, a worldwide social community such as Gedda-Headz will have the possibility for members to help and cooperate with each other. However, before discussing those potentials in detail, we will explain the concept of Gedda-Headz [11] in a nutshell.

The Main Concept of Gedda-Headz

Gedda-Headz targets creating a mobile gaming community combined with social networking and multi-platform support. The most important part of Gedda-Headz is a mobile application which is fully compatible with any mobile platform that supports Java ME with the JSR-82 Bluetooth API (for example, mobile devices from manufacturers like Nokia, Sony Ericsson, Motorola, RIM, Samsung, LG and others), as shown in Fig. 9.1. In order to achieve a large community, Gedda-Headz is also available on the Apple iPhone and iPod Touch and gaming between the two platforms is one of the core features of the system. There are two options available for players to connect to each other. The first is creating a local connection directly between the phones via Bluetooth. The second is connecting to each other over the Internet using wireless technologies such as WiFi, GSM, UMTS, HSDPA, LTE, WiMAX or others.

Fig. 9.1 Gedda-Headz collectibles in front of the cool tin that they are shipped in. Furthermore some cross-platform examples of the games on the iPhone, iPod touch, and Java ME phones

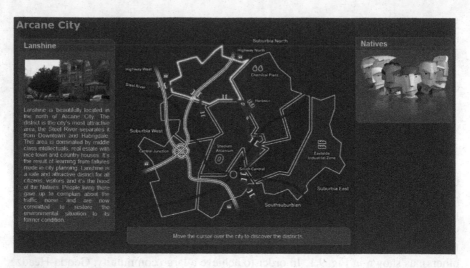

Fig. 9.2 Arcane city showing the districts of the six different clans – currently selected are the natives

The heart of the gaming concept are the so called 'Headz', shown in Fig. 9.1. Every player needs at least one of them to join the gaming community. They are collectible figurines coming in cool designer cans, each can holding three different Headz. Each Head has a metal disc identifier ("dog-tag") attached to it containing the Head's name, clan, abilities and unique code that has to be entered in the mobile application in order to have a virtual copy of the Head living in the app. There is a large variety of Headz available for the gamers: six different clans (located in Arcane City, a virtual place where the gangs live, see Fig. 9.2), each made up of six Headz which means 36 different Headz altogether, each having unique abilities offering unique possibilities and gaming experiences for players. These abilities differ in terms of swiftness, cleverness, and toughness, influencing the mobile games themselves which are available free of charge to members of the community.

Playing games in Gedda-Headz is only part of the big picture: the real goal is to become a respected member of the community. This can be achieved by earning 'respect points' through winning games and reaching different kinds of achievements connected to playing, collecting Headz and being an active member of the community. Users can also make friends using their mobile phones creating real bonds between community members. Security for the users is very important, so friendship queries require confirmation and are available only via Bluetooth.

Figure 9.3 shows the Gedda-Headz communication architecture. Users can play games over Bluetooth as long as they are close to each other (players *A* and *B*). The mobile application stores the respect points earned by playing games and users can upload them later whenever they have Internet access. Users with WiFi or 2G/3G Internet access can connect directly to the Online Arena where they can meet and challenge other players from around the world. For users whose phone does not have a WiFi or 2G/3G flat-rate data tariff, Gedda-Headz offers a PC tool, the so-called

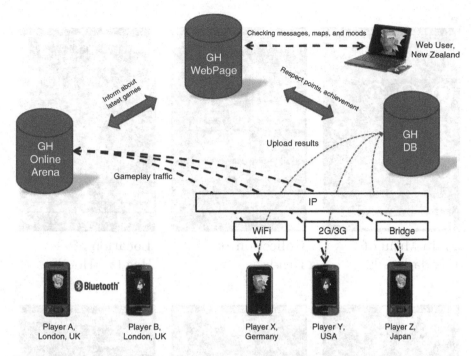

Fig. 9.3 The Gedda-Headz architecture: two users are playing with each other via Bluetooth, three worldwide gamers are playing via the Online Arena and a Web user is checking out the latest results

PC Bridge. The main idea behind this tool is to provide Internet access to the mobile application (and therefore access to the Online Arena) by creating a Bluetooth connection between the mobile phone and the PC then forwarding all traffic between the phone and the Gedda-Headz servers over the fixed Internet connection of the PC. The Online Arena then processes all game requests of each player and acts as a relay between the two participants of each challenge. The latest game results are always sent to a web server which announces them to the community. After they finish playing, users can also upload their scores (respect points) to the Gedda-Headz database.

Gedda-Headz on the Mobiles

The Gedda-Headz mobile application or 'app' is available publicly for Java ME phones with the JSR-82 Bluetooth API and the iPhone/iPod touch devices. This section will describe the main features of the application through the version for iPhones and iPod touches. Figure 9.4a shows the main menu which is designed and optimized for touch screens. The first icon (from top-left) allows the user to manage his collection of Headz (see Fig. 9.4b). The next icon shows the Hood. As given in

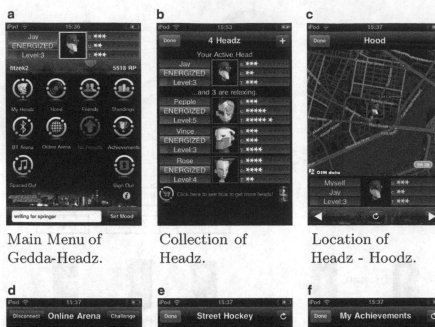

a Main Menu of Gedda-Headz.

b Collection of Headz.

c Location of Headz - Hoodz.

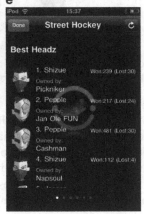

d Online Arena.

e Highscore list of Gedda-Headz.

f User's Achievement List.

Fig. 9.4 Screenshots of the Gedda-Headz application for iPhone and iPod touch. (**a**) Main menu of Gedda-Headz. (**b**) Collection Headz. (**c**) Location of Headz-Hoodz. (**d**) Online Arena. (**e**) Highscore list of Gedda-Headz. (**f**) User's achievement list

Fig. 9.4c the Hood shows a map of the user's vicinity (with the user displayed in the middle) and displays the location of nearby users as well. The user is also displayed on the global *Maps and Moods* web page at the same time. As the users of Gedda-Headz come from all around the globe, location based services are integral parts of the Gedda-Headz concept. Players are represented by their currently active heads on the map. Users are displayed on the map only if they agree to it. To retrieve the

Fig. 9.5 Gedda-Headz Maps and Moods web page with the latest 20 Mood messages

location of the users, the application uses a GPS (or Assisted GPS where available), or calculates the location using access-point information (mainly on iPod touches and iPhones). The local rankings (nearby players with the highest score) and the latest Mood messages are also displayed on the map. Figure 9.4d shows the Online Arena. The player has connected to the Gedda-Headz game server where he or she can play with people from around the world. When the games end, users can upload the respect points they earned to the Gedda-Headz server where the highscore lists (the global rankings as well as the rankings for each game) are updated (Fig. 9.4e) and the user's achievements are recalculated (see Fig. 9.4f).

In Fig. 9.5 the latest 20 Mood messages are displayed together with the location of the associated Headz for parts of Germany, France, Benelux and others. With the Maps and Moods the location of Headz in the world or in your neighbourhood can be derived. This allows users to view the latest Mood messages or the highscore for a given area. It is Gedda-Headz's location service, based on OpenStreetMap [12].

Getting the App to the Users

It is important to make the Gedda-Headz application available for every interested gamer. Depending on their devices, different installation methods are available for the users. The iPhone and iPod touch users have only one choice: download and install the app. from Apple's AppStore. Users with Java ME phones can choose from three options: direct download, PC installation and viral distribution.

Direct download is the most straightforward method. The user has to type 'dl.gedda-headz.mobi' in the web browser of the mobile device. After that, the browser will display the download link. Clicking on this link will start the installation of the application.

The second option is to download the installer of the Gedda-Headz application to a PC and then either send it to the phone directly via Bluetooth or WiFi then run it on the phone, or install the application using phone manufacturers' tools like the Nokia PC Suite. This approach is a bit more complex, but this is necessary for users who have phones without WiFi or 2G/3G flat-rate Internet access (or whose phones have no Internet access at all). This installation method is well known and common among mobile users.

The first two methods are generally available for any mobile (Java) application. However, viral distribution is specific for Gedda-Headz. This concept involves dedicated users downloading the installers of the Gedda-Headz application to their phone then sending one of them to other devices. These users need to have multiple installers, because the Gedda-Headz application is available for different screen sizes and there is a different installer for each size. This means that these users make a great effort to contribute to the community, so they are rewarded with respect points and achievements for spreading the Gedda-Headz application. This method will be discussed in detail later in section "Conventional Methods for Viral Expansion".

The Gedda-Headz Games

Gaming is the main source of respect points for the users, thus the games are the core of the mobile application. Every game is affected by the attributes of the selected Headz playing with each other. For example, in the Street Hockey game, the size of the sewer, the size of the puck and the speed of the can are influenced by the cleverness, toughness and swiftness of both Headz respectively. Every game can be played over Bluetooth, however, that is not entirely true for the Online Arena. Larger and more variable delays caused by communicating over the Internet reduces the available game types. The users' concerns about their data traffic (as discussed in section "The Gedda-Headz User Profile") has to be taken into consideration as well when making a game available to be played in the Online Arena. Below, we will describe the current games in Gedda-Headz in alphabetical order. Furthermore, a screenshot of each game is shown in Fig. 9.6.

AD-Rivals

You play turn-by-turn. Open up two cards, find the pairs. The player who found more pairs wins the game. Be careful, there is a timeout for your turn, but it's not

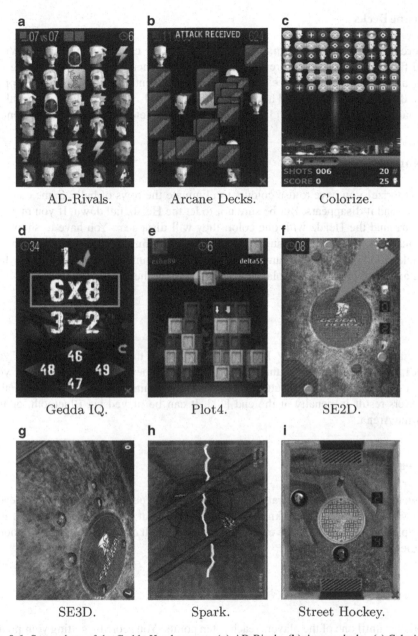

Fig. 9.6 Screenshots of the Gedda-Headz games. (**a**) AD-Rivals. (**b**) Arcane decks. (**c**) Colorize. (**d**) Gedda IQ. (**e**) Plot 4. (**f**) SE2D. (**g**) SE3D. (**h**) Spark. (**i**) Street Hockey

all about being fast. Be sure you know where to find the pairs. And there is a special pair too: The Flash! It closes the pairs your opponent found and steals score from your opponent – so it may be your last chance to win the game! [11] It can be played via Bluetooth, or the Online Arena.

Arcane Decks

There are 30 cards face down. Your goal is to flip the cards and make pairs. When you flip two cards over and reveal the headz under them. If they match, you got a pair and they will remain face up! If the two cards dont match, they will be flipped face down again and you will have to try different cards. The first player to reveal all 15 pairs, wins the game! [11] It can be played via Bluetooth, or the Online Arena.

Colorize!

In Colorize! you have to use colours to eliminate the rows of balls. Same color in a row, and it disappears. But be sure not to let the Headz fall down. If you manage to surround the Headz with one color, they will disappear. You have to shoot the colours fast, otherwise the auto-fire function will ruin your gameplay. When the attack button is active, you can randomize the playground of your opponent. Be fast and accurate! [11] It can be played via Bluetooth, or the Online Arena.

Gedda IQ

Calculate fast and accurately. Hit the button showing the correct result, or – if you can't solve it quickly – skip the answer by pressing the skip button. The faster you enter the correct result, the better. The less wrong results you enter, the better. False answers result in penalty at the end [11]. It can be played via Bluetooth, or the Online Arena.

Plot 4

Power of deduction, concentration, and a fast eye – if you have these, you are already the winner! The concept is known for along time, but the new features make it a complete new game – and it's even in color now! [11] It can be played via Bluetooth, or the Online Arena.

SE2D and SE3D

You play until one of the players reaches ten points. You score by getting your pucks into the middle area of the playground by flipping your pucks with the finger. Using a wiping movement with your finger allows for choosing the discus you want to shoot [11]. SE2D is the Java ME version of the game, while SE3D is the iPhone version. They can be played via Bluetooth, or the Online Arena.

Spark

Spark is a racing game in a sewer of Arcane City. Race your spark through the dark and electrify the rats, so they have fun too! Be fast. Be first. Get respect [11]. This game is for Bluetooth only.

Street Hockey

Score by shooting the can into your opponent's sewer. One hit, one point. Play until your reach ten points. Be sure to use the right Head to rule the street [11]. This game is for Bluetooth only.

The Gedda-Headz User Profile

There are three types of users in Gedda-Headz, namely mobile users with and without a flat-rate data tariff and nomadic users. *Mobile users with a flat fee* do not care about how much data is sent over the air as they always pay the same amount. Flat-fee users and nearly-flat-fee users can be considered the same, since the data traffic in Gedda-Headz is so low that users will not notice any difference even if their flat fee is not totally flat. These users always connect to the Gedda-Headz world immediately when the application starts.

Mobile users without a flat fee are users who pay per traffic. They can still connect to the Internet and thus the Gedda-Headz servers via their network operators, but are more concerned about the amount of data traffic involved.

Nomadic users are users who do not use a data connection provided by their network operator (either because they do not have any, or they are unwilling to use it). These players can connect to the Internet and Gedda-Headz via a WiFi access point at home, office, school, etc. In case no WiFi hotspot is available, or the user's phone does not support WiFi at all, Gedda-Headz provides the so-called PC Bridge. It is a small PC tool that relays the messages between the phone and the Gedda-Headz servers, maintaining the connection as long as the Gedda-Headz application is running. The number of these users is expected to decrease over the years (and because of decreasing data-rate costs). However, the Bridge concept should help them minimize (even eliminate) their connection costs. Even when no Internet connection is available for the phones, Gedda-Headz gamers can still play with nearby opponents via Bluetooth.

The different types of users will look for different cooperative strategies, so it is important to design the strategies based on the preferences of each user type.

Music and Video Content in Gedda-Headz

The Gedda-Headz concept also involves songs from the hip-hop/rap band Gedda-Headz. The Los Angeles-based band, which published their first single "Spaced Out" in 2009, will support life in the virtual metropolis of the Gedda-Headz with cool music videos and an intoxicating beat. At first, the identities of the band members Jasper, Frank, and Zoe will be secret – they appear in the video as Gedda-Headz characters. The idea with the music is to create viral marketing effects and to strengthen the community.

The GH Community

In parallel to the mobile phones, the Gedda-Headz users can access the community on the web. This feature is very important to Gedda-Headz, as people usually want to know who they play against, or players may wish to form friendships, or view the rankings, and so on. As given in Fig. 9.7, users may fill out a detailed profile page that other users may see, and view their rank, list of Headz, friends, achievements, mood and location. With the addition of user ranks and achievements, users can be motivated further to be even more active members of the community. Gedda-Headz also provides a Discussion Board, where users may interact directly with each other, help others, or get help from other people, strengthening the community even more.

User Cooperation in Gedda-Headz

As discussed in [1–5], cooperation among mobile phone users brings them numerous advantages. However, both [1] and [10] explain, that users will not share their resources (disk space, Internet connection, battery, the time and effort to spread the word about something, etc.) and will not cooperate with others unless they are motivated to do so. In this section the cross over between cooperation and social mobile networks shall be highlighted in the context of Gedda-Headz, focusing on how to motivate the users as well.

Fitzek and Katz [1] describes three different aspects of cooperation in wireless networks. The first one is known as communicational cooperation, where nodes interact with each other using different techniques to improve performance or resource usage or bring other advantages. The second aspect is the operational cooperation where cooperation mainly occurs to ensure end-to-end connectivity between nodes in different networks. To achieve this goal, certain negotiating procedures are required to maintain the connections. It is commonly used in heterogeneous networks. The third angle is the social cooperation where nodes (users) may decide to participate in the network and cooperate with others or not. In such networks these decisions ultimately influence the performance of the whole network.

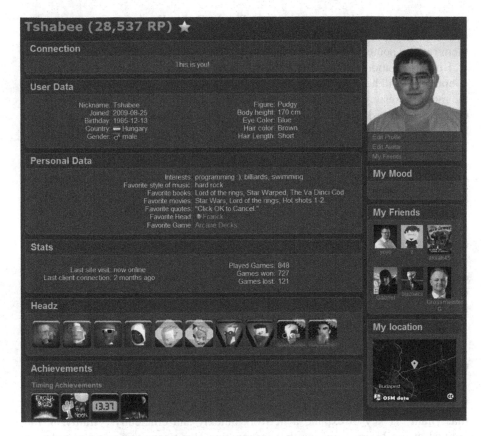

Fig. 9.7   A Gedda-Headz user profile

The Gedda-Headz concept already has cooperative functionalities implemented. However, instead of creating relay channels, which is the classical example of cooperation that was introduced in [13] and [14], Gedda-Headz offers different ways for users to cooperate with each other. First of all, the uploading of the scores has certain cooperative aspects. In case two players are gaming over Bluetooth, only one gamer needs to upload the scores for both players to benefit from it. In this case it might be the mobile user with a flat fee (see section "The Gedda-Headz User Profile"). Figure 9.8 shows this procedure: Player A and B play over Bluetooth then Player B uploads the scores to the Gedda-Headz database, as Player A does not have an Internet connection. This is a good example of both the communicational and social cooperation, as users without a connection to the Gedda-Headz web servers gain access to their services this way. Furthermore, the user who uploads the scores, is highly motivated to do so, as he receives his share of the respect points right away for the games they played.

Another example of the social aspect of cooperation is the spreading of the software from phone to phone as described in sections "Getting the App to the Users" and "Conventional Methods for Viral Expansion". In this case, helping others does not include a reward in itself. But the Gedda-Headz concept ensures that users, who spread the application, will receive the respect they deserve by awarding them respect points and achievements as well.

But cooperation is a two-way street. So far we have had some examples how cooperation will help the Gedda-Headz concept and more will come over time. But the more interesting side is how Gedda-Headz will support cooperation among users even for other tasks (e.g. cooperative video retrieval). The Gedda-Headz concept holds several tools to build up trust and to motivate users to help each other. As long as the users-to-cooperate are of the Gedda-Headz community, they might help each other based on pure altruism, just like helping friends or close relatives in everyday life. But the Gedda-Headz concept can also reward users for helping by giving them respect points or just showing on to the community who is helping who. For example, a user may let others use his Internet connection (in case he has one), thus providing them access to the Gedda-Headz API, or the Online Arena, or other websites, or other services that involve cooperation. Sharing the Internet connection is not rewarding in itself, however, combining it with Gedda-Headz enables the system to reward the users who share their resources with respect points, or achievements based on the other users' traffic, or other metrics. These aspects are left for further research.

Gedda-Headz and Virality

It has been shown by networks like Facebook, or MySpace, and explained in [10] that virality is key to expand a network quickly and efficiently. Virality, in the context of the Internet, means that information about something (e.g. a video, a network, etc.) spreads extremely fast, and the number of people who watch that video, or use that network grows exponentially.

In a social network, virality can in fact be measured, based on the acts of spreading that are tracked down, or simply looking at the growth rate of the network. For the latter method, one needs to know the time it takes for users to convince their friends to join. The metric for virality is called the *virality index* [10]. It basically means how valuable the average user is to the network. If this index is below 1 then the network is not viral and the number of users will eventually stop growing and existing users will also leave the network. If it is exactly 1 then it means that each user is worth one user, resulting in a constant (small fluctuations are possible, of course) number of users. However, when it goes above 1, then each user is worth more than one user, which means that users are constantly bringing others to the network, creating a viral network. In this section we will discuss the basic factors that affect virality in the context of Gedda-Headz, and also introduce a novel method to increase the virality of a social network, which is very useful in a mobile environment.

In order to make anything (e.g. a video, a network, etc.) viral, people need to be motivated to spread the word about it, similarly to user cooperation, where

Fig. 9.8 Player B uploading the scores after playing with Player A over Bluetooth

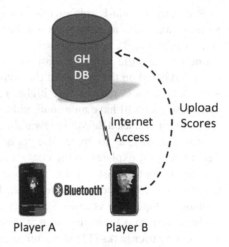

people need to be motivated to cooperate with others in a wireless network (see section "User Cooperation in Gedda-Headz"). In classical cases the act of spreading itself is motivating enough, as people like sharing good/funny/interesting things with their friends or family, as explained in [10]. In the case of a social network, the two most important things are providing services that people *want to* use and ensuring that they *can* use them. It does not matter how useful a service might be, if it is too complex for the users to understand its usage. If a network meets these two requirements, the system can further increase the motivation by giving incentives to users who bring new people to the network. Gedda-Headz is a fine example of that, as users get a boost of respect points and achievements when they spread the word. However, the system needs to track down every act of spreading that occurs, in order to give rewards to the users. This section will also show how it is done in Gedda-Headz.

Conventional Methods for Viral Expansion

First of all, as already discussed in section "Music and Video Content in Gedda-Headz", Gedda-Headz has a hip-hop/rap band that makes music videos to create viral marketing effects. This is one of the most common viral methods on the Internet, as viral videos can be used to promote lots of different things besides social networks. According to [10], a viral video, or generally a viral content is such content that people find interesting enough to share it with their friends/family. This sharing takes place outside Gedda-Headz, through video sharing portals, such as YouTube, which means it cannot be tracked down, so boosting its virality with further incentives is not possible.

Secondly, Gedda-Headz enables users to send invitations to their friends via e-mail. This is also a common (if not the most conventional) way to increase virality in a social network. In contrast to viral content, the invitations can be tracked down if one can map the invited e-mail addresses to new users then the inviters can be rewarded based on the actions of the invited users. That way, users who invite more active/useful users may receive higher rewards. However, one cannot assume that each new user will have an e-mail address, as we will see later, which may pose a problem (or at least a delay) in rewarding the inviters.

Another way is to make the registration procedure as simple as possible. Penenberg [10] explains in the context of an online social network that users may give up trying to register if it is too complex, or takes too long, even if they would like to use the services of the network. In a social mobile network, this aspect is even more important, as a mobile device cannot be expected to have constant access to the servers, thus the registration process can easily become too complex for users. That is why user ranks [11] were introduced in Gedda-Headz. This concept requires users to enter only the most necessary data (nickname and password) to complete the registration in the mobile client and become a member of the lowest rank of players (that is not even recognized on the server yet), then they can start playing Bluetooth games right away. Eventually, they will have to connect to the Internet, for example to upload game results. That is when the new user's account is created on the server. This step is automatic in case the new nickname is not used already by another user, otherwise the server will require the new user to change his nickname. Completing this step results in the user moving up the ranks, and after this he will be able to use more features of Gedda-Headz, for example play in the Online Arena. Higher ranks have higher requirements for a user, e.g. entering his e-mail address (sending e-mail invitations becomes available after this step) on the website, filling out his profile, keeping his mood message up-to-date, playing regularly, or adding more Headz to his profile. The concept of user ranks also motivates the users to perform these tasks by rewarding higher-ranked users with access to more and more features, while providing the most basic features to lower-ranked users as well.

The Gedda-Headz Spreader

Besides the conventional ways, Gedda-Headz involves a novel method to increase virality, and that is the Gedda-Headz spreader. In order to use Gedda-Headz (or any other social mobile network), people need to install a client application on their phones (as discussed in section "Getting the App to the Users"). The spreader application (downloadable from the Gedda-Headz website) enables users to send the installer of the Gedda-Headz client to the phones of their friends and ensures that they receive appropriate rewards for this action. It is only capable of spreading the Java ME client of Gedda-Headz, as installing any application on an iPhone has to be done through the AppStore of Apple.

The spreader uses Bluetooth to transfer the installer of the client application to other devices. Nowadays, even the most simple phones have Bluetooth support, and it is also the main wireless technology required by the Gedda-Headz client, making Bluetooth the best choice to use for the spreading. It also provides an identifier (called Bluetooth address). The spreader stores the Bluetooth address of the target device, if the transfer of the installer was successful, and the user can upload it to the Gedda-Headz server along with the exact date and time of the spreading (and the ID of the spreader user, of course). The server can then use it to match newly registered users with uploaded spreader data. If the server successfully finds a match, it can reward the appropriate users right away.

The spreader application is also designed to be easy to use. It has a similar UI to the Java ME client (see Fig. 9.9) and it contains the same login procedure (necessary for identifying the spreader user), ensuring that the users who wish to use the spreader are already familiar with it. Login is required only on the first start of the application, to make it more comfortable for the users. From the main menu (Fig. 9.9a), the user can start looking for nearby devices right away and choose the device that should receive the installer (Fig. 9.9d). If the transfer is successful, an information screen is displayed (Fig. 9.9e) and the transfer data is saved on the phone. After that, the user can upload this data to the server anytime he has access to the server (the same way as game results are uploaded) then the rest (rewarding the users) is done automatically by the server: at the moment the reward is based on the amount of respect points the invited users earn in the first 2 weeks of playing Gedda-Headz.

The Gedda-Headz client (and the spreader as well) supports phones with lots of different screen resolutions, therefore it is available in eight UI profiles to make sure that it looks good on each device. This raises an important question: which profile(s) should be available in the spreader? If only one is made available, the transferred application will not look good on most devices it is sent to. This would result in bad user experience, which in turn would decrease the virality of Gedda-Headz. Therefore, we opted to making all eight profiles available, so the optimal one could be sent to each device. However, this raises another question: how to determine which profile should be sent to a given phone? In order to determine that, the spreader application would need to know the screen resolution of the target device. To answer this question, as a first step we moved the device database of the server to the spreader application, that contains the manufacturer and screen resolution for each model. That modified the question to: how to determine the model of the target device? Using Bluetooth, it cannot be done automatically, as the Bluetooth info of a device that can be retrieved does not contain information about the model. Therefore, one needs the users' assistance to ensure that *the optimal profile* is sent to the target devices, meaning that the user needs to select the appropriate manufacturer from a list of available ones (Fig. 9.9b) then he needs to select the device model from another list that can be filtered for better user experience (Fig. 9.9c). However, this step is not mandatory, as it might be considered too complex by users. When a user does not select a device model, the default profile will be sent to the target devices. Making this step completely automatic is left for further research.

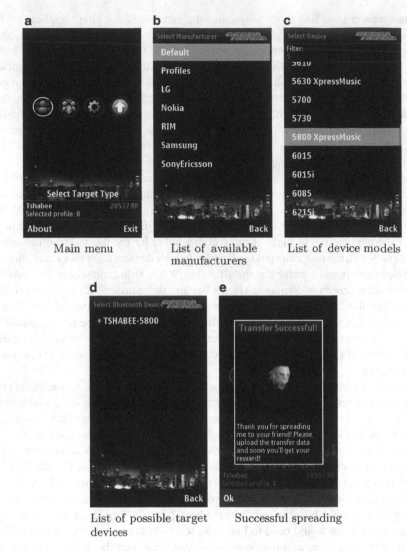

Fig. 9.9 Screenshots of the Gedda-Headz spreader. (a) Main menu. (b) List of available manufacturers. (c) List of device models. (d) List of possible target devices. (e) Successful spreading

Virality or Security?

Viral features in a social network always involve security concerns that people with ill intentions can exploit. Addressing these security problems results in a reduced virality index, as security makes using the services of the network more complex, slowing down the growth of the network. That is why it is an important and difficult decision for social networks how to address security problems or weaknesses, or even whether to address certain issues or not. For example, sending e-mail invitations enables a user with ill intentions to send lots of spam, while requiring passing a CAPTCHA test [15] makes sending invitations more complex, thus less users will use it. Another example is whether to require users to have strong (secure) passwords or not: strong passwords offer better protection for the users' personal data, while they are more difficult to enter, especially on a mobile phone, which is the main reason why social networks do not have strict requirements for passwords.

In the context of games, exploiting these weaknesses is called cheating. Preventing cheating usually upsets users who try to cheat (as it did in Gedda-Headz), which may result in the network losing those users. However, allowing cheating will upset the users who do not cheat. That is why in Gedda-Headz we opted to eliminating any kind of exploits in the system from the start. There were three main questions that we had to address in Gedda-Headz before making the system available for the gamers around the world.

The first one was what to do when a player disconnects from the server or turns off his phone in the middle of a game, as it could be exploited by players who are about to lose the game if not handled properly. The system cannot prevent it from happening of course, but it can detect it at least. This enables the client application of the opponent to generate a game result and thus win the game instantly. This means that it is the user's responsibility to ensure that he remains connected to his opponent in a game and does not lose connection unintentionally.

The second one was what to do with players who have more than one account, as these players can easily gain respect points with one of the accounts by playing against the other ones. Even detecting these players is not as straightforward as detecting disconnecting players. However, the servers store every game result that is uploaded and certain patterns (e.g. two players playing very much against each other and only one of them losing all the time) among those results help detection and thus the proper punishment of the cheater.

Finally, the third one was connected to the Gedda-Headz spreader: as nobody can stop a user from transferring the installer to a device that will never be used for playing (e.g. a desktop computer with Bluetooth support), or transferring the installer to the same device multiple times, we needed a reward system that would not reward these transfers, only those that indeed brought new users to the network. That is why the rewards are based on the new users' activity, rather than the transfers themselves.

Conclusion

In this chapter we introduced the concept of Gedda-Headz, a social network that focuses on gaming in a mobile environment. We have also underlined the importance of and opportunities for cooperation in a social mobile network, and described several ways for enhancing the services of the network with the help of user cooperation in the context of Gedda-Headz.

Furthermore, we have discussed virality in a social mobile network, and introduced several methods for increasing the virality of a network. One of these methods is spreading the client application of the network from phone to phone using a spreader application. This method is unique to mobile networks, and it is a great way to involve users in spreading the word about a network. We have also shown that user motivation is very important for all of these methods and that the motivation can be boosted by giving rewards to people who bring new users to the network. Finally, we have discussed the security problems/weaknesses these methods cause and shown ways for dealing with these problems.

As part of future work, we would like to investigate how social mobile networks may help user cooperation outside the network itself, by giving rewards to users who cooperate with others, or by other ways, as it may enhance the efficiency of other services as well, and reduce the data traffic and energy use of mobile devices. We would also like to enhance the efficiency of the viral aspects of social mobile networks, in particular the viral spreading of the client among mobile devices. So far we have focused on the distribution of the client from one mobile phone to another. It is important to note that the presented approach is limited to one source and one destination and that all of the data needs to be transmitted between both of them. In case the conveying gets interrupted the spreading has to be restarted.

Therefore we advocate the possibility to use random linear network coding (RLNC) [16] for the viral distribution of the client applications. In [17] the usage of Fountain codes is suggested to distribute programmable codes among sensor nodes. But the shortcoming of that paper and others focusing on end to end coding schemes is, that it overcomes the problem of interrupted downloads but does not allow the distributed information injection over multi hop. Therefore RLNC is the right choice for viral content distribution.

Acknowledgements This work is connected to the scientific program of the "Development of quality-oriented and cooperative R+D+I strategy and functional model at BUTE" project. This project is supported by the New Hungary Development Plan (Project ID: TÁMOP-4.2.1/ B-09/1/KMR-2010-0002).

References

1. Fitzek, F.H.P., Katz, M. (eds.): Cooperation in Wireless Networks: Principles and Applications: Real Egoistic Behavior Is to Cooperate! Springer, Dordrecht (2006). ISBN 1-4020-4710-X
2. Fitzek, F.H.P., Katz, M. (eds.): Cognitive Wireless Networks: Concepts, Methodologies and Visions Inspiring the Age of Enlightenment of Wireless Communications. Springer, Dordrecht (2007). ISBN 978-1-4020-5978-0
3. Kristensen, J.M., Fitzek, F.H.P.: Cognitive Wireless Networks Cellular Controlled P2P Communication Using Software Defined Radio, pp. 435–455. Springer, Dordrecht (2007). ISBN 978-1-4020-5978-0 22
4. Perrucci, G.P., Fitzek, F.H.P., Zhang, Q., Katz, M.: Cooperative mobile web browsing. EURASIP J. Wirel. Commun. Netw. **2009**, 1–9 (2009)

5. Perrucci, G.P., Fitzek, F.H.P., Petersen, M.V.: Heterogeneous Wireless Access Networks: Architectures and Protocols Energy Saving Aspects for Mobile Device Exploiting Heterogeneous Wireless Networks, pp. 277–304. Springer, New York (2008). ISBN 978-0-387-09776-3 10

6. Fitzek, F.H.P.: "Cooperative mobile gaming", a contributing Nokia's "Mobile Games 2010" white paper NRC-TR-2007-011 (2007)

7. Fitzek, F.H.P., Schulte, G., Reisslein, M.: System architecture for billing of multi-player games in a wireless environment using GSM/UMTS and WLAN services. In: Proceedings of the First Workshop on Network and System Support for Games (NetGames 2002), Braunschweig, pp. 58–64 (2002). ISBN:1-58113-493-2

8. Blazovics, L., Varga, Cs., Bamford, W., Zanaty, P., Fitzek, F.H.P.: Future Cooperative Communication Systems Driven by Social Mobile Networks. Wireless Personal Communications, Special Issue on "5G Networks, Services and Applications", pp. 1–15, Springer, Dordrecht (2010)

9. Brosnan, S.F., Schiff, H.C., de Waal, F.B.: Tolerance for inequity may increase with social closeness in chimpanzees. Proc. Biol. Sci. **272**, 253–258 (2005)

10. Penenberg, A.L.: Viral Loop: From Facebook to Twitter, How Today's Smartest Businesses Grow Themselves. Hyperion, New York (2009)

11. Gedda-Headz. [Online]. Available: http://www.gedda-headz.com (2010)

12. OpenStreetMap. [Online]. Available: http://www.openstreetmap.org (2010)

13. van der Meulen, E.C.: Transmission of information in a T-terminal discrete memoryless channel. Ph.D. thesis, Department of Statistics, University of California, Berkeley (1968)

14. van der Meulen, E.C.: Three-terminal communication channels. Adv. Appl. Probab. **3**, 120–154 (1971)

15. Completely Automated Public Turing Test To Tell Computers and Humans Apart. [Online] Available: http://www.captcha.net/ (2010)

16. Koetter, R., Medard, M.: An algebraic approach to network coding. IEEE/ACM Trans. Netw. **11**(5), 782–795 (2003)

17. Rossi, M., Zanca, G., Stabellini, L., Crepaldi, R. Harris, A.t.F. III, Zorzi, M.: SYNAPSE: a network reprogramming protocol for wireless sensor networks using fountain codes. In: Fifth Annual IEEE Communications Society Conference on Sensor, Mesh and Ad Hoc Communications and Networks, pp. 188–196, San Francisco (2008)

Chapter 10
An Effective User-Driven Framework for Selection of Social Network Services

Salaja Silas, Kirubakaran Ezra, and Elijah Blessing Rajsingh

Abstract The social network services have tremendously grown during the recent years and have a promising future ahead. Many organizations are coming forward with wide variety of interesting social networking services. In fact, most of the social network services are almost identical and the users select the services based on public perceptions; trial and error method which sometimes provide lower level of satisfaction to the users. Therefore, discovering and providing the best social network service based on user's interest is really a challenge. Discovering a set of feasible social services and selecting the most appropriate social network service based on the user preferences can be modeled as multi-criteria decision making problem. In this chapter, an effective framework for service selection of social network is proposed. The experimental results on overhead, social service deduction time, average delay have also been obtained. The results show that the proposed framework is effective.

Introduction

Social Networking can be defined as the set of services provided by an organization to the larger community where the social networking sites have the characteristics such as constructing a community within a bounded system, articulate a list of other users with whom to share a connection, view and traverse their list of connections made by others in the social networking system [1]. Today many social networking sites are provided by various organizations which support same or different type of services. These organizations can be classified by their goal of providing the

S. Silas • E.B. Rajsingh (✉)
Department of Information Technology, Karunya University, Coimbatore, India
e-mail: blessingsalaja@gmail.com; elijahblessing@gmail.com

K. Ezra
BHEL, Trichy, India

A. Abraham (ed.), *Computational Social Networks: Security and Privacy*,
DOI 10.1007/978-1-4471-4051-1_10, © Springer-Verlag London 2012

services such as professional, personal, gaming and so on. FaceBook, Twitter, LinkedIn, MySpace are few examples of the popular social networking sites. Social Networking has gained popularity in spite of age, profession and region. The selection of the service provided by the social networking sites by the user is influenced by individual user perspective and also the group perspective. The selection of the service is also influenced by the gender, attitude, privacy concern, age [2–4]. Therefore, selecting [5] a suitable service based on social and individual preferences of the user and requirements is a challenging research area. In this paper, selecting a suitable service based on user criteria has been modeled as a multi-criteria decision making problem and an efficient, user-driven service selection framework for social networking services is proposed adopting PROMETHEE I methodology.

Literature Survey

Hsi-Peng Lu et al. [6] broadly classified the users of social network into two categories as Extroverts and Introverts. The factors such as social value, emotional value, value of money and quality value were studied and were found that extroverts had more impact in the social network than the introverts. It was also been found that many were reluctant to pay to the services provided by the social networking sites paving way for the lack of a viable revenue model. Fred Stutzman et al. [7] had discerned about the factors mediating the disclosure of social networking sites such as the privacy attitudes, privacy behavior, Privacy policy consumption and disclosure behavior. Based on the evidence from the survey, it was ascertained that the social network sites could help mitigate concerns about disclosure by providing transparent privacy policies and privacy controls.

Teresa Correa et al. [8] suggested that the factors such as extraversion, emotional stability and openness to experience were related to use of social applications on the Internet. The experimental results had been revealed that while extraversion and openness to experiences were positively related to social media use, emotional stability was a negative predictor, controlling for socio-demographics and life satisfaction. These findings differed by gender and age. Ohbyung Kwon et al. [3] had proposed a Technology Acceptance Model (TAM) to construct an amended model that focused on three individual differences: social identity, altruism and telepresence. The users' perception was based on either human relationship-oriented service or a task-oriented service. Based on the experimentation of the users' perception, the perceived encouragement and perceived orientation were found to be significant constructs that affect actual use of social network services.

Flora S. Tsai et al. [9] had developed mobile social software which helped to bring people together by discovering, communicating and sharing resources through mobile devices. The software was based on peer-to-peer technology and was tested on various mobile devices. Sonia Ben Mokhtar et al. [4] had proposed a middleware which provided the concept of social networking in the pervasive environment.

It enabled users to accurately recommend the activities by dynamically combining both the social and physical proximity relations. Social preferences such as users' social networks and the mobility patterns were considered while selecting a particular activity.

Qin Gao et al. [10] had made an extensive study and had identified the factors that affect the social networking. The main factor considered for the success of social networking was found to be sociability. Apart from these there were many factors categorized under the topics such as purpose and benefit, people, social climate, mediated communication and technological system which had an impact on the user's perception, performance and the choice of the social networking sites. Even though system competency was not a sociability factor, still it influenced the user's experience to a greater extent.

Yutu Liu et al. [11] had proposed an extensible QoS model which performs a preference oriented ranking of services based on an open fair computation. This method also obtains the feedback from the user and also monitors the execution duration based on which the credibility of the service varies. L. Taher et al. [12] had proposed a data model which collects the factors influencing the service selection and has a computational model which performs the process of finding the best possible match by using the Euclidean distance and also performs the validation of the credentials by using validation manager.

Stefania Galizia et al. [13] had proposed a trust based methodology for selection of web services because trust plays a major role in providing the service by the service provider. The paper classifies the models of trust as policy based; reputation based and trusted third party models. The paper has proposed a hybrid technique with policy combined with trusted third party model to select the service dynamically. Baopeng Zhang et al. [14] had proposed a semantic based service selection in selecting the services provided in the pervasive environment. André C. Santos et al. [15] had proposed a methodology where the sensors play a major role to study the environment of the user's. Based on the sensor data, required services are provided to the user. This chapter discusses about a user friendly environment where the users are requested to provide their preferences based on which the social network service will be selected.

Factors That Influence Social Network Service Selection

Service type (St) – the type of service being provided to the user to meet a particular category either professional or personal or nostalgic etc.,

Paid or Unpaid Service (PuP) – the service for which an amount has to be paid is termed as paid service and those which can be used free of cost are termed as unpaid services.

Reliability (Re) [10] – the extent to which social online activity can be performed reliably and continuously, without any failure or interruption.

Searchability (Se) [10] – the ability of the system to search for services relevant to social interaction, such as people or events.

Privacy Aware (Pa) [16] – the extent to which the user's private information can be controlled by themselves.

Information Richness (Ir) – the amount and types of information which can be stored and retrieved from the system.

Platform Independence (Pi) – the extent to which the social networking services can be accessed by various handheld devices.

Customizability (Cu) – the ease at which the content and format of exchanged information can be controlled.

Activity Support (As) – the extent to which groups of special interests can be established and maintained easily.

Prevention from disturbance (Pd) – the extent to which the user can distinguish between wanted and unwanted information and can block the latter.

Proposed Framework for Social Network Service Selection

The social network organizations are clustered in group based on their objectives. Each group (G) consists of a set of social network organizations. In general

$$G_n = \{O_{n1}, O_{n2}, ..., O_{nm}\} \tag{10.1}$$

where n is the number of group and m is the number of services provided by a single organization.

Figure 10.1 shows that there are four different social network groups G_1, G_2, G_3, G_4. The social network organizations O_{11}, O_{12}, O_{13} and Users $U_{11}, U_{12}, U_{13}, U_{14}$ are available in a particular group G_1 and are handled by Social Network Service Authority $SNSA_1$. The communication between Social Network Service Authority's takes place through Master Social Network Service Authority $MSNSA$.

Therefore for the example shown in Fig. 10.1,

$$
\begin{aligned}
G_1 &= \{O_{11}, O_{12}, O_{13}, U_{11}, U_{12}, U_{13}, U_{14}, SNSA_1\} \\
G_2 &= \{O_{21}, O_{22}, O_{23}, O_{24}, U_{21}, U_{22}, U_{23}, SNSA_2\} \\
G_3 &= \{O_{31}, O_{32}, O_{33}, O_{34}, U_{31}, U_{32}, U_{33}, U_{34}, SNSA_3\} \\
G_4 &= \{O_{41}, O_{42}, O_{43}, O_{44}, U_{41}, U_{42}, U_{43}, SNSA_4\} \\
G_n &= \{O_{n1}, O_{n2}, O_{n3}, , O_{nm}, U_{n1}, U_{n2}, U_{nl}, SNSA_n\}
\end{aligned}
\tag{10.2}
$$

Let each social network organization provide a set of social services such as

$$O_{11} = \{s_{111}, s_{112}, s_{113}\}$$

$$O_{12} = \{s_{121}, s_{122}, s_{123}\} \tag{10.3}$$

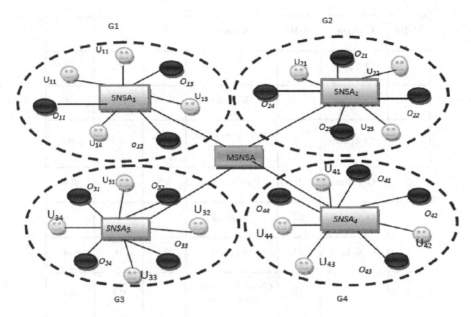

Fig. 10.1 Social network environment

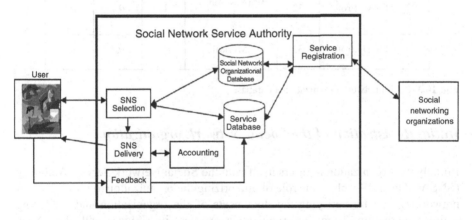

Fig. 10.2 Proposed user-driven framework for social network service selection

Figure 10.2 shows the proposed user-driven framework for social network service selection. The Social Network Service Authority consists of Service Registration Unit, User Registration Unit, Social Network Service (SNS) Selection Unit and Social Network Service (SNS) Delivery Unit. Each social network organization furnishes the services it wishes to provide and registers it with the service registration unit (Figs. 10.3, 10.4).

O_ID	O_Name	S_ID	S_name	Re	Se	Pa
1	O_Space	11	Musical	0.97	0.2	.98
1	O_Space	12	Bike race	0. 97	0.2	.98
1	O_Space	13	cloud computing community	0. 97	0.2	.98
2	O_Gamer	21	Virtual forest	0.5	0	0.4
2	O_Gamer	22	Musical	0.5	0	0.4
2	O_Gamer	23	Bike race	0.5	0	0.4
3	O_Profe	31	Cloud computing community	0.5	0.1	0.3
3	O_Profe	32	Wireless sensor community	0.5	0.1	0.3
3	O_Profe	33	Musical	0.5	0.1	0.3

Fig. 10.3 Social network organizational database

Initial Registration of the Social Network organization

Initially the organization registers itself with the Social Network Service Authority (SNSA). The SNSA plays the role of authorizing the organization to provide social networking site by verifying the documents of the organization and producing a digital signature. Then the organization registers its services with the SNSA by sending a *Service_Registration* message. The SNSA on receiving the message updates the information both in the social network organizational database and the service database (Fig. 10.5).

The SNSA sends a service identity number (S_ID) for all the services registered by the particular organization through the *Acknowledgement* message. The *Ack* message format is shown in Fig. 10.6

If an organization has n_s services, then the initial registration overhead O_{oreg} is found to be

$$O_{oreg} = 2\,(n_s + 1) \tag{10.4}$$

S_Name	S_ID	O_ID	St	PuP	Ir	Pi	Cu	As	Pd
Musical	11	1	Personal	0	0.5	0.99	0.9	0.6	0.77
Bike race	12	1	Personal	0	0.5	0.77	0.9	0.4	0.99
cloud computing community	13	1	Personal	1	0.5	0.65	0.9	0.45	0.88
Virtual forest	21	2	Game	1	0.99	0	0.77	0.2	0.55
Musical	22	2	Game	1	0.78	0	0.6	0.2	0.66
Bike race	23	2	Game	1	0.78	0.80	0.9	0.3	0.89
Cloud computing community	31	3	Edu.	0	0.78	0.30	0.2	0.4	0.77
Wireless sensor community	32	3	Edu.	0	0.89	0.4	0.5	0.5	0.83
Musical	33	3	Edu.	1	0.67	0.5	1	0.5	0.77

Fig. 10.4 Service database

HDR	O_ID	Re	Se	Pa	S_HDR	S_name	St	PuP	Ir	Pi	Cu	As	Pd	S_Tail	...	Tail

Fig. 10.5 Service_Registration message

HDR	SNSA_ID	O_ID	No. of services	S_1_name	S_1_ID	...	S_n_name	S_n_ID	Tail

Fig. 10.6 Ack message

If there are n_o organizations offering n_s services, then O_{oreg} is found to be

$$O_{\text{oreg}} = 2\left(\sum_{i=1}^{n_o} n_{si} + n_o\right) \qquad (10.5)$$

HDR	O_ID	SHDR	S_Name	PuP	St	Ir	Cu	As	Pd	Pi	Stail	...	Tail

Fig. 10.7 Service_New message

Fig. 10.8 Org_Upgrade message

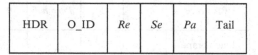

HDR	O_ID	Re	Se	Pa	Tail

A New Service/Multiple Services Are Offered by a Registered Social Network Organization

When an already existing social network organization wishes to offer a new service or multiple services, it sends a *Service_New* message which is shown in Fig. 10.7 to the SNSA. The SNSA updates the social network organizational database and the service database.

The SNSA sends a service identity number (S_ID) for the services registered by the particular organization through the *Acknowledgement* message. If an organization has $n_{s(\text{new})}$ services, then the new service registration overhead O_{sreg} is found to be

$$O_{sreg} = 2\left(n_{s(\text{new})} + 1\right) \tag{10.6}$$

If there are n_o organizations offering $n_{s(\text{new})}$ services, then O_{sreg} is found to be

$$O_{sreg} = 2\left(\sum_{i=1}^{n_o} n_{s(\text{new})i} + n_o\right) \tag{10.7}$$

Upgradation of the Social Network Organization

If the registered social network organization wishes to upgrade the factors influencing the services provided by the organization, then the organization sends the *Org_Upgrade* (Fig. 10.8) message to the SNSA with the common parameters. The *Org_upgrade* message format is as follows.

Upon receiving the *Org_Upgrade* message, the SNSA updates the social network organizational database. If an organization has n_s services, the organization upgrade overhead O_{upg} is found to be

$$O_{\text{upg}} = n_s + 1 \tag{10.8}$$

HDR	O_ID	S_ID	St	PuP	Ir	Pi	Cu	As	Pd	Tail

Fig. 10.9 Ser_Upgrade message

If there are n_o organizations offering n_s services, then O_{upg} is found to be

$$O_{\mathrm{upg}} = \sum_{i=1}^{n_o} n_{si} + n_o \qquad (10.9)$$

Upgradation of a Service Provided by a Registered Social Network Organization

If the registered social network organization wishes to upgrade the factors influencing a particular service provided by the organization, then the social network organization sends the *Ser_Upgrade* message to the SNSA with the parameters influencing that service. The *Ser_Upgrade* message format is as follows (Fig. 10.9).

Upon receiving the *Ser_Upgrade* message the SNSA updates the service database.

Social Network Service Selection

The Social Network Service Authority (SNSA) uses the PROMETHEE I methodology (Preference Ranking Organization METHod for Enrichment Evaluation) [17–21] concept to select the best social network organization based on the users' requirement. This methodology provides the social network users to select the criteria of their own interest based on their requirement and also to give preferences to those criteria in terms of weights.

Step 1: Requirements for Social Network Selection

1. Information from the Social network user
   The social network user's preference for each criteria Cr provided by the user is obtained in terms of weights and a set $\{w_j, j = 1, 2, ..., k\}$ representing the preference of the different criteria in terms of weight is tabulated and the weights are normalized [22] to 1.

Fig. 10.10 Evaluation table

S	$Cr_1(.)$	$Cr_2(.)$	...	$Cr_j(.)$	...	$Cr_k(.)$
s_1	$Cr_1(s_1)$	$Cr_2(s_1)$	...	$Cr_j(s_1)$	...	$Cr_k(s_1)$
s_2	$Cr_1(s_2)$	$Cr_2(s_2)$	...	$Cr_j(s_2)$	...	$Cr_k(s_2)$
$\vdots$	$\vdots$	$\vdots$	$\ddots$	$\vdots$	$\ddots$	$\vdots$
s_i	$Cr_1(s_i)$	$Cr_2(s_i)$	...	$Cr_j(s_i)$	...	$Cr_k(s_i)$
$\vdots$	$\vdots$	$\vdots$	$\ddots$	$\vdots$	$\ddots$	$\vdots$
s_n	$Cr_1(s_n)$	$Cr_2(s_n)$	...	$Cr_j(s_n)$	...	$Cr_k(s_n)$

$Cr_1(.)$	$Cr_2(.)$	...	$Cr_j(.)$	...	$Cr_k(.)$
w_1	w_2	...	w_j	...	w_k

$$\sum_{j=1}^{k} w_j = 1 \qquad (10.10)$$

2. Information from the Social Network organizations
   An evaluation table (Fig. 10.10) with corresponding weights is generated based
   on the information available in the social network organizational database and
   service that influences the selection of a particular social network service from n
   feasible services.

Step 2: Calculation of Preferences of the Social Network Service for Different Criterion

The preference function is calculated for maximization criterion as well as the minimization criterion. For maximization criterion, the preference function $P_j(s_x, s_y)$
gives the preference of s_x over s_y for the observed deviations as defined below

$$P_j(s_x, s_y) = F_j[d_j(s_x, s_y)] \forall s_x, s_y \in S \qquad (10.11)$$

where $d_j(S_x, S_y) = Cr_j(S_x) - Cr_j(S_y)$ for which $(0 \le P_j(S_x, S_y) \le 1)$ where
$S = \{s_1, s_2, ..., s_n\}$, a set of n feasible services provided by the organizations. The
preference function equals 0, when the deviation is negative and also the following
property holds.

$$P_j(S_x, S_y) > 0 \Rightarrow P_j(S_y, S_x) = 0 \qquad (10.12)$$

For minimization criterion, the preference function is calculated by the following $P_j(s_x, s_y)$ and is defined as

$$P_j\left(s_x, s_y\right) = F_j[-d_j(s_x, s_y)]\forall s_x, s_y \in S \qquad (10.13)$$

where $d_j\left(S_x, S_y\right) = Cr_j\left(S_x\right) - Cr_j\left(S_y\right)$ for which $\left(0 \leq P_j\left(S_x, S_y\right) \leq 1\right)$

The pair $\{Cr_j(.), P_j(s_x, s_y)\}$ is termed as the generalized criterion associated to the criterion $Cr_j(.)$ for which the preference function has to be defined. The Qualitative Preference function is defined as

$$P(d) = \begin{cases} 0, d \leq 0 \\ 1, d > 0 \end{cases} \qquad (10.14)$$

Step 3: Calculation of Aggregated Preference Indices

The pair wise comparisons of various criteria are performed from the feasible set of social network services and the aggregated reference indices are defined. Let $s_x, s_y \in S$, where S is a set of social network services offering the same functionality, then the Aggregated Preference Indices is given by

$$\begin{cases} \pi(s_x, s_y) = \sum_{j=1}^{k} w_j P_j(s_x, s_y) \\ \pi(s_y, s_x) = \sum_{j=1}^{k} w_j P_j(s_y, s_x) \end{cases} \qquad (10.15)$$

$\pi\left(S_x, S_y\right)$ is expressing with which degree s_x is preferred to s_y over all the criteria and $\pi(s_y, s_x)$ is expressing with which degree s_y is preferred to s_x.

Step 4: Calculation of Positive and Negative Outranking Flows

Each social network service s_a is compared with $n - 1$ other services from S. The positive outranking flow is calculated as:

$$\phi^+(s_a) = \frac{\sum_{x \in S} \pi(s_a, s_x)}{n - 1} \qquad (10.16)$$

where n is the number of social network service which provide identical functionality. The negative outranking flow can be calculated as:

$$\phi^-(s_a) = \frac{\sum_{x \in S} \pi(s_x, s_a)}{n - 1} \qquad (10.17)$$

Fig. 10.11 Ranking table

	s_1	s_2	s_3	s_4	s_5
s_1	-	R^I	I^I	P^I	P^I
s_2	R^I	-	R^I	P^I	P^I
s_3	I^I	R^I	-	P^I	P^I
s_4	R^I	P^I	P^I	-	P^I
s_5	P^I	P^I	P^I	P^I	-

Step 5: Construction of Ranking Table

A ranking table is built based on the positive and negative outranking flows calculated for all the feasible social network services. The entries in the ranking table are inferred by the three properties given in Eq. 10.18.

$$\begin{cases} s_x\,P^I\,s_y & \textit{iff} \\ s_x\,I^I\,s_y & \textit{iff} \\ s_x\,R^I\,s_y & \textit{iff} \end{cases} \begin{cases} \left(\phi^+(s_x) \geq \phi^+(s_y)\ and\ \phi^-(s_x) \leq \phi^-(s_y)\right) \\ \left(\phi^+(s_x) = \phi^+(s_y)\ and\ \phi^-(s_x) = \phi^-(s_y)\right) \\ \left(\phi^+(s_x) > \phi^+(s_y)\ and\ \phi^-(s_x) > \phi^-(s_y)\right) \\ \left(\phi^+(s_x) < \phi^+(s_y)\ and\ \phi^-(s_x) < \phi^-(s_y)\right) \end{cases} \quad (10.18)$$

where P^I, I^I, R^I represents preference, indifference and incomparability respectively. The sample of the ranking table (Fig. 10.11) is given below

Step 6: Selection of Best Social Network Service

The social network service which has the highest number of preferences over other social network services and also has the highest positive outranking flow is the best social network service.

Implementation and Results

The proposed user-driven framework was implemented and the experimental results were obtained.

Fig. 10.12 Service registration overhead

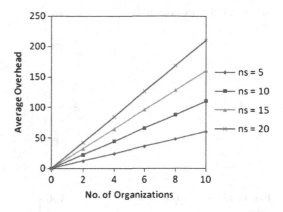

Fig. 10.13 Social network organization upgrade overhead

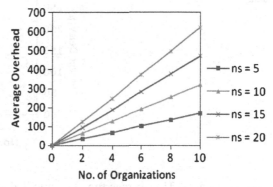

A Social Network environment with different social networking organizations was generated. The social network organizations were permitted to register initially with the Social Networking Service Authority for providing social network services to the users. Each social network organization was permitted to offer 5, 10, 15, 20 services and the effect of the number of social services on the service registration overhead is studied for various social network organizations.

Figure 10.12 shows that the variation of service registration overhead for different number of social network organizations for different number of social network services. It is found that the overhead increases linearly with the number of service network organization.

During the operation of network, few of the social network organizations were permitted to upgrade themselves. The overhead due to this event was studied.

Figure 10.13 shows the variation of Overhead due to social network organization upgrade for various numbers of social network services. It is found that as the number of social network organization upgrade increases; it contributes to additional overhead which increases almost linearly to the increase in the number of organizations.

The social network users who are interested in availing the services from the social network were permitted to register along with their service requirements

Fig. 10.14 Service deduction time

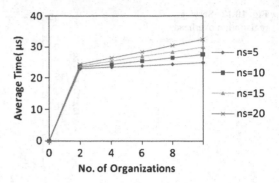

Fig. 10.15 Service deduction delay

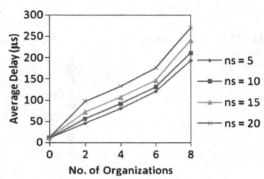

and preferences. The average time taken to deduct the best social network service as required by the user was determined for different number of social network organizations with different services and is shown in Fig. 10.14. The average delay experienced by the social network user for five preferences is shown in Fig. 10.15.

Case Study

Three social networking organizations were created in a closed group with 150 users and they were designed to offer different services with different criteria. These social networking organizations were registered with the SNSA. Users were permitted to register with SNSA and provide their preferences in selecting their desired social networking services. The proposed framework was used in selecting the best service for each user based on their preferences. A study was conducted to obtain the user satisfaction from the registered user. The user's requirements, the social network organization selected by the PROMETHEE method and satisfaction of the users are tabulated in Fig. 10.16. It is found that 95% expressed that they are excellently satisfied and the satisfaction levels are shown in Fig. 10.17.

Us-ers	Service Name	Pu P	Re	Se	Pa	Ir	Pi	Cu	Selected Or-ganization	Satisfac-tion
U1	Musical	1	0.85	0.325	0.9	0.75	0.55	0.625	O_Gamer	0.75
U2	Musical	0	0.45	0.65	0.75	0.56	0.9	0.95	O_Space	0.9
U3	Musical	0	0.55	0.77	0.77	0.80	0.2	0.78	O_Space	0.98
U4	Musical	1	0.6	0.3	0.8	0.9	0	0.8	O_Profe	0.65
U5	Bike Race	0	0.77	0.4	0.5	0.8	0.2	0.3	O_Space	0.75
U6	Bike Race	0	0.9	0.3	0.4	0.75	0.2	0.4	O_Space	0.8
U7	Bike Race	0	0.8	0.3	0.4	0.6	0.9	0.8	O_Gamer	0.45
U8	Cloud Community	1	0.9	0.2	0.6	0.7	0.2	0.2	O_Space	1
U9	Cloud Community	1	0.2	1	0.5	1	0	0	O_space	1
U10	Cloud Community	0	0.5	1	0.5	0.75	0	0	O_Gamer	0.25

Fig. 10.16　Case study

Fig. 10.17　User satisfaction

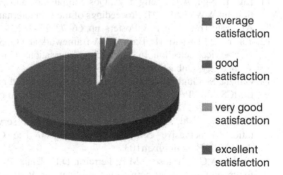

■ average satisfaction

■ good satisfaction

■ very good satisfaction

■ excellent satisfaction

Conclusion

In this chapter, an effective user-driven framework for selection of social network services was proposed. The social network service selection has been as modeled as multi-criteria decision making problem. Many criteria such as information richness, reliability, searchability, paid/unpaid services, customizability, platform independence and activity support that influences the service selection was considered. The experimental analysis was performed on the proposed framework and was found to be effective.

References

1. Sauerbier, R.A., Grant, A.E., Meadows, J.H.: Social networking, Chapter 20. In: Communication Technology Update and Fundamentals, 12th edn. Elsevier, Amsterdam (2010). ISBN 978-0-240-81475-9
2. Lin, Kuan-Yu, Hsi-Peng, Lu: Why people use social networking sites: an empirical study integrating network externalities and motivation theory. Comput. Hum. Behav. 27, 1152-1161 (2011). doi:10.1016/j.chb.2010.12.009
3. Kwon, O., Wen, Y.: An empirical study of the factors affecting social network service use. Comput. Hum. Behav. 26, 254-263 (2010). doi:10.1016/j.chb.2009.04.011
4. Mokhtar, S.B., McNamara, L., Capra L.: A middleware service for pervasive social networking. In: M-PAC '09 Proceedings of the International Workshop on Middleware for Pervasive Mobile and Embedded Computing. ACM Press, New York (2009). doi: 10.1145/1657127.1657130
5. Wang, H.-C., Lee, C.-S., Ho, T.-H.: Combining subjective and objective QoS factors for personalized web service selection. Exp. Syst. Appl. 32, 571-584 (2007). doi:10.1016/j.eswa.2006.01.034
6. Hsi-Peng, Lu, Hsiao, K.-L.: The influence of extro/introversion on the intention to pay for social networking sites. Inf. Manage. 47, 150-157 (2010). doi:10.1016/j.im.2010.01.003
7. Stutzman, F., Capra, R., Thompson, J.: Factors mediating disclosure in social network sites. Comput. Hum. Behav. 27, 590-598 (2011). doi:10.1016/j.chb.2010.10.017
8. Correa, T., Hinsley, A.W., Gil de Zúñiga, H.: Who interacts on the Web?: the intersection of users' personality and social media use. Comput. Hum. Behav. 26, 247-253 (2010). doi:10.1016/j.chb.2009.09.003
9. Tsai, F.S., Han, W., Junwei, Xu, Chua, H.C.: Design and development of a mobile peer-to-peer social networking application. Exp. Syst. Appl. 36, 11077-11087 (2009). doi:10.1016/j.eswa.2009.02.093
10. Gao, Q., Dai, Y., Fan, Z., Kang, R.: Understanding factors affecting perceived sociability of social software. Comput. Hum. Behav. 26, 1846-1861 (2010). doi:10.1016/j.chb.2010.07.022
11. Liu, Y., Ngu, A.H., Zeng, L.Z.: Qos computation and policing in dynamic web service selection. In: WWW Alt. '04: Proceedings of the 13th International World Wide Web Conference on Alternate Track Papers & Posters, pp. 66-73, 17-22 May 2004. doi: 10.1145/1013367.1013379
12. Taher, L., El Khati, H., Bash, R.: A framework and QoS matchmaking algorithm for dynamic web services selection. In: The Second International Conference on Innovations in Information Technology, Dubai, UAE, 26-28 Sept 2005
13. Galizia, S., Gugliotta, A., Domingue, J.: A trust based methodology for web service selection. In: ICSC '07 Proceedings of International Conference on Semantic Computing, pp. 193-200, 17-19 Sept 2007. doi: 10.1109/ICSC.2007.8
14. Zhang, B., Shi, Y., Xiao, X.: A policy-driven service composition method for adaptation in pervasive computing environment. The Comput. J. 53(2), 152-165 (2007). doi:10.1093/comjnl/bxm103
15. Santos, A.C., Cardoso, J.M.P., Ferreira, D.R., Diniz, P.C., Chaínho, P.: Providing user context for mobile and social networking applications. Pervasive Mob. Comput. 6, 324-341 (2010). doi:10.1016/j.pmcj.2010.01.001
16. Shin, D.-H.: The effects of trust, security and privacy in social networking: a security-based approach to understand the pattern of adoption. Interact. Comput. 22, 428-438 (2010). doi:10.1016/j.intcom.2010.05.001
17. Behzadian, M., Kazemzadeh, R.B., Albadvi, A., Aghdasi, M.: Decision support PROMETHEE: a comprehensive literature review on methodologies and applications. Eur. J. Oper. Res. 200, 198-215 (2010). doi:10.1016/j.ejor.2009.01.021
18. Gül Özerol and Esra Karasakal: A parallel between Regret theory and outranking methods for multicriteria decision making under imprecise information. Theor. Decis. 65, 45-70 (2008). doi:10.1007/s11238-007-9074-y

19. Roux, O., Duvivier, D., Dhaevers, V., Meskens, N., Artiba, A.: Multicriteria approach to rank scheduling strategies. Int. J. Prod. Econ. **112**, 192–201 (2008). doi:10.1016/j.ijpe.2006.08.020
20. Jian-jun, W.A.N.G., Cai-min, W.E.I., De-li, Y.A.N.G.: A decision method for vendor selection based on AHP/PROMETHEE/GAIA. J. Dalian Univ. Technol. **46**, 926–931 (2006). doi:cnki:ISSN:1000-8608.0.2006-06-027
21. Brans, J.-P., Mareschal, B.: The PROMCALC & GAIA decision support system for multi-criteria decision aid. Decis. Support Syst. **12**, 297–310 (1994). doi:10.1016/0167-9236(94), 90048-5
22. Wei-xiang, L., Bang-yi, L.: An extension of the Promethee II method based on generalized fuzzy numbers. Exp. Syst. Appl. **37**, 5314–5319 (2010). doi:10.1016/j.eswa.2010.01.004

Part III
Anonymity

Chapter 11
Providing Group Anonymity in Social Networks

Oleg Chertov and Dan Tavrov

Abstract In today's world, there are almost no borders between people. Using Internet technologies, especially social networks, people can communicate and share different information regardless of where they live or work. However, giving out any sensitive information can pose significant security threats for the owner of the information. As more privacy challenges arise, people become concerned about their security. Many social networking websites provide various types of privacy policies, but this proves to be insufficient. All existing security methods aim at gaining individual anonymity. Nevertheless, information about user groups, which could be determined inside social networks, is not protected. Still, this information might occur to be security-intensive information is present in this data set.

In this chapter, the task we have set is providing group anonymity in social networks. By group anonymity we understand the property of a group of people to be indistinguishable within a particular dataset. We also propose a technique to solve the task using wavelet transforms.

Introduction

The phenomenon of social networks (SNs) is a completely outstanding feature of Web 2.0 which allows different people all over the world to express their own personalities, share information, and find new friends or partners. The popularity of SNs has risen dramatically in recent years, which makes it a topical subject for different researches and studies.

However, the widespread occurrence of SNs has a flip side. The greater the amount of information we give out freely to the greater number of people, the more vulnerable we become. By analyzing a SN user's content and his/her activity, we can

O. Chertov (✉) • D. Tavrov
Kyiv Polytechnic Institute, National Technical University of Ukraine, 03056 Kyiv, Ukraine
e-mail: chertov@i.ua; dan.tavrov@i.ua

A. Abraham (ed.), *Computational Social Networks: Security and Privacy*,
DOI 10.1007/978-1-4471-4051-1_11, © Springer-Verlag London 2012

disclose not only some factual (biographical) data, but also his/her habits, interests, intentions etc. All the problems connected with providing individual anonymity and protection of personal information have been discussed for many years now with respect to SNs as well.

But, in this chapter we would like to pay attention to those features of SNs that do not concern providing individual anonymity. They rather deal with issues such as national security and terror threats. All the challenges arising here can be divided into direct and indirect ones.

However, SNs have today become a convenient and fast method of communication and influence. That is why they can be successfully abused by fraudsters to organize so-called "pump and dump" financial spam schemes. At the same time, they can be used by the British criminal investigation departments while solving crimes. Special services and security agencies of different states try to influence the performance of SNs to a greater and greater extent. Let us recall only the latest facts. For instance, on December 19, 2010 in Minsk all social networks which were being used to coordinate a protest against the expected rigging of the presidential elections were disconnected. Another example is a subpoena issued by The U.S. District Court for the Eastern District of Virginia on December 14, 2010 ordering Twitter Inc. to hand over all data on people tied to the Wikileaks site (all connection records and session times, IP addresses used to access Twitter, e-mail and residential addresses plus billing records and details of bank accounts and credit cards).

In relation to this, having somehow gotten access to the information stored in a SN, and analyzed the activity of many users, one can violate the privacy not only of a distinct person, but of a certain group of people. This group might not even be explicitly defined. For instance, basing on how SN users participate in discussing particular topics, it is possible to reveal the territorial distribution of informal group members. This distribution could possibly indicate some restricted military, scientific, or, perhaps, terrorist centers. An abnormal quantity of messages from a certain region or of a certain tendency might suggest the planning or implementation of a certain move. By analyzing previous network activity of detected malefactors, one can construct their behavior model (an SN portrait). With its help, it is worth trying to track down similar criminals. Of course, such methods can be used for some "civil" purposes as well, for example in marketing, when suggesting goods for specific categories of SN users. Such external interference isn't always pleasant or desirable. That's why we consider that SNs ought to not only improve individual user anonymity, but also pay severe attention to the open problems of providing group anonymity.

In this chapter, we formalize a term of "group anonymity" and propose a method for providing it in SNs. We use wavelet transforms (WT) since they are rather sufficient in this case. Also, we introduce a quite comprehensive metric to measure possible data utility loss when providing data anonymity.

In section "Related Work", we analyze existing works in the field of preserving privacy in SNs. Then, in section "Data Representation", we address the problem of interpreting SNs users' profiles in a way suitable for our method. Section "Providing Group Anonymity" explains how to provide group anonymity in a given dataset.

Then, in section "Practical Example", we present a practical example built upon real-life data. Eventually, section "Conclusion" is devoted to drawing conclusions and pointing out goals to be achieved in the nearest future.

Related Work

The main purpose of SNs is helping people to go public, and link to other people with similar interests and intentions. Still, most users wouldn't like to give away any of the sensitive information contained in their "profiles" to totally random strangers. Therefore, privacy is likely to be a topic of great concern to every SN user.

Indeed, almost every online SN gives certain means of designing the user's own privacy policy. This means the user can explicitly choose which kind of information provided in his profile can be publicly available, and which can not. However, this only seems to be an appropriate solution.

In [1, 2], the authors performed a rather thorough and deep analysis of SN users and their privacy preferences. In [1], they analyzed the online profiles of more than 4,000 Carnegie Mellon University students present in the SN Facebook. The authors came to the conclusion that the majority of users do not take possible privacy risks seriously, and use default though rather weak privacy preferences instead of applying limiting ones. A similar result was obtained in [3]. This means that, when it comes to real life, many SN users simply do not make use of the possibilities provided to protect their own privacy. Though, we have to add that in 2010 things became a little better. According to a report by Forrester Research [4], about 36% of American adults said they were "very concerned" about their privacy on social networking sites in 2010, compared with 30% who felt that way the year before. The shift was particularly noticeable among people over age 44; 50% of people aged 54 to 64 described themselves as "very concerned," compared with 32% who said that in 2009.

So, the problem of providing privacy in SNs hasn't been solved completely yet. Though, this theme is being studied a lot, and many interesting results have been achieved. Some of them will be covered later on in this chapter.

In general, all existent works which deal with the problem of protecting privacy in SNs can be categorized according to how the authors treat a social network.

Papers of the first type do not propose any techniques to preserve privacy. Their main purpose is supplying readers with thorough analysis of current online SNs so that privacy violation challenges become clearer to researchers. The works [1–3] all represent this category.

Other researchers tend to refer to SNs as an abstract mathematical entity. For instance, the authors of [5] propose a mathematical model of a social network which takes into consideration cases where data may belong to many users. They provide a detailed formal representation of a SN, and also suggest formal definitions for various types of privacy policies to be applied by users. On this basis, they introduce and implement a solution which builds on some results from game theory freeing the users from the routine activity of selecting privacy preferences for every photo they upload. In [6], a social network is viewed as a simple graph, and an appropriate algorithm for its l-diversity anonymization is proposed.

Another way to treat SNs is to think of them as real-life online web services prone to external attacks and unwanted data leakage. In [7], the authors address a problem of defining possible ways of violating privacy in SNs, and try to propose solutions to protect people's privacy in each case. Such works as [8,9] propose quite effective solutions in the form of software applications that can aid in protecting individual privacy. For example, [8] introduces a novel privacy-by-proxy technique to decrease the risk of malicious data harvesting. At the same time, the authors of [9] developed a Firefox browser plugin that modifies the SN page allowing users to encrypt their profiles. In [10], the authors even propose a special access control system named Lockr. It can be integrated with various online applications helping users to control their own social information.

Nevertheless, there exists yet another way to represent SNs. It often becomes relevant when the data about SN users are being published, or passed to some third-party organizations. This is not a far-fetched situation. On October 2, 2006, the world's largest online DVD rental company, Netflix, published a dataset containing movie ratings created by 480,189 users. In [11], the authors proved that this dataset contains security-intensive information (even with all explicit user identifiers omitted), especially when using suitable auxiliary information. The same thing happened in 2006 when America Online posted a file containing three months of anonymized search queries of 658,000 users. Although there was no personally identifiable data linked to these accounts, there was no defense against obtaining security-intensive information; these data helped determine concrete personal information about some users [12].

Moreover, SN data might come in handy when performing marketing research. Marketers could make use of data collected from profiles of users who show interest in particular goods or activities. These are not some groundless statements. Harris Interactive accomplished a survey of US brand managers [13] for Buddy Media Reaching Customers in Local Markets. It turned out that 43% of those managers used Facebook to find customers all over the world. Besides, in the already mentioned paper [6], the authors study the problem of providing l-diversity in SN data that is published for research.

Taking all this into account, we will consider a social network to be a dataset containing miscellaneous pieces of information about its users, and our aim will be to provide anonymity for such a dataset before it is given away.

All the problems and solutions mentioned above are way too unlike and dissimilar, each pointing at its own subject of research. But, what ties them all together is individual anonymity.

All the studies in the field of preserving privacy in SNs, regardless of how they treat a particular social network, deal with protecting single individuals. In a way there is no major difference between users of online SNs and vertices in a graph. As a matter of fact, these all are individuals. At the same time, we previously introduced

[14] a completely new type of anonymity which can be achieved in a given dataset. We named it group anonymity.

Group anonymity, as opposed to the individual one, means that different data patterns and distributions are protected, and cannot lead to unwanted information disclosure. Such collective data features cannot be basically distinguished when analyzing single users' profiles only. The importance of such anonymity can be illustrated with an example. Suppose that a particular third-party takes interest in researching the age distribution of people working at power plants. But, if by chance the possessor of the corresponding SN data decides to analyze where nuclear plant workers work exactly, it may very likely reveal some concealed nuclear research center. This could be tracked down by discovering the maximum quantity of power plant workers in a region with few officially registered stations.

Herein, we will presume that the only data source available for a potential adversary is the dataset we mentioned above.

Data Representation

As has been stated before, we propose to treat a social network under analysis as a certain statistical dataset. That is why we need to define a convenient way of representing SN data. The most common and comprehensive one is presenting all the information about each user as a tuple consisting of several entries. Usually, this is not hard to accomplish since in most SNs popular nowadays users are invited to fill in so-called profiles.

The entire set of tuples corresponding to all the users of a SN could be gathered into a table. We would like to note here that such tables do not reflect all the relations inside a network. Their main purpose is to provide researchers and miscellaneous third-parties with statistical information only.

Nevertheless, giving away such tables almost inevitably leads to security-intensive information leaking (as we clearly showed in section "Related Work"). That is why necessary precautions should to be taken beforehand. Possibly the simplest (but not quite as sufficient) thing to accomplish is to remove all the *identifiers* (i.e., entries unambiguously defining a person such as one's full name). Also, quite a lot of other methods for providing anonymity of an individual might be applied to such tables. Though, we won't discuss them in this chapter.

Instead, we will present a method for providing *group anonymity* in a given SN dataset.

Firstly, we need to slightly readjust the data representation discussed above. To guarantee at least some level of individual anonymity, we need to remove all the identifiers from this dataset. And to be able to perform the necessary calculations, we need to replace all the entries with suitable numerical substitutes. Every column of the resultant table is called an *attribute* (with respect to a similar term used in statistics). After performing these preliminary actions, we obtain the dataset (often called a *microfile*) presented in Table 11.1.

Table 11.1 Microfile
representation of SN data

	w_1	w_2	$\cdots$	w_η
u_1	y_{11}	y_{12}	$\cdots$	$y_{1\eta}$
u_2	y_{21}	y_{22}	$\cdots$	$y_{2\eta}$
$\cdots$	$\cdots$	$\cdots$	$\cdots$	$\cdots$
u_μ	$y_{\mu 1}$	$y_{\mu 2}$	$\cdots$	$y_{\mu\eta}$

Here, u_i stands for the ith SN user, w_j stands for the jth attribute, y_{ij} stands for a particular data element.

To provide group anonymity within any given microfile **M**, we need to rearrange specific y_{ij} so that potential adversaries cannot determine security-intensive data distribution. At the same time, the data itself shouldn't be altered drastically, which we will discuss in section "Practical Example".

To start redistributing data elements, we need to determine which attribute values we would like to modify, and according to what rule. For that matter, we need to introduce several important definitions.

Definition 1. A vital set S_v is a subset of Cartesian product $w_{v_1} \times w_{v_2} \times \ldots \times \times w_{v_l}$ of columns from Table 11.1, where v_i, $i = \overline{1,l}$ are integers. Respectively, each $w_{v_i}, i = \overline{1,l}$ is called a vital attribute.

Definition 2. We will call an element $s_k^{(v)}$ from S_v, $k = \overline{1, l_v}$, $l_v \le \mu$ a vital value combination, whereas each element of $s_k^{(v)}$ itself will be called a vital value.

Definition 3. A parameter set S_p is a subset of microfile data elements corresponding to the pth attribute, $p \ne v_i$ $\forall i = \overline{1,l}$. We will call elements $s_k^{(p)}$ from S_p, $k = \overline{1, l_p}$, $l_p \le \mu$ parameter values. Analogously, the pth attribute will be called a parameter attribute.

Vital and parameter attributes serve to specify user groups to be redistributed (defined by vital value combinations) and the method of their arrangement (determined by parameter values). For instance, if we take "Places to Spend Holiday" as a vital attribute, we can define groups of people who enjoy mountaineering, or love scuba diving. At the same time, picking "Age" as a parameter attribute could reveal their distribution by age. Such information could be very useful for marketing research though security-intensive in some cases.

Providing Group Anonymity

A Generic Scheme of Providing Group Anonymity

When providing group anonymity in any microfile, including SN datasets, one has to carry out certain steps common for all the tasks of similar origin. In this subsection,

we will present a generic scheme of providing group anonymity regardless of its
type, aim, or complexity. For detailed information, refer to [15].

Let us introduce more definitions.

Definition 4. A group $G(V, P)$ is a set consisting of several vital attributes
$V = V_1, V_2, \ldots, V_{l_v}$ and a parameter attribute P, $P \neq V_j$ $\forall j = \overline{1, l_v}$.

Each group represents a certain SN user category that needs to be protected.

In almost all cases, it is mostly inconvenient to work with a microfile as it is. To
achieve valuable results, we would rather convert the dataset to a more appropriate
form.

Definition 5. A goal representation $\Omega(\mathbf{M}, G)$ of a dataset $\mathbf{M}$ with respect to a
group G is a certain dataset presenting data within the microfile in a way proper
for providing group anonymity.

Definition 6. A mapping function $\Upsilon : \mathbf{M} \rightarrow \Omega(\mathbf{M}, G)$ is any function, algorithm,
or procedure transforming the initial microfile $\mathbf{M}$ into its goal representation
$\Omega(\mathbf{M}, G)$.

In general, the goal representation is a dataset of any possible form, either one-dimensional or multidimensional. In this chapter, we will work with one-dimensional
goal representations only.

After having defined a concrete goal representation, we need to determine how to
modify it precisely (which is possibly the most important part of the whole thing).

Definition 7. A modifying functional $\Xi : \Omega(\mathbf{M}, G) \rightarrow \Omega'(\mathbf{M}, G)$ of a dataset
$\mathbf{M}$ with respect to a group G is any function, algorithm, or procedure leading
to transformation of the initial goal representation into another one with group
anonymity achieved.

In this chapter, we will present one particular modifying functional based upon
applying a wavelet transform (WT). The necessary background for that topic will
be presented in section "Wavelet Transform Basics".

Generally speaking, all the operations mentioned above can be divided into the
following stages:

1. Build up a (depersonalized) microfile $\mathbf{M}$ with SN data to be modified.
2. Choose one or several groups $G_i(V_i, P_i)$, $i = \overline{1, k}$.
3. For each i from 1 to k:

   (a) Pick a proper goal representation $\Omega_i(\mathbf{M}, G_i)$ for a group $G_i(V_i, P_i)$.
   (b) Define a mapping function $\Upsilon : \mathbf{M} \rightarrow \Omega_i(\mathbf{M}, G_i)$. Obtain needed goal
       representation.
   (c) Define a modifying functional $\Xi : \Omega_i(\mathbf{M}, G_i) \rightarrow \Omega_i'(\mathbf{M}, G_i)$. Obtain a
       modified goal representation.
   (d) Define an inverse goal mapping function $\Upsilon_i^{-1} : \Omega_i'(\mathbf{M}, G_i) \rightarrow \mathbf{M}'$. Obtain a
       modified microfile.

4. Prepare the modified microfile for publishing.

Wavelet Transform Basics

In this subsection, we will cover only the most important wavelet theory results necessary for its practical application. The detailed information can be found in [16].

Let $s = (s_1, s_2, \ldots, s_m)$ denote a discrete *signal* consisting of numerical values. Also, let us denote by $h = (h_1, h_2, \ldots, h_n)$ a *high-pass wavelet filter*, whereas $l = (l_1, l_2, \ldots, l_n)$ will represent a *low-pass wavelet filter*. In the next few equations, we will refer to both h and l simply as f.

To calculate the convolution of signal s and filter f, we need to perform the following operation:

$$(s * f)(i) = \sum_{j \in \mathbb{Z}} s(j) f(i + 1 - j). \tag{11.1}$$

In (11.1), $\mathbb{Z}$ stands for a set of integer numbers.

Then, to dyadic downsample the output (i.e., leave out those array elements which come at odd positions), we can carry out the following operation denoted by $\downarrow 2$:

$$s_{\downarrow 2}(i) = s(2i), \quad 2i \leq m. \tag{11.2}$$

Also, we can define an inverse operation of dyadic upsampling (i.e., inserting zero value after every array element) denoted by $\uparrow 2$:

$$\begin{cases} s_{\uparrow 2}(2i - 1) = s(i) \\ s_{\uparrow 2}(2i) = 0 \end{cases}, \quad 2i \leq m. \tag{11.3}$$

To guarantee ideal signal wavelet reconstruction, we need to introduce two additional operations. The first one is signal extension:

$$s^{\langle L|R \rangle} y = (y_1, y_2, \ldots, y_L, s_1, s_2, \ldots, s_m, y_{L+1}, \ldots, y_{L+R}). \tag{11.4}$$

Also, we need an operation of signal K-length central-part selection:

$$z = \langle s \rangle_K. \tag{11.5}$$

Now, we will define consequent operations (11.4), (11.1), (11.5), and (11.2) as follows:

$$s *_{\downarrow 2} f = \left(\left\langle \left(s^{\langle L|R \rangle} \breve{s} \right) * f \right\rangle_K \right)_{\downarrow 2}, \tag{11.6}$$

and consequent operations (11.3), (11.4), (11.1), and (11.5) as follows:

$$s *_{\uparrow 2} f = \left\langle \left(s_{\uparrow 2}^{\langle L|R \rangle} \breve{s} \right) * f \right\rangle_K. \tag{11.7}$$

In (11.6) and (11.7), $\breve{s}$ is a signal consisting of s elements and zero values.

Let us introduce some useful notations to shorten our further explanation:

$$z = (\underbrace{((s *_{\downarrow 2} f) *_{\downarrow 2} f) \ldots *_{\downarrow 2} f}_{k-1 \text{ times}}) = \prod_{i=1}^{k} s *_{\downarrow 2} f; \qquad (11.8)$$

$$z = (\underbrace{((s *_{\uparrow 2} f) *_{\uparrow 2} f) \ldots *_{\uparrow 2} f}_{k-1 \text{ times}}) = \prod_{i=1}^{k} s *_{\uparrow 2} f. \qquad (11.9)$$

To perform signal s one-level wavelet decomposition, we need to apply (11.8) and (11.9) to the signal and both filters separately:

$$a_1 = s *_{\downarrow 2} l; \qquad (11.10)$$

$$d_1 = s *_{\downarrow 2} h. \qquad (11.11)$$

An array a_1 consists of approximation coefficients at level 1, whereas d_1 stands for an array of detail coefficients at the same decomposition level.

To obtain coefficients at any level k, we need to apply (11.10) and (11.11) to approximation coefficients at level $k - 1$. Generally speaking, to obtain approximation and detail coefficients at any level k, we need to apply the following transformations to our initial signal:

$$a_k = \prod_{i=1}^{k} s *_{\downarrow 2} l; \qquad (11.12)$$

$$d_k = \left(\prod_{i=1}^{k-1} s *_{\downarrow 2} l \right) *_{\downarrow 2} h. \qquad (11.13)$$

It has been shown in the wavelet theory that we can obtain signal *approximation* at level k and signal *detail* at the same level by performing the following operations:

$$A_k = \prod_{i=1}^{k} a_k *_{\uparrow 2} l; \qquad (11.14)$$

$$D_k = \prod_{i=1}^{k-1} \left[(d_k *_{\uparrow 2} h) *_{\uparrow 2} l \right]. \qquad (11.15)$$

Signal approximation is a smoothed version of the initial numerical array. Signal details reflect high-frequency fluctuations and deviations in a signal. So, wavelet transforms help to divide any initial numerical array into low-frequency and high-frequency components. This means that the initial signal s can always be obtained as the following sum:

$$s = A_k + \sum_{i=1}^{k} D_i. \qquad (11.16)$$

In many situations, the formulae presented above are not very computationally efficient. Sometimes, it is better to use the matrix wavelet transform described in [17]. Here, we will present only how to obtain signal approximation using matrix multiplications.

To complete this task, we need to introduce matrix equivalent forms of operations (11.1), (11.3), (11.4), and (11.5):

$$
s * f = \mathbf{M}^c_{(m+n-1) \times m}(f) \cdot s = \begin{pmatrix}
f_1 & 0 & 0 & \ldots & 0 & 0 \\
f_2 & f_1 & 0 & \ldots & 0 & 0 \\
f_3 & f_2 & f_1 & \ldots & 0 & 0 \\
\multicolumn{6}{c}{\ldots\ldots\ldots\ldots\ldots\ldots} \\
0 & 0 & 0 & \ldots & f_n & f_{n-1} \\
0 & 0 & 0 & \ldots & 0 & f_n
\end{pmatrix} \cdot s; \tag{11.17}
$$

$$
s_{\uparrow 2} = \mathbf{M}^u_{2m \times m}(f) \cdot s = \begin{pmatrix}
1 & 0 & 0 & 0 & \ldots & 0 \\
0 & 0 & 0 & 0 & \ldots & 0 \\
0 & 1 & 0 & 0 & \ldots & 0 \\
0 & 0 & 0 & 0 & \ldots & 0 \\
\multicolumn{6}{c}{\ldots\ldots\ldots\ldots\ldots\ldots} \\
0 & 0 & 0 & 0 & \ldots & 1 \\
0 & 0 & 0 & 0 & \ldots & 0
\end{pmatrix} \cdot s; \tag{11.18}
$$

$$
s^{\langle L | R \rangle} \check{s} = \mathbf{M}^e_{(m+L+R) \times m} \cdot s; \tag{11.19}
$$

$$
\langle s \rangle_K = \mathbf{M}^s_{K \times m} \cdot s. \tag{11.20}
$$

Matrix $\mathbf{M}^c_{(m+n-1) \times m}$ is called a *convolution matrix*. Its lower index explicitly shows the size of the matrix. Matrix $\mathbf{M}^u_{2m \times m}$ is called an *upsampling matrix*. *Extension matrix* $\mathbf{M}^e_{(m+L+R) \times m}$ and *central-part selection matrix* $\mathbf{M}^s_{K \times m}$ are not presented here, because their structure varies depending on the particular wavelet scheme being applied.

Now, we can present the matrix form of (11.14):

$$
A_k = \mathbf{M}^s_{m \times \left(2\left[\frac{K_1}{2}\right]+L_1+R_1+n-1\right)} \cdot
$$
$$
\cdot \mathbf{M}^c_{\left(2\left[\frac{K_1}{2}\right]+L_1+R_1+n-1\right) \times \left(2\left[\frac{K_1}{2}\right]+L_1+R_1\right)}(l) \cdot
$$
$$
\cdot \mathbf{M}^e_{\left(2\left[\frac{K_1}{2}\right]+L_1+R_1\right) \times 2\left[\frac{K_1}{2}\right]} \cdot \mathbf{M}^u_{2\left[\frac{K_1}{2}\right] \times \left[\frac{K_1}{2}\right]} \cdot
$$
$$
\cdots \cdot \mathbf{M}^s_{\left[\frac{K_{k-1}}{2}\right] \times \left(2\left[\frac{K_k}{2}\right]+L_k+R_k+n-1\right)}.
$$

$$\cdot \mathbf{M}^c_{\left(2\left[\frac{K_k}{2}\right]+L_k+R_k+n-1\right)\times\left(2\left[\frac{K_k}{2}\right]+L_k+R_k\right)}{}^{(l)} \cdot$$

$$\cdot \mathbf{M}^e_{\left(2\left[\frac{K_k}{2}\right]+L_k+R_k\right)\times 2\left[\frac{K_k}{2}\right]} \cdot$$

$$\cdot \mathbf{M}^u_{2\left[\frac{K_k}{2}\right]\times\left[\frac{K_k}{2}\right]} \cdot a_k \equiv \mathbf{M}_{\mathrm{rec}} \cdot a_k. \tag{11.21}$$

Matrix $\mathbf{M}_{\mathrm{rec}}$ is called a *wavelet reconstruction matrix* (WRM). Its size is $m \times \times \left[\frac{K_k}{2}\right]$.

Providing Group Anonymity Using Wavelet Transform

Recalling the group anonymity scheme from section "A Generic Scheme of Providing Group Anonymity", we can see that we need to define the goal representation, mapping function, and modifying functional to be able to provide group anonymity in an SN dataset. In this subsection, we will define all three of them.

First, let us define a suitable goal representation. In [14], we introduced a so-called *quantity signal*. It can be obtained by counting up all the users that share the same vital value combination and parameter value (determined by a group definition). A quantity signal gives us a quantitative distribution of SN users with particular qualities over a range distinguished by parameter values. Certain extreme values of this signal could lead to a privacy breach, that is why we need to group-anonymize it.

In [14], we showed that to provide group anonymity one needs to modify the quantity signal wavelet approximation. At the same time, all the details should be left as they are (or changed at most proportionally). The latter restriction ensures that a certain amount of data utility is preserved. Also, we demonstrated that any arbitrary alteration of a signal approximation is unacceptable. This is why the only option is to replace approximation coefficients.

But, in general it is hard to define which approximation coefficients to take in order to gain the needed signal distribution. However, it is possible to obtain them as a solution to a simple linear programming problem (we will delve deeper into this topic in section "Practical Example").

In most cases, a new quantity signal (a sum of new approximation and old details) might consist of negative values. To overcome this undesired result, we need to add a reasonably big value to all the signal elements. After that, it is important to multiply the resultant signal by a coefficient which guarantees that mean values of both modified and initial quantity signals are the same (we need to make sure that the total number of SN users remains stable).

Summarizing the above, we can present a step-by-step algorithm which can be treated as a modifying functional:

1. Construct a quantity signal q by calculating all the users with the same vital value combination and parameter value.
2. Decompose the signal using a certain wavelet basis.
3. Modify approximation coefficients (for example, by solving a linear programming problem with constraints obtained from (11.21)).
4. Obtain a new quantity signal as the sum of the new approximation and old details.
5. Obtain a non-negative signal $\hat{q}$, and fix its mean value: $\tilde{q} = \hat{q} \cdot \sum_{i=1}^{m} q_i / \sum_{i=1}^{m} \hat{q}_i$.

Modifying the Initial Dataset with Minimum Distortion

After having obtained the new quantity signal, we obviously need to reconstruct our initial dataset $\mathbf{M}$ so that it corresponds to the new quantities. One option is to change the vital attribute values of particular users. Though, this technique does not provide any feasible estimation of likely data utility loss.

Another choice lies in swapping parameter attribute values between two users (moving users from one group to another). In this case, we might want to measure how much distortion is being introduced into our dataset during such data perturbations.

For that matter, we need to define *influential* attributes. These attributes' values should be distorted as little as possible. To explain this, let us consider one typical situation. Suppose we need to exchange one person of a certain occupation living in a certain region for another one of a different occupation, and living in a different region. To provide group anonymity, we have to make sure that these two people have the same occupations. But, the level of anonymity does not depend on their age, income level, family members and so on. So, in general we could pick these two people without paying attention to such attributes. Nevertheless, it would be much better to take those people who are of similar age, have similar families, and earn a similar amount of money.

To evaluate "closeness" between two users, we propose use of the following metric:

$$Inf\,M(u, u^*) = \sum_{p=1}^{n_{\text{ord}}} \omega_p \left(\frac{u(I_p) - u^*(I_p)}{u(I_p) + u^*(I_p)} \right)^2 +$$

$$+ \sum_{k=1}^{n_{\text{nom}}} \gamma_k \left(\chi_k \left(u(J_k), u^*(J_k) \right) \right)^2 . \qquad (11.22)$$

Metric (11.22) is called the *influential* metric. I_p stands for the pth ordinal influential attribute (making a total of n_{ord}), J_k stands for the kth nominal influential attribute (making a total of n_{nom}). Besides, $u(\cdot)$ denotes an appropriate attribute value for user u. The $\chi(v_1, v_2)$ operator equals χ_1 if values v_1 and v_2 fall into one category. If they don't, the operator equals χ_2. Coefficients ω_p and γ_k regulate the importance of each attribute (e.g., for those attributes which are not to be changed at all they should be as big as possible).

With the help of the influential metric, we can propose a strategy of modifying the initial dataset while distorting it as little as possible. This lies in examining all potential pairs of SN users $\langle u, u^* \rangle$ for swapping their parameter values, and choosing those that yield the lowest $Inf M(u, u^*)$ value. In our opinion, this strategy seems to be NP-hard. Though, there might also be proposed heuristics providing not optimal but quite acceptable solutions.

Practical Example

To construct an appropriate quantity signal for our practical analysis, we decided to refer to the social network which is most popular in Russia, Ukraine, and neighboring countries. This network is called "VKontakte" (vk.com), or "In Touch," translated into English. According to vk.com's Worldwide Traffic Rank provided by Alexa Internet [18], it is the third most visited web site in Russia, Ukraine, and Belarus, with nearly 108 mln user accounts registered as of January 13th, 2011.

So, let us presume that all the user data from this SN is presented in microfile form (see Table 11.1). As we've pointed out in the previous subsections, our initial task is to define which group of SN users we would like to protect. Therefore, we need to pick acceptable vital and parameter attributes and values.

We decided to choose a vital value "Nuclear Energy" of a vital attribute "Interests." Also, we chose a parameter attribute "University Location Region." The values of this attribute stand for regions of Ukraine where SN users study, or have graduated. Actually, we set a task of protecting the regional distribution of people somehow connected with the field of nuclear energy (which in some cases can lead to classified information disclosure).

With these attributes in mind, we browsed through two formal groups, i.e., "Atomic Energetics" and "I am an Atomic Scientist" (appropriate screenshots can be found in Fig. 11.1), and built up the following quantity signal:

$$q = (4, 1, 7, 7, 1, 1, 6, 76, 2, 3, 6, 14, 150, 4, 4, 84, 2, 2, 23, 2, 5, 2, 2, 3).$$

Each element of q corresponds to a particular Ukrainian region. A comprehensive graph illustration is presented in Fig. 11.3a.

As we can see, there are three evident maximums in this signal. They all correspond to those regions of Ukraine where relevant universities are located. For instance, the maximum in the 13th signal element corresponds to Odessa National Polytechnic University which has a Nuclear Power Stations Department, and so on.

But, this example gives a very good understanding of the group anonymity problem. Suppose that such quantity signal maximums correspond to some half-concealed scientific centers which are not thought to be accessible publicly. Then, it is very easy to locate them just by analyzing appropriate quantity signals!

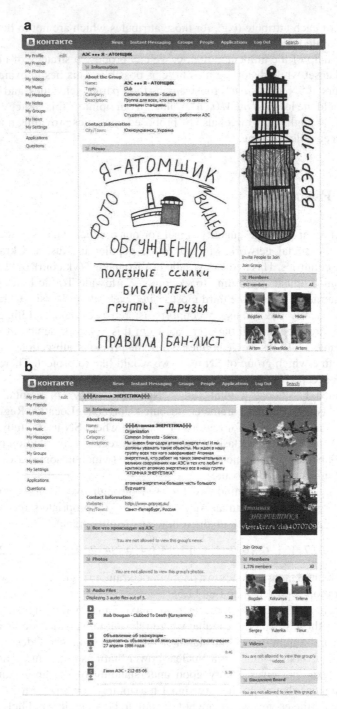

Fig. 11.1 Screenshots taken of the "I am an Atomic Scientist" (**a**) and "Atomic Energetics" (**b**) "VKontakte" groups' main pages

So, our task would rather be to redistribute our signal according to the algorithm from section "Providing Group Anonymity Using Wavelet Transform". There are two basic approaches to such redistribution. On one hand, we might want to transit existent extremums from one signal position to another. Though, this isn't all that satisfactory for us, because all existent maximums are clearly understandable, and have to persist to some extent. The other possibility is to deliberately create alleged signal maximums which would distract potential adversaries.

We have to decompose our signal using a certain wavelet basis first. We decided to choose Daubechies second-order low-pass wavelet decomposition filter $l = \left(\frac{1-\sqrt{3}}{4\sqrt{2}}, \frac{3-\sqrt{3}}{4\sqrt{2}}, \frac{3+\sqrt{3}}{4\sqrt{2}}, \frac{1+\sqrt{3}}{4\sqrt{2}} \right)$, and performed the signal's two-level wavelet decomposition (11.12) and (11.13):

$$a_2 = (6.0592, 6.8628, 23.4167, 106.1072, 48.5322, 14.2219).$$

(We presented all the results with four decimal numbers, though the calculations had been carried out with higher precision.)

Also, we can obtain $\mathbf{M}_{rec}$ according to (11.21):

$$
\mathbf{M}_{rec} =
\begin{pmatrix}
0.6373 & 0 & 0 & 0 & 0 & -0.1373 \\
0.2958 & 0.2333 & 0 & 0 & 0 & -0.0290 \\
0.0792 & 0.4040 & 0 & 0 & 0 & 0.0167 \\
-0.0123 & 0.5123 & 0 & 0 & 0 & 0 \\
-0.1373 & 0.6373 & 0 & 0 & 0 & 0 \\
-0.0290 & 0.2958 & 0.2333 & 0 & 0 & 0 \\
0.0167 & 0.0792 & 0.4040 & 0 & 0 & 0 \\
0 & -0.0123 & 0.5123 & 0 & 0 & 0 \\
0 & -0.1373 & 0.6373 & 0 & 0 & 0 \\
0 & -0.0290 & 0.2958 & 0.2333 & 0 & 0 \\
0 & 0.0167 & 0.0792 & 0.4040 & 0 & 0 \\
0 & 0 & -0.0123 & 0.5123 & 0 & 0 \\
0 & 0 & -0.1373 & 0.6373 & 0 & 0 \\
0 & 0 & -0.0290 & 0.2958 & 0.2333 & 0 \\
0 & 0 & 0.0167 & 0.0792 & 0.4040 & 0 \\
0 & 0 & 0 & -0.0123 & 0.5123 & 0 \\
0 & 0 & 0 & -0.1373 & 0.6373 & 0 \\
0 & 0 & 0 & -0.0290 & 0.2958 & 0.2333 \\
0 & 0 & 0 & 0.0167 & 0.0792 & 0.4040 \\
0 & 0 & 0 & 0 & -0.0123 & 0.5123 \\
0 & 0 & 0 & 0 & -0.1373 & 0.6373 \\
0.2333 & 0 & 0 & 0 & -0.0290 & 0.2958 \\
0.4040 & 0 & 0 & 0 & 0.0167 & 0.0792 \\
0.5123 & 0 & 0 & 0 & 0 & -0.0123
\end{pmatrix}
$$

Also, we obtained signal approximation at level 2, and a sum of its details at both levels according to (11.14) and (11.15):

A_2 = (1.9092, 2.9803, 3.4910, 3.4413, 3.5417, 7.3160, 10.1058, 11.9113, 13.9805, 31.5463, 44.9598, 54.2210, 64.5948, 42.1113, 28.4319, 23.5566, 16.3222, 14.5844, 11.3737, 6.6903, 2.4015, 4.2118, 4.3878, 2.9295);

$D_1 + D_2$ = (2.0908, −1.9803, 3.5090, 3.5587, −2.5417, −6.3160, −4.1058, 64.0887, −11.9805, −28.5463, −38.9598, −40.2210, 85.4052, −38.1113, −24.4319, 60.4434, −14.3222, −12.5844, 11.6263, −4.6903, 2.5985, −2.2118, −2.3878, 0.0705).

Old approximation and details are presented in Fig. 11.2a, c.

From the structure of the WRM, we can construct rather simple linear constraints. For example, they might guarantee that signal elements from 6 to 9 and from 17 to 20 become bigger, and that the elements from 10 to 16 become smaller. The solution to such a linear programming problem goes as follows:

$\hat{a}_2$ = (22.9291, −5.4643, 87.4289, 21.7521, −8.5747, 87.4289).

We can obtain a new approximation:

$\hat{A}_2$ = (2.6113, 2.9708, 1.0736, −3.0802, −6.6294, 18.1119, 35.2728, 44.8533, 56.4649, 31.0896, 15.6249, 10.0709, 1.8613, 1.8972, −0.2763, −4.6591, −8.4500, 17.2261, 35.0066, 44.8914, 56.8919, 31.4544, 16.0484, 10.6738).

This approximation is depicted in Fig. 11.2b.

When we sum up this approximation and the details D_1, D_2, we get a new quantity signal:

$\hat{q}$ = (4.7021, 0.9905, 4.5826, 0.4785, −9.1711, 11.7959, 31.1670, 108.9420, 44.4844, 2.5433, −23.3349, −30.1501, 87.2664, −36.2141, −24.7082, 55.7843, −22.7722, 4.6418, 46.6329, 40.2011, 59.4903, 29.2426, 13.6606, 10.7443).

In order to make the signal strictly positive and to preserve its mean value, we might, for instance, carry out the following operation:

$$\tilde{q} = (\hat{q} + 40) \cdot \left(\sum_{i=1}^{24} q_i\right) \bigg/ \left(\sum_{i=1}^{24} \hat{q}_i + 40\right).$$

The rounded version of the resultant signal goes as follows:

$\tilde{q}$ = (13, 12, 13, 12, 9, 16, 21, 45, 25, 13, 5, 3, 38, 1, 5, 29, 5, 13, 26, 24, 30, 21, 16, 15).

It is also presented in Fig. 11.3b.

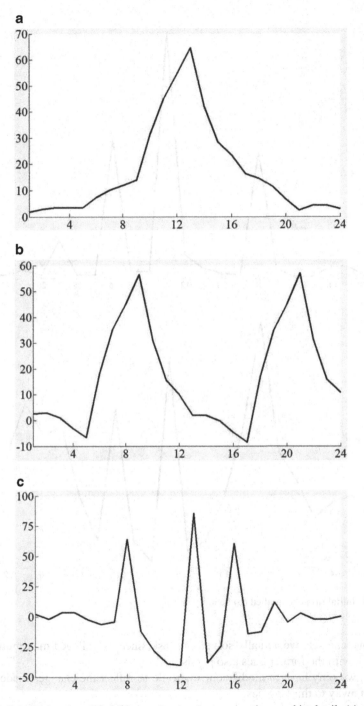

Fig. 11.2 Initial (**a**) and modified (**b**) quantity signal approximations, and its details (**c**)

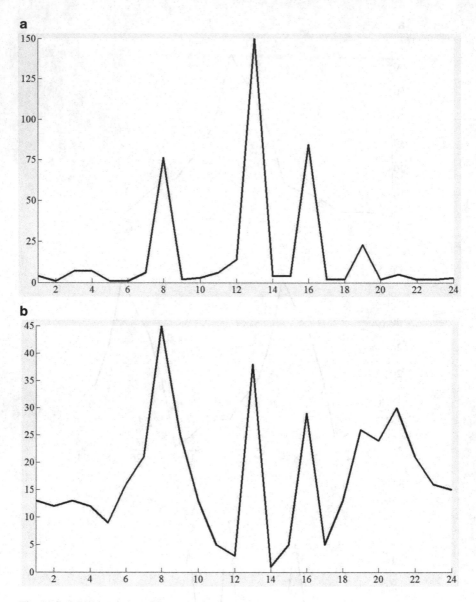

Fig. 11.3 Initial (**a**) and modified (**b**) quantity signals

As one can see, we actually solved our task since two alleged maximums have emerged, with the former ones also persisting.

Now, we only have to modify our microfile to reflect the changes made before giving it away to third-parties.

Conclusion

In this chapter, we discussed the problem of providing a completely new kind of anonymity in SNs. This kind of anonymity is often required when passing SN data on to third-party organizations for various types of statistical and marketing research.

We also suggested an effective technique to anonymize the SN dataset, which proves to be rather easy to implement. Moreover, we also addressed the problem of introducing minimum distortion into the dataset so that other kinds of statistical analysis could yield close results for both initial and perturbed microfiles.

Still, we consider some topics not to be covered thoroughly. They need to be studied in more depth in the future. These include:

- Developing heuristics for perturbing the initial dataset which yield satisfactory results at acceptable computational cost;
- Examining how applying different wavelet bases leads to obtaining different quantity signals.

References

1. Gross, R., Acquisti, A.: Information revelation and privacy in online social networks. In: Proceedings of the 2005 ACM Workshop on Privacy in the Electronic Society, pp. 71–80. ACM, New York (2005)
2. Acquisti, A., Gross, R.: Imagined communities: awareness, information sharing, and privacy on the Facebook. In: International Workshop on Privacy Enhancing Technologies. Lecture Notes in Computer Science, vol. 4258, pp. 36–58. Springer, Berlin/Heidelberg (2006)
3. Krishnamurthy, B., Wills, C.E.: Characterizing privacy in online social networks. In: Proceedings of the First Workshop on Online Social Networks, pp. 37–42. ACM, New York (2008)
4. Augie, R., Jennifer, W., Emily, R.: Fight social media stagnation. Build trust and advocacy with targeted content and engagement strategies. Forrester Research report (2010)
5. Squicciarini, A.C., Shehab, M., Paci, F.: Collective privacy management in social networks. In: Proceedings of the 18th International Conference on World Wide Web, pp. 521–530. ACM, New York (2009)
6. Panda, G.K., Mitra, A., Prasad, A., Singh, A., Tour, D.: Applying l-diversity in anonymizing collaborative social network. Int. J. Comput. Sci. Inf. Secur. 8(2), 324–329 (2010)
7. Chew, M., Balfanz, D., Laurie, B.: (Under)mining privacy in social networks. In: Proceedings of Web 2.0 Security and Privacy Workshop, Oakland (2008)
8. Felt, A., Evans, D.: Privacy protection for social networking platforms. In: Proceedings of Web 2.0 Security and Privacy Workshop, Oakland (2008)
9. Guha, S., Tang, K., Francis, P.: NOYB: privacy in online social networks. In: Proceedings of the First Workshop on Online Social Networks, pp. 49–54. ACM, New York (2008)
10. Tootoonchian, A., Saroiu, S., Ganjali, Y., Wolman, A.: Lockr: better privacy for social networks. In: Proceedings of the 5th International Conference on Emerging Networking Experiments and Technologies, pp. 169–180. ACM, New York (2009)
11. Narayanan, A., Shmatikov, V.: Robust de-anonymization of large sparse datasets. In: Proceedings of the 2008 IEEE Symposium on Security and Privacy, pp. 111–125. IEEE Computer Society, Washington (2008)
12. Barbaro, M., Zeller Jr., T.: A face is exposed for AOL searcher no. 4417749. New York Times Aug 9, p. C4 (2006).

13. Buddy Media. "Corporate Brand Manager Poll—Reaching Customers in Local Markets" conducted by Harris Interactive, Aug 3 (2010)
14. Chertov, O., Tavrov, D.: Group anonymity. In: Hüllermeier, E., Kruse, R. (eds.) IPMU-2010. Communications in Computer and Information Science, vol. 81, pp. 592–601. Springer, Heidelberg (2010)
15. Chertov, O., Tavrov, D.: Data group anonymity: general approach. Int. J. Comput. Sci. Inf. Secur. **8**(7), 1–8 (2010)
16. Mallat, S.A.: Wavelet Tour of Signal Processing. Academic, New York (1999)
17. Chertov, O.: Group Methods of Data Processing. Lulu.com, Raleigh (2010)
18. Alexa Internet. Vkontakte.ru, http://www.alexa.com/siteinfo/vkontakte.ru (2012)

Chapter 12
Anonymisation of Social Networks and Rough Set Approach

Bala Krishna Tripathy

Abstract Scientific study of network data can reveal many important behaviors of the elements involved and social trends. It also provides insight for suitable changes in the social structure and roles of individuals in it. There are many evidences (HIPAA (2002) Health insurance portability and accountability act. Available online http://www.hhs.gov/ocr/hipaa; Lambert, J Off Stat 9:313–331, 1993; Xu (2006) Utility based anonymisation using local recording. In: KDD'06, Philadelphia) which indicate the precious value of social network data in shedding light on social behavior, health, and well-being of the general public. For this purpose, the social network information needs to be published publicly or before a specialized group. But, depending upon the privacy model considered, this information may involve some sensitive data of individual participants in the social network, which are undesirable to be disclosed. Due to this problem, social network data need to be anonymized before its publication in order to prevent potential reidentification attacks. Data anonymization techniques are abundantly used in relational databases (Aggarwal et al. J Priv Technol, 2005; Backstrom et al. (2007) Wherefore art thou R3579X? Anonymized social networks, hidden patterns, and structural steganography. In: International world wide web conference (WWW). ACM, New York, pp 181–190; Bayardo and Agrawal (2005) Data privacy through optimal k-anonymisation. In: IEEE 21st international conference on data engineering, April 2005; Bamba et al. (2008) Supporting anonymous location queries in mobile environments with privacy grid. In: ACM world wide web conference; Byun et al. (2007) Efficient k-anonymisation using clustering techniques. In: International conference on database systems for advanced applications (DASFAA), pp 188–200; Campan and Truta (2008) A clustering approach for data and structural anonymity in social networks. In: ACM SIGKDD workshop on privacy, security, and trust in

B.K. Tripathy (✉)
Senior Professor, School of Computing Science and Engineering, VIT University,
Vellore, Tamil Nadu 632 014, India
e-mail: tripathybk@rediffmail.com

A. Abraham (ed.), *Computational Social Networks: Security and Privacy*,
DOI 10.1007/978-1-4471-4051-1_12, © Springer-Verlag London 2012

KDD (PinKDD), Las Vegas; Chakrabarti et al. (2004) R-MAT: a recursive model for graph mining. In: SIAM international conference on data mining; Chawla et al. (2005) Toward privacy in public databases. In: Proceedings of the theory of cryptography conference, Cambridge, MA; Evfimievski et al. (2003) Limiting privacy breaches in privacy preserving data mining. In: ACM principles of database systems (PODS). ACM, New York, pp 211–222; Getoor and Diehl, A surv SIGKDD Explore Newsl 7(2):3–12, 2005; Ghinita et al. (2007) Fast data anonymisation with low information loss. In: Very large data base conference (VLDB), Vienna, pp 758–769; Lefebvre et al. (2006) Mondrian multidimensional K-anonymity. In: IEEE international conference of data engineering (ICDE), p 25; Liu and Terzi (2008) Towards identity anonymisation on graphs. In: Wang (ed.) SIGMOD conference. ACM, New York, pp 93–106; Lunacek et al. (2006) A crossover operator for the k-anonymity problem. In: Genetic and evolutionary computation conference (GECCO), Seattle, Washington, pp 1713–1720; Machanavajjhala et al. (2006) L-diversity: privacy beyond K-anonymity. In: IEEE international conference on data engineering (ICDE), Atlanta, p 24; Malin, J Am Med Inform Assoc 12(1):28–34, 2004; Nergiz and Clifton (2006) Thoughts on k-anonymisation. In: IEEE 22nd international conference on data engineering workshops (ICDEW), Atlanta, April 2006, p 96; Nergiz and Clifton (2007) Multirelational k-anonymity. In: IEEE 23rd international conference on data engineering posters, April 2007). However, most of the known anonymisation approaches such as suppression or generalization do not directly apply to social network data. One major challenge in social network anonymization is the complexity. In (Gross and Yellen (2006) Graph theory and its applications. CRC, Boca Raton), it has been proved that a particular k-anonymity problem trying to minimize the structural change to the original social network is NP-hard. Research in anonymization of social networks is a relatively new field. In this chapter, we provide a systematic study of different approaches and studies done so far in this direction. There is no doubt that social network nodes can have imprecise data as their attributes. So, normal methods proposed for anonymization are not suitable for such type of social networks. Recently, a very efficient rough set-based algorithm was established in (Tripathy and Prakash Kumar, Int J Rapid Manuf 1(2):189–207, 2009) to handle clustering of tuples in relational models. We shall describe how this algorithm can be used for anonymization of social networks. Also, we shall present some recent algorithms which use isomorphism of graphs for anonymization of social networks. In the end, we shall discuss the current status of research on anonymization of social networks and present some related problems for further study.

Introduction

A social network consists of a finite set or sets of actors (social entities, which can be discrete individual, corporate, or collective social units) and the relation (a collection of the defining feature that establishes a linkage between a pair of actors) or relations defined on them. The presence of relational information is a critical and defining feature of a social network. For example, the entities may be individuals and the connections between them being relationships, friendships, or flows of information. Social network analysis is concerned with uncovering patterns in the connections between entities. It has been widely applied to organizational networks to classify the influence or popularity of individuals and to detect collusion and fraud. Social network analysis can also be applied to study disease transmission in communities, the functioning of computer networks, and emergent behavior of physical and biological systems. The network analyst would seek to model these relationships to depict the structure of a group. One could then study the impact of this structure on the functioning of the group and/or the influence of this structure on individuals within the group. The social network perspective thus has a distinctive orientation in which structures, their impact, and their evolution become the primary focus [25]. Since structures may be behavioral, social, political, or economic. The advent of social network sites in the last few years seems to be a trend that will likely continue in the years to come. This has accelerated the research in this field. Online social interaction has become very popular around the globe, and most sociologists agree that this will not fade away. Such a development is possible due to the advancements in computer power, technologies, and the spread of the World Wide Web.

Social Network Representation

Social network analysts use two kinds of tools from mathematics to represent information about patterns of ties among social actors: graphs and matrices. Network analysis uses one kind of graphic display that consists of points (or nodes) to represent actors and lines (or edges) to represent ties or relations. These are called sociograms. There are a number of variations on the theme of sociograms, but they all share the common feature of using a labeled circle for each actor in the population we are describing, and line segments between pairs of actors to represent the observation have a tie existing between the two. Graphs are very useful ways of representing information about social networks. However, when there are many actors and/or many kinds of relations, they can become so visually complicated that it is very difficult to see the patterns. It is also possible to represent information about social networks in the form of matrices. Representing the information in this way also allows the application of mathematical and computer tools to summarize and find patterns. The most common form of matrix in social network analysis is a very simple one composed of as many rows as columns as there are actors in our data set and where the elements represent the ties between the actors. The simplest and most common matrix is binary. That is, if a tie is present, a one is entered in a cell; if there is no tie, a zero is entered. This kind of a matrix is the starting point for almost all network analysis, and is called an "adjacency matrix," because it represents who is next to, or adjacent to whom in the "social space" mapped by the relations that we have measured. In representing social network data as matrices, the question always arises: what do I do with the elements of the matrix where i = j? This part of the matrix is called the main diagonal. If it is unimportant, it is ignored. But, sometimes the main diagonal can be very important and can take on meaningful values. Some of the most fundamental properties of a social network have to do with how connected the actors are to one another. Those networks that have a few or weak connections or where some actors are connected only by pathways of great length may display low solidarity, a tendency to fall apart. Networks that have more and stronger connections with shorter paths among actors may be more robust and more able to respond quickly and effectively. Measuring the number and lengths of pathway among the actors in a network allow us to index these important tendencies of whole networks. Individual actors' positions in networks are also usefully described by the number and lengths of pathways that they have to other actors. Actors who have many pathways to other actors may be more influential with regard to them. Actors who have short pathways to more other actors may be more influential or central figures. So, the number and lengths of pathways in a network are very important to understanding both individual's constraints and opportunities, and for understanding the behavior and potentials of the network as a whole. There are many measures of individual position and overall network structure that are based on whether there are pathways of given lengths between actors, the length of the shortest pathway between two actors, and the numbers of pathways between actors. Indeed, most of the basic measures of network groupings and substructures are based on looking at the numbers and lengths of pathways among actors [18].

Social Network Analysis

Scientific study of social network data can reveal many important behaviors of the elements involved and social trends and provides insight for suitable changes in the social structure and roles of individuals in it. There are many evidences [4] which indicate the precious value of social network data in shedding light on social behavior, health, and well-being of the general public. Social network analysis provides a formal, conceptual means for thinking about the social world. Freeman has argued that the methods of social network analysis provide formal statements about social properties and processes. Social network analysis thus allows a flexible set of concepts and methods with broad interdisciplinary appeal. Social network analysis provides a formal, conceptual means for thinking about the social world. Social network analysis is based on an assumption of the importance of relationships among interacting units. Of critical importance for the development of methods for social network analysis is the fact that the unit of analysis in network analysis is not the individual but an entity consisting of a collection of individuals and the linkages among them. The concept of a network emphasizes the fact that each individual has ties to other individuals, each of whom in turn is tied to a few, some, or many others, and so on. Social network analysis attempts to solve analytical problems that are nonstandard. The data analyzed by network methods and are quite different from the data typically encountered in social methods are quite different from the data typically encountered in social and behavioral sciences. However, social network analysis is explicitly interested in the interrelatedness of social units. The dependencies among the units are measured with structural variables. Theories that incorporate network ideas are distinguished by propositions about the relations among social units. Such theories argue that units are not acting independently from one another but rather influence each other. Focusing on such structural variables opens up a different range of possibilities for, and constraints on, data analysis and model building.

Anonymization

Many naive technology users may not always realize that the information they provide online is stored in massive data repositories and may be used for various purposes. Researchers has pointed out for some time the privacy implications of massive data gathering [14], and a lot of effort has been made to protect the data from unauthorized disclosure [26, 31, 49, 52]. However, most of the data privacy research has been focused on more traditional data models such as microdata (data stored as one relational table, where each row represents an individual entity) [1, 2, 4–12, 19, 22–25, 28, 29]. More recently, social network data has begun to be analyzed from a different, specific privacy perspective. Since the individual entries in social networks, besides the attribute values that characterize them, also have relationships with other entities, the possibility of privacy breaches increases [35]. Technological advances have made it easier than ever to collect the electronic records that describe social networks. However, agencies and researchers who collect such data often face with two undesirable problems. They can publish data for others to analyze, even though that analysis will create severe privacy threats [4], or they can withhold data because of privacy concerns, even though that makes further analysis impossible. Therefore, the goal should be to enable the useful analysis of social network data while protecting the privacy of individuals [39]. Most of the recent works have focused on managing balance between privacy and utility in data publishing but applicable only to some limited type of data sets. For the purpose of analysis, the social network information needs to be published publicly or before a specialized group. But, depending upon the privacy model considered, this information may involve some sensitive data of individual participants in the social network, which are undesirable to be disclosed. Due to this problem, social network data need to be anonymized before its publication in order to prevent potential reidentification attacks. Most of the recent works have focused on managing balance between privacy and utility in data publishing but applicable only to some limited type of data sets [10, 11]. Some efforts in this direction are the k-anonymity [1, 5, 19, 23, 27–29, 36, 38, 48] and its many variants, its extensions l-diversity [24] and t-closeness [20], which are data perturbation techniques designed for tabular micro-data, which typically consists of a table of records, each of which describes an entity. These algorithms are not suitable to tackle the anonymization problem of social networks. A common assumption underlying all these techniques is that the records are independent and can be anonymized (more or less) independently [14]. In contrast, social network data forms a graph of relationships between entities. Existing tabular perturbation techniques are not equipped to operate over graphs, and they will tend to ignore and destroy important structural properties [8]. Likewise, graph structure and background knowledge combine to threaten privacy in many new ways.

Problems in Social Network Anonymization

Anonymizing social network data is much more challenging than anonymizing relational data due to many problems, some of which we list below:

- It is much more challenging to model the background knowledge of adversaries and attacks about social network data than that about relational data. In a social network, many pieces of information can be used to identify individuals, such as labels of vertices and edges, neighborhood graphs, induced subgraphs, and their combinations. So, all these make modeling social networks difficult.

- It is also challenging to measure the information loss in anonymising relational data. In this case, it is unlike for relational data for which the sum of the information loss for tuples solves the purpose.

- It is hard to compare two social networks by comparing the vertices and edges individually.

- Anonymizing a social network is much more difficult since changing labels of vertices and edges may affect the neighborhoods of other vertices, and removing or adding vertices and edges may affect other vertices as well as the properties of the network.

Chapter Structure

In the subsections above, we have introduced the concept of social networks, their analysis, and the requirement of anonymization techniques. The organization of the rest of the chapter is as follows: Different types of expected attacks are to be discussed in section "Privacy Attacks." In section "Privacy in Social Networks," we present the different types of privacy in social networks, and in section "Background knowledge of adversaries," we describe the background knowledge of the adversaries, which play a crucial role in handling the different types of attacks. Uncertainty in databases and information systems is a common feature nowadays. Rough set theory is one of the approaches to handle such type of characteristics. We present the basics of rough set theory and information systems in section "Rough Set Theory." Though research in analysis of social networks is relatively a new venture, several algorithms have been developed so far. In section "Social Network Anonymization Algorithms," we shall discuss on two such approaches to handle neighborhood attacks in social networks and the preserving privacy of sensitive relationships. In neighborhood attacks, the adversity may have knowledge about the neighborhood node structure of a target node. It may be a single neighborhood or any finite number of neighborhoods of the target. We shall present two algorithms to handle this problem in section "Social Network Anonymization Algorithms." Rough set theory is one of the latest and perhaps the best technique to handle uncertainty and vagueness in data. A clustering algorithm is established in [47]. We shall present this algorithm and its use in the context of social network anonymization in section "Handling Uncertainty in Node Data." An algorithm which takes care of maintaining minimum cluster size and also maximum cluster size, called the union-split algorithm, is to be discussed in section "The Union-Split Algorithm." Also, we shall present an algorithm which is fast and takes care of l-diversity in the process and has been developed recently [46] in section "A Fast l-Diversity Algorithm." In the next section, that is, in section "Problems for Further Study," we discuss on some problems which are yet to be tackled in the anonymization of social networks. Finally, we provide some concluding remarks on the chapter in section "Conclusion." We conclude the chapter with a compilation of the papers, monographs, reports, and books used in compiling the contents of the chapter.

Privacy Attacks

As more and more rich social media, popular online social networking sites, and various kinds of social network analyzing and mining techniques are available, privacy in social networks becomes a serious concern [50], particularly when social network data is published. An adversary may intrude privacy of some victims using the published social network data and some background knowledge. Importantly, many of the richest emerging social network data come from settings such as e-mails, instant messages, or telephone communication. Users have strong expectations of privacy on such data. When social network data is made public in one way or other, it is far from sufficient to protect privacy by simply replacing the identifying attributes such as name and SSN of individuals by meaningless unique identifiers.

Background Knowledge-Based Attacks

A family of attacks have been identified by Backstrom, Dwork, and Kleinberg [2] such that even from a single anonymized copy of a social network hiding the identifying attributes, it is possible for an adversary to learn whether edges exist or not between some specific target pairs of vertices. The attacks are based on the uniqueness of some small random subgraphs embedded in an arbitrary network using ideas related to those found in arguments from Ramsey theory [13]. Two categories of attacks are addressed in [2]. The first category is active attacks. Before releasing the anonymized network G of $(n - k)$ vertices, the attackers can choose a set of b target users, randomly create a subgraph H containing k vertices, and then attach H to the target vertices. After the anonymized network is released, if the attackers can find the subgraph H in the released graph G, then the attackers can follow edges from H to locate the b target vertices and their locations in G and determine all edges among those b vertices. To implement the attacks, the random graph H should satisfy the following requirements:

1. H must be uniquely and efficiently identifiable regardless of G.
2. There is no other subgraph S in G such that S and H are isomorphic.
3. H has no automorphism.

Backstrom et al. [2] provide two methods to construct subgraphs satisfying the above requirements. The second category is passive attacks, which are based on the fact that most vertices in social networks usually belong to a small uniquely identifiable subgraph. Thus, an attacker can collude with other $(k - 1)$ friends to identify additional vertices connected to the distinct subset of the coalition. The attacks are possible under the following assumptions:

1. All colluders should know edges among themselves, that is, the internal structure of H.
2. All colluders should know the name of their neighbors outside the coalition.
3. There exists no Hamiltonian path linking $x_1, x_2, \ldots x_n$, where x_i is a vertex in G.

The experiments on a real social network with 4.4 million vertices and 77 million edges show that the creation of 7 vertices by an attacker can reveal on an average 70 target vertices and compromise the privacy of approximately 2,400 edges between them.

Neighborhood Attacks

To define the problem of privacy preservation in publishing social network data, we need to formulate the following issues: First, we need to identify the privacy information to be preserved. Second, we need to model the background knowledge that an adversary may use to attack the privacy. Last, we need to specify the usage of the published social network data so that an anonymization method can try to retain the utility as much as possible while the privacy information is fully preserved. In order to attack the privacy of a target individual in the original network, that is, analyze the released anonymization network and reidentify the vertex, an adversary needs some background knowledge and plays a critical role in both modeling privacy attacks on social networks and developing anonymization strategies to protect privacy in social network data. Suppose the background knowledge about the neighborhood of some target individuals. This assumption is realistic in many applications. Among many types of information about a target victim that an adversary may collect to attack is how the neighbors are connected. Generally, we can consider the d-neighbors of the target vertex, that is, the vertices within distance d to the target vertex in the network where d is a positive integer. However, when d is large, collecting information about the d-neighbors of a vertex may often be impractical for an adversary since the adversary may often have a limited access to a large social network. Moreover, as found in many social networks, the network diameter is often small. So, an adversary may have to collect information about many vertices in the case when $d > 1$. Therefore, in [55], the discussions were confined to only immediate neighbors. But considering the case when $d = 1$ only seems to be too restrictive. In fact, techniques used in [55] is not convenient to extend to tackle the case $d > 1$. However, Tripathy et al. [43,44] have modified the algorithm by suitable changes in the approach so that it is more efficient and also tackles the case $d > 1$.

An adversary may attack the privacy using the neighborhoods. For a social network G, suppose an adversary knows $Neighbor_G(u)$ for a vertex $u \in V(G)$. If $Neighbor_G(u)$ has k instances in G' where G' is an anonymization of G, then u can be reidentified in G' with confidence 1/k.

Similar to the philosophy of k-anonymity model [37, 40, 41], to protect the privacy of vertices sufficiently, we want to keep the reidentification confidence lower than a threshold. Let k be a positive integer. For a vertex $u \in V(G)$, u is k-anonymous in anonymization G' if there are at least (k − 1) other vertices v_1, $v_2, \ldots v_{k-1} \in V(G)$ such that $Neighbor_G(A(u))$, $Neighbor_G$ $(A(v_1()), \ldots Neighbor_G$ $(A(v_{k-1}))$ are isomorphic. G' is k-anonymous if every vertex in G is k-anonymous in G'. A theorem parallel to that for relational data is as follows:

Theorem 1. *Let G be a social network and G' an anonymization of G. If G' is k-anonymous, then with the neighborhood background knowledge, any vertex in G cannot be reidentified in G' with confidence larger than 1/k.*

Privacy in Social Networks

In privacy preservation on relational data, the attributes in a table are divided into two groups: non-sensitive attributes and sensitive attributes. The values in sensitive attributes are considered to be private for individuals. However, in social network data, much more pieces of information can be considered as privacy of individuals. These are:

- *Vertex existence.* In social network data, whether a target individual appears in the network or not can be considered as the privacy of the individual. If a target individual can be determined appearing in the network, an attacker knows the sensitive attribute value of the target.

- *Vertex properties.* In social network data, some properties of a vertex such as degree can be considered as privacy of the individual.
- *Sensitive vertex labels.* In social network data, vertices may carry labels, which can be divided into two categories: non-sensitive vertex labels and sensitive vertex labels. Similar to the case of relational data, the values of sensitive vertex labels are considered to be privacy of individuals.
- *Link relationship.* In social network data, an edge between two vertices indicates that there is a relationship between the two corresponding individuals. The link relationship among vertices can be considered as privacy of individuals.
- *Link weight.* Some social networks may be weighted. The weights of edges can reflect affinity between two vertices or record the communication cost between two individuals.
- *Sensitive edge labels.* In social network data, edges may carry several labels as well. The edge labels may be divided into non-sensitive edge labels and sensitive edge labels. The values of sensitive edge labels are considered as privacy for the corresponding two individuals.
- *Graph metrics.* In social network analysis, many graph metrics have been proposed to analyze graph structures, such as betweenness (that is, the degree an individual lies between other individuals in the network directly or indirectly), closeness (that is, the degree an individual is near to all other individuals in the network directly or indirectly) , centrality (that is, the count of the number of relationships to other individuals in the network), path length (that is, the distances between pairs of vertices in the network), reachability (that is, the degree any member of a network can reach other members of the network), and so on.

Background Knowledge of Adversaries

In relational data, a major type of privacy attacks is to reidentify individuals by joining the published table with some external tables modeling the background knowledge of the users. Specifically, the adversaries are assumed knowing the values on the quasi-identifier attributes of the target victims. In privacy preservation in publishing social networks, due to the complex structures of graph data, the background knowledge of adversaries may be modeled in various ways:

- *Identifying attribute of vertices.* A vertex may be linked uniquely to an individual by a set of attributes, where the set of identifying attributes play a role similar to a quasi-identifier in the reidentification attacks on relational data. Vertex attributes are often modeled as labels in a social network. An adversary may know some attribute values of some victims. Such background knowledge may be abused for privacy attacks.
- *Vertex degrees.* The degree of a vertex in the network captures how many edges the corresponding individual is connected to others in the network. Such

information is often easy to collect by adversaries. For example, the neighbor of a target individual may easily estimate the number of friends the victim has. An adversary equipped with the knowledge about the victim's degree can reidentify the target individual in the network by examining the vertex degrees in the network.

- *Link relationship.* An adversary may know that there are some specific link relationships between some target individuals. For example, in a social network about friendship among people, edges may carry labels recording the channels people use to communicate with each other such as phone, e-mail, and/or messaging. An adversary may try to use the background knowledge that a victim uses only e-mails to contact her friends in the network to link the victim to vertices in the network. Privacy attacks using link relationship as the background knowledge are studied.

- *Neighborhoods.* An adversary may have the background knowledge about the neighborhood of some target individuals. For example, an adversary may know that a victim has four good friends who also know each other. Using this background knowledge, the adversary may reidentify the victim by searching the vertices in the social graph whose neighborhoods contain a clique of size at least four. Generally, we can consider the d-neighbor of a target vertex, that is, the vertices within a distance d to the target vertex in the network, where d is a positive integer.

- *Embedded graphs.* An adversary may embed some specific subgraphs into a social network before the network is released. After collecting the released network, it is possible for the adversary to reidentify the embedded subgraph if the subgraph is unique. As shown in [16], the creation of 7 vertices by an attacker can reveal an average of 70 target vertices.

- *Graph metrics.* As mentioned above, graphs have many metrics, such as betweenness, closeness, centrality, path length, reachability, and so on. Graph metrics can be used as background knowledge for the adversaries to breach the privacy of target individuals.

Rough Set Theory

The notion of rough sets as a model to capture impreciseness in data was introduced by Pawlak [33, 34]. Since its inception, many fruitful applications have been found in various fields. The basic assumption in rough set theory is that human knowledge depends upon their capability to classify objects. As classification of universes and equivalence relations are interchangeable notions, for mathematical reasons, equivalence relations are used to define rough sets. A rough set is represented by a pair of crisp sets, called the lower approximation, which comprises of elements belonging to it, and upper approximation, which comprises of elements possibly in the set with respect to the available information. Let U be a universe of discourse and A be a set of attributes. With every attribute $a \in A$ we associate a set V_a of its values, called the domain of a. Any subset B of A determines a binary relation I(B) on U, which is called an indiscernibility relation and is defined as follows: x I(B) y if and only if $a(x) = a(y)$ for every $a \in B$, where $a(x)$ denotes the value of attribute a for element x. It is clear that I(B) is an equivalence relation. The family of all equivalence classes of I(B), that is, partition determined by B, will be denoted by U/I(B) or simply U/B; an equivalence class of I(B), that is, block of the partition U/B containing x, will be denoted by B(x). If (x, y) belongs to I(B), we will say that x and y are B-indiscernible. Equivalence classes of the relation I(B) (or blocks of the partition U/B) are referred to as B-elementary sets. In the rough set approach, the elementary sets are the basic building blocks (concepts) of our knowledge about reality. The indiscernibility relation I(B) is used next to define approximations and other basic concepts of rough set theory.

Definition 1. For every subset X of the universe U, we associate two approximation sets, which are defined as follows:

$$\underline{X_B} = \{x \in U : B(x) \subseteq X\}, \overline{X_B} = \left\{x \in U : B(x) \bigcap X \neq \phi\right\}.$$

The two sets $\underline{X_B}$ and $\overline{X_B}$ are called the B-lower and the B-upper approximation of X, respectively. The set $BN_B(X) = \overline{X_B} - \underline{X_B}$ is referred to as the B-boundary region of X.

Definition 2. If the boundary region of X is the empty set, that is, $BN_B(X) = \phi$, then the set X is crisp (exact) with respect to B; in the opposite case, that is, if $BN_B(X) \neq \phi$, the set X is to as rough (inexact) with respect to B. We denote the equivalence class of x_i in the relation I (B) by $[x_i]_{I(B)}$, which is also known as elementary set in B.

Definition 3. The ratio of the cardinality of the lower approximation and the cardinality of the upper approximation is defined as the accuracy of approximation, which is a measure of roughness. It is represented as $R_B(X) = 1 - (\overline{X_B}/\underline{X_B})$.

Definition 4. Given $a_i \in A$, X is a subset of objects having one specific value α of attribute a_j, $\underline{X_{a_j}}(a_i = \alpha)$ and $\overline{X_{a_j}}(a_i = \alpha)$ refer to the lower and upper approximation with respect to $\{a_j\}$, then $R_{a_j}(X)$ is defined as the roughness of X with respect to $\{a_j\}$, that is,

$$R_{a_j}(X/a_i = \alpha) = 1 - [\underline{X_{a_j}}(a_i = \alpha)/\overline{X_{a_j}}(a_i = \alpha)].$$

Social Network Anonymization Algorithms

As a first step to hide information, the released social network has to go through the anonymization procedure which replaces social entity names with meaningless unique identifiers [6], although this kind of anonymization may still leak a lot of information. Protection against the threat of reidentification presents novel challenges for graph-structured data. In tabular data, identified attributes can be generalized, suppressed, or randomized easily, and the effects are largely restricted to the individual entities affected. It is much harder to generalize or perturb the structure around a node in a graph, and the impact of doing so can spread across the graph. In order to ensure anonymity, we require that the adversary has a minimum level of uncertainty about the reidentification of any node in the vertex set. The condition implies that there are at least k-candidate nodes for any node x in the original data, and furthermore, all the candidates are equally likely. This is a generalization of basic k-anonymity in the sense that if the probability distribution over candidates is uniform, this definition simply requires at least k candidates. Graph anonymization by edge perturbation results in a more complex probability distribution over candidates, for which this general definition is required. Hay et al. [2] presented a framework for assessing the privacy risk of sharing anonymized network data. They modeled the adversaries' background knowledge as vertex requirement structural queries and proposed a privacy requirement k-candidate anonymity which is similar to k-anonymity in tabular data.

Privacy Preservation Against Neighborhood Attacks

Recently, Zhou and Pei proposed an anonymization technique for social networks to prevent the neighborhood attacks [55]. The following definitions are used in [55].

Definition 5 (Modeling a Social Network). A social network is modeled as a simple graph $G = (V, E, L, \zeta)$, where V is a set of vertices, $E \subseteq V \times V$ is a set of edges, L is a set of labels, and a labeling function assigns each vertex a label. For a graph G, V(G), E(G), L_G , and ζ_G are the set of vertices, the set of edges, the set of labels, and the labeling function in G, respectively. However, in this chapter edges have been taken without labels to maintain simplicity.

Definition 6 (Label Hierarchy). The items in the label set L forms a hierarchy. For example, if the occupations are used as labels of vertices in a social network, L contains not only the specific occupations such as dentist, general physician, optometrist, high school teacher, and primary school teacher but also general categories like medical doctor, teacher, and professional. It is assumed that there exists a meta symbol $* \in L$, which is the most general category generalizing all labels.

Definition 7 (Neighborhood of a Vertex and Neighborhood Component). In a social network G, the neighborhood of $u \in V(G)$ is the induced subgraph of the neighbors of u, denoted by $Neighbor_G(u) = G(N_u)$, where $N_u = \{v/(u, v) \in E(G)\}$. The components of the neighborhood graph of a vertex are the neighborhood components. In a social network G, a subgraph C of G is a neighborhood component of $u \in V(G)$ if C is a maximal connected subgraph in $Neighbor_G(u)$.

Definition 8 (d-Neighborhood). The d-neighborhood graph of a vertex u includes all the vertices that are within the distance "d" from the vertex u.

The basic aim of this chapter was to protect the privacy of the individuals, represented as vertices in the social network. Consider a graph $G = (V, E, L, \zeta)$ and its published anonymized graph $G' = (V', E', L', \zeta')$. The vertices in the network should not be identified in the anonymized graph. For a positive integer k, the privacy of u is preserved in G if it cannot be re identified in G' with a confidence larger than 1/k. Secondly, the background knowledge of an adversary will be having information about the neighborhood of a few vertices. The anonymization also depends on the purpose for which the anonymized graph will be used. In [55], the purpose was to use the anonymized social networks for answering aggregate network queries. In order to establish the isomorphism of two graph, a different technique called DFS code is used in this chapter. The depth-first search tree (DFS tree for short) is popularly used for navigating connected graphs. Thus, it is natural to encode the edges and vertices in a graph based on its DFS tree. All the vertices in G can be encoded in the preorder of T. However, the DFS tree is generally not unique for a graph. To solve the uniqueness problem, a minimum DFS code notation of [17] is used, which is as defined below.

Definition 9. For any connected graph G, let T be a DFS tree of G. Then, an edge is always listed as (v_i, v_j) such that $i < j$. A linear order $\prec$ on the edges in G is defined as follows: Given edges e=(v_i, v_j) and $e' = (v_{i'}, v_{j'})$, we say $e \prec e'$:

1. When both e and e' are forward edges (that is in DFS tree T), $j < j'$ or ($i > i'$ and $j = j'$)
2. When both e and e' are backward edges (that is edges not in DFS tree T), $i < i'$ or ($i = i'$ and $j < j'$)
3. When e is a forward edge and e' is a backward edge, $j \leq i'$
4. When e is a backward edge and e' is a forward edge, $i < j'$

For a graph G and a DFS tree T, a list of all edges in E(G) in order $\prec$ is called the DFS code of G with respect to T, denoted by code(G, T). Suppose there is a linear order over the label set L. Then, for DFS trees T_1 and T_2 on the same graph G, their DFS codes can be compared lexically according to the vertex pairs as labels of edges. The lexically minimum DFS code is selected as the representation of the graph, denoted by DFS(G). Minimum DFS code has a nice property ([17]) that two graphs G and G' are isomorphic if and only if DFS(G) = $DFS(G')$.

Definition 10. For two neighborhood components C_i and C_j in $Neighbor_G(u)$, we define $C_i \prec C_j$ if (1) $|V(C_i)| < |V(C_j)|$ or (2) $|V(C_i)| = |V(C_j)|$ and $|E(C_i)| = |E(C_j)|$ or (3) $|V(C_i)| = |V(C_j)|$, $|E(C_i)| = |E(C_j)|$, and $DFS(C_i)$ is smaller than $DFS(C_j)$.

Based on the neighborhood component code, we can assign a canonical label for each neighborhood. In a social network G, for vertex $u \in V(G)$, the neighborhood component code of $Neighbor_G(u)$ is a vector $NCC(u) = (DFS(C_1), \ldots, DFS(C_m))$, where $C_1, \ldots C_m$ are the neighborhood components of $Neighbor_G(u)$, that is,

$Neighbor_G(u) = \bigcup_{i=1}^{m} C_i, C_i \preceq C_j$ for $1 \leq i < j \leq m$.

Using neighborhood component code, we can easily identify isomorphic neighborhoods.

Theorem 2. *For two vertices* u, $v \in V(G)$, *where* G *is a social network,* $Neighbor_G$ *and* $Neighbor_G(u)$ *are isomorphic if and only if* $NCC(u) = NCC(v)$.

Anonymization Preliminaries

The main objective is to anonymize a social network to satisfy k-anonymity requirement. In this anonymization algorithm, neighborhoods of all vertices in the network are extracted. To facilitate the comparisons among neighborhoods of different vertices, similarity among these neighborhoods are found out by using isomorphism. For grouping vertices, greedy techniques are used, and the neighborhoods of vertices in the same group are anonymized. The major challenge in designing anonymization techniques is that adding edges or changing the labels of the vertices may affect the neighborhoods of some other vertices as well as the properties of the networks. The k-anonymity requires that each vertex $u \in V(G)$ is grouped with at least $(k-1)$ other vertices such that their anonymized neighborhoods are isomorphic. The following properties of social networks are useful in devising the anonymization algorithm:

Property 1 (Vertex Degree in Power Law Distribution). The degrees of vertices in a large social network follow a power law distribution, that is, only a small number of vertices have a high degree. Processing the higher degree vertices first can keep the information loss about those vertices low. Often, there are many vertices of lower degrees. It is relatively easier to anonymize those lower degree vertices and retain high quality.

Property 2 (Small-World Phenomenon [50]). This phenomenon states that large practical social networks often have surprisingly small average diameters. Anonymization can be done in following two ways, both of which involve some information loss. The approaches to cope up with these losses are as discussed below:

Anonymization Quality Measure

The two approaches adopted for anonymizing the neighborhoods of vertices are generalizing vertex labels and adding edges. There is loss of information in both these cases. An estimation of these losses is measured as follows:

1. *Loss due to generalization of labels:* The information loss can be measured by normalized certainty penalty [9]. Consider a vertex u of label l_1, where l_1 is at the leaf level of the label hierarchy. Suppose l_1 is generalized to l_2 for u, where l_2 has a higher order in label hierarchy when compared to l_1. Let size(l_2) be the number of descendants of l_2 that are leaf nodes in the label hierarchy, and size(*) is the total number of leaves in the label hierarchy then the normalized certainty penalty of l_2 is given by NCP(l_2) = size(l_2)/size(*).

2. *Loss due to addition of edges:* It can be measured by the total number of edges added and the number of vertices those are linked to the anonymised neighborhood during the process of anonymisation. Suppose, two vertices $u_1, u_2 \in V(G)$, where G is a social network. Suppose $Neighbor_G(u_1)$ and $Neighbor_G(u_2)$ are generalized to $Neighbor_G(A(u_1))$ and $Neighbor_G(A(u_2))$, which are isomorphic. The anonymization cost is given by Cost $(u, v) = \alpha \sum_{v' \in H'} NCP(v') + \beta \left| \left\{ (v_1, v_2) / (v_1, v_2) \notin E(H), (A(v_1), A(v_2)) \in E(H') \right\} \right| + \mu (|V(H')| - |V(H)|)$, where α, β, μ are the weights proposed by the user. The anonymization cost of two vertices u and v measures the similarity between $Neighbor_G(u)$ and $Neighbor_G(v)$. The smaller the anonymization cost, the more similar are the two neighborhoods.

Anonymizing Two Neighborhoods

A greedy method is used to anonymize two neighborhoods $Neighbor_G(u)$ and $Neighbor_G(v)$. First, all perfect matches of neighborhood components in $Neighbor_G(u)$ and $Neighbor_G(v)$ are found out. Two components perfectly match each other if they have the same minimum DFS code. Those perfect matches are marked as "matched" and pass over for further consideration. For the unmatched components, the anonymization algorithm tries to pair similar components and anonymize them. The similarity between two components is based on the anonymization cost. To calculate the similarity between two components, as much as possible, the similarity of vertices in two components is tried. Instead of computing the optimal matching, a greedy matching [55] is conducted as the structure similarity problem has been proved to be NP-hard [55].

Anonymization of Social Network Algorithm

The following algorithm is used in [55] for the anonymization process:

Input: A social network G = (V, E), the anonymization requirement parameter k, and the cost function parameters $\alpha, \beta, and \gamma$
Output: An anonymized graph G'

1. Initialize $G' = G$;
2. Mark $v_i \in V(G)$ as "unanonymized";
3. Sort $v_i \in V(G)$ as VertexList in neighborhood size descending order;
4. WHILE (VertexList $\neq \phi$) DO
5. Let Seed Vertex = VertexList.head () and remove it from VertexList;
6. FOR each $v_i \in VertexList$ DO
7. Calculate Cost (Seed Vertex, v_i) using the anonymization method for two vertices;
8. END FOR
9. IF $(VertexListsize() \geq 2k - 1)$ DO
10. Let CandidateSet contain the top $k - 1$ vertices with the smallest Cost;
11. ELSE
12. Let CandidateSet contain the remaining unanonymized vertices;
13. Suppose CandidateSet = $\{u_1, \ldots, u_m\}$, anonymize Neighbor(Seed Vertex) and Neighbor( )
14. FOR $j = 2$ to m DO
15. Anonymize Neighbor(u_j) and Neighbor(SeedVertex),Neighbor(u_1), Neighbor (u_{j-1}), mark them as "anonymized";
16. Update VertexList;
17. END FOR
18. END WHILE

An Improved Algorithm

Very recently, the above algorithm has been modified by Tripathy et al. [44] to obtain an algorithm which has several advantages over the above algorithm. This alternative anonymization algorithm adheres to the k-anonymity security model. The social network graph is considered to be represented by its adjacency matrix [8]. The algorithms required for the process are explained in this section.

Algorithm to Check Component Similarity

The neighborhood graphs of all the vertices are separated into their components and are represented in the form of adjacency matrices. The adjacency matrix is constructed in the decreasing order of the vertices and their label in the component. When two or more vertices have the same degree, the ordering is done according to decreasing label. Two components with the same degree and having same adjacency matrices are isomorphic according to their structure. Next, if the labels also match, then they are isomorphic. Else the labels are generalized to their parent label. The similarity between the components with different number of vertices is done by comparing the first submatrices of the adjacency matrices of the components with highest number of vertices. In non-matching cases, vertices or edges can be added for anonymization or making them isomorphic.

Revised Brute Force Graph-Isomorphism Testing

Two graphs are isomorphic if it is possible to order their respective vertex sets so that their adjacency matrices are identical, called the Brute force algorithm for graph isomorphism. We modify this algorithm as follows to make it more efficient:

Input: Graphs G and H
Output: YES or NO, according to whether G is isomorphic to H or not

1. Let V_G and V_H denote the set of vertices of the graphs G and H, respectively.
2. If $V_G \neq V_H$, return NO.
3. Else, put the vertices in G and H in the descending orders of their degrees.
4. If degree sequences are not equal return NO.
5. Write the adjacency matrices A_G and A_H of G and H respectively with respect to the ordering of their vertices as above.
6. Let the number of vertices of order "i." i $= 1, 2 \ldots$ k, in the graphs G and H be G_{n_i} and H_{n_i}.
7. For j $=$ k,... 1.
8. If $G_{n_i} \neq H_{n_i}$ for some i, then return NO.
9. Else, let $[A_G]_j$ and $[A_H]_j$ denote respectively the submatrices of A_G and A_H corresponding to the vertices of order j, respectively.
10. For a particular ordering of $[A_G]_j$, write $[A_H]_j$ in that order.
11. If $[A_G]_j \neq [A_H]_j$, then return NO.
12. Else, return YES.

Note The complexity of the Brute force graph isomorphism is n!, where n is the number of nodes in the graph. However, the complexity of this algorithm is $n_1! + n_2! + \ldots + n_k! = O(n_j!)$, where $n_j = max(n_1, n_2, \ldots, n_k)$. The worst case complexity of this algorithm occurs for a complete graph in which all nodes are of same degree n (a rare possibility). The best case occurs when all the nodes form a cycle or a chain and are equal to $O(1)$.

Theorem 3. *Let G be a graph with adjacency matrix A_G. Then the value of the entry $A_G^r[u, v]$ of the rth power of matrix A_G equals the number of u-v walks of length r.*

Algorithm to Check Component Similarity

The neighborhood graphs of all the vertices are separated into their components and are represented in the form of adjacency matrices. The adjacency matrix is

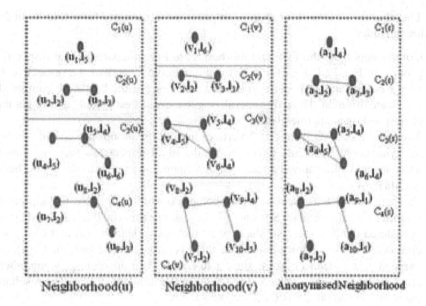

Fig. 12.1 Illustration of anonymization of two neighborhoods

constructed in the decreasing order of the vertices and their label in the component. When two or more vertices have the same degree, the ordering is done according to decreasing label. Two components with the same degree and having same adjacency matrices are isomorphic according to their structure. Next, if the labels also match, then they are isomorphic. Else the labels are generalized to their parent label. The similarity between the components with different number of vertices is done by comparing the first submatrices of the adjacency matrices of the components with highest number of vertices. In non-matching cases, vertices or edges can be added for anonymization or making them isomorphic.

Algorithm to Anonymize Two Vertices

Consider two neighborhoods of $u, v \in V(G)$ as shown in Fig. 12.1. The components in each neighborhood are ordered in descending order and are grouped and named based on the number of vertices of the component. Thus $[C_1(u)], [C_2(u)] and [C_3(u), C_4(u)]$ are the three groups formed from Neighborhood(u) and $[C_1(v)], [C_2(v)], [C_3(v)], and [C_4(v)]$ are the four groups formed from Neighborhood(v).

The adjacency matrices for all the components are compared for similarity in the following order:

1. Components from the two neighborhoods are first compared in the respective groups. In Fig. 12.1, $C_1(u)$ and $C_1(v)$ are the components of the respective 1-vertex groups and have same adjacency matrices. So, the labels are compared, which are different. Thus, by generalizing to their nearest parent 'l_4', we get the corresponding anonymized neighborhood is $C_1(a)$.

2. The next respective groups of 2 vertices in both the groups are considered for anonymization. $C_2(u)$ and $C_2(v)$ are similar in all respects, so they are simply anonymized without any changes. The corresponding anonymized neighborhood is $C_2(a)$.

3. The components $C_3(u)$ and $C_4(u)$ are compared with $C_3(v)$. Here, the adjacency matrices are not similar. So, one of the components (in this case $C_3(u)$) is considered that has more similarity with the labels. Thus, $C_3(u)$ and $C_3(v)$ are considered for anonymization. Since there is an edge deficiency in $C_3(u)$, an extra edge is added to make it similar to $C_3(v)$. Then the corresponding labels are compared and generalized to make the neighborhoods similar. The resultant anonymized component is $C_3(a)$.

4. The final component '$C_4(u)$' is compared with $C_4(v)$. Since $C_4(u)$ has one vertex deficient, a vertex $w \in V(G)$ that is neither in Neighborhood(u) or Neighborhood(v) is brought into Neighborhood(u) and is added to $C_4(u)$ to make $C_4(u)$ and $C_4(v)$ similar. The generalization of labels is carried, and the resultant anonymized component is as $C_4(a)$. Thus, the final anonymized neighborhood is as shown in Fig. 12.1.

Network Anonymization Procedure

1. Neighborhood Extraction: For all the vertices of the graph, the G vertices that fall in its d-neighborhood are considered. The neighborhood components are obtained for each of the vertex neighborhood.

2. First, mark all vertices in the network as "unanonymized." Maintain a list VertexList of "unanonymized" vertices according to the descending order of the number of vertices in the neighborhood. The vertices with the same number of vertices in neighborhood are arranged arbitrarily.

3. Iteratively, we pick the first vertex Seed Vertex in the list VertexList. The anonymization cost of Seed Vertex and any other vertices in VertexList is calculated using the anonymization method for two vertices discussed in Sect.V.B. If the number of unanonymized vertices in VertexList is at least $2k - 1$, we select a CandidateSet of the top $k - 1$ vertices in the VertexList with the smallest anonymization cost.

4. It is not possible that every vertex in a graph can find at least one other vertex with isomorphic neighborhoods. So, a factor known as "Anonymization Quality

Measure" also known as "Anonymization Cost" is calculated for every pair of vertices that do not find a match. The vertices with the minimum cost difference can be grouped together for anonymization.

5. The Seed Vertex and the vertices in the CandidateSet $= u_1, u_2, \ldots, u_m$ are anonymized in turn using the anonymization method for two vertices discussed in Sect. V. B. The anonymization of Seed Vertex and u_1 is straightforward. After these two vertices are anonymized, their neighborhoods are identical. When we anonymize them with respect to u_2, any change (e.g., adding an edge or a neighbor node) to the neighborhood of Seed Vertex will be applied to u1 as well, so that the neighborhoods of Seed Vertex, u_1 and u_2, are same. The process continues until the neighborhoods of Seed Vertex and $u_1, u_2, \ldots u_m$ are anonymized.

6. During the anonymization of a group of vertices, some changes may occur to some other vertices v that have been marked as "anonymized" in another group (e.g., adding edges between an anonymized vertex and a vertex being anonymized based on vertex matching). In order to maintain the k-anonymity for these vertices, we apply the same changes to every other k − 1 vertices having the isomorphic neighborhoods as v. Once those k vertices are changed, they are marked as "unanonymized" and inserted into the VertexList again.

7. When the number of unanonymized vertices in VertexList is less than 2k, to satisfy the k-anonymity, the remaining vertices in VertexList have to be considered together for anonymization. They are added to the CandidateSet in a batch. The social network anonymization algorithm continues until all the vertices in the graph are marked as "anonymized."

Comparison with the Existing Algorithm

In this section, we provide some logical comparative statements between our modified algorithm and the algorithm of Zhou and Pei [55]:

1. Our algorithm is applicable for cases where the adversary has knowledge of d-neighborhoods. Obviously, the earlier algorithm cannot be applicable to this case. Though it is not practicable for an adversary to have knowledge of larger neighborhoods of target nodes, it is highly possible that they can have knowledge about neighborhoods with $d > 1$.

2. The DFS tree of a graph is not unique. So, the DFS code is used instead of the DFS code in the existing algorithm. The complexity of computation of a DFS tree is of order $\ominus(n^2)$ [13], where n is the number of nodes in the graph. Also, the computation of the DFS code adds to this complexity.

3. The modified graph isomorphism used by us is simple as for as computation is concerned. If the neighborhood graphs have structural dissimilarities, like having unequal number of nodes of same degrees or nodes of different degrees, then we

can come up with a negative answer with a few matching. We need not go for even construction of the adjacency matrix for such cases as it is to be done in "2" above.

4. Even in the case in which the graphs are isomorphic, we shall get a positive answer after comparing the adjacency matrix of one graph with permutation of the corresponding submatrices of the other graph for which we have computed the complexity as shown earlier. This complexity can be of order $O(n_j!)$, where n_j is the largest size neighborhood.

5. Perhaps the worst case occurs in our algorithm when we find a negative answer in matching of the submatrix corresponding to the lowest order vertices. But properties 1 and 2 mentioned in section "Anonymisation Preliminaries" take care of this.

Preserving Privacy of Sensitive Relationships

Zheleva and Getoor [54] have proposed a different type of social network model, which is more general than the standard social network model. In fact, they have assumed that the anonymized data will be useful only if it contains both structural properties and node attributes. Another distinction of their approach is that, unlike other works on privacy preservation which concentrates on hiding the identity of entities, the relationships between the entities are considered to be kept private. Finding out the existence of these sensitive relationships leads to a privacy breach. The problem of inferring sensitive relationships from anonymized graph data is referred as link reidentification. Campan and Truta [7] continued this study further. In this approach, a node represents an individual entity and is described by identifier, quasi-identifier, and sensitive attributes. A relationship is between two nodes, and it is unlabeled. To protect the social network data, it is masked according to the k-anonymity model in terms of nodes' attributes and nodes' associated structural information (neighborhood). This anonymization method tries to disturb as little as possible the social network data, both the attribute data associated to the nodes, and the structural information. The anonymization method used is generalization. For structural anonymization, a new method called edge generalization that does not insert or remove edges from the social network data set. Although it incorporates a few ideas similar to [54], this approach is different in several aspects. The k-anonymity model presented by Hay et al. [15] is touched, but a richer data model is assumed which contains much higher structural information. The distinct contribution of this chapter is to develop a greedy privacy algorithm for anonymizing a social network and the introduction of a structural information loss measure that quantifies the amount of information lost due to edge generalization in the anonymization process. A generalized definition of a social network model was put forth in [7], which we present below.

Definition 11. A social network is modeled as a simple undirected graph G = (N, E), where N is the set of nodes and $E \subseteq N \times N$ is the set of edges. Each node represents an individual entity. Each edge represents a relationship between two entities. The set of nodes, N, described by a set of attributes that are classified into the following three categories:

1. $I_1, I_2, \ldots I_m$ are identifier attributes such as the name and SSN that can be used to identify an entity.
2. $Q_1, Q_2, \ldots Q_q$ are quasi-identifier attributes such as zip code and sex that may be known by an intruder.
3. $S_1, S_2, \ldots S_r$ are confidential or sensitive attributes such as diagnosis and income that are assumed to be unknown to an intruder.

Binary relationships are used in the model, and all relationships are considered as being of the same type, and as a result, the relations are represented as undirected edges. The graph structure may be known to an intruder and used by matching it with known external structural information, therefore serving in privacy attacks that might lead to identity and/or attribute disclosure. While the identifier attributes are removed from the published social network data, the quasi-identifier and the confidential attributes, as well as the graph structure, are usually released to the researchers. A general assumption, as noted, is that the values for the confidential attributes are not available from any external source. This assumption guarantees that an intruder cannot use the confidential attribute values to increase his/her chances of disclosure. However, there are multiple techniques that an intruder can use to try to disclose confidential information. As pointed out in the microdata privacy literature, an intruder may use record linkage techniques between quasi-identifier attributes and external available information to glean the identity of individuals. Using the graph structure, an intruder is also able to identify individuals due to the uniqueness of the neighborhoods of various individuals. It is shown in [15] that when the structure of a random graph is known, the probability that there are two nodes with identical 3-radius neighborhoods is less than 2^{-cn}, where n represents the number of nodes in the graph and c is a constant value, $c > 0$; this means that the vast majority of the nodes can be uniquely identified based on their 3-radius neighborhood structure.

For social network data, the k-anonymity model has to impose both the quasi-identifier attributes and the quasi-identifier relationship homogeneity for groups of at least k individuals. The only equivalent method for the generalization of a quasi-identifier relationship that exists in the research literature appears in [54] and consists of collapsing clusters together with their component nodes' structure. Edge additions or deletions are currently used, in all the other approaches, to ensure nodes' indistinguishability in terms of their surrounding neighborhood; additions and deletions perturb to a large extent the graph structure, and therefore, they are not faithful to the original data. These methods are equivalent to randomization or perturbation techniques for a microdata. In [7], a generalization method is employed for the quasi-identifier relationship similar to the one exposed [54], but enriched with extra information, that will cause less damage to the graph structure, that is, a smaller structural information loss.

Let n be the number of nodes from the set N. Using a grouping strategy, one can partition the nodes from this set into v totally disjoint clusters: $cl_1, cl_2, \ldots cl_v$. With the assumption that the nodes are not labeled (that is do not have attributes), and they can be distinguished only based on their relationships, an edge generalization process, with two components, is introduced: edge intra-cluster generalization and edge inter-cluster generalization is introduced in [7].

Edge Intra-cluster Generalization

Given a cluster cl, let $G_{cl} = (cl, E_{cl})$ be the subgraph of G = (N, E) induced by cl. In the masked data, the cluster cl will be generalized to (collapsed into) a node, and the structural information we attach to it is the pair of values $(|cl|, |E_{cl}|)$, where $|cl|$ represents the cardinality of the set cl. This information permits assessing some structural features about this region of the network that will be helpful in some applications. From the privacy standpoint, an original node within such a cluster is indistinguishable from the other nodes. At the same time, if more internal information was offered, such as the full nodes' connectivity inside a cluster, the possibility of disclosure would be too high [7].

Edge Inter-cluster Generalization

Given two clusters cl_1 and cl_2, let $E_{cl1,cl2}$ be the set of edges having one end in each of the two clusters ($e \in E_{cl1,cl2}$ if and only if $e \in E$ and $e \in cl_1 \times cl_2$). In the masked data, this set of inter-cluster edges will be generalized to (collapsed into) a single edge, and the structural information released for it is the value $|E_{cl1,cl2}|$. While this information permits assessing some structural features about this region of the network that might be helpful in some applications, it does not represent any disclosure risk.

Masked Social Networks

Let us return to a fully specified social network and how to anonymize it. Given G = (N, E), let X_i, i = 1...n, be the nodes in N, where n = |N|. We use the term tuple to refer only to the corresponding node attribute values (nodes' labels) without considering the relationships (edges) the node participates in. Also, we use the notation $X_i[C]$ to refer to the attribute C value for the tuple X_i tuple (the projection operation). Once the nodes from N have been clustered into totally disjoint clusters $cl_1, cl_2, \ldots cl_v$, in order to make all nodes in any cluster cl_i indistinguishable in terms of their quasi-identifier attributes values, we generalize each cluster's tuples to the least general tuple that represents all tuples in that group. There are several types of generalization available. Categorical attributes are usually generalized using generalization hierarchies, predefined by the data owner based on domain attribute characteristics (see Fig. 12.1). For numerical attributes, generalization may be based on a predefined hierarchy or a hierarchy-free model. In our approach, for categorical attributes, we use generalization based on predefined hierarchies at the cell level [23]. For numerical attributes we use the hierarchy-free generalization [19], which consists of replacing the set of values to be generalized with the smallest interval that includes all the initial values. We call generalization information for a cluster the minimal covering tuple for that cluster, and we define it as follows. (Of course, in this paragraph, generalization and coverage refer only to the quasi-identifier part of the tuples.)

Definition 12. (*Generalization Information of a Cluster*): Let $cl = \{X^1, X^2, \ldots X^u\}$ be a cluster of tuples corresponding to nodes selected from N, $QN = \{N_1, N_2, \ldots N_s\}$ be the set of numerical quasi-identifier attributes, and $QC = \{C_1, C_2, \ldots C_1\}$ be the set of categorical quasi-identifier attributes. The generalization information of cl with respect to the quasi-identifier attribute set $QI = QN \cup QC$ is the "tuple" gen (cl), having the scheme QI, where:

- For each categorical attribute $C_j \in QI$, $gen(cl)[C_j]$ = the lowest common ancestor in H_{C_j} of $\{X^1[C_j], \ldots X^u[C_j]\}$. H_C denotes the hierarchies (domain and value) associated to the categorical quasi-identifier attribute C.
- For each numerical attribute $N_j \in QI$,

$$gen(cl)[N_j] = \left[min\left\{X^1[N_j], \ldots X^u[N_j]\right\}, max\left\{X^1[N_j], \ldots X^u[N_j]\right\} \right].$$

For a cluster cl, its generalization information gen(cl) is the tuple having as value for each quasi-identifier attribute, numerical or categorical, the most specific common generalized value for all that attribute values from cl tuples. In an anonymized graph, each tuple from cluster cl will have its quasi-identifier attribute values replaced by gen(cl).

Given a partition of nodes for a social network G, we are able to create an anonymized graph by using generalization information and edge intra-cluster generalization within each cluster and edge inter-cluster generalization between any two clusters.

Definition 13. (*Masked Social Network*): Given an initial social network, modeled as a graph G = (N, E), and a partition $S = \{cl_1, cl_2, \ldots cl_v\}$ of the nodes set N, $\bigcup_{j=1}^{v} cl_j = N$, $cl_i \cap cl_j = \phi$, $i, j = 1, \ldots v, i \neq j$; the corresponding masked social network MG is defined as MG = (MN, ME), where:

- MN = $\{Cl_1, Ccl_2, \ldots Cl_v\}$, cl_i is a node corresponding to the cluster and is described by the "tuple" gen(cl_j) (the generalization information of cl_j, with respect to the quasi-identifier attribute set) and the intra-cluster generalization pair $(|cl_j|, |E_{cl_j}|)$.

- $ME \subseteq MN \times MN$, $(Cl_i, Ccl_j) \in ME$ if and only if $cl_i, cl_j \in MN$ and $\exists\, X \in cl_j$, $Y \in cl_j$ such that $(X, Y) \in E$. Each generalized edge $(Cl_i, Cl_j) \in ME$ is labeled with the inter-cluster generalization value $\left| E_{cl_i, cl_j} \right|$.

By construction, all nodes from a cluster cl collapsed into the generalized (masked) node Cl are indistinguishable from each other. To have the k-anonymity property for a masked social network, we need to add one extra condition to Definition 13, namely, that each cluster from the initial partition is of size at least k. The formal definition of a masked social network that is k-anonymous is presented below.

Definition 14. (*k-Anonymous Masked Social Network*): A masked social network $MG = (MN, ME)$, where $MN = Cl_1, Cl_2, \ldots Cl_v$ and $Cl_j = [gen(cl_j), (\left| cl_j \right|, \left| E_{cl_j} \right|)]$, $j = 1, \ldots v$ is k-anonymous if and only if $\left| cl_j \right| \geq k$ for all $j = 1, \ldots v$.

The SaNGreeA Algorithm [7]

The algorithm SaNGreeA (Social Network Greedy Anonymization) performs a greedy clustering processing to generate a k-anonymous masked social network given an initial social network modeled as a graph $G = (N, E)$. Nodes from N are described by quasi-identifier and sensitive attributes and edges from E are undirected and unlabeled. First, the algorithm establishes a "good" partitioning of all nodes from N into clusters. Next, all nodes within each cluster are made uniform with respect to the quasi-identifier attributes and the quasi-identifier relationship. This homogenization is achieved by using generalization, both for the quasi-identifier attributes and the quasi-identifier relationship, as explained in the previous section. But how is the clustering process conducted such that a good partitioning is created and what does "good" mean? In order for the requirements of the k-anonymity model to be fulfilled, each cluster has to contain at least k tuples. Consequently, a first criterion to lead the clustering process is to ensure each cluster has enough elements. As it is well known, (attribute and relationship), generalization results in information loss. Therefore, a second criterion used during clustering is to minimize the information lost between initial social network data and its masked version, caused by the subsequent cluster-level quasi identifier attributes and relationship generalization. In order to obtain good quality masked data, and also to permit the user to control the type and the quantity of information loss he/she can afford, the clustering algorithm uses two information loss measures. One quantifies how much descriptive data detail is lost through quasi-identifier attributes generalization – we call this metric the generalization information loss measure. The second measure quantifies how much structural detail is lost through the quasi-identifier relationship generalization, and it is called structural information loss. In the remainder of this section, these two information loss measures and the SaNGreeA algorithm are introduced.

Generalization Information Loss

The generalization of quasi-identifier attributes reduces the quality of the data. To measure the amount of information loss, several cost measures were introduced [6, 12, 19]. In this social network privacy model, the generalization information loss measure as introduced and described in [6] is used.

Structural Information Loss

A measure to quantify the structural information which is lost when anonymizing a graph through collapsing clusters into nodes, together with their neighborhoods, is introduced, which has two components, the intra-cluster structural loss and the inter-cluster structural loss. An analysis has established that a smaller structural information loss corresponds to clusters in which nodes have similar connectivity properties with one another or, in other words, when cluster's nodes are either all connected (or unconnected) among them and with the nodes in other clusters. A normalized structural information loss measure is defined and used to put it in the range [0, 1].

The Anonymization Algorithm

We put together in clusters nodes that are as similar as possible, both in terms of their quasi-identifier attribute values and in terms of their neighborhood structure. By doing that, when collapsing clusters to anonymize the network, the generalization information loss and the structural information loss will both be in an acceptable range. To assess the proximity between nodes with respect to quasi-identifier attributes, we use the normalized generalization information loss. However, the structural information loss cannot be computed during the clusters creation process as long as the entire partitioning is not known. Therefore, we chose to guide the clustering process using a different measure. This measure quantifies the extent in which the neighborhoods of two nodes are similar with each other, that is, the nodes present the same connectivity properties, or are connected/disconnected among them and with others in the same way. To assess the proximity of two node neighborhoods, we proceed as follows: Given $G = (N, E)$, assume that nodes in N have a particular order, $N = \{X^1, X^2, \ldots X^n\}$. The neighborhood of each node X^i can be represented as an n-dimensional Boolean vector $B_i = (b_1^i, b_2^i, \ldots b_n^i)$, where the jth component of this vector, b_j^i, is 1 if there is an edge $(X^i, X^j) \in E$, and 0 otherwise, $\forall j = 1, \ldots n; j \neq i$. We consider the value b_i^i to be undefined and therefore not equal with 0 or 1. A classical distance measure called the symmetric binary distance [7] is used for this type of vectors.

Algorithm SaNGreeA[7]

Input $G = (N, E)$, a social network; k, as in k-anonymity; α and β, -user-defined weight parameters

Output $S = \{cl_1, cl_2, \ldots cl_v\}$; $\bigcup_{j=1}^{v} cl_j = N$; $cl_j = \phi, i, j = 1 \ldots v, i \neq j$; $|cl_j| \geq K, j = 1..v$ – a set of clusters that ensures k - anonymity

1. $S = \phi$; i = 1;
2. Repeat
3. X^{seed} = a node with maximum degree from N;
4. $cl_i = X^{seed}$;
5. $N = N - X^{seed}$; // N keeps track of nodes not yet distributed to clusters
6. Repeat $X^* = argmin_{X \in N}(\alpha * NGIL(G_1, S_1) + \beta * dist(X, cl_i))$; //$X^*$ is the node within N (unselected nodes) //that produces the minimal information loss growth when added to cl_i. // G_1 – the subgraph induced by $cl \bigcup X$ in G; S_1 – a partition with one cluster $cl \bigcup X$;
7. $cl_i = cl_i \bigcup X^*$; $N = N - X^*$;
8. Until (cl_i has k elements) or (N == ϕ);
9. If ($|cl_i| \leq k$) then DisperseCluster(S,cl_i); // this happens only for the last cluster
10. Else
11. $S = S \bigcup cl_i$; i++;
12. End If;
13. Until N = ϕ;
14. End GreedyPKClustering.
15. Function DisperseCluster(S, cl)
16. For every $X \in cl$ do
17. cl_u = FindBestCluster(X, S); $cl_u = cl_u \bigcup X$;
18. End For;
19. End DisperseCluster;
20. Function FindBestCluster(X, S)
21. BestCluster = null; $infoLoss = \infty$;
22. For every $cl_j \in S$ do
23. If $\alpha * NGIL(G_1, S_1) + \beta * dist(X, cl_j) < infoloss$ then
24. InfoLoss = $\alpha * NGIL(G_1, S_1) + \beta * dist(X, cl_j)$;
25. BestCluster = cl_j;
26. End If; End For; Return BestCluster; End FindBestCluster;

Using the above introduced measures, we explain how clustering is performed for a given initial social network $G = (N, E)$. The clusters are created one at a time. To form a new cluster, a node in N with the maximum degree and not yet allocated to any cluster is selected as a seed for the new cluster. Then the algorithm gathers nodes to this currently processed cluster until it reaches the desired cardinality k. At each step, the current cluster grows with one node. The selected node has to be unallocated yet to any cluster and to minimize the cluster's information loss growth quantified as a weighted measure that combines NGIL and dist. The parameters α and β, with $\alpha + \beta = 1$, control the relative importance given to the total generalization information loss and the total structural information loss and are user-defined. It is possible, when n is not a multiple of k, that the last constructed cluster will contain less than k nodes. In that case, this cluster needs to be dispersed between the previously constructed groups. Each of its nodes will be added to the cluster whose information loss will minimally increase by that node addition.

Experimental Results

Since the model used in [7] is different from the models used in other social network anonymization papers, it can only be compared with the work by Zheleva and Getoor [53]. Experiments performed to compare the SaNGreeA algorithm with Zheleva and Getoor's algorithm to measure the quality of results they produce, measured against the normalized generalization information loss and the normalized structural loss, established the superiority of SaNGreeA over the other in all aspects.

Handling Uncertainty in Node Data

As in the case of relational data, it is very likely that the attributes of nodes and the relations among these attributes may contain information which is uncertain, numerical, or categorical. To handle such situations, normal algorithms developed are not suitable. A rough set-based clustering algorithm which can be used for clustering of hybrid uncertain data has been developed by Tripathy and Kumar [47]. This algorithm can be extended and used for anonymization of social networks very much in the direction of Zheleva and Getoor [53] and its extension due to Campan and Truta. We present below this algorithm for completion and use.

Definitions and Notations

We have introduced the notion of basic rough sets in section "Rough Set Theory." We introduce some more definitions in this section which are to be used in the context of the algorithm MMeR [47].

Definition 15. The mean roughness on attribute a_i with respect to a_j is defined as

$$Rough_{a_j}(a_i) = \frac{R_{a_j}(X|a_i = \alpha_1) + \ldots R_{a_j}(X|a_i = \alpha_{|V(a_i)|})}{|V(a_i)|}$$ where $a_i, a_j \in A$ and $a_i \neq a_j$.

Definition 16. Given n attributes, MR, min-roughness of attribute a_i ($a_i \in A$) refers to the minimum of the mean roughness, that is, $MR(a_i) = Min(Rough_{a_1}(a_i), \ldots Rough_{a_j}(a_i) \ldots)$, where $a_i, a_j \in A, a_i \neq a_j, a_i \neq a_j, 1 \leq i, j \leq n$.

And we define $MMR = Min(MR(a_1), \ldots MR(a_i), \ldots)$, where $a_i \in A$, i goes from 1 to cardinality(A).

Definition 17. Let A be a given set of n attributes and ($a_i \in A$). X be a subset of objects having a specific value α of the attribute α_i. Then we define the mean roughness for the equivalence class $a_i = \alpha$, denoted by MeR($a_i = \alpha$) and is given by

$$MeR(a_i = \alpha) = \sum_{\substack{j=1 \\ j \neq 1}}^{n} (X/a_i = \alpha)/(n-1).$$

We define as MMeR as
$$MMeR = \underset{1 \leq i \leq n}{Min} \, min\{MeR(a_i = \alpha_1), \ldots .MeR(a_i = a_{k_j})\},$$
where k_j is the number of equivalence classes in Dom(a_i).

The Clustering Algorithm (MMeR)

We are using the unaltered algorithm MMeR for clustering of heterogeneous data as in Tripathy and Prakash Kumar [47]. The algorithm is as follows:

Procedure MMeR (U, k)

1. Begin
2. Set current number of cluster CNC = 1
3. Set ParentNode = U
4. Loop1:
5. If $CNC < k$ and $CNC \neq 1$ then
6. ParentNode = ProcParentNode(CNC)
7. End if // Clustering the ParentNode
8. For each $a_i \in A$(i = 1 to n, where n is the number of attributes in A)
9. Determine $[X_m]_I(a_i)$(m = 1 to number of objects)
10. For each $a \in A$(j = 1 to n, where n is the number of attributes in A, $j \neq i$)
11. Calculate $Rough_{a_j}(a_i)$
12. Next
13. Mean-Roughness $(a_i) = Mean(Rough_{a_j}(a_i))$
14. Next
15. Set Min-Mean-Roughness = Min (Mean-Roughness (a_i)), i = 1,. . .,n
16. Determine splitting attribute a_i corresponding to the Min-Mean-Roughness
17. Do binary split on the splitting attribute a_i

18. CNC = the number of leaf nodes
19. Go to Loop1:
20. End
21. ProcParentNode (CNC)
22. Begin
23. Set i = 1
24. Do until $i < CNC$
25. If Avg-distance of cluster i is calculated
26. Go to label
27. Else
28. n = Count (Set of Elements in Cluster i).
29. $Avg-distance(i) = 2*(\sum_{j=1}^{n-1} \sum_{k=j+1}^{n}$ (Hamming distance between objects $a_j and a_k))/(n*(n-1))$
30. Label:
31. Increment i
32. Loop
33. Determine Max (Avg-distance(i))
34. Return (Set of Elements in cluster i) corresponding to Max (Avg-distance (i))
35. End

Efficiency and Superiority of MMeR

It is shown in [47] that the algorithm MMeR is applicable to categorical data and can handle uncertainty, which is an inherent property of the rough set model. MMeR is an extension of an existing algorithm MMR[32], which used rough set theory for the first time in clustering relational data.

In order to compare MMeR with MMR and all other algorithms which have taken initiative to handle categorical data, we developed an implementation. The data sets are taken from UCI Machine Learning Repository [30] (http://www.ics.uci. edu//mlearn/MLRepository.html). The traditional approach for calculating purity of a cluster is given below:

$$\text{Purity (i)} = \frac{\text{the number of data occurring in both the ith cluster and its corresponding class}}{\text{the number of data in the data set}}$$

$$\text{Over all Purity} = \frac{\sum_{i=1}^{\text{no. of clusters}} \text{Purity(i)}}{\text{no. of clusters}}$$

Purity of a cluster reflects the relevance of objects in the cluster. The purity value ranges from 0 to 1. Table 12.1 summarizes the overall purity of the different algorithms on clustering relational data on two of the widely used data sets.

Overall purity of MMeR algorithm for another relatively large data set, Mushroom data, has been shown to be 0.9641 [47].

Table 12.1 Summarizes the overall purity of the different algorithms on clustering relational data on two of the widely used data sets

Data set	K-modes	Fuzzy K-modes	Fuzzy centroids	MMR	MMeR
Soyabean	0.69	0.77	0.97	0.83	0.83
Zoo	0.60	0.64	0.75	0.787	0.902

The Union-Split Algorithm

In [42], Thomson and Yao have presented an algorithm called the union-split algorithm, in which it is strongly considered that an important and unique graph property for social networks is the social role of an individual. A social role can be defined as the position or purpose that someone or something has in a situation, organization, society, or relationship. A social network contains the information about the social role of each participant that has usually reflected in the way people interact with each other and in social connections in particular. So, an anonymization algorithm for social network needs to preserve the connectivity of the individuals in the network as much as possible. As mentioned in [42], the lack of a simple and efficient algorithm for minimum size clustering in the literature has led to develop two such algorithms: the bounded t-means algorithm and the union-split clustering algorithm. However, we shall see that a simple clustering algorithm has been developed in [42], which takes care of the minimum cluster size and the l-diversity of clusters in their sensitive attribute values. This algorithm however does not take care of interrelations. If this algorithm can be extended to take care of this point then shall be one of the most efficient algorithms available so far. We describe below the two algorithms in [42]. The following new definitions are necessary to introduce these two algorithms.

Definition 18 (Distance Metric). In the (0-hop) degree-based model, we define the distance between vertices u and v as $D(u, v) = |d(u) - d(v)|$. In the 1-hop degree-based model, we define the distance between vertices u and v as $D(u, v) = |d(u) - d(v)| + \sum |d(x_j) - d(y_j)|$, where $x_1, x_2, \ldots \in N(u, 1)$ with $d(x_1) \geq d(x_2) \geq \ldots$, and $y_1, y_2, \ldots \in N(v, 1)$ with $d(y_1) \geq d(y_2) \geq \ldots$ The distance from a vertex u to a cluster c is defined as $D(u, c) = D(u, v_c)$, where v_c is the center of the cluster c.

Definition 19 (Marginal Cost). Let G(V, E) be a social network graph and let $c_1, \ldots c_t \subset V$ be disjoint clusters. Let $v \in V$ be any vertex in the graph and let be two arbitrary clusters. We define the marginal cost $a(v, c_i, c_j) = |D(v, c_i) - D(v, c_j)|$.

Definition 20 (Surrogate). Let G(V, E) be a social network graph and let $c_1, \ldots c_t \subset V$ be disjoint clusters. A surrogate of v is defined as the cluster of size $< k$ whose center is closest to v, where k is the privacy parameter.

Bounded t-Means Clustering Algorithm

1. Let $t = \text{Floor}(n/k)$. Arbitrarily choose t vertices to be cluster centers and denote them as $v_{c1}, \ldots v_{ct}$. Denote the t clusters by $c_1, \ldots c_t$. Initially all clusters are empty.
2. For each vertex $v \in V$.

   (a) *Cluster assignment:* Add vertex v to the nearest cluster c_i according to a chosen distance metric defined above.
   (b) *Bumping:* If $|c_i| = k + 1$, that is, C_i was full and already had k members, then perform the following procedure: For each vertex $u \in c_i$, compute the marginal cost $g(u, c_i, c_j)$, where C_j the surrogate cluster of u. Bump is the vertex u^* with the lower marginal cost to its surrogate cluster C_j .
   (c) *Extra vertices:* If $|V|$ is not a multiple of k, then the remainder vertices may be safely placed in their nearest cluster, without fear of violating the minimum size constraint.

3. *Cluster update:* For each cluster C_i, a new cluster center $v_{c_i}^*$ is computed. If the new cluster centers are the same as for the previous iteration, then equilibrium has been reached and the algorithm terminates. Otherwise repeat from step 2.

Union-Split Clustering Algorithm

The above algorithm does not guarantee to produce a globally optimum clustering solution. Also, the initial choice of cluster centers may affect the outcome. So, another deterministic algorithm is introduced in [42] as follows:

1. Initialize each vertex to be in its own cluster.
2. Compute all pair wise distances between cluster centers. For each cluster, maintain the next nearest cluster to it using a min heap data structure.
3. While there exists an undersized cluster(¡k members), (a) Choose an undersized cluster c whose distance to its nearest cluster (full or undersized) is the shortest. Form the union of cluster c with its nearest cluster. (b) If the combined cluster c' is overfull ($size \geq 2k$), split it into two clusters, each of size $\geq k$. Splitting may be accomplished by finding the two vertices in c'' that are farthest from each other and then applying the bounded t-means algorithm above with $t = 2$ to ensure that the size constraint is satisfied. (c) Update all relevant cluster distances.
4. When all clusters are full, stop.

It has been established that the union-split clustering algorithm converges after a finite number of steps and the complexity of the union-split algorithm is $O(n^2 log n)$.

After the vertices of a graph have been clustered, the anonymization of the vertices inside the clusters are done. For this, the graph generalization method in [15] is used. The next step is to anonymize the clusters using inter-cluster matching.

Basic Inter-cluster Matching Method

This is applicable to the 0-hop degree-based privacy model, where the adversary has prior knowledge about the degree of the target node but not its neighbors. The approach is to transform the degrees of the vertices such that all the vertices inside a cluster has the same degree:

1. Cluster using any clustering algorithm and compute the average degree of nodes within each cluster.
2. For each node, determine how many edges it must add or remove in order to match the degree of its cluster center.
3. Match up vertices that are adjacent, but both have too many edges, and remove the edges between them.
4. If there are still vertices with too many edges, remove the necessary number of edges arbitrarily.
5. Finally, match up vertices that have too few edges and join them with an edge.
6. Add a fake vertex if needed. At most one such vertex is needed and also easy to anonymize.

Extended Inter-cluster Matching Method

This algorithm is designed in such a way that the resulting anonymized graph is robust against 1-hop degree-based attacks. The steps are:

1. Cluster using any clustering algorithm and compute the cluster centers using the mode-based method.
2. Match up vertices that are adjacent, but both desire to lose their common edge, and remove it.
3. If there are still vertices who desire to lose edges, remove those edges accordingly.
4. Precompute a neighborhood matching table such that the rows represent the anonymized degree of a vertex and the columns represent the neighbor degrees that need to be gained. The cell (X, Y) contains a multi-set of all vertices with anonymized degree X that need to gain a neighbor of degree Y.
5. Match up remaining vertices in a way that brings them mutual benefit. For each vertex at cell (X, Y) in the table, pair it up with a vertex at cell (Y, X), adding an edge between the two and removing them from the table. Anytime multiple options are available, heuristics may be used to choose the edge that best preserves the social roles of the vertices involved.
6. If there are vertices left in the table for which the complementary table entry is vacant, then create fake vertices with the required degrees to pair up with these leftover vertices.

A Fast l-Diversity Algorithm

In this section, we present a fast l-diversity algorithm [46], which can be used instead of the bounded t-means and the union-split algorithm so that the process of clustering can be fast and take care of l-diversity in the sensitive attribute values of the nodes [45]. We need the following concepts to introduce the algorithms. The notion of information loss is used to quantify the amount of information that is lost due to k-anonymization. The description in this section is based upon that in Byun, Kamra, Bertino, and Li [6]. Let T denote a set of records, which is described by m numeric quasi-identifiers $N_1, N_2, \ldots N_m$ and q categorical quasi-identifiers $C_1, C_2, \ldots C_q$. Let $P = P_1, P_2, \ldots P_p$ be a partition of T. Each categorical attribute C_i is associated with a taxonomy tree T_{C_i} that is used to generalize the values of this attribute. Consider a set $P \subseteq T$ of records. Let $\underline{N}(P)$ and $\overline{N}(P)$ denote the minimum and maximum values of the records in P with respect to the numeric attribute N_i. Also, let $C_i(P)$ denote the set of values of records in P with respect to the categorical attribute C_i and let $T_{C_i}(P)$ denote the maximal subtree of T_{C_i} rooted at the lowest common ancestor of the values of $C_i(P)$. Then, the diversity of P, denoted by D (P), is defined as $D(P) = \sum_{i \in [1,\ldots m]} (\overline{N_i}(P) - \underline{N_i}(P))/(\overline{N_i}(T) - \underline{N_i}(T)) + \sum_{i \in [1,\ldots q]} H(T_{C_i}(P))/H(T_{C_i})$, where H (T) represents the height of the tree T. Let r' and r^* be two records, then the distance between r' and r^* is defined as the diversity of the set r', r^*. The centroid of P is a record whose value of attributes is at minimum distance from all other attribute values in P. To anonymize the records in P means to generalize these records to the same values with respect to each quasi-identifier. The amount of information loss occurred by such a process, denoted as L(P), is defined as $L(P) = |P| \times D(P)$, where $|P|$ represents the number of records in P. When we consider a partition $P = \{P_1, P_2, \ldots P_p\}$ of T, the total information loss of P is the sum of the information loss of each $P_{i \in 1,\ldots p}$. To ensure the data quality of T after anonymization, an anonymization method should try to construct a partitioning P such that total information loss of P is minimized. It may be noted that the notion of centroid of a cluster was defined differently in [22], and it is followed in [21]. There the average values of the records in a cluster P are computed, and the record whose value matches with this average value is taken as the centroid. But this creates many problems, like there may not be any record whose value matches with this average value. Also, there may be several records matching this value. Again, for categorical attributes C_i, the centroid record should have its value equal to the lowest common ancestor of the values of $C_i(P)$ in the taxonomy tree T_{C_i}. Both conditions may not be satisfied by any record to be considered as the centroid. So, we have changed the definition of a centroid record as defined above to avoid the delicate situations where the algorithm is likely to collapse. The algorithm has three stages. However, in practical applications, it has been found that in most of the cases, the second and third stages are becoming redundant. So, one can think of modifying the first stage suitably so that the second and third stages are not at all necessary. A proof should solve the purpose after suitable modification. But, to be on the safer side, we present all the three stages as these may be necessary in certain cases to achieve l-diversity.

Clustering Algorithm

Input: A set T of n records; the value k for k-anonymity
Output: A partition $P = P_1, P_2, P_K$

1. Sort all records in T by their quasi-identifiers;
2. Let K:= $\lfloor n/k \rfloor$;
3. Select K distinct records based on their frequency in sensitive attribute values;
4. Let $P_i := r_i$ for i = 1 to K;
5. Let $T := T/\{r_1, r_2, \ldots r_K\}$;
6. While $(T \neq \phi)$ do
7. Let r be the first record in T
8. Order P_i according to their distances from r;
9. Let i=1;
10. Flag = 0;
11. While $((i < K)$ and(Flag= 0))
12. Let $s(P_i)$ be the set of distinct sensitive attribute values of P_i;
13. Let s (r) be the sensitive attribute value of r;
14. If $((|P_i| < k) or s(r) \notin s(P_i)$ then add r to P_i;
15. Update centroid of Pi;
16. Flag = 1;
17. Else i:= i+1;
18. If(Flag = 0) add r to the nearest cluster
19. Let T:=T/r;
20. End of while

The Adjustment Algorithm

The adjustment stage algorithm proposed by Lin and Wei [21] for the second stage takes the outputs of the first stage and applies a procedure, using which the clusters having less than k elements are compensated with elements taken from those clusters which have more than k elements. However, after adding suitable number of elements to make the number of elements in all the clusters more than k, the rest of the elements if any are again distributed among all the clusters such that they are placed in the clusters to which they are closet. But, it obviously increases the complexity in terms of processing time. It is clear from the first stage that the elements are clearly closest to the clusters from which they have been chosen. So the algorithm can be modified to take care of the return of the excess elements, if any, to their parent clusters. We present the slightly modified algorithm as follows:

Input: a partitioning $P = \{P_1 \ldots . P_K\}$ of T
Output: an adjusted partitioning $P = \{P_1 \ldots . P_K\}$ of T

1. Let $S := \phi$;
2. For each cluster $P \in P$ with $|P| < k/2$ do
3. Do $S = S \bigcup P$;
4. While $(S \neq \phi)$ do
5. Randomly select a record r from S;
6. If P contains cluster P_i with $k/2 < |P_i| < k$ do
7. Add r to the closest such cluster;
8. Else add r to the closest cluster in P
9. End of While
10. Let $R := \phi$;
11. For each cluster $P \in P$ with $|P| > k$ do
12. Sort records in P by distance to centroid of P;
13. While $(|P| > k)$ do
14. $r \in P$ is the record farthest from centroid of P ;
15. Let $P := P/r$; $R := R \bigcup r$ and $c = Index(P)$;
16. End of While
17. End of For
18. While $(R \neq \phi)$ do
19. Randomly select a record r from R;
20. Let $R := R/r$;
21. If P contains cluster Pi such that $|P_i| < k$ then
22. Add r to its closest cluster P satisfying ;
23. Else
24. Add r to its cluster P_c;
25. End if
26. End While

After the completion of adjustment stage, the following algorithm is to be used to achieve l-diversity in the clusters:

Algorithm for l-Diversity

Input: Clusters formed after adjustment stage (m in number) *Output:* Clusters satisfying l-diversity

1. Let P be the matrix of frequencies of attribute values, whose columns correspond to the clusters and rows correspond to the different attribute values in the domain of the sensitive attribute. The last row contains the diversity values (di) for the clusters (equal to the number of nonzero values in the corresponding column). The entries in P other than those in the last row contain frequencies of attribute values in the clusters.
2. Order the columns in P according to the ascending order of the diversity values.
3. Let $q = max i : d_i < l$

4. For each cluster C_i with $1 \le i \le q$ compare with cluster $C_j, j = q + 1 \ldots m$.
5. F = the sensitive attribute values which are in C_j but not in C_i and have frequency greater than 1. Find $m_i = min(l - d_i), |F|$ of them which are closest to the tuples in C_i.
6. Interchange m_i tuples between C_i (those tuples with sensitive $values > 1$) and C_j s.
7. Increment the diversity of C_i by m_i.
8. Continue the process till the diversity of all C_i is "l" or no cluster is left in $C_i, q + 1 \le j \le m$ for comparison.
9. Let S = $\{C_i : \text{diversity} of C_i < l\}$.
10. If $|s| > 1$ then
11. C be the first element of S. Compare it with other clusters in S.
12. Perform steps 5 to 8;
13. Else merge the element in S with the nearest of the clusters with diversity 1 or more obtained above.

Problems for Further Study

In this section, we present some problems which can be considered for further study. The following problems can be studied in connection with the SaNGreeA algorithm:

1. Extend the anonymity model to achieve protection against attribute disclosure in social networks. Similar models such as l-diversity [24], (α, k)-anonymity [51], and t-closeness [20] exist for microdata.
2. Study the change in utility of an anonymized social network for various application fields.
3. Formally analyze how the similarity measure is tied to the total structural information loss measure and improve the greedy selection criteria. The following problems can be studied in connection with handling uncertainty in data values of nodes.
4. Though the algorithm presented takes care of clustering of similar nodes, it is primarily suitable for relational data. Though there is a distinct possibility that it can be suitably modified to handle relation among attribute of nodes in order that it is suitable for social networks, it will be interesting to work out the details of it. In connection with the union-split algorithm, we have provided an extension algorithm to take care of l-diversity. However, the following problems can be tackled.
5. Attacks other than the reidentification of target, like the social relationship attack and link disclosure.
6. The l-diversity algorithm described here takes care of distinct l-diversity. However, the other types of l-diversity remain to be tackled.
7. An extension to handle the t-closure property would be interesting.

Conclusion

In this chapter, we presented different types of social network attacks and provided several algorithms developed so far. However, the analysis of social network in general and the anonymization problem in particular are being researched recently. It needs some deep studies further because of the reasons mentioned in section "Introduction" of the chapter. Of particular interest are the methods to handle uncertainty and providing diversity in sensitive attribute values and the t-closure property. We have also presented some problems at the end which remain to be worked out. We have initiated the use of rough set theory in the context of anonymization of social networks. However, it needs extensive work to come out with successful applications.

References

1. Aggarwal, G., Feder, T., Kenthapadi, K., Motwani, R. , Panigrahy, R., Thomas, D., Zhu, A.: Approximation algorithms for k-anonymity. J. Priv. Technol. pp. 1–8 (2005)
2. Backstrom, L., Dwork, C., Kleinberg, J.: Wherefore art thou R3579X? Anonymized social networks, hidden patterns, and structural steganography. In: International World Wide Web Conference (WWW), pp. 181–190. ACM, New York (2007)
3. Bader, D.A., Madduri, K.: GTGraph: a synthetic graph generator suite. Available online http://www.cc.gatech.edu/~kamesh/GTgraph/ (2006)
4. Bamba, B., Liu, L., Pesti, P., Wang, T.: Supporting anonymous location queries in mobile environments with privacy grid. In: ACM World Wide Web Conference, Beijing, China (2008)
5. Bayardo, R., Agrawal, R.: Data privacy through optimal k-anonymisation. In: IEEE 21st International Conference on Data Engineering, Tokyo, Japan, April 2005
6. Byun, J.W., Kamra, A., Bertino, E., Li, N.: Efficient k- anonymisation using clustering techniques. In: International Conference on Database Systems for Advanced Applications (DASFAA), pp. 188–200. Bangkok, Thailand (2007)
7. Campan, A., Truta, T.M.: A clustering approach for data and structural anonymity in social networks. In: ACM SIGKDD Workshop on Privacy, Security, and Trust in KDD (PinKDD), Las Vegas, (2008)
8. Chakrabarti, D., Zhan, Y., Faloutsos, C.: R-MAT: a recursive model for graph mining. In: SIAM International Conference on Data Mining, Florida, USA (2004)
9. Chawla, S., Dwork, C., Mcsherry, F., Smith, A., Wee, H.: Toward privacy in public databases. In: Proceedings of the Theory of Cryptography Conference, Cambridge, MA, (2005)
10. Evfimievski, A., Gehrke, J., Srikant, R.: Limiting privacy breaches in privacy preserving data mining. In: ACM Principles of Database Systems (PODS), pp. 211–222. San Diego, CA (2003)
11. Getoor, L., Diehl, C.P.: Link mining. A surv. SIGKDD Explore Newsl. 7(2), 3–12 (2005)
12. Ghinita, G., Karras, P., Kalinis, P., Mamoulis, N.: Fast data anonymisation with low information loss, In: Very Large Data Base Conference (VLDB), pp. 758–769, Vienna (2007)
13. Gross, J., Yellen, J.: Graph Theory and Its Applications. CRC, Boca Raton (2006)
14. Han, J., Kamber, M.: Data Mining, Concepts and Techniques, 2nd edn. Morgan Kaffmann, San Francisco, CA (2006)
15. Hay, M., Miklau, G., Jensen, D., Weiss, P., Srivastava, S.: Anonymising social networks. Technical Report No. 07–19, University of Massachusetts Amherst (2007)
16. HIPAA: Health insurance portability and accountability act. Available online http://www.hhs.gov/ocr/hipaa (2002)

17. Horowitz, E., Sahani, S., Rajasekaran, S.: Fundamentals of Computer Algorithms. Galgotia Publications, Darya Ganj, Galgotia Publications, New Delhi, India (2004)
18. Lambert, D.: Measures of disclosure risk and harm. J. Off. Stat. **9**, 313–331 (1993)
19. Lefebvre, K., DeWitt, D., Ramakrishnan, R.: Mondrian multidimensional K-anonymity. In: IEEE International Conference of Data Engineering (ICDE), p. 25, Atlanta, Georgia, USA (2006)
20. Li, N., Li, T., Venkitasubramaniam, S.: t-closeness: privacy beyond k-anonymity and l-diversity. In: Proceedings of the 23rd International Conference on Data Engineering (ICDE), Istanbul, pp. 106–115, Istanbul, Turkey (2007)
21. Lin, J.-L., Wei, M.-C.: An efficient clustering method for k-anonymization. In: Proceedings of the 2008 International Workshop on Privacy and Anonymity in Information Society, Nantes, pp. 29–29, March 2008
22. Liu, K., Terzi, E.: Towards identity anonymisation on graphs. In: Wang, J.T.L., (ed.) SIGMOD Conference, pp. 93–106. ACM, New York (2008)
23. Lunacek, M., Whitley, D., Ray, I.: A crossover operator for the k-anonymity problem. In: Genetic and Evolutionary Computation Conference (GECCO), Seattle, Washington, pp. 1713–1720 (2006)
24. Machanavajjhala, A., Gehrke, J., Kifer, D.: L-diversity: privacy beyond K-anonymity. In: IEEE International Conference on Data Engineering (ICDE), Atlanta, p. 24, Georgia, USA (2006)
25. Malin, B.: An evaluation of the current state of genomic data privacy protection technology and a roadmap for the future. J Am. Med. Inform. Assoc. **12**(1), 28–34 (2004)
26. Miklau, G., Suciu, D.: A formal analysis of information disclosure in data exchange. In: ACM Conference on Management of Data (SIGMOD), Paris, pp. 575–586 (2004)
27. Nergiz, M.E., Clifton, C.: Thoughts on k-anonymisation. In: IEEE 22nd International Conference on Data Engineering Workshops (ICDEW), Atlanta, Istanbul, Turkey, April 2006, p. 96
28. Nergiz, M.E., Clifton, C.: Multirelational k-anonymity. In: IEEE 23rd International Conference on Data Engineering Posters, Istanbul, Turkey, April 2007
29. Nergiz, M.E., Atzori, M., Clifton, C.: Hiding the presence of individuals from shared databases. In: 26th ACM SIGMOD International Conference on Management of Data, Beijing, June 2007
30. Newman, D.J., Hettich, S., Blake, C.L., Merz, C.J.: UCI repository of machine learning databases. Available online at: www.ics.uci.edu/~mlearn/MLRepository.html (1998)
31. Pang, R., Paxson, V.: A high-level programming environment for packet trace anonymisation and transformation. In: ACM SIGSOMM, Karlsruhe, Germany (2003)
32. Parmar, D., Wu, T., Blackhurst, J.: MMR: an algorithm for clustering categorical data using rough set theory. Data Knowl. Eng. **63**, 879–893 (2007)
33. Pawlak, Z.: Rough sets. Int. J. Comput. Inf. Sci. **11**, 341–356 (1982)
34. Pawlak, Z.: Rough Sets: Theoretical Aspects of Reasoning about Data. Kluwer, Dordrecht (1991)
35. Pearl, J.: Probabilistic Reasoning in Intelligent Systems: Networks of Plausible Inference. Kaufmann, San Mateo (1988)
36. Samarati, P.: Protecting respondents identities in microdata release. IEEE Trans. Knowl. Data Eng. **13**(6), 1010–1027 (2001)
37. Samarati, P., Sweeney, L.: Generalizing data to provide anonymity when disclosing information. In: PODS'98, Seattle, Washington (1998)
38. Singliar, T., Hauskrecht, M. Noisy-or component analysis and its application to link analysis. J Mach. Learn. Res. **7**, 2189–2213 (2006)
39. Stein, R.: Social networks' sway may be underestimated. Washington Post, 26 May 2008
40. Sweeney, L.: k-anonymity: a model for protecting privacy. Int. J. Uncertain. Fuzziness Knowl. Based Syst. **10**(5), 557–570 (2002)
41. Sweeney, L.: Achieving k-anonymity privacy protection using generalization and suppression. Int. J. Uncertain. Fuzziness Knowl. Based Syst. **10**(5), 571–588 (2002)
42. Thompson, B., Yao, D.: The union-split algorithm and cluster-based anonymisation of social networks. ASIACCS'09, Sydney, 10–12 March 2009

43. Tripathy, B.K., Lakshmi Janaki, K., Jain, N.: Security against neighborhood attacks in social networks. In: Proceedings of the National Conference on Recent Trends in Soft Computing (NCRTSC'09), pp. 216–223, Bangalore, India (2009)
44. Tripathy, B.K., Panda, G.K.: A new approach to manage security against neighborhood attacks in social networks. In: Proceedings of the 2010 International Conference on Advances in Social Networks Analysis and Mining, Odense, pp. 264–269 (2010). DOI 10.1109/ASNOM.2010.69
45. Tripathy, B.K., Panda, G.K., Kumaran, K.: A rough set approach to develop an efficient l-diversity algorithm based on clustering, accepted for presentation at the 2nd IIMA international conference on "Advanced Data Analysis, Business Analytics and Intelligence", Ahmedabad, January 2011
46. Tripathy, B.K., Panda, G.K., Kumaran, K.: A fast l – Diversity anonymisation algorithm, accepted for presentation at ICCMS 2011, Mumbai, 7–9 January 2011
47. Tripathy, B.K., Prakash Kumar, Ch.: MMeR: an algorithm for clustering heterogeneous data using rough set theory. Int. J. Rapid Manuf. **1**(2), 189–207 (2009)
48. Truta, T.M., Bindu, V.: Privacy protection: P-sensitive k-anonymity property. In: PDM Workshop, with IEEE International Conference on Data Engineering (ICDE), Atlanta, p. 94 (2006)
49. Wang, T., Liu, L.: Butterfly: protecting output privacy in stream mining. In: IEEE International Conference on Data Engineering (ICDE), Cancun, pp. 1170–1179 (2008)
50. Wasserman, S., Faust, K.: Social Network Analysis, Cambridge University Press, Cambridge/ New York (1994)
51. Wong, R.C.W., Li, J., Fu, A.W.C., Wang, K.: (α, k)- anonymity: an enhanced k-anonymity model for privacy-preserving data publishing. In: SIGKDD, pp. 754–759, Philadelphia, PA (2006)
52. Xu, J., Wang, W., Pei, J., Wang, X., Shi, B., Fu, A.W.C: Utility based anonymisation using local recording. In: KDD'06, Philadelphia, PA (2006)
53. Xu, J., Wang, W., Pei, J., Wang, X., Shi, B., and Fu, A. W.C.: gspan: graph-based substructure pattern mining. In: ICDM'02, Maebashi City (2002)
54. Zheleva, E., Getoor, L.: Preserving the privacy of sensitive relationships in graph data. In: ACM SIGKDD Workshop on Privacy, Security, and Trust in KDD (PinKDD), San Jose, pp. 153–177 (2007)
55. Zhou, B., Pei, J.: Preserving privacy in social networks against neighborhood attacks. In: Proceedings of the 24th International Conference on Data Engineering (ICDE), Cancún, pp. 506–515, Simon Fraser University (2008)

Chapter 13
Behavioural Patterns and Social Networks in Anonymity Systems

Kamil Malinka and Petr Hanáček

Abstract This chapter deals with anonymous communication. Our aim is to extend knowledge of the security limits of anonymity systems with information based on real-world traffic data. We perform a set of analyses targeting the behavioural patterns of users and their impact on such systems. The first part of the analyses are focused on the properties of email communication relevant to the designers of anonymous systems. The two parameters we are interested in are inter-arrival times and the number of messages sent by an individual user. The importance of our analyses' results for the design and implementation of anonymity systems is discussed. The second part of the analyses are focused on social networks. Information about user profiling, properties of identifiable social networks and their development in time are presented in the context of the security of anonymous systems.

Introduction to Anonymity Systems

Almost everyone is familiar with the term "Big Brother". Is it still only an emanation of our fantasy, or do we meet him with every step? We provide plenty of information about ourselves every time we access the Internet – IP address, version of operating system we are running, etc. When appropriately combined, this, at first sight valueless information, can reveal much about you including your geographic position, or which firm you are working at. Most of us do not care about this information, but there are also others – for example firms dealing with targeted advertisement – who do care and find this information very interesting and useful.

K. Malinka (✉) • P. Hanáček
Faculty of Information Technologies, Brno University of Technology, Božetechova 1/2,
612 66 Brno, Czech Republic
e-mail: malinka@fit.vutbr.cz; hanacek@fit.vutbr.cz

A. Abraham (ed.), *Computational Social Networks: Security and Privacy*,
DOI 10.1007/978-1-4471-4051-1_13, © Springer-Verlag London 2012

Thus, the need to preserve privacy and ensure confidence of not only sensitive data, but also of information about the behaviour of information system users, is an important problem of current research into IT security. It also appears that it is necessary to view privacy as a fundamentally new security property and analyze it as such.

There are plenty of reasons for preservation of privacy. What can be imagined exactly by the terms privacy and anonymity?

Privacy belongs to elemental human rights and is usually defined as the capability of a person to control access to their personal information. Our main interest relates to communication privacy. One of the existing approaches to providing this type of privacy is the deployment of so-called anonymity systems. Anonymity systems allow their users to hide relations with particular persons or activities. As we are interested in the anonymity of communication, we deal with systems ensuring it. Some services could not work without high-quality anonymization. Electronic votes are a typical example, where the need for voters' identities to remain hidden is essential.

We can see that privacy is strongly connected to humans as well as systems providing privacy and anonymity. For this reason, we are very interested in the impact of repetitive human behaviour on the systems providing anonymity.

This chapter is dedicated to behavioural patterns and social networks that can be detected in email communication and their impact on anonymity systems.

One of the biggest problems in research of communication anonymity systems is the lack of real-world data. This problem is reflected in many areas, as we will show later. In this chapter, we want to pinpoint some of these problems and discuss their solution. We aim to provide an empirical basis for the properties of email communications from the social networks point of view, which are also relevant to the designers of anonymous systems.

We were able to obtain anonymized logs from a main SMTP server dispatching emails for the four faculties of the Brno University of Technology: the Faculty of Civil Engineering, the Faculty of Fine Arts, the Faculty of Chemistry, and the Faculty of Architecture. These faculties do not have their own SMTP servers and instead rely on the central university's computing services.

A detailed description of the data is given later, but this data represents a sufficiently large amount of real-world communication data for us to conduct our research oriented towards behavioural patterns in anonymity communication. We use this data as the input for our analysis, which is targeted towards answering problems connected with lack of real data. Findings presented in this chapter are based on this dataset.

In the first part of this chapter, the necessary terminology is given. Then, we briefly discuss the requirements for ensuring anonymity, current implementations of systems ensuring it, and approaches used by these systems. The security of anonymity systems is discussed together with an overview of the existing threats. We mention the lack of analysis executed on real data. In this overview, we are focused on threats that take advantage of social networks existing in the user communication.

In the second part of the chapter, we present repetitive user behavioural patterns detectible in real-world communication. We present examples of user profiling and the possibility of creating long-term profiles, with very small variations over a longer time period. The impact of these profiles on security is discussed.

The third part of the chapter describes social networks detectible in real-world email communication. An appropriate abstraction for the expression of these networks is given and the long-term evolution of the social network is described and discussed.

Basic Terminology

Before we move on to our main point of interest – behavioural patterns and their impact on systems dealing with anonymity, it is necessary to correctly define terms used in this area. Rapid development in the field of anonymous communication has been accompanied by many papers dealing with terms such as anonymity, unlinkability, pseudonymity, etc. Definition of these terms is not easy as there is no consistency in the literature in regard to meanings and definitions. We decided to use the definitions specified in [21], which we consider consistent and the most consolidated of those available.

This terminology was developed in the usual setting of senders and recipients in a communication network, sending messages to each other. The same terminology can also be adopted in other settings (e.g. database queries, online shopping) by abstracting the special names. But for ease of explanation, we use the specific setting here. Irrespective of whether we speak of senders or recipients, we regard a subject as a possibly acting entity such as, for example a human being (i.e. a natural person), a legal person, or a computer.

As is specified in [21]: "All statements are made from the perspective of an attacker who may be interested in monitoring what communication is occurring, what patterns of communication exist, or even in manipulating the communication".

For our area of research, further definitions are crucial.

- *Anonymity of a subject means that the subject is not identifiable within a set of subjects, the anonymity set.*
- *Anonymity of a subject from an attacker's perspective means that the attacker cannot sufficiently identify the subject within a set of subjects, the anonymity set.*
- *Unlinkability of two or more items of interest (IOIs, e.g. subjects, messages, actions, ...) from an attacker's perspective means that within the system (comprising these and possibly other items), the attacker cannot sufficiently distinguish whether these IOIs are related or not.*

A group of tools called anonymizers help users to hide their identity on the Internet and prevent their tracing by an attacker. It is necessary to point out that they do not remove, but only minimize, danger of disclosure. Not all of the available tools can also be considered as completely safe.

Implementations of Anonymous Communications Systems

The first approach in ensuring unlinkability of a sender and message was introduced by Chaum in [4]. His initial ideas have led to many implementations of anonymity systems in the following decades [3, 8–11, 13–15, 25]. These systems, in turn, not only bolstered the notions of privacy in information systems but also sparked research in developing attack techniques.

The basic concept assumes the existence of a "mix" – a kind of router that has the ability to receive and forward messages. Simultaneously, it must hide information about the sender. This is provided by two mechanisms. The first is the impossibility of linking input messages to output messages, the second is mixing.

The first mechanism ensures that if an attacker compares all relevant input and output messages, they are not able to find correspondent couples (neither via length nor content). This is often solved by the division of incoming messages to smaller blocks of stable length, where each block is sent in a different way. Thus, each part of the message travels on a distinct path.

Conversely, mixing destroys time patterns. There will be no effect from an anonymity point of view in the case that the mix just forwards messages in the same order as they arrive, because with the assistance of statistical methods, it may be possible to link related blocks of the message. Thus, the messages are operated in batches and forwarded in groups.

Because the number of mixes is not limited, they can be grouped into mixnets–networks of routers that cooperate with each other in ensuring anonymity of communication. They provide the mixing of each message in the scope of a bigger set of messages; this mixing is repeated several times. Computers that are used for the mixing of a specific message are chosen in many different ways (depending on design), but essentially this choice should be unpredictable. During the forwarding of a message, each mix knows only the mix that delivered the message to its actual position and mix, to which the message should be subsequently forwarded. Thus, on the occasion of the corruption of the specific mix by an attacker, only part of the path will be revealed.

The mechanism of the mix can be applied to different areas: sending emails, web browsing or ensuring payment protocol. Conversely, we can not afford delays that result from the delivering of single packets if we want to anonymize streams of data, for example voice, video. For that reason, systems demanding stream connection use a prior channel establishment setup. These channels differ for each connection. This principle is used in another approach in path anonymization – onion routing, which was derived from the concept of mixnets.

Onion routing is based on the establishment of a communication path randomly assembled from other participants from the network. Every participant serves as a router – receives messages from other nodes in the network and forwards them to selected addresses. The point is that the intermediator that forwards messages does not know either the contents of the message, the sender or the target. Every message

Fig. 13.1 Format of message for Alice sent via onion routing

must contain the whole routing data in order to continue operation of the service. Concealment is reached by asymmetric cryptography.

Let us imagine a situation where Bobs want to send a message to Alice. To hide this communication Bob establishes a communication channel:

$$\text{Bob} \Rightarrow A \Rightarrow B \Rightarrow C \Rightarrow \text{Alice}$$

Further, Bob must encipher the transferred message using Alice's public key. Additional information is then added to the encrypted message – routing information for node C and the new message, encrypted by the public key of node C. The same scenario is repeated for node B and node A. Here we get an "onion message" with four layers of information, see Fig. 13.1. The sent message is transferred to node A which removes the outer layer of the message, and the resultant message is transferred to node B. In this manner the message is transferred the whole way from start (Bob) to final destination (Alice), and the contents of the message remains secret to routing nodes.

We can see that anonymity likes company. Although it can sound paradoxical, the degree of anonymity is dependent on the number of participants in the process. A bigger amount of messages provides a bigger number of combinations and significantly makes attacks on anonymity systems more difficult.

Security of Anonymity Systems

In every area of security (privacy is not an exception) one argument is valid – a system is safe until someone breaks in. Although there are theoretical and practical attacks on anonymity systems (e.g. based on the analysis of network traffic), real security appears sufficient. The other side of the coin is the systems that keep records of incoming and outgoing connections. They grant only pseudoanonymity, because it is theoretically possible to trace users. In a situation that an anonymity system is located in the country where the local authorities are interested in these records, it is highly likely that they can get access to them using a court order. As with other technologies anonymity can also be used for both good and bad purposes.

Anyway, we are interested in security analysis of real anonymity systems and the impacts of user behaviour on the effectivity and security of these systems.

One of the first papers on traffic analysis of anonymous message systems, which belongs to one of the attack techniques, appeared in 1993 [19]. Papers on traffic analysis started appearing regularly from 2000 and there is a very good understanding of the security limits of anonymity systems. Computational boundaries for successful attacks on anonymity systems have been defined [9, 13, 14, 20] in the last few years. Thus, knowledge of security limits of anonymity systems is now at a relatively high level [10, 24] but there is no validated concept about user behaviour which is necessary for the successful modelling and simulation of anonymity systems.

There are several types of anonymity systems and ways to attack them. For our purposes, we briefly introduce only attacks relevant to behavioural patterns. Proposed attacks are not based on some specific implementation; we give only a general concept that can be mounted at the high level descriptions of the schemes.

Model of Attacker

If we want to set the level of security in anonymity systems, it is necessary to define the strength of the attacker against whom we want to be protected. Without this specification, we can get a (maybe) generally secure system, but surely this system will be useless in practice. In the area of anonymity systems, the strength of the attacker is determined by assessing their ability to access hidden information and how large a part of the communication of an anonymity system it is able to capture [22]. We consider the following attacker properties [23]:

- *Internal-External: An adversary can compromise communication mediums (external) and mix nodes, recipients and senders (internal).*
- *Passive-Active: An active adversary can arbitrarily modify the computations and messages (adding and deleting) whereas a passive adversary can only listen. For example, an external active adversary can remove and add messages from the wire(s) they control and a passive internal adversary can easily correlate messages coming into a compromised node with messages going out (but cannot modify them).*
- *Static-Adaptive: Static adversaries choose the resources they compromise before the protocol starts and cannot change them once the protocol has started. Conversely, adaptive adversaries are allowed to change the resources they control while the protocol is being executed. They can, for example "follow" messages.*
- *Local-Global: Local adversaries have access only to a subset of a network, unlike the global, which embraces the whole network.*

An adversary can, of course, have any combination of these properties. There are of course certain boundaries and limits. We constantly assume that the use of cryptographic primitives is secure and an attacker is not able to break them, for example they are not able to decipher messages encrypted with a strong symmetrical algorithm. They are also not able to detect what is happening in the nodes that are not under their control. They can be used only as a black box.

Behavioural Attacks: Attacks Based on Repetitive Behaviour

It this section, we describe attacks based on user behaviour analysis. These attacks belong to the most powerful attacks, if we consider the stability of human behaviour and its tendency to converge to a specific form. Thus, it is relatively difficult to develop proper protection at a reasonable price.

Communication Patterns Attacks

We can reveal a great deal of interesting information by simply looking at the communication patterns: the time when participants of communication are active, area of interests of users, etc. Increasing the time of observations allows better filtering of these patterns from the noise of other communication. This attack can be mounted by a passive adversary that can monitor the entry and exit mix nodes.

We also assign to this subset attacks focused on social networks such as MySpace, Facebook, etc. There has been a significant increase in the usage of these social networks and hand in hand with this comes abuse. Many people place a lot of private information on their profile with no idea of the possible dangers. We already have referenced cases of people getting fired because of information published on their personal sites. Also personnel departments usually use these sites to screen people they are interested in. Thus, it is very close to privacy issues.

Intersection Attacks

An intersection attack is a very powerful approach for attacking any anonymity system to discover the recipients of a message (link senders and recipients of messages). Intersection attacks can be launched on two different scales. An attacker observes the communication lines between users and the first mix to determine whether the user is active or not. An attacker also observes the number of messages leaving the mixnet. On the basis of these observations, some messages can be linked to a sender [2].

The attack assumes that it is possible to create a profile describing the behaviour of a selected user. This profile is then used to compute intersections with anonymized traffic. The attacker creates a set of possible recipients of the selected user. This set is then intersected with the user's profile. The power of the attack is assumed to be very high due to the existence of behavioural stereotypes.

Disclosure Attacks

Disclosure attacks belong to the family of attacks that takes advantage of patterns in human behaviour.

Disclosure attack and statistical disclosure attack are the most cited. The disclosure attack [19] assumes simplified user behaviour. An adversary monitors only public parameters of communication, such as who is sending and who is receiving messages. From this knowledge, the adversary can reveal the contacts of a specific user.

A different style of attack, the Statistical Disclosure Attack (SDA) [7], considers the same user behaviour and communication model, but reduces the computation complexity by using statistical models and approximations to reveal the same information to an attacker. This basic attack is also enhanced in some ways [19].

In SDA Alice's behaviour is considered as uniform and is represented by the vector $\mathbf{v}$, whose elements correspond to the probability of Alice sending a message to each of the N recipients in the system. The elements of $\mathbf{v}$ corresponding to Alice's m recipients will be $1/m$; the other $N - m$ elements of $\mathbf{v}$ will be 0.

Vector $\mathbf{u}$ represents the probability of distribution used by all other senders to select their recipients for each round of mixing. This serves as a model for the background traffic.

During an attack the attacker derives a set of vectors $\mathbf{o}_1, ..., \mathbf{o}_t$. Each vector represents the recipient anonymity set observed corresponding to the t messages sent by Alice.

Taking this arithmetic means $\mathbf{O}$ of a large set of these observation vectors gives (by the law of large numbers):

$$\mathbf{O} = \frac{\sum_{i=1...t} \mathbf{o}_i}{t} = \frac{\mathbf{v} + (b - 1)\mathbf{u}}{b} \tag{13.1}$$

From the knowledge of observation the attacker can estimate Alice's behaviour:

$$\mathbf{v} = b\frac{\sum_{i=1...t} \mathbf{o}_i}{t} - (b - 1)\mathbf{u} \tag{13.2}$$

We have presented a few ways of attacking anonymity systems. Being aware of the power of attacks based on repetitive patterns, it is necessary to understand the details of human behaviour. Knowledge about the appearance of a development of such patterns can help us to create sufficient protection against related attacks.

Problems of Anonymity Systems

The first problem we will deal with herein is the impact of user behaviour on anonymous communication. One great challenge for designers of anonymity systems is to aggregate predictable user behaviour so that it appears as random noise. Any deviations from pure randomness can often be exploited to undermine the security properties of anonymity systems. There are many assumptions about how user behaviour may deviate from randomness, yet precious little is known about how users actually operate. For example, one common "rule-of-thumb" is that X% of the effects come from (1–X)% of the causes – the so-called Pareto principle observable in many, not only social, types of phenomena. However, no existing analysis of communication patterns has been used to verify this rule for email communication.

Another problem related to the lack of real data is the efficiency of existing attacks. The real power of attacks on anonymity systems is questionable because of their design, which is based on simplified models of communication that differ, to some level, from real-world communication. There is a family of attacks based on searching for a human behaviour pattern. To be able to develop a proper measure against these attacks, it is necessary to have a better understanding of the properties of the behaviour patterns. One step towards this knowledge is determining the properties of social networks that occur in communication.

What exactly are these social networks or user behaviour patterns in terms of anonymity systems? People tend to create communication patterns and repeat them in such a way that every user has a group of people that he/she usually communicates with. These patterns represent social networks, which are essentially the maps of relations between individuals. These social networks can be detected and used to compromise the anonymity system because knowledge of this social network can considerably ease the attack. Protection against disclosure attacks is the object of the research. We can protect against them, but the price is very high. Our target is to develop a method that will make patterns of behaviour invisible.

Despite the fact that knowledge of the security limits of anonymity systems is now at a relatively high level [10, 24], there is no validated concept about user behaviour which is necessary for the successful modelling and simulation of anonymity systems. There are very few works [9] covering the evaluation of anonymity systems and even less works focusing on social profiling [12]. Research into how a user environment influences the success of attacks represents an interesting topic that is very hard to perform, as a large amount of data is needed. A large number of results related to anonymity systems assume that user behaviour can be described with simple probabilistic models. We want to show some basic interesting characteristics of email communication that we have identified in a log of SMTP traffic and demonstrate that user behaviour cannot be easily described with simple models.

We will also describe the basic properties of existing social networks. One of the characteristics of social networks is their correspondence with scale-free networks. The scale-free networks can be briefly described as networks where there is a small amount of nodes with a large quantity of connections (edges) with other nodes in the network. The assumption is that this very strong imbalance can lead to a successful attack on users' communication privacy. One of the weaknesses is that it allows the easy creation of unique communication profiles.

We analyze the network traffic from two main viewpoints: intra-domain and complete communication. We have created subsets of communication within university faculties to analyze their social networks. For the creation of these social networks the whole traffic that took place in these domains was used. The second viewpoint is represented by an analysis of all traffic initiated by users from these email domains.

We would also like to know if, once revealed, a social network could lead to an absolute or partial compromise of the system, and if this state is permanent or if it is possible to return to a safe state after further use of the system. Directly connected to this is the knowledge about short-term and long-term development of social networks.

In the next part, we deal with the problems described above and show the results of our analysis of real-world data.

Analyses of Real Email Traffic Properties

We have presented a few ways of attacking anonymity systems. Being aware of the power of attacks based on repetitive patterns, it is necessary to understand the details of human behaviour. Knowledge about the appearance of a development of such patterns can help us to create sufficient protection against related attacks.

The main problem of current research is the lack of real data that can be used for the testing of new systems or models of new systems for ensuring privacy. This deficiency comes with the problems of acquiring data flow because of the protection of personal information. One exception from the main stream is [11] where results based on data from a specific anonymity system are published.

On the basis of the lack of real data in research related to privacy, we have decided to provide the strong empirical evidence that the field of anonymity systems has been lacking. We were able to obtain anonymized logs from a main SMTP server dispatching emails for four faculties of the Brno University of Technology: the Faculty of Civil Engineering, the Faculty of Fine Arts, the Faculty of Chemistry, and the Faculty of Architecture. These faculties do not have their own SMTP servers and instead rely on the central university computing services. We run several analyses on this data [16]. The first area is related to mixes and their parameterization, the second is related directly to social networks in email communication.

Data Set

The first data set that we discuss in this work contains emails sent between 1st July 2006 and 8th August 2006. Since this is a university environment, these dates fall into a period of slightly lower traffic due to the summer break.[1] We also mention that this is only a subset of data we have available for analysis, later we also study data gathered over a 10-month period.

There are approximately 790,000 records (email messages) in our log file. A virus was detected in around 4,000 of them, while 311,000 messages were marked

---

[1] Surprisingly, the fall in traffic is very slight. There are 670,000 messages in July compared to 867,000 messages in October, 635,000 in November, and 717,000 in December. The average number of messages is 735,000 per month.

```
       1B2M2Y8AsgTpgAmY7PhCfg | chXunH2dwinSkhpA6JnsXw |
kIV5zAmuZjBgoNwtF7OFzg | QyfwyB/Tfd E/hGz0DDyBdQ | 2006-07-01
   09:41:04 | 5TUrF1P3W48zBGB L1edsoQ | -3.432 | ok | 9817
```

Fig. 13.2 Example of a log record

as spam by SpamAssassin (the number is so low due to gray-listing applied to the traffic before logging). Each processed record in the log file contains the following information (see Fig. 13.2 for an example):

1. MD5 hashes of sender and recipient email address – the addresses were appropriately processed before hashing (display name was removed and the address converted to lower case).
2. MD5 hashes of sender and recipient address domain – domain stands for the whole part of the address after @.
3. Exact time when the message reached our SMTP server.
4. MD5 hash of the message ID if one exists – this hash enables us to link several copies of the same message.
5. SpamAssassin scoring – only messages smaller than 100 KB are evaluated, the scoring is set to 0 for larger messages.
6. Flag whether the email contains a virus or is spam.
7. Size of the email – in bytes.

Email addresses were carefully processed to remove unnecessary text information that could cause a duplicate hash for factually same addresses before applying the MD5 algorithm .

During this time our first data set grew into a much bigger form. These new logs record email communication of university staff and students of several faculties of a large university (Brno University of Technology). There are approximately ten million records in our log files with almost five million messages marked as spam by SpamAssassin. Each processed record in the log file has a standardized format and contains the same information as specified above: MD5 hashes of sender and recipient email address and their address domain, exact time when the message reached our SMTP server, an MD5 hash of the message ID if one exists, SpamAssassin scoring, and the size of the email.

The email traffic logs come from a server that is used for all the email traffic within some faculties of the university.

Analysis of Social Networks' Effects on Anonymity Systems

The main goal of this section is to demonstrate properties of real-world email traffic from a social networks point of view. We will show that there are indeed social networks identifiable in the email traffic and that these networks correspond to communication patterns of users.

Table 13.1 Characteristics of the largest email domains

Domain	Number of nodes	Largest component	2nd largest component	# of components
1	781	481(62%)	130	47
2	714	665(93%)	6	19
3	894	666(74%)	23	35
4	931	858(92%)	16	12
5	3,127	2,844(91%)	14	65
6	4,207	4,066(97%)	21	38

The existence of these networks and the possibility of their disclosure may therefore have a substantial impact on the level of anonymity provided by any anonymity system. We carried out an analysis of real data – SMTP logs. This section focuses on the analysis of social networks for domains (usually faculties) within the university, the comparison of the social networks topology with scale-free networks, and the potential impact of the communication topology on the anonymity, and possible user profiling.

Topology of Real Email Communication

This section describes the several, most important, aspects that would allow reasonably precise modelling of user behaviour. The first aspect we were interested in was the structure of intra-domain communication. We have identified eight domains with more than 500 email addresses. All these domains consisted of one large graph component consisting of more than 50% of all the nodes of the domain (see Table 13.1). The rest of the nodes usually form very small communication networks of up to around 30 nodes.

This means that a potential attacker can very successfully diminish the anonymity of a possibly large portion of users in the domain that communicates only within their small social network. The possibility to completely separate groups of users and their communication is a very strong tool as it is efficient to implement.

At the same time, the anonymity of users in the main graph is also weakened. This effect is not that serious as the amount of communication in the small graph components is relatively small. This is also due to the fact that the amount of communication per user is lower in the small graph components when compared to the main component.

Another observation is that the majority of domains contain a few users sending large numbers of emails. These seem to be administrators and their traffic can again be used for attacks on anonymity as it causes strong skews in the message's distributions.

Fig. 13.3 Approximation of social networks with a scale-free network characteristic

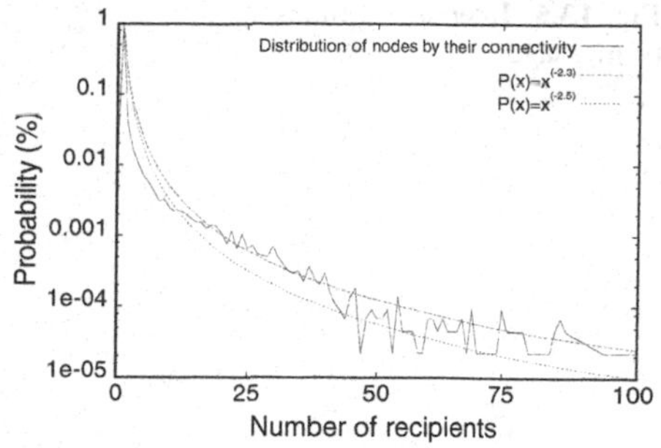

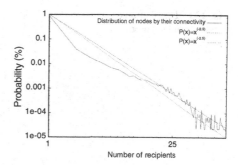

Fig. 13.4 Approximation of social networks with a scale-free network characteristic (log–log)

Scale-Free Networks: Analytical Model of Social Networks

Analysis of social networks deserves a bit more attention as the data we use contain relatively rich details about user behaviour. We want to introduce a few basic results of discovered social networks' properties in this section.

A general assumption is that social networks can be, in analytical models, replaced by scale-free networks [1]. The internal structure of scale-free networks can be described by a very simple Eq. 13.3 defining the connectivity of graph nodes.

$$P(x) = x^{-\alpha}, \tag{13.3}$$

where x is the connectivity of a node (expressed via an arbitrary metric such as the number of neighbours or amount of forwarded data), $P(x)$ is a probability of nodes with a given connectivity x in a network. α is a constant parameter. The following graph (Fig. 13.3) shows what social networks inside email domains look like.

It seems that a social network that is computed from a communication inside the largest domain (one of the university faculties) can be abstracted with a scale-free network with a coefficient α =2.3–2.5. Such values fit graphs of particular inter-domain communications as well as for the overall communication, as we have seen in our data. The abstraction is not perfect as can be seen in Fig. 13.4.

Fig. 13.5 Inter-arrival times
of messages

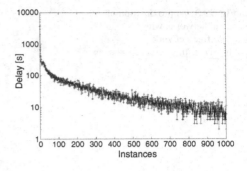

Fig. 13.6 Distribution of
messages among users

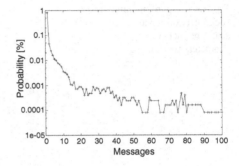

Message Distribution

Further important parameters for reasonable modelling of email communication
are message distributions among users and message inter-arrival times. You can
see graphs of the two related distributions in Figs. 13.5 and 13.6, respectively. The
first observation is that they cannot be described with any of the commonly used
probability distributions. These real-world graphs have the very long characteristic
tails that we have identified in many other properties of the email communication.

Realistic models of the email communication parameters we have just named
should allow the creation of reasonably good abstractions that might be used for
reasoning about the privacy provided by various anonymity systems.

User-Level Distribution of Recipients

Distribution of messages among recipients is the part of the analysis that has brought
the biggest surprise so far.

In the introduction we mentioned the Pareto principle commonly used in
sociology and economics. This rule, if true, would state that, for example four fifths
of each user's messages are addressed to only one fifth of the user's communication
partners. This was an expectation we were not able to confirm. What we found

Fig. 13.7 User-level distribution of messages among recipients

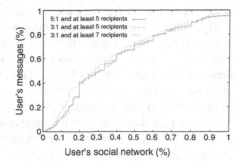

Fig. 13.8 Analysis of user behaviour for addressing 20%, 30%, and 40% of emails

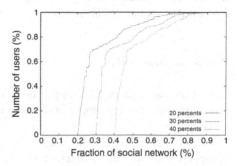

instead, was a linear function mapping the proportion of recipients to the fraction of messages. This is not to say that all users are so balanced in disseminating their communications. While the average user respects linearity, a minority of users do concentrate their messages on a few recipients. Trying a bit harder, we were able to break the linearity by carefully selecting a subset of users but we could never approach the, for example 80/20 rule.

Figure 13.7 shows the distribution of messages among recipients, selecting only users that send three to five times more messages than their total number of recipients. At the same time, a minimum number of recipients are required. Even such a crafted selection ensures only a 67/33 or 60/40 rule.

Notice the slow take off of the graph. This is due to the small number of users sending messages to a high number of recipients, so the aggregates for less than 10% of recipients are lower than expected.

Figure 13.7 presents an aggregate measure of the distribution of messages to recipients, so it would be a misinterpretation to suggest that all users evenly distribute messages among recipients. We more closely examine the behaviour of particular users in Fig. 13.8. This graph shows the number of recipients per user for particular x fractions of top messages ($x = 0.2, 0.3$, and 0.4) from Fig. 13.7. The left-most line shows the fraction of all emails that are addressed to 20% of number of recipients per user for particular fractions of top messages.

The graph contains the distribution for users that sent at least 15 messages, which is a small portion (302 to be precise) of all users. One can see that there is only a small fraction (less than one fifth of the 302) of users whose messages are spread really non-linearly among their recipients. For instance, for the middle 30% of the graph, around 20% of users distribute their top 30% of messages to at least 50% of their total recipients. Furthermore, only a few users (around 1%) distribute 20% of their messages among 80% of users. This graph demonstrates that while the average distribution of messages remains linear, a small number of users do exhibit the kind of concentrated message patterns that could be exploited by traffic analysis.

Figure 13.8 is affected by rounding errors. When we use exact numbers then 174 users out of 302 from the plot sent exactly one message to each of their recipients (through the university SMTP server). This means that more than 50% of these users would still be immune to any intersection attacks after 40 days of observing all the email traffic on our SMTP server.

Provided Anonymity

Each mix has a theoretical upper bound for the anonymity level provided. The difference between this upper bound and the real anonymity depends on the users' behaviour.

The simplest aspect is the sizes of messages being sent through a mix and their comparison to the size of message blocks processed by the mix. We would like to see as few messages being split as possible, while limiting the increase in the volume of the transmitted data. The number of blocks per messages decreases exponentially while the volume of the data increases linearly in the mix block size [16]. This allows the increase of the mix block size, for example from 50 kB up to 100 kB with the data "overhead" going up from 80% to 170%.

Kesdogan et al. [15] prove an optimality of exponential distribution for the delay of messages in Stop-and-Go mixes assuming $M/M/\infty$ queuing system with Poisson distribution of message arrivals. We show that this assumption is not true and, as a result, such a mix will not mix the messages perfectly, and the anonymity provided will be lower than expected – the difference is, however, unclear at the moment.

We used the distribution of message sizes to compute the optimum mix block size, but there is more to be said. We have shown that although the total number of messages larger than a megabyte is very low, messages of up to tens of megabytes tend to appear regularly. Such a message can cause an effective $(n - 1)$ attack on the mix. Obviously, an attack may let such messages appear when most convenient.

Another interesting aspect affecting the anonymity of users is the distribution of messages among users. The data set covering 40 days of email traffic contains messages to over 102 thousand recipients. However, only 7,700 recipients received ten email messages or more, covering almost 20% of all the traffic.

On the side of senders, only 2% of non-spam users sent at least ten messages. This number increased to 8% in a subset of internal users (the data set contains all their email traffic). Local static attackers controlling "random" mixes would use the former number, while a dynamic local attacker controlling adaptively chosen mixes – closest to the selected victim – would use the latter one. In both cases, however, a large majority of users would have to sustain a long-term (several months) traffic analysis attack to lose their privacy.

The last finding in this section relates to the behaviour of users. We have shown that the distribution of recipients is far from the expected Pareto principle. When we analyzed the behaviour of users that sent more than 500 messages (108 in total), two thirds addressed their messages to only one recipient. The analysis further showed that the distribution of messages according to, for example the 80/20 rule is far from reality. This again potentially influences the results of statistical traffic analysis attacks.

Delivery Delay Variation

The timely delivery of messages is an important factor from a user's perspective, especially if the anonymity technologies are to be widely accepted. We show that there is not that much difference in the amount of traffic throughout the day, but the variation is very substantial between working days and weekends (particularly when combined with bank holidays). There seems to be another open question of whether it is possible to sacrifice anonymity provided by mixes during low-traffic periods because of different traffic patterns?

Statistical Disclosure

Statistical disclosure attacks are very simple but also very powerful attacks against privacy technologies. There are several interesting aspects influencing the efficiency of these attacks that we have identified during our analysis.

- We have not found, for a large portion of users, any analytical statistical distribution that would describe the distribution of messages onto recipients.
- Many users send messages in batches – especially users with a higher number of different recipients. The average number of messages within one mixing window of 100 messages went easily over 5. The reason seems to be the use of off-line emailing. We believe that this is another aspect of users' behaviour whose effects on statistical attacks are worth further research.
- Even though the assumptions of uniform message distribution by Serjantov et al. [24] do not hold in real-world traffic, it is very easy to create a general traffic profile that can be successfully used for automated statistical disclosure attacks.
- Several experiments we have conducted indicate that false-positives start appearing much faster than false-negatives. In other words, the attacker can substantially limit the set of recipients with a high probability that actual recipients will be picked.

We have run several simple experiments to verify the results for statistical disclosure attack by Danezis [7] (later extended by Mathewson and Dingledine [19]).

Table 13.2 Number of messages needed for a successful attack

m	1	2	3	4	5	6	7	8	9	13	20
t	1	12	14	22	35	45	57	72	84	142	295

The basic equation estimating the amount of data for a successful attack against "Alice" is (95% confidence):

$$ t > \left[2.m \left(\sqrt{\frac{N-1}{N^2}(b-1)} + \sqrt{\frac{N-1}{N^2}(b-1) + \frac{m-1}{m^2}} \right) \right]^2 \tag{13.4} $$

where N is the number of recipients, m the number of Alice's recipients, b the size of the mix's pool, and t is the number of mix rounds that must be collected.

The simple experiments we did were using a mix of the size $b = 100$. N was then in the region of 5,000, and m lower than 50. The large N and relatively small b allows us to simplify the equation:

$$ t > \left[2.m \left(\sqrt{\frac{b}{N}} + \sqrt{\frac{b}{N} + \frac{m-1}{m^2}} \right) \right]^2 \tag{13.5} $$

The first square root is around 0.15, while the second is 0.15 for just one recipient (which does not sound right), and then monotonically decreases from 0.72 down to 0.14 (0.22 is for 40 recipients) – the sum is therefore between 0.86 and 0.28, and the evaluation of the whole equation is in Table 13.2.

The experiments we have carried out suggest that the attack complexity is undervalued for low numbers of recipients, while over valued when more recipients are to be identified. The non-uniform distribution of messages also causes different anonymity levels for differently "popular" recipients. We believe that this attack can be elaborated and made more efficient with the use of real-world data.

Open Questions

Parts of this chapter's analysis elaborate on the performance properties of mixes. These mixes were not applied to the data in real time but we have instead written a simulator of a mix system.

The analysis assumes that there is a mix server deployed on the SMTP server that has produced the traffic data. We have analyzed two basic constructions of mixes: with a fixed time delay and with a fixed pool size.

There are a few open questions that could cause objections that we cannot answer yet. The first is the question about emails written as replies to previous emails.

There are emails written as replies to previous emails and the deployment of a mix would change the time line of this part of the traffic. The significance of this problem is very hard to estimate as SMTP servers do not store "In-reply-to" headers and it is unclear how the delay of the responses would influence the results of our analysis. To assess the potential influence, we can provide the following numbers: there were 522,000 independent emails to which 50,000 automatic responses were generated within 60 s. Non-automatic replies (the delay was longer than 60 s) were sent for 500 different email threads.

We also assume real-world data but a large portion of spam messages blocked on the SMTP server is ignored.

We agree with these objections, but we have not found a way around them. It can be overcome by delaying quick responses during simulations and we are implementing programs that would allow us to do this. However, it is not quite clear how much better the simulations will be when compared to real traffic. We have therefore decided to use the results without data traffic manipulation.

Another question is the relevance of the data. Traffic from a university may suffer from oscillations like holidays, weekends, and so on. Obviously, it would be slightly more interesting to analyze the data of email traffic of common users but it is very hard to get these. Conversely, we have been lucky in a sense, because the collected data come from non-engineering departments and the users reflect the general population much better than would users with an IT background.

The last question is related to the validity of the data set because of an incredibly high number of users that sent very few messages. This was a surprise for us as well and we have verified this on a data set covering a 14-month period. The distribution of messages among users was invariant.

Social Networks and Attacker Models

The anonymity research assumes two types of attackers. There is a global attacker that is able to eavesdrop on all communication – this is the model for which the analysis of the characteristics of complete social networks is most useful.

Much weaker is a local attacker model when access to traffic of a (small) part of social networks is only available. Even such an attacker may be able to discover the social networks of users that we would assume are outside the monitored network. This is possible due to "Cc" and "Bcc" items in email headers. These headers disclose the relations of outside users – assuming that addressees of the same email will know each other. The potential of this attack amplification can be estimated from the number of messages that are sent to more than one recipient. We have counted numbers of message copies using a simple criterion that the sender, time, and size are the same for all the copies. The results are on the graphs in Fig. 13.9. We have to keep in mind that there are only around 600 users that sent at least ten messages. The attack therefore works very well (i.e. they compromised at least five external users) on 20% of such users.

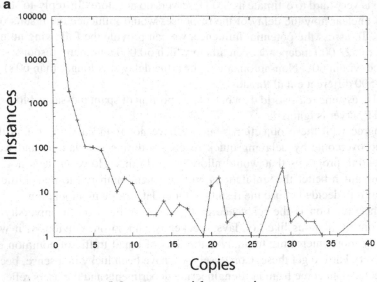

Messages with more instances.

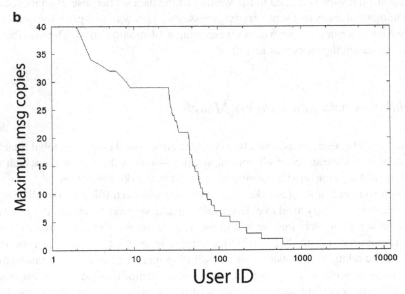

Users disclosing outer social networks.

Fig. 13.9 Graphs of number of messages and users disclosing outer social networks.

$$D_x = \frac{\sum_{i=1..|U|}\left[P(U_i) - \frac{P_x(U_i)*|M|}{|M_x|}\right]}{|M|} \quad (6) \qquad D_x = \frac{\sum_{i=1..|U|}\left[P(U_i) - \frac{P_x(U_i)*|M|}{|M_x|}\right]^2}{|M|^2} \quad (7)$$

Fig. 13.10 Equations for computing the difference between two profiles

User Profiling

An intersection attack is a very powerful approach for attacking any anonymity system to discover the recipients of a message (link senders and recipients of messages). The attack assumes that it is possible to create a profile describing the behaviour of a selected user. This profile is then used to compute intersections with anonymized traffic. The attacker creates a set of possible recipients when the user is selected. This set is then intersected with the user's profile. The power of the attack is assumed to be very high due to the existence of behavioural stereotypes.

We tried several approaches to profile the users. We started with comparing the profiles of the users against each other but any reasonable quantification was too expensive and hard to use. What we were looking for were metrics that would make it hard to cluster users into groups with similar behaviour. If this were possible, there would be email addresses that were hard to discern as their behaviour would be very similar.

The final approach was to create a general profile of the whole domain – this is also quite easy to do even when only anonymized traffic is available. We then compared the profiles of the users against this aggregated profile of the domain. We tried several metrics to compare the similarity of the profiles. One has to remember that relative numbers of messages are important and so the easiest equation is Eq. 13.6 in Fig. 13.10,

$$D_x = \frac{\sum_{i=1..|U|}\left[P(U_i) - \frac{P_x(U_i)*|M|}{|M_x|}\right]}{|M|} \qquad (13.6)$$

$$D_x = \frac{\sum_{i=1..|U|}\left[P(U_i) - \frac{P_x(U_i)*|M|}{|M_x|}\right]^2}{|M|^2} \qquad (13.7)$$

D_x is the difference in the profiles between user U_x and the domain she/he belongs to. U is the set of users in the domain and M, M_x are the set of all messages, and messages sent by user U_x, respectively. $P(U_i)$ and $P_x(U_i)$ are the probabilities of user U_i being the recipient of a message sent by anybody in the domain and user U_x, respectively. The results for the largest domain are shown in Fig. 13.11a.

Much more interesting is, however, to use geometric distance (Fig. 13.10, Eq. 13.7) – the square of the differences divided by the square of the total message number. The results after using this metric are shown in Fig. 13.11b. You can see that the users are very nicely spread in space. It is also clearly visible that there exist

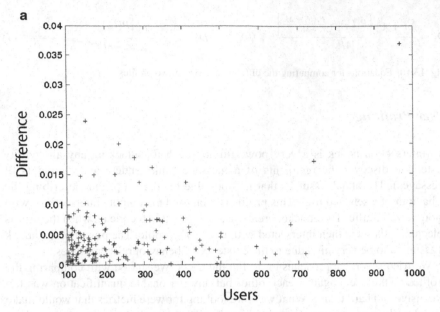

Messages with more instances.

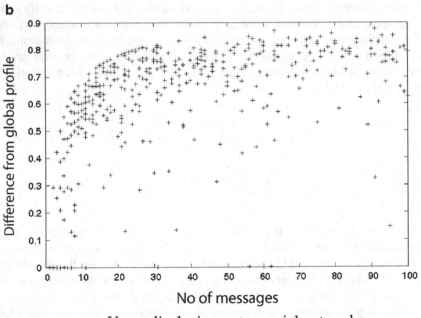

Users disclosing outer social networks.

Fig. 13.11 Profiles created from the number of messages sent during an interval and the similarity of the recipient sets.

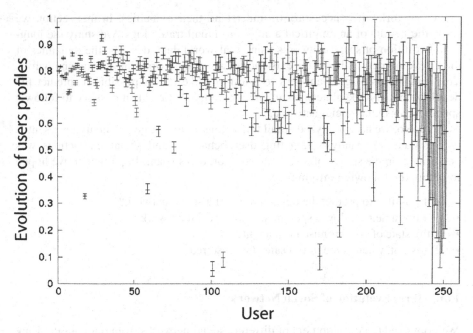

Fig. 13.12 Evolution of user profiles in time. Users sending more than 100 messages in 6 months

values of the maximum possible similarity of profiles dependent on the number of messages sent by a particular user. These values are repeated with different sets of messages.

The largest domain, and its traffic, was sufficiently large to allow the splitting of the traffic into 2-month intervals. We created three intervals for the period October 2006–March 2007 to determine how much user behaviour changes over time. We set a limit on the minimum number of messages sent by the users to filter out possible large variations caused by the very small numbers of messages sent by some users. Figure 13.12 shows the results for users sorted by the difference between minimum and maximum values.

About two thirds of the users have profiles varying within 10%. This may allow the creation of long-term profiles for a large number of users. This is an aspect that, we believe, deserves much more attention and a deeper analysis of users with vastly varying profiles.

Development of Social Networks in Email Communication

Disclosure attacks use eavesdropping communication to rebuild a social network and further use this knowledge to reveal the users' identity. We should use the same principle to protect the user. To be able to develop protective methods based on social networks, it is necessary to understand their dynamics. In this section we show the results of an empirical analysis of email traffic logs. We study the long-term evolution of social networks using real-world data, describe the dynamics of their development and how the existence of a social network impacts on anonymity. This enables us to give answers to questions like: "Is it possible to predict the development of a social network in email communication? Is it possible to follow a specific user in this social network?"

To do so, we have analyzed email traffic logs from a large university represented in our data set. Analysis targeting user behaviour and social interactions was performed on the subset of messages not marked as spam. In particular, we hoped to obtain the following information:

- Is it possible to predict the development of a social network?
- Is it possible to follow a specific user in a social network?
- Is the state of compromise permanent?
- If it is not, when is the initial safe state restored?

Long-Term Evolution of Social Networks

We compared the development of different social networks from our dataset. They converge to a similar shape corresponding to the mathematical model of a scale-free network. Incremental development of one communication domain from ten of the most significant domains is depicted in Fig. 13.13. We can see increments after every 2 months of communication, where the nodes represent users, edges represents relation between users and the weight of edge represents the number of messages transferred between two nodes.

We can see an incremental creation of a relationship between nodes. Notice the few nodes, the so-called strong nodes, which are easy to identify and contain substantially more bindings than an ordinary node. A great amount of communication is transferred through these strong nodes, which gives them a privileged role. The significance of this role is discussed later.

A few properties common to all detected communication domains can be observed through visualization. We also verified these observations on the numerical expression of the social network.

- Nodes in the role of strong node remain in their position during long-term development. The set of strong nodes is relatively small (from one to ten nodes).
- A main component of graphs is usually similar in all communication domains (corresponding to the structure of scale-free networks). It also contains more than 50% of all inter-domain communication.
- Weights of edges are low. (Probably particularity of academic correspondence in a given period.)

Before we discuss these three observations, let's first deal with something else – the properties of month accumulation. Observation of independent accumulation is inconsistent. To get obvious results, it is necessary to combine this knowledge

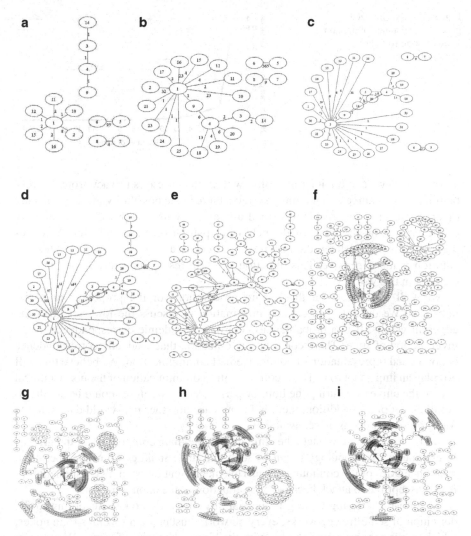

Fig. 13.13 Incremental development of a communication domain. From (**a**) first 2 months of data set to (**i**) last 2 months

with previous accumulations. The development of the social network is gradational and converges to a specific stationary shape. From this we can conclude that once the identity or social network is revealed, it is very difficult to return it back to its previous safe state because it is almost impossible to change the pattern of user behaviour. And moreover, we do not want to change this pattern.

An attacker can reuse the acquired knowledge of user behaviour and make their attacks more effective. Our capability to create long-term profiles of the email users discussed in the previous section supports this argument [6].

Fig. 13.14 Normalized geometric distance of domain nodes in one round of accumulation

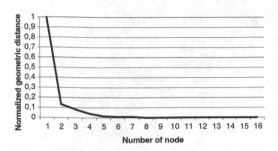

From this we can elicit an idea of how to protect a user's privacy from the very beginning. In a range of anonymity systems there is the possibility to use some kind of noise. It may be possible to extend a commonly used approach – the dummy traffic created on the basis of the behaviour pattern of a specific user. A sort of parametrical personalized dummy traffic. There is a question as to whether this solution is too expensive. This direction is worth researching further but it is not covered in this work.

We will focus now on three main observations of the properties of social networks. We do not have enough information to discuss the low weight of the edges in graphs. It is a probable particularity of academic correspondence in the given period of time. There could be the objection that academic correspondence is not a good representation of common email communication. We believe this will not play an important role. The record contains communication of the non-technical part of the university during the holiday period, so its structure should be similar to common people. In addition, there is in any case no other real-world data suitable for our research that is as yet available.

In the second item we state the similarity of the main components of the graphs. In communication topology it can be seen that these main components operate in more than 90% of the communication. This means that other small components are more susceptible to attack because of a reduction of the anonymity set.

The most interesting finding is the stability of strong nodes. According to the definition of scale-free networks, every network must contain several strong nodes, which in our case represents nodes with the highest capacity of traffic. We can use their stability for improving disclosure attacks.

The strength of a node is expressed by the geometric distance from all other nodes. The normalized results are shown in Fig. 13.14. We can see the privileged position of a few nodes. When we have knowledge about their position, we can approximate their position with a function (Fig. 13.15), where the x-axis represents every round of accumulation. This could help us predict their next behaviour. The distance could not be lower, it has ascending tendency.

The set of strong nodes is stable, thus once detected it is easy to follow them over time. Despite the fact that they are well protected against disclosure attack because of the high number of neighbours, they could represent a weakness for other nodes as described in the attack of a proper selection [16].

Fig. 13.15 The development of selected strong nodes in all rounds of accumulation

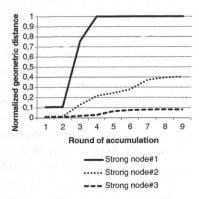

Note: In our interpretation, strong nodes are for the whole domain as well as the social network. We are not focussed on individuals in this case, but on the overall behaviour of the group. For the group, the strong node represents the most-communicating node; in the context of an individual, a strong node is only a sender.

Summary

We have described some basic properties of social networks in email traffic in general. These properties can be used for rather realistic simulation models. We believe to have shown that social networks are a very important aspect of our behaviour influencing the results of possible attacks on the privacy of our email communication – particularly the linkability of senders and recipients.

We have shown that social networks that appear in email communication can be detected and modelled with scale-free networks in an appropriate way. Then an analysis of the development of social networks was given. We described the properties common to all communication domains and discussed the similarities. The main focus was on the development of social networks.

We presented simple examples of how to create user profiles allowing intersection attacks to identify the recipients of their messages. We are certain that it is possible to create profiles that are valid over long time periods and the results will improve when more context information is used. The intersection attacks will not work only for a small fraction of traffic. Also, there seem to be users that are very hard to profile with general approaches. However, existing attacks on anonymity systems will probably work on the vast majority of users.

We have also shown the stability and traceability of a specific part of the network – strong nodes, and discuss the possibilities of predicting their behaviour.

Conclusion

This chapter is focused on the impacts of behaviour on the security of anonymity systems. We point out the main weaknesses of current security analysis of anonymous communication networks – the lack of real data. We show the performance of various analyses with one joint attribute – all are performed on the above-described data from real email communication. We provided an empirical basis for the properties of email communications relevant to the designers of anonymous systems. We hope, it will enable a better understanding of the security limits of anonymity systems with real-world traffic data.

We want to emphasize how important a role repetitive human behaviour plays in the security of anonymous systems and that it is necessary to take it into account. We show that some assumptions (such as the Pareto principle or some models of user behaviour) used in security analyses are wrong or at least misleading. We also determined that most users balance their messages across recipients, but a minority of users concentrate their messages on a few recipients. A detailed discussion can be found in the results of the analysis.

The second part is oriented towards behavioural features of people, their ability to create social networks and the development of social networks. We provided a tool for the modelling of social networks and the stability and traceability of a specific part of the network was discussed.

The summary of the properties of email communication presented in this chapter is not complete, but it represents a solid basis for future research. We show a few discrepancies that appear in other works. Specifically we are talking about the assumptions that are usually considered to be valid overall, but our data did not confirm this. A great surprise for us was the result of the distribution of messages between users. The inability to confirm the 80/20 rule brings us to the idea of a deeper analysis of user behaviour and mapping of their social networks.

The main conclusion of the analysis performed on features of the email communication are the findings that theoretical assumptions, which are currently used for attack simulations and the design of defence systems, are built on shaky foundations and it is necessary to further consider the creation of more suitable behaviour models that better correspond to real life. The analyses and results described in this part of the chapter were published previously [18].

Another part of the research is devoted to social networks that are detectable in real e-mail communications. From the description of the properties of communication topology, we move on to the expression of social networks via a suitable model. We have shown that this model is appropriate for the description of detectable social networks.

One of the main contributions of this part is the discussion of intersection attack on real data. We have shown that it is possible to relatively easily create profiles of user behaviour, which are applicable for a further attack. In addition, we found that for a large number of users, (about 2/3) it is possible to create long-lasting profiles that have only small variations over a longer time period. These properties can be used for a simplification of intersection attack. It is therefore necessary to calculate this possibility in the design of protection. Results acquired by examining user behaviour were published previously [5, 6].

We have further expanded the direction of long-term user profile development to the development of the whole social network. We tried to answer the question concerning the predictability of network behaviour. It appeared that disclosure of social networks is persistent and a return to a safe state is difficult.

Our findings are applicable to anonymity systems, but also to areas of privacy other than anonymity systems. Types of services such as Facebook, etc., may serve as an example. People voluntarily reveal their social networks, without any possibility of remedy. There may be a possibility to correct this, but only with the assumption of total loss of identity and a condemnation of their circle of friends. Our findings about the long-term development of social networks were published previously [17].

All these findings show the importance of behavioural patterns, occurring in the real behaviour of people. We believe that our findings will help to create a better picture of a user behaviour model.

Further research in applying real data to theoretical models appearing in anonymous communications could reveal which parameters are the most important and have the highest impact on the security of anonymity systems. These findings can then be reflected in the design of new defences.

Acknowledgements This work was partially supported by the BUT FIT grant FIT-10-S-1 and the research plan MSM0021630528.

References

1. Barabasi, A.-L., Albert, R.: Emergence of scaling in random networks. Science **286**, 509–512, (1999)
2. Berthold, O., Langos, H.: Dummy traffic against long term intersection attacks. In: Dingledine, R., Syverson, P. (eds.) Proceedings of Privacy Enhancing Technologies workshop (PET 2002), San Francisco. LNCS, vol. 2482. Springer (2002)
3. Berthold, O., Federrath, H., Köpsell, S.: Web mixes: a system for anonymous and unobservable internet access. In: Federrath, H. (ed.) Proceedings of Designing Privacy Enhancing Technologies: Workshop on Design Issues in Anonymity and Unobservability, Berkeley. LNCS, vol. 2009, pp. 115–129. Springer (2000)
4. Chaum, D.: Untraceable electronic mail, return addresses, and digital pseudonyms. Commun. ACM **24**(2), 84–88 (1981)
5. Cvrček, D., Malinka, K.: Chování uživatelů elektronické pošty. In: Datakon 2007 -Sborník databázové konference, Brno, pp. 92–101. Faculty of Informatics MU (2007)
6. Cvrček, D., Malinka, K.: Effects of social networks on anonymity systems. In: Proceedings of ISAT 2007, Wroclaw, p. 8 (2007)
7. Danezis, G.: Statistical disclosure attacks: traffic confirmation in open environments. In: Gritzalis, D., Vimercati, S., Samarati, P., Katsikas, S. (eds.) Proceedings of Security and Privacy in the Age of Uncertainty, (SEC2003), Athens, pp. 421–426. IFIP TC11, Kluwer (2003)

8. Danezis, G.: The traffic analysis of continuous-time mixes. In: Proceedings of Privacy Enhancing Technologies workshop (PET 2004), Toronto. LNCS, vol. 3424, pp. 35–50 (2004)
9. Danezis, G., Dingledine, R., Mathewson, N.: Mixminion: design of a type III anonymous remailer protocol. In: Proceedings of the 2003 IEEE Symposium on Security and Privacy, Oakland, pp. 2–15 (2003)
10. Diaz, C., Seys, S., Claessens, J., Preneel, B.: Towards measuring anonymity. In: Dingledine, R., Syverson, P. (eds.) Proceedings of Privacy Enhancing Technologies Workshop (PET 2002), San Francisco. LNCS, vol. 2482. Springer (2002)
11. Diaz, C., Sassaman, L., Dewitte, E.: Comparison between two practical mix designs. In: Proceedings of ESORICS 2004, Sophia Antipolis. LNCS (2004)
12. Diaz, C., Troncoso, C., Serjantov, A.: On the impact of social network profiling on anonymity. In: Borisov N., Goldberg, I. (eds.) Proceedings of the Eighth International Symposium on Privacy Enhancing Technologies (PETS 2008), Leuven, pp. 44–62. Springer (2008)
13. Dingledine, R., Mathewson, N., Syverson, P.: Tor: the second-generation onion router. In: Proceedings of the 13th USENIX Security Symposium, San Diego (2004)
14. Freedman, M.J., Morris, R.: Tarzan: A peer-to-peer anonymizing network layer. In: Proceedings of the 9th ACM Conference on Computer and Communications Security (CCS 2002), Washington, DC, pp. 193–206 (2002)
15. Kesdogan, D., Egner, J., Büschkes, R.: Stop-and-go MIXes: providing probabilistic anonymity in an open system. In: Proceedings of Information Hiding Workshop (IH 1998), Portland. LNCS, vol. 1525, Springer (1998)
16. Malinka, K.: On selected issues of behavioural patterns in computer security. Ph.D. thesis, Brno University of Technology (2010)
17. Malinka, K., Schäfer, J.: Development of social networks in email communication. In: The Fourth International Conference on Internet Monitoring and Protection, Venice/Mestre, p. 5 (2009)
18. Malinka, K., Hanáček, P., Cvrček, D.: Analyses of real email traffic properties. Radioengineering 18(4), 7 (2009)
19. Mathewson, N., Dingledine, R.: Practical traffic analysis: extending and resisting statistical disclosure. In: Proceedings of Privacy Enhancing Technologies workshop (PET 2004), Toronto. LNCS, vol. 3424, pp. 17–34 (2004)
20. Newman, R.E., Moskowitz, I.S., Syverson, P., Serjantov, A.: Metrics for traffic analysis prevention. In: Dingledine, R. (ed.) Proceedings of Privacy Enhancing Technologies Workshop (PET 2003), Dresden. LNCS, vol. 2760, pp. 48–65. Springer (2003)
21. Pfitzmann, A., Hansen, M.: Anonymity, unlinkability, undetectability, unobservability, pseudonymity, and identity management – a consolidated proposal for terminology. Available at: https://dud.inf.tu-dresden.de/Anon_Terminology_v0.31.bib (2008)
22. Rackoff, C., Simon, D.R.: Cryptographic defense against traffic analysis. In: Proceedings of ACM Symposium on Theory of Computing, San Diego, pp. 672–681 (1993)
23. Raymond, J.-F. Traffic analysis: protocols, attacks, design issues, and open problems. In: Federrath, H. (ed.) Proceedings of Designing Privacy Enhancing Technologies: Workshop on Design Issues in Anonymity and Unobservability, Berkeley. LNCS, vol. 2009, pp. 10–29. Springer (2000) Jean-François Raymond.
24. Serjantov, A., Danezis, G.: Towards an information theoretic metric for anonymity. In: Dingledine, R., Syverson, P. (eds.) Proceedings of Privacy Enhancing Technologies Workshop (PET 2002), San Francisco. LNCS, vol. 2482. Springer (2002)
25. Serjantov, A., Dingledine, R., Syverson, P.: From a trickle to a flood: active attacks on several mix types. In: Petitcolas, F. (ed.) Proceedings of Information Hiding Workshop (IH 2002), Noordwijkerhout. LNCS, vol. 2578. Springer (2002)

Index

A. Abraham (ed.), *Computational Social Networks: Security and Privacy*,
DOI 10.1007/978-1-4471-4051-1, © Springer-Verlag London 2012